The Center for South and Southeast Asia Studies of the University of California is the coordinating center for research, teaching programs, and special projects relating to the South and Southeast Asia areas on the nine campuses of the University. The Center is the largest such research and teaching organization in the United States, with more than 150 related faculty representing all disciplines within the social sciences, languages, and humanities.

The Center publishes a Monograph Series, an Occasional Papers Series, and sponsors a series of books published by the University of California Press. Manuscripts for these publications have been selected with the highest standards of academic excellence, with emphasis on those studies and literary works that are pioneers in their fields, and that provide fresh insights into the life and culture of the great civilizations of South and Southeast Asia.

RECENT PUBLICATIONS OF THE CENTER FOR SOUTH AND SOUTHEAST ASIA STUDIES:

Frank F. Conlon
A Caste in a Changing World: The Chitrapur Saraswat Brahmans

Kenneth Jones
Arya Dharm: Hindu Consciousness in 19th-Century Punjab

Leonard Nathan
The Transport of Love: The Meghaduta of Kalidasa

M. N. Srinivas
The Remembered Village

Social History
of an Indian Caste

This volume is sponsored by the
CENTER FOR SOUTH AND SOUTHEAST ASIA STUDIES,
University of California, Berkeley

Raja Girdhari Pershad, better known as Bansi Raja or Baqi (his pen name), was a typical nineteenth-century Kayasth. He supervised both household and military units for the Nizam's government and was a skilled writer of Persian and Urdu. Photograph, ca. 1890, courtesy of Ami Chand & Sons, Secunderabad.

Social History of an Indian Caste

The Kayasths of Hyderabad

Karen Isaksen Leonard

UNIVERSITY OF CALIFORNIA PRESS

Berkeley / Los Angeles / London

University of California Press
Berkeley and Los Angeles, California
University of California Press, Ltd.
London, England
ISBN 0-520-03431-7
Library of Congress Catalog Card Number: 76-52031
Printed in the United States of America

1 2 3 4 5 6 7 8 9

Contents

Contents

Part Four: / Incorporation into India

Figures, Tables, and Maps

Figures, Tables, and Maps

Preface

Before visiting the Indian city of Hyderabad to learn about the Kayasths, I was interested chiefly in the unique eclectic culture for which the Kayasth caste is famous throughout India. The Hindu Kayasths worked closely with Muslim rulers for centuries, and a Muslim Nizam ruled Hyderabad state until 1948. I imagined that I would be able to discern and analyze a cultural synthesis both Muslim and Hindu in origin, developed and elaborated by a single caste over time. I assumed that the presence of this caste and its culture had proved significant to the successful maintenance of a Muslim political kingdom in the predominantly Hindu south.

This historical hypothesis assumed the existence of a structural entity termed the Kayasth caste, composed though it might be of several endogamous subcastes, whose members followed the traditional occupation of administrative service. I expected to find both traditional and modern caste or subcaste organizations, such as councils of elders and voluntary associations, uniting the Kayasths, and I planned to focus on these structures to assess social change. This expectation stemmed from social science theories of modernization, particularly those concerned with caste-based voluntary associations.

On my first research trip to Hyderabad in 1965–1966, I found that the Kayasths there were not so easily analyzed. Kayasths had not retained a favored political position in the state right up to 1948 (when Hyderabad was incorporated into India), with all that that would have implied for cultural preservation. The extent of cultural change, both before and after 1948, was far greater than I had anticipated.

Attempts to formulate a standard body of cultural beliefs and practices proved frustrating because even families of the same nominal subcaste did not share similar concepts or ritual observances. There were no councils of elders or, with one exception, tightly structured subcastes, in the city. While efforts to build a formal caste-based association did occur in the twentieth century, those efforts were not clearly linked to modernization or to increased participation in a democracy. The caste associational efforts, in fact, had declined after Hyderabad state became part of independent democratic India in 1948. I did write my dissertation—a descriptive history of the Kayasth families in the city that emphasized their roles in Hyderabad politics and society until 1900—after that visit.

On my second major research trip, in 1970–1971, I collected contemporary as well as historical material. The expanded time period and detailed new data led to a re-evaluation of the Kayasths. I found that what I had been describing were really kin groups, not subcastes or a caste, and that their persistence and adaptation over time could be directly related to changes in the opportunity structure of the city and state. Quantitative measurements, possible with the fuller research data, substantiated this analysis. On a brief visit in 1976 I added a few final details.

Many people helped me write this book. Most were Kayasths, and I want to thank especially the four men upon whom I called most often: Gurucharan Das Saxena, Dr. Brij Mohan Lal, Roy Mahboob Narayan, and Hakim Vicerai. One hundred fifteen other Kayasths are credited in the footnotes and bibliography, and still others were present for interviews or social occasions: I thank them all. For the acquisition of necessary language skills, I am grateful to the National Defense Foreign Language Fellowship Program, Professors K. A. Faruqi and G. C. Narang of the University of Delhi, and Dr. Muhammad Khalidi and Mujahid al Ansari of Hyderabad. I thank the Fulbright-Hays Foreign Language Fellowship Program for funding the dissertation research in 1965-1966, and the American Institute of Indian Studies for funding the postdoctoral trips of 1970-1971 and 1976. Osmania University twice provided me with a research affiliation, and I have profited from many discussions with Dr. Sarojini Regani and Dr. V. K. Bawa, fellow historians of Hyderabad. The Newberry Library's summer seminar in quantitative methods for family history, with Richard Jensen and Daniel Scott Smith, and discussions with other historians of India, notably Bernard Cohn, Burton Stein, and John Broomfield, stimulated my thinking about the material. John Leonard helped organize the successive drafts of the manuscript and contributed rigorous criticism and valuable insights. I am also grateful to Gerald Barrier, Tom Kessinger, Pat Peebles, and Burton Stein for comments on the manuscript.

Finally, I owe much to the many women, individuals and groups, who have given me support during the last few years of teaching and writing. Special thanks are due to Elizabeth Armour, the friend who typed the manuscript several times, and to Meryl Lanning, copy editor for the University of California Press.

Transliteration and Abbreviations

To encourage readers who are not India specialists, commonly recognized English spellings for Urdu and Persian words are employed even in the bibliography (thus, "register" and "general," not "rejister" and "jinarāl"; "H.E.H. the Nizam," not "a'c ī a'c dī Nizam").

In both footnotes and bibliography I have changed Hijri, Deccani Fasli, and Samvat dates to dates A.D. to simplify and standardize the references. When a month has not been specified in the three other dating systems, sometimes the A.D. dates must span two years: 1289 Fasli equals 1879–1880, for example.

Abbreviations of libraries used throughout

APSA Andhra Pradesh State Archives, Hyderabad

BGVS Bharat Guna Vardhak Sanstha (Indian Cultural Center and Library), Hyderabad

BM British Museum, London

IAU Idara-e-Adabiyat-e-Urdu (Institute of Urdu Literature), Hyderabad

IOL India Office Library, London

OUL Osmania University Library, Hyderabad

NAI National Archives of India, Delhi

SCL State Central Library, Hyderabad

SJL Salar Jung Museum Library, Hyderabad

SOAS School of Oriental and African Studies, London

Abbreviations used in the footnotes

CC Clippings Collection, APSA: three scrapbooks of press cuttings, 1890–1904

CIS Contributions to Indian Sociology, The Hague; new series, Delhi.

[xiii

Transliteration and Abbreviations

FCS Files of the Chief Secretariat, APSA.
HA *Hyderabad Affairs.* Mahdi Syed Ali, ed. 10 vols. (Bombay, 1883–1889)
IESHR *Indian Economic and Social History Review,* Delhi.
JAS *Journal of Asian Studies,* Chicago.
KH *Kayasth Herald.* Gurucharan Das Saxena, ed. 7 vols. (Hyderabad, 1941–1948).

Glossary

abdarkhanah public booth serving water or (during Muharram) sherbet

al Hindu patrilineage or clan, designated by common name, within which marriage is not allowed

alam relic or banner associated with Muharram; banner awarded to nobles along with titles

anna 1/16th of a rupee

Arbab-i Nishat department of dancers, singers, musicians

ashurkhanah Muslim shrine for Muharram *alams*

Basant Hindu springtime festival, held the fifth day of the lunar month of Megh

bavarchikhanah kitchens

bhoi, plural *bhois* or *bhoyan* water-carriers, palanquin-bearers, lamp-carriers

biradari brotherhood

bismillah ceremony marking the formal commencement of a Muslim boy's education, usually held at the age of four years, four months, and four days; formula praising Allah used on that and other occasions.

chowk street

daftar office, place where records and documents were kept

daftardar head of an office

dargah tomb of a Muslim, often a saint

daroga supervisor of a department or office

dashtah "kept" in Persian, used in reference to a concubine

Dasserah Hindu festival honoring Durga, or the tools of one's traditional occupation

dastar distinctive turban worn by the Nizam's officials

devrhi palatial residence, usually of nobles

Divali Hindu festival of lights

Diwan chief minister, Prime Minister, in Mughal or Mughlai administration

diwankhanah reception room, drawing room, in male apartments of wealthy homes

durbar royal audience, reception; the court

farman royal order, decree, grant

fatihah annual ceremony for a dead person, in which the first chapter of the Quran is read

fauj army

Glossary

ghardamad see *khanadamad*

ghat platform or place

gotra exogamous unit in the Hindu kinship system

hakim physician, doctor

hamzulf literally, same hair; men married to sisters, or, sometimes, cousin-sisters

Holi Hindu festival just before the full moon of Phalgun, featuring the throwing of powdered colors

huliyah written description of one's physical appearance; part of military records kept by *serrishtahdars*

inam hereditary rent-free land grant; variety of grants

inamdar holder of an inam

jagir conditional or unconditional land assignment from which the holder collected revenue

jagirdar holder of a *jagir* and recipient of its revenues

jamadar commander of a military unit

jama nima Deccani long-skirted court costume for men

jati endogamous unit of the Hindu caste system

jatra annual Hindu festival of a given temple

karkhanah Mughlai administrative or production unit, usually under the household or palace division

khanahdamad son-in-law residing with his wife's family; another term for this is *ghardamad*

khandan family; patrilineal descent group

khillat robes of honor, presented with titles or with appointment to nobility

linewalla one who stands in line; European-trained soldier

mal revenue

mansab rank in the Hyderabad Mughlai service, often hereditary; consisted of two parts, the *savar* and *zat* figures

mansabdar holder of a *mansab*

mardanah men's quarters

mashalkhanah department of torches

mehlat palace; often used particularly for women's quarters

moulvi Muslim teacher, cleric

muash payment, salary

Muharram Shia commemoration of the martyrdom of Imam Husain at Qarbala

mulki countryman, as opposed to non-*mulki*, or outsider

munshi clerk

munsif subordinate judge

mushrif examiner or officer of a treasury who authenticated documents

naubatkhanah place where kettledrums played at entrance to a palace

Nazm-i Jamiat unit of soldiers; military organization; in Hyderabad, used for Irregular Forces, under both Diwani and Sarf-i Khas administrations

nazr or nazranah token gift of cash offered to the Nizam in return for an interview or favor; customary gift at audience with superiors

parvanah official letter with appropriate seal

peshkar in general usage an agent, deputy, or manager; in Hyderabad, also a specific office (and family) just below the Diwan in traditional rank

purdah cloth curtain or cloak; refers to the seclusion of women

qaum community, subcaste, or caste

rae, plural *rais* gentleman; plural, respectable men

Ramzan the Islamic month of fasting, the ninth month in the Hijri calendar

sabha society, organization

sahukar banker, moneylender

samasthan noble or chief family; area ruled by such a family

samdhi co-fathers-in-law; men whose children have married each other

sanad document, grant, patent, conferring titles, land, or other rights to individuals from ruler

sardaftar head of an office; same as *daftardar*

Sarf-i Khas Nizam's private estate, or privy purse

sati Hindu widow burned on her husband's funeral pyre

savar horseman; part of *mansab* rank referring to cavalry maintained by *mansabdar*

serrishtah unit of employees, civil or military

serrishtahdar supervisors, managers, of *serrishtahs*

shadikhanah wedding hall (*shadi* means wedding)

sherwani high-collared men's coat, becoming fashionable in late nineteenth-century North India

subah province

subahdar governor of a *subah*

suratval illegitimate Hindu children of Hyderabad Kayasths

taluk division of a revenue district

talukdar revenue contractor (in Hyderabad)

taziyah replica of shrine of Hasan and Husain, associated with Muharram

urs annual commemoration of a Muslim saint's death or union with the divine; annual offerings to a saint's tomb

vakil agent, representative, ambassador; later, a lawyer

vaqai nigar letter-writer, reporter

varna designates one of the four or five general categories of castes making up the "caste system" in India. The traditional four *varnas* are those of the Brahmans, Kshatriyas, Vaishyas, and Sudras (priests, warriors, merchants, peasants, and some service groups); a fifth *varna,* of outcastes or untouchables, is sometimes included.

zamindar landholder

zat personal, as in *zat mansab*; a personal stipend as distinguished from one including payments for others

zenanah women's quarters

Introduction

The Problem

The Kayasth, Sabha Chand, set out in the 1750's from Delhi for Hyderabad, a journey of nearly a thousand miles that required about two months' time. He was a clerk well trained in Persian, and he accompanied a Mughal official with letters for the Nizam, provincial governor of the Deccan. Sabha Chand found himself a better position, as paymaster of troops in the Nizam's army, married the daughter of another Kayasth similarly employed, and settled in Hyderabad city. Upon his death, Sabha Chand left his residence and his records as paymaster to his sister's son, who later shared the responsibilities and salary with other relatives.

Two centuries later, Sabha Chand's descendants were completing higher educations in English-medium schools. Brij Raj, employed in a bank in England, flew home to marry a young woman doctor from another Kayasth subcaste. His younger sisters, both graduates, started careers as schoolteachers before their marriages were arranged. Many things have changed for Sabha Chand's descendants, among them language, occupation, inheritance practices, and marriage patterns. But they are still Kayasths, and the relation between marriage alliances and economic resources is still crucial.[1]

Sabha Chand and his descendants have faced a series of recurring problems over the generations. How can individuals best advance their

1. I am not using the term marriage alliance in the technical sense defined by Dumont and other anthropologists, although kinship specialists may be struck by the repetition of intermarriages over the course of generations among these members of a North Indian caste.

[1

careers and perpetuate their families? What are the criteria for desirable marriages, and which social boundaries can or cannot be crossed for marriage purposes? What happens to hereditary positions and property when a family has no sons? The Kayasths of Hyderabad have developed a range of solutions to these problems over the last two centuries. Their decisions and strategies have depended upon the opportunities available to them. How they and their contemporaries have determined kinship boundaries and occupational choices has raised important issues in Indian social history.

Descriptive and theoretical writings about social change in modern India rest upon an understanding of Indian society in the past; but there is considerable disagreement about the nature of that society. What were the important kinship units, and how did they relate to other social units? Was mobility an individual or corporate phenomenon? How did the caste system in urban centers differ from that in rural India? How have family, kin, and caste units changed over time?[2] Attempts to answer these questions usually involve a great deal of theoretical ingenuity and little evidence.

The Kayasths (pronounced Kīyȧsths) of Hyderabad provide some striking answers to questions about family history and social change. Although they appear to be a cohesive North Indian caste isolated in southern India, their internal history reveals surprising diversity. Individual Kayasth immigrants began arriving in the Deccan in the eighteenth century. They shared cultural attributes to a large extent, but in most cases they had no previous kinship ties with other Kayasth immigrants. These Kayasths, who were from several different subcastes, either made or rejected marriage alliances with each other. This study relates the kin groups and marriage networks developed by Kayasths over a span of two hundred years to the external environment—the political, economic, and cultural conditions in Hyderabad.

This is necessarily a history of Hyderabad city and state, seen from the vantage point of people closely connected to the governmental structure since the eighteenth century. There have been four periods of administrative and economic change through which the Kayasths can be traced:

2. See the general discussion and references provided by McKim Marriott and Ronald Inden, "Caste Systems," *Encyclopaedia Britannica,* Macropaedia, III (Chicago, 1974), 982-999. On mobility, McKim Marriott, "Multiple Reference in Indian Caste Systems," and Burton Stein, "Social Mobility and Medieval South Indian Hindu Sects," in James Silverberg, ed., *Social Mobility in the Caste System in India* (The Hague, 1968); and M. N. Srinivas, "Mobility in the Caste System," in Milton Singer and Bernard S. Cohn, eds., *Structure and Change in Indian Society* (Chicago, 1968). On urbanization and social change, articles by Pauline Kolenda, Harold Gould, and Milton Singer in Singer and Cohn, *Structure and Change*; A. M. Shah, *The Household Dimension of the Family in India* (Berkeley, 1974); Sylvia Vatuk, *Kinship and Urbanization* (Berkeley, 1974); Richard G. Fox, ed., *Urban India: Society, Space and Image* (Durham, N.C., 1970).

the initial "frontier society" of eighteenth-century Hyderabad, when the state rested on a primarily military aristocracy; the consolidation of the Mughlai (meaning: derived from the Mughal) bureaucracy in the early nineteenth century, when recordkeepers at all levels attained political power; the transition to an Anglo-Indian bureaucracy in the second half of the nineteenth century, when Western-educated men began to prosper; and the mid-twentieth-century incorporation of the state into independent India. This last, perhaps the period of most rapid and disruptive change, has not yet ended.

At first, the different social units formed among the Kayasths seemed to correspond to these historical periods. In the eighteenth-century military aristocracy, an individual and his immediate family were the important social unit. In the nineteenth century, kin groups formed, and these small groups of closely related families controlled hereditary positions within the Mughlai administration. Due to the educational and administrative changes of the late nineteenth century, some Kayasths organized on the basis of common subcaste membership; in the twentieth century, they have organized on the basis of common caste membership.

But this convenient progression has proven analytically inadequate, especially after 1940, when the proportion of marriages beyond caste as well as subcaste boundaries rose. Marriages between members of different, formerly endogamous, subcastes could be seen as a shift from caste to ethnicity, and the expansion beyond caste boundaries as a transition from caste to class. Such interpretations, however, depend upon prior acceptance of the familiar tradition-modernity dichotomy, itself a basically ahistorical model.

These most recent changes, instead, challenge the assumption that ascriptive status was the most fundamental element in social definition in Hyderabad in the past. The determination of social boundaries and the continuity of families and kin groups always depended upon economic resources and occupational strategies, far more than upon any elaboration of purity and pollution concepts. In the modern period, Kayasth occupational and marriage strategies have changed, partly because of the nature of education and of administrative and professional positions. The expansion of marriage networks to provide a broader range of educational and occupational contacts has enlarged the social boundaries for individuals and families. The purpose of the new marriage networks, like the kin groups, is primarily to secure economic resources.

The terms distinguishing the social units formed by Kayasth families over time are familiar, but my usage should be clarified here. I follow the older convention and use caste to refer to all those who call themselves Kayasths. I use subcaste most frequently to indicate membership in one or another of the caste's named subdivisions, formerly the endogamous units, like Mathur or Saksena.[3] But the most characteristic structural units have been the kin groups, based upon control of hereditary positions which Kayasths transmitted bilaterally, through both sides of the family. The kin groups, consisting of a few closely related families, were thus property groups. They distributed not only social but economic and political resources.[4] There is one exception: I have called the Mathur Kayasths a subcaste, following local usage and differentiating them from the other kin groups. All designated Mathurs were in fact related to each other, and they were ranked internally according to their marriages with one central, dominant family. They all resided in one locality and shared the reputation of the dominant family, which distributed economic resources and exercised social control over the others.[5] Kin groups as defined above did develop within this subcaste when the Mathurs began taking up modern occupations and ceased to be dependent upon the centrally distributed resources.

Finally, I use the term marriage network for social units in transition, relatively unbounded and not property groups in the same sense as the kin groups. The boundaries of the networks are changing or unknown, ranging outside of Hyderabad or expanding beyond former boundaries. The marriage networks are broader than the kin groups, and they provide access and influence, rather than control, with respect to economic resources.

Focusing on the relation between marriage alliances and economic resources emphasizes differences of income and status within a single caste. Discussions of the caste system tend to emphasize the cultural attributes shared by members of a caste and the interactional behavior among members of different castes. The differential achievements and patterns of interaction within a caste have received less attention; too

3. Recently the term caste category, or caste cluster, has been used by specialists on India for the large category of people sharing cultural attributes and similar occupations; caste has been reserved for the *jati* or endogamous unit.

4. This contrasts with Leach's position. He remarks on "the total absence of kinship as a factor in extra-caste systemic organization," and states that "the cultural rules of caste behaviour establish a dichotomy in the total field of social relationships—political, economic and ritual relations are external, kinship relations are exclusively internal." E. R. Leach, ed., *Aspects of Caste in South India, Ceylon, and North-west Pakistan* (Cambridge, Eng., 1969), 7.

5. Here Mayer's "kindred of cooperation" coincides with subcaste membership: Adrian C. Mayer, *Caste and Kinship in Central India* (London, 1960). Mayer recognizes that we need more empirical work on kin, subcaste, and caste units. See also Hamza Alavi, "Kinship in West Punjab Villages," *CIS*, n.s. VI (1972), 1-12; Leighton W. Hazlehurst, "Multiple Status Hierarchies in Northern India," *CIS*, n.s. II (1968), 38; Anthony Carter, "Caste 'boundaries' and the principle of kinship amity: a Maratha caste Purana," *CIS*, n.s. IX (1975), 123-137.

many scholars have assumed that caste members who share cultural attributes and a characteristic occupation also share a common economic level.[6]

Historians of modern India have seldom studied family, kin, and caste groups, though these are believed to be the fundamental social units in Indian society. Most have preferred to study social change by focusing on administrative policies and practices, perhaps documenting the growth of an educated elite or middle class or noting the prominence of members of a particular caste or community in administrative service. But these new or newly prominent groups are the products of change, and the data concerning them has been drawn from the administrative unit. As Bernard Cohn has pointed out, this kind of source material tells more about those who collected and used it than it does about indigenous social units and their relation to social change.[7]

Most indigenous family and caste histories produced since the eighteenth century also have limited historical value. Responding to the British Census classification of castes, such histories argue for the "correct" ranking of a particular caste in the classical four-*varna* system, citing Sanskrit texts, the opinions of learned pandits, and specific regulations and customs.[8] Other family and caste histories were composed to earn titles and awards from the British government for their authors or subjects. These usually included material on a few eminent individuals rather than an entire kin group or caste.[9] Most Indological discussions of the distant origins of the caste system are even harder to utilize because they draw upon Vedic and later Brahmanical Hindu texts. There are few similarities to the castes designated in more recent sources or to current problems and methods of research in the social sciences.[10]

6. Leighton Hazlehurst has discussed this emphasis on "status equivalence" rather than "status inversion" aspects of caste: "Urban Space and Activities," in Fox, *Urban India*, 186–195.

7. Bernard S. Cohn, "Notes on the History of the Study of Indian Society and Culture," in Singer and Cohn, *Structure and Change*, 3–25.

8. The *varna* system is explained in the glossary. For a typical Kayasth claim to be Kshatriya, see Munshi Kali Prasad, *The Kayastha Ethnology* (Lucknow, 1877); non-Kayasths dismissed such claims, as in Kumar Cheda Singh Varma, *Kshatriyas and Would-be Kshatriyas* (n.p., 1904). An Urdu translation of the famous Patna High Court decision for Kshatriya status has been widely circulated among Kayasths: Kamta Pershad, ed., *Patna High Court ke Faislah ka Urdu Tarjumah* (Lucknow, 1928).

9. For example [Lala Maharajah Lal], *A Short Account of the Life of Rai Jeewan Lal Bahadur, late Honorary Magistrate, Delhi, and Extracts from his diary* (Delhi, 1888), IOL pamphlet, or biography collections such as Shiv Narayan Saksenah, *Kayasth Sajjan Caritra*, 3 vols. (Jaipur, 1912–1913). In contrast, Gaur family histories of real historical value were collected by Ram Das Gaur: *Tazkirah-i Sucaru Vanshi* (Allahabad, 1911).

10. An exception is Ronald B. Inden's work on the formation of castes and clans in medieval Bengal: *Marriage and Rank in Bengali Culture* (Berkeley, 1976).

Introduction

A few historians of India have contributed pioneering work on kin groups or a local caste system. Bernard Cohn has pointed to the rural *biradari*, or brotherhood, the localized exogamous unit, as the "first-level" unit in the system.[11] Richard Fox has also used historical materials to analyze rural landholding lineages or clans and their role in the centralized states of preindustrial North India.[12] Both writers emphasize the economic functions of these unilineal descent and inheritance groups. Tom Kessinger's excellent study of families in one Punjabi village over time, because North Indian kinship requires village exogamy, is, in fact, a study of male property groups.[13] His finding is that rural social change must be studied through these groups, which were the units of economic activity.[14] My study, in contrast, is an historical reconstruction of both sides of family histories of an urban caste population. It shows that kin groups transmitted bilaterally "property" that consisted of major and minor administrative positions.

Most work on caste by anthropologists, sociologists, and political scientists contains implicit historical assumptions that have been influential and need to be challenged. Among anthropologists, the organizing principle of caste has overshadowed that of kinship in empirical studies.[15] Concern with the system as a whole has centered debate on the corporate units, assumed to be subcastes and castes, and their reciprocal perceptions and behavior. Edmund Leach's model of the caste system as a set of complementary ranked occupational groups has led many, even those who disagree with him, to argue at that level and to overlook stratification within the units. Furthermore, in Leach's model, changes so disruptive as to destroy the noncompetitive relationships between castes meant the end of the true caste system.[16] He holds that such changes have occurred

11. Bernard S. Cohn, *India: The Social Anthropology of a Civilization* (Englewood Cliffs, N.J., 1971), 124–147.

12. Richard G. Fox, *Kin Clan Raja and Rule* (Berkeley, 1971).

13. Tom G. Kessinger, *Vilyatpur, 1848–1968* (Berkeley, 1974).

14. Two other historians working on castes in the modern period, Frank Conlon and Lucy Carroll, emphasize institutions and organizations rather than kinship units: Frank Conlon, "Caste by Association: The Gauda Sarasvata Brahmana Unification Movement," *JAS*, XXXIII, no. 3 (1974), 351–365; Lucy Carroll, "Caste, Social Change, and the Social Scientist: A Note on the Ahistorical Approach to Indian Social History," *JAS*, XXXV, no. 1 (1975), 63–84. An anthropologist, R. S. Khare, also focuses on a caste organization: *The Changing Brahmans* (Chicago, 1970). A sociologist, Maureen Patterson, uses source materials which explicitly link marriage alliances to educational and occupational patterns: "Chitpavan Brahman Family Histories," in Singer and Cohn, *Structure and Change.*

15. See note 5 above. Dumont, Vatuk, Khare, and others are looking closely at kinship, but chiefly at terminology and in the context of theoretical debates generated by structuralism: *CIS*, n.s. IX, no. 2 (1975), special issue on kinship and marriage.

16. Leach, *Aspects of Caste*, 1–10; and for a summary of arguments about the nature

recently; the implication, which others have extended, is that the caste system has been a relatively static and unchanging system in the past. Thus anthropologists attempting to provide historical backgrounds commonly preface their studies of present-day castes in a specific locality with generalized cultural accounts drawn from Sanskritic literature and early British administrative records.[17] Such juxtapositions easily accomplish contrasts between tradition and modernity, since recently collected structural data shows organizational change from the cultural model.

For sociologists and political scientists, issues of caste have frequently been raised in the context of modernization. Definitions of modernization usually include urbanization, extension of political and economic opportunities, Western education, experience of the nationalist movement, extension of the adult franchise, and the enactment of anti-caste legislation.[18] The impact of modernization upon caste has been seen most clearly in the formation of caste associations. Kothari and Maru state: "In all cases it is the secular potential of caste that is brought out by its adopting an associational form of organization and then functioning in an interactional framework;" and "Cross-cutting interactions and identities in the communication between society and politics . . . is the essence of secularization in a caste society."[19] Again, the implication is that internal cultural features, such as religious beliefs and ritual, were emphasized in the past, but that structural adaptations and increased interaction with the external society are recent features of castes.

Yet the Kayasths who began migrating to Hyderabad in the eighteenth century participated in many of the processes associated above with modernization. Traditionally a "writing caste," their historical prominence dates from the establishment of Muslim rule in India.[20] Following

---

of the system, Stephen A. Barnett, "Approaches to Changes in Caste Ideology in South India," in Burton Stein, ed. *Essays on South India* (Honolulu, 1975), 149–180.

17. L. W. Hazlehurst, *Entrepreneurship and the Merchant Castes in a Punjabi City* (Chapel Hill, 1966); L. P. Vidyarthi, *The Sacred Complex in Hindu Gaya* (New York, 1961); R. G. Fox, "Resiliency and Change in the Indian Caste System: The Umar of U. P.," *JAS,* XXVI, no. 4 (1967) 575–587; and a political scientist, Robert Hardgrave, *The Nadars of Tamilnad* (Berkeley, 1969).

18. Susanne H. and Lloyd Rudolph, *The Modernity of Tradition* (Chicago, 1967), 3; R. Kothari and R. Maru, "Caste and Secularism in India," *JAS,* XXV, no. 1 (1965), 33–34.

19. "Caste and Secularism," 34, 49.

20. Some find Kayasths mentioned in the Laws of Manu and certain Puranas: Gopi Nath Sinha Varma, *A Peep into the Origin, Status, and History of the Kayasthas,* 2 vols. (Bareilly, 1929 and 1935); Ramcharan, *Kayasth Dharm Darpan,* trans. from Sanskrit to Urdu by Lala Lalji (Lucknow, 1928). Good overviews are by P. V. Kane, "The Kayasthas," *New Indian Antiquary,* I (1929), 739–743, and Pandit Raghuvara Mitthulal Shastri, "A Comprehensive Study into the Origin and Status of the Kayasthas," *Man in India,* XI, no. 2 (1931), 116–159.

the rise of the Mughal Empire in the sixteenth century, Kayasths were noted as a group of men proficient in Persian, the language of the Mughal administrations. The Kayasth men functioned in the secular and inter-actional framework of the Mughal administration. They were associated with the development of Persian education, urban administrative centers, and the extension of political and economic opportunities to Indians by a new government.

The Kayasths present us clearly with a case of social mobility. Most writers have assumed that a literate Hindu community, previously over-shadowed by Brahmans, attained administrative employment through rapid adaptation to the Persian language and culture of India's new rulers.[21] But it is also possible that Hindus of diverse caste backgrounds who learned Persian and staffed the Muslim administration began inter-marrying and formed a new caste known as the Kayasths. Whatever their origin, the Kayasths have been portrayed as a bridge between the rulers and their subjects, mediating between Muslim and Hindu in both admin-istrative and cultural capacities.[22] They have long been associated with social change, whether as products or agents of it.

This study concentrates more on changes in social structure among the Kayasths than on their cultural attributes; it relates families, kin groups, and marriage networks to the opportunities and resources avail-able to the Kayasths in Hyderabad over time.

Research Methods and Sources

Two very different kinds of sources had to be utilized in this study. First, men and women had to be placed within marriage networks. Second, men (and, very recently, women) had to be placed by occupational spe-cialty and rank in the Hyderabad government and other professional frameworks.

I have collected and compared family histories to discover marriage patterns. Oral information obtained in interviews has been the chief source for the reconstitution of each *khandan,* an Urdu term translated most simply as family. *Khandan* usually denotes a minimal patrilineage,

21. Two twentieth-century Hyderabad Kayasth authors with opposing views of the merit of Kayasth adaptation to Muslim culture believe that the caste existed prior to Muslim rule: Surya Pratap [Haq Prast], *Hamari Zaban* (Hyderabad, 1940), 14-15; Mahender Raj Suxena, "Hyderabad aur Kayasth," *KH,* IV-V (1944-1945), 4.

22. Yusuf Husain, "Les Kayastnas, ou 'scribes,' caste Hindoue Iranisée, et la culture musulmane dans l'Inde," *Revue des études islamiques,* I (1927), 455-458; Aziz Ahmad, *Studies in Islamic Culture in the Indian Environment* (Oxford. 1964), 105-106.

with a depth of about three generations. Since few Kayasth immigrant families have genealogies going back more than seven generations, *khandan* means both family and lineage in Hyderabad, including all patrilineal descendants of a "founder."

The reconstruction of genealogies, begun as a method of conducting interviews, differentiating individuals, and outlining an anticipated common caste structure, became the major research task. This task might be termed family reconstitution, though there were no official records of births, marriages, and deaths maintained by the state or religious institutions. The cross-checks on this kinship data came from interviews with other Kayasths, particularly families related by marriage. As I met more and more Kayasths and learned the history of their families, walking about the old city and being referred from one household to another, the diversity within the caste proved its most striking feature. Some individuals and families could not even be definitely assigned to one or another of the seven Kayasth subcastes represented in the city; indeed, whether they were Kayasths at all depended upon the informant.

Written materials also provided checks on the oral information. Some families had their own records to document inheritance, property acquisition, and so forth. In many cases, checking the official records in the Andhra Pradesh State Archives (APSA) verified the information given concerning employment. For the Mughlai bureaucracy, the bundles of Persian and Urdu records provided names, dates, and salary figures. Civil and military lists dating from the late nineteenth century did the same for the modern bureaucracy. Collections of biographies of city and state leaders published since the late nineteenth century supplemented the official records; and the older Persian and Urdu histories of Hyderabad had similar biographical sections. Finally, for those who held *mansabs* (titles) and *jagirs* (salary and land grants) awarded by the Nizam, the APSA preserved documents detailing their transmission over the generations.

The written and oral materials were certainly biased in favor of propertied and titled families. But because Kayasths often served in low-level clerical positions in the Mughlai administration, many who were not propertied did appear as the recordkeepers in archival materials. And since inheritance in the past had been bilateral, the oral information concerning female relatives, that is, both sides of the marriage alliances, was fuller than it might have been had the caste ideology of patrilineal inheritance been practiced. The genealogical data is summarized in Appendix A: the quantity exceeded expectations, as did accuracy of the initially oral information.

The second research effort involved writing and rewriting an administrative history of Hyderabad state. Political and economic opportunities can be documented rather well by the late nineteenth century; but for the eighteenth and early nineteenth centuries only an approximate reconstruction of the Mughlai military and civil service has been attempted. I have outlined the administrative divisions of the Mughlai bureaucracy and placed most Kayasths in those divisions. The distribution of occupations among Kayasths for the earliest periods has been related to the kin groups, providing insights into the nature of the Mughlai bureaucracy. The fuller records of the late nineteenth and twentieth centuries allowed accurate measurement of Kayasth movement into the modern administration. Useful secondary works for the later periods also greatly simplified that part of the research effort.

Frequent problems were encountered when attempting to relate the written to the oral data. A detailed example will suffice to show how I used or discarded materials. Written sources tell of a famous late-eighteenth-century poet, Lala Dooleh Rae Dabir (Dabir was his pen name), nephew of one Lala Khushal Chand Farhat (Farhat, again, was the pen name), who moved to Aurangabad from Burhanpur in 1802 and died in 1808.[23] Is this the same Dooleh Rae whose transcriptions, done in 1761 and 1771, survive in Hyderabad libraries?[24] And what might the connection be with the Dooleh Rae who appears on the genealogy of the Malwalas, the leading Mathur Kayasth family in Hyderabad, as a great-nephew of one Khushal Chand? The coincidence of the names and the nearly identical relationship made such an identification tempting. But the Malwala family oral tradition did not include residence in Burhanpur or Aurangabad; neither Malwala man is remembered as a poet; the Malwala genealogy places Dooleh Rae in the mid-nineteenth century; and, finally, the Malwala Dooleh Rae converted to Islam.[25] Since that fact would hardly have escaped the notice of the Muslim compiler of poets' biographies,[26] this connection could not be made.[27]

23. Muhammad Abdul Jabbar Khan, *Mahbub us Zaman, Tazkirah-i Shora-i Dakan,* 2 vols. (Hyderabad, 1911), I, 434.

24. I take the transcriber of these two manuscripts to be the same Dooleh Rae, as the subject matter is similar and the dates close: OUL, Persian manuscript acquisition no. 1328, "Nigar Namah-i Munshi," transcribed in Hyderabad in 1761; APSA, Persian manuscript no. 250, "Munshi Malikzada," transcribed in 1771–1772.

25. Interviews with Hakim Vicerai and Raja Mahbub Karan.

26. A conversion was invariably well publicized.

27. There was another Dooleh Rae in one of the Srivastava families, about whom little is known save that he was a noble and *jagirdar* at the court of Nizam Ali Khan in the 1780's: Makhan Lal, *Tarikh-i Yadgar-i Makhan Lal* (Hyderabad [1829]), 69; Register Asnad-i Jagir (APSA) II, no. 13, Hyderabad *subah* (province), nos. 288/25 and 225/11. That possibility cannot be ruled out entirely, for the time is right, and we do not know

Even for the nineteenth and twentieth centuries, uncertain chronology and inadequate detail created problems in using materials about individuals. Poor calligraphy and misspellings were as frequent as in the earlier materials, and sometimes knowledge of additional details only complicated matters. This was particularly true with the use of double or alternative names: one individual was known as Ram Pershad alias Ram Lal, and another as Govind Raj alias Govind Sahae alias Basanti Raja. The difficulties and judgments involved in use of the historical materials are sufficiently clear from these examples. Particularly for the eighteenth century, positive identifications between the men named in written sources and the ancestors recalled orally by present-day Hyderabad Kayasth families could not be made with certainty; therefore they were not made.

Some quantitative methods have been employed, although a late-eighteenth-century base line could not be established with confidence. In any case, the urban environment and the Hyderabad administration have changed so much since then that it would not do to evaluate all later data with respect to such a base line. Many measurements of comparable data over shorter periods of time have been used to simplify and illustrate the discussion.

A cultural account of the Kayasths (such as I have criticized others for placing at the beginning of studies of social change) follows here. It is set in smaller type as a reminder that it is derived almost entirely from North Indian twentieth-century materials and that its relevance to the Hyderabad Kayasths is somewhat uncertain, since their historical experience has differed from that of the North Indian Kayasths. Its presentation here is justified: first, it exemplifies what has been thought of as an historical background for the caste under study, and it is a useful introduction for readers unfamiliar with Indian caste society. Second, it serves as a reminder of the type of model constructed during the first stages of research, to which further empirical discoveries may or may not correspond.[28]

---

whether this Dooleh Rae was a poet, or the name of his uncle, or where the family resided earlier. But Dooleh Rae is a common name among Khatris and Brahmo-Khatris as well as Kayasths, and Dooleh Rae Dabir was not designated by one or another caste label in the source.

28. Save where specific sources are given, the account that follows is drawn from: Prasad, *Kayastha Ethnology*; Ramcharan, *Kayasth Dharm Darpan*; Kane, "The Kayasthas"; Shastri, "A Comprehensive Study"; Varma, *A Peep into the Origin*; Gopinath Singh Varman (the same author but as transliterated from Urdu), *Mukhtasir Tarikh-i Aqvam ul-Kayasth, Prabhu, va Thakur,* 2 vols. (Bareilly, 1921); Jogendra Nath Bhattacharya, *Hindu Castes and Sects* (Calcutta, 1896), 186–191; William Crooke, *The Tribes and Castes of North-western Provinces and Oudh,* 4 vols. (Calcutta, 1896), III, 184–216; Syed Siraj al-Hassan, *Castes and Tribes in H.E.H. the Nizams Dominions* (Bombay, 1920), 322–323.

Introduction

A Cultural Account of the Kayasths

Three regional communities in India lay claim to the name "Kayasth" or "Kayastha." These are the Chitragupta Kayasths of North India, the Prabhu Kayasths of Maharashtra, and the Bengal Kayasths of Bengal. Both culturally and structurally, these have always been three different communities, with mother tongues of Hindustani, Marathi, and Bengali respectively.[29] But each fulfilled a similar function in its respective regional political system. All three were "writing castes"—their traditional occupation was administrative service with the reigning political power. Today these three groups tend to see themselves as divisions of a single Kayasth caste. But when the designation Kayasth is used alone, it usually refers to the North Indian or Chitragupta community, and most histories of the Kayasths concentrate on this group.

The Chitragupta Kayasths had in common particular myths of origin and of relations to one another. They subscribed to similar sets of regulations governing social intercourse and marriage. They maintained traditional relations with specific service castes, primarily Brahmans and barbers, and they shared a generally high rank with respect to other castes in their regions. They followed a similar set of religious and domestic practices. Finally, they shared a traditional occupation: clerical and administrative service.

The origins of the Kayasths and their ranking within the all-India *varna* system postulated by Brahmanical tradition are matters of controversy. The Kayasths have been variously classified as Brahmans, Kshatriyas (rulers), or Sudras (peasants), thus ranking first, second, or fourth in the four-fold system, depending largely upon legal decisions in different areas of India. They might be Brahmans because of their literacy, Kshatriyas because of their association with rulers and military service, or Sudras (in Bengal) because of a failure to adhere scrupulously to the orthodox practices enjoined upon the twice-born (the first three categories in the *varna* system).

But the difficulty of their placement has been overcome in the favorite Kayasth myth of origin. The ambiguity is resolved by postulating the creation of a fifth *varna*, the Kayasths, to keep records concerning the other four *varnas*. Brahma created the four *varnas*, then summoned forth the first Kayasth, with pen and inkpot already in hand, to record the activities of all other men. This first Kayasth was named Chitragupta, and he became revered as founder and patron deity of the community.[30] Chitragupta's chief employment was as recordkeeper for Yama, the god of death in Hindu mythology, for whom he recorded all the good and bad deeds of men.

All North Indian Kayasths are said to be descendants of Chitragupta. The twelve Kayasth subcastes, or endogamous divisions, are traced to his twelve sons by two wives. (See Figure 1.)[31] From Chitragupta's first wife were born the Mathurs, Bhatnagars, Saksenas, and Srivastavas; from the second wife the Gaurs, Nigams, Asthanas, Surajdwaj, Amasthas, Karans, Kulsirishtas, and Balmiks (the last five are usually held to be extinct). A founding family, a patron deity, and a home

---

29. Kayasth is the correct transliteration of the customary Urdu spelling; in Bengali, Hindi, and Marathi, a final short "a" appears. Since the Hyderabad Kayasths used Urdu, I use that spelling.

30. This tale is recounted in full in a Hyderabad journal: Fateh Chand, "Kaifiyat Ibtida-i Kayast," *Dabdabah-i Asafi,* 11, no. 3 (1899), 13–14.

31. Picture from Baldev Pershad. *Kayasth Kul Utpatti* (Bijnur, 1911), facing p. 57.

1: Chitragupta with his two wives and twelve sons

area were designated for each of these twelve subcastes. The subcastes were also assigned nominal *gotras,* exogamous divisions within an endogamous caste. *Gotras* were an especially strong feature of Brahman caste organization and allegedly the major determinant of marriage patterns. It is doubtful that these nominal *gotras* were ever functional within the Kayasth subcastes, but the Kayasths had similar prohibitions based on *als,* or family distinctions. An *al* could refer to a distinguished ancestor or place of origin, or it could refer to a characteristic acquired during migrations. As members of the same *al* were not allowed to marry, these units performed the same function that *gotras* did in other castes. There were other restrictions on marriages, such as prohibited degrees of relationship. Fifth cousins (and according to some regulations, seventh cousins) could not marry, and Kayasth widows were not allowed to remarry.

Chitragupta Kayasths adhered to other typically high-caste Hindu restrictions on social intercourse, such as prohibitions on interdining. Upon occasion members of the Kayasth caste could eat certain foods together, but generally speaking, members of one Kayasth subcaste did not dine with members of another, much less with members of other Hindu castes or with Muslims.[32]

Relationships typical of the caste system, among them the hereditary ties between Kayasth families and their family priests and barbers, were maintained. When Chitragupta Kayasths moved from North India to other areas, members of their particular Brahman and barber families are supposed to have accompanied them. The family priests employed by the Kayasths were Kanya Kubya, or Kanaujya, Brahmans, usually those of the Katyayan *gotra.* Like the Kayasths,

32. Kayasths of different subcastes could eat fried food like *puris* together, but not boiled food like rice. For these and many other details of food, serving, and eating distinctions, see Kamta Pershad, *Ittehad al Akhwan,* 2 vols. (Agra, 1895), II, 15, 20, 35–38, 40, 60.

[13

Introduction

these Brahmans were originally from the region now known as Uttar Pradesh. Kanaujya Brahmans performed domestic religious ceremonies for Kayasth families, and sometimes they served as cooks in Kayasth households. Hindi-speaking barbers, Nais, were similarly attached to Kayasth families. It is said that there were twelve Kayasth brothers, and then their half-brother the Nai. In addition to his services as barber, the Nai was an intermediary in marriage arrangements and had an important role in the marriage ceremony. His wife traditionally served as a midwife.[33]

Their traditional relationship with Kanaujya Brahmans of the Katyayan *gotra* indicates the Kayasths' relatively high place in the North Indian regional caste system, where these Brahmans are held in high repute. The Kayasth claim to *gotras*, even if nominal, and the numerous regulations concerning social intercourse also lay claim to a high-caste Hindu style of life. This impression is confirmed by the religious practices of the Kayasths, for they follow a sequence of domestic religious observances which conforms to that of other high-ranking North Indian castes. This Hindu life cycle begins with purification rites after the birth of a baby, and the naming ceremony of the infant and the first shaving of its head; it ends with the cremation and ceremonial observances after death. The family priest and barber participate in most of the ceremonies.

Despite all these Hindu credentials—adherence to Hindu mythology and religious observances, relationships to others within the caste system, and postulated internal organization and regulations—the Kayasth community has been noted throughout India as a heavily Islamicized one. The reasons have to do with the traditional education and occupation of Kayasths. Boys were well educated in Persian and Urdu, and sometimes even Arabic. They, like Muslim boys, were taught by *moulvis* (Muslim clerics), privately or in Islamic schools affiliated with mosques. Their education commenced with the ceremony called *bismillah* (part of the Islamic life cycle).[34] Kayasth men associated closely with Muslims in their jobs. They wore the customary court dress and could converse fluently in Persian and Urdu, following the conversational and social mannerisms appropriate to Mughal court society. Kayasths prided themselves on their literary skills and made substantial contributions to prose and poetry of the Mughal period.

Some of the essentially occupational patterns followed by Kayasth men carried over into domestic life, particularly in nomenclature, diet and manner of eating, and amusements. Kayasths often took personal names customarily used by Muslims, as in Jahangir Pershad, Iqbal Chand, and Mahbub Karan. Kayasth diets and eating practices were similar to those of Muslims. They ate meat regularly (usually a high-caste Hindu prohibition) and enjoyed a reputation as gourmets of Mughlai cuisine. They were famous wine-drinkers too; this was certainly not an

33. R. S. Khare, "The Kanya-Kubja Brahmins and their Caste Organization," *Southwestern Journal of Anthropology*, XVI (1960), 348–367; Hassan, *Castes and Tribes*, 322–323; and interviews with two Hyderabad Kanaujya Brahmans, Dev Shanker Sharma and Dixit Maharaj.

34. An account of the ceremony as performed in late-nineteenth-century Hyderabad appears in Brij Mohan Lal, "The Story of My Life" (manuscript, 1956 with Kunj Behari Lal, Asthana), 4: "The Moulvi dressed in spotless white sat next to me, and after repeating the usual Muslim formula 'Bismillah ur Rahman ur Rahim' . . . he handed me the chalked takhti or wooden board and helped me to write with a broad pointed reed pen the first alphabets of Urdu."

14]

orthodox Muslim trait, but it was characteristic of the court culture under most Mughal emperors. Wine-drinking has often been mentioned as evidence of Islamic influence on the Kayasths; it could also be attributed to their use of wine (and meat) as worshippers of Devi and Shakti.[35] Indeed, drinking was the one characteristic which set the Kayasths apart from other "writing castes." As a popular proverb in Hyderabad put it:

> Reading, writing, so many do this;
> But if he doesn't drink wine, he can't be a Kayasth.[36]

Feasting and wine-drinking were major elements of Kayasth entertainments. Weddings featured the Hindustani classical music and dancing patronized by the Mughals. Other entertainments linked with Mughal culture were the popular games of chess and parcheesi and the composition and recitation of Persian and Urdu poetry.

In many respects, then, the Kayasths reflected their close association with the Mughal administration and culture. Of course, many aspects of Mughlai culture had spread throughout northern India, even to peasants in village communities. The Kayasths, as a heavily urban, literate group employed in the Mughal administration, adopted more Mughlai characteristics than did other groups; and perhaps they did so more conspicuously and more consciously. But in their stated principles of caste organization and regulation, and in their domestic religious observances, Kayasths conformed to the basic patterns of Hindu civilization.

The Kayasths migrating to Hyderabad were members of the North Indian Chitragupta caste. While their North Indian kin accommodated themselves to British rule, the Hyderabad Kayasths retained an allegiance to Mughlai administration and culture as it continued under the Nizams of Hyderabad. We turn now to Hyderabad state in the late eighteenth century, as the Kayasths established themselves there.

35. In an analagous case, members of the Katyayan *gotra* of the Kanaujya Brahmans, like the Kayasths, were noted as meat-eaters and wine-drinkers; yet their "purity rating" was high among Brahmans. See R. S. Khare, "A Case of Anomalous Values in Indian Civilization: Meat-eating among the Kanya-Kubja Brahmans of Katyayan Gotra," *JAS*, XXV, no. 2 (1966), 229–240.
36. Recited to me by Shakamber Raj Saxena, the anonymous Deccani Urdu poem reads:
> likhna parhna jaisa vaisa,
> daru nain pie, so Kayasth kaisa.

PART ONE

The Nizam
Under Siege

CHAPTER 1

The Administration
of a Military Regime

The eighteenth century was one of warfare and turbulence throughout India, as the Mughal Empire lost supremacy in the subcontinent. European-trained forces and imported military technology helped bring new men to power in the mid-eighteenth century. In southern India, the expanding power of the Marathas in the western Deccan, the rise of new regional powers in Mysore and Madras, and the expanded activities of the French and English trading companies heightened diplomatic and military competition in the Deccan.[1] (See Map 2.)

Nizam ul Mulk, Mughal governor of the Deccan province in the early eighteenth century, held the Deccan for the Mughals by military force. Maintaining nominal allegiance to Delhi, he founded a separate dynasty and administration which his successors firmly established by the end of the century.[2] Shifting military alliances and constant diplomatic negotiations contributed to Hyderabad's political survival. Individuals, local rulers, and states switched sides often. The state was threatened most frequently by the Marathas and the Muslim ruler of Mysore; British and French companies based on the Madras coast played decisive roles as allies of one or another of the rulers.

In his will, Nizam ul Mulk (titled Asaf Jah I) stressed the personal nature of his rule and the military basis of the state. According to him, the ruler's life is best spent touring with the army. He exhorted his successor to "spend your life under the canvas . . . [as] this is the best

---

1. Basic histories are Yusuf Husain Khan, *The First Nizam*, 2d ed. (Bombay, 1963); P. Setu Madhava Rao, *Eighteenth Century Deccan* (Bombay, 1963); and Sarojini Regani, *Nizam-British Relations 1724–1857* (Hyderabad, 1963).
2. Karen Leonard, "The Hyderabad Political System and its Participants," *JAS*, XXX, no. 3 (1971), 569–582.

[19

method of administration." He spoke of the need to keep part of the treasury on the march for the satisfaction of the soldiers and army officers because they were the strongest support of the state and made proper administration possible.[3] These statements accurately characterized the new state to the end of the eighteenth century.

The second half of the eighteenth century was the formative period for Hyderabad state. An autonomous administrative system developed steadily; and the capital was moved to Hyderabad city. The long reign of Nizam Ali Khan Asaf Jah II, from 1762 to 1803, contributed to internal stability. Hyderabad, seventeenth-century capital of the Qutb Shahi Empire, had been conquered by the Mughal Emperor Aurangzeb in 1687. For almost a century after that, the city of Aurangabad in the west served as the administrative and cultural center of the Deccan province, though the political center moved about with the Nizam and the army. Increasing pressures from the Marathas in the west and Tipu Sultan in Mysore made Hyderabad city a more strategic center. As late as 1777, Nizam Ali Khan still maintained establishments in both Aurangabad and Hyderabad and preferred to reside in Aurangabad;[4] but by the end of the century Hyderabad had become the permanent center of administrative and court establishments.

A well-planned and attractive administrative city for the Qutb Shahi Empire, Hyderabad had declined when Aurangabad served as the Mughal capital, and considerable repair and rebuilding was necessary in the late eighteenth century.[5] After Nizam Ali Khan had improved the military fortifications, the residential areas were resettled and the city began to expand. Some of the Nizam's nobles, particularly the Shia Muslim families, settled in the old Qutb Shahi nobles' locality near the river. But many Qutb Shahi palaces had been destroyed, and the Nizam and other nobles built new ones.

Military encampments dominated the landscape to the south of the city. The splendid residences of the French officers of the Nizam, surrounded by gardens, were as impressive as those of the nobles. Most European officers of the Nizam's forces were quartered in the Ghazibanda and Shahalibanda localities. Typical was the French officer Monsieur Raymond and his famous force of Deccani soldiers trained in the European fashion, called *linewallas*. In the older areas of the city, high-walled

3. Rao, *Eighteenth Century Deccan*, 66.
4. Jadunath Sarkar, "Old Hyderabad," *Islamic Culture*, XI, no. 4 (1937), 527.
5. For the city in this period, see H. K. Sherwani, *Muhammad-Quli Qutb Shah: Founder of Haiderabad* (New York, 1967); S. A. Asgar Bilgrami, *The Landmarks of the Deccan* (Hyderabad, 1927); Sarkar, "Old Hyderabad," and Jadunath Sarkar, "Hyderabad and Golkonda in 1750 seen through French Eyes," *Islamic Culture*, X, no. 2 (1936), 237.

compounds sheltered the nobles and their dependents from curious eyes; the large establishments were separated from each other by narrow lanes. But in Shahalibanda, both the buildings and the style of life were more open and expansive.[6]

The nobility was a military one in the eighteenth century, and the administration was based on the collection and deployment of resources for warfare. The Nizam and leading nobles exercised highly personal military leadership and were the most important dispensers of patronage in the late-eighteenth-century political system. Their resources depended initially upon military and diplomatic success. Later, when the court was fixed in Hyderabad city, they received regular income from their *jagirs*. The Nizam himself, with personal control over the largest revenue, military, and household establishments, was the best source of financial support in Hyderabad. Nobles maintained establishments patterned on the Nizam's. They too could dispense administrative posts or cash grants. Also, depending upon their status and the strength of their recommendations, nobles could secure places for their clients in the Nizam's establishment. Successful provision for a large number of diverse clients— relatives, employees, artisans, poets, and religious men—was a mark of noble status.

The patron-client relation was the key to maintenance of position and advancement for the clients. Employees with ability could switch allegiance from one patron to another, improving their positions in the process. Access to the Nizam's administrative service, and eventually perhaps to the nobility, depended upon a connection with an influential patron or sponsor. An aspirant to even a relatively low appointment in the Nizam's service had to be presented to the Nizam by someone already in good standing at court. Such sponsors were not necessarily relatives of the applicants. Patron-client relationships appear to have been formed on an individual basis in this early period and did not follow caste or kinship lines.[7]

6. On Raymond, see Jadunath Sarkar, "General Raymond of the Nizam's Army," *Islamic Culture,* VII, no. 1 (1933), 95–113, and O. S. Crofton, *List of Inscriptions on Tombs or Monuments in H.E.H. The Nizam's Dominions* (Hyderabad, 1941), 33–34. For the European officers and the French Gardens, see Henry George Briggs, *The Nizam,* 2 vols. (London, 1861), II, 95–97, and the appendix of Herbert Compton, *A Particular Account of the European Military Adventurers of Hindustan from 1784–1803* (London, 1892). On urban life, see Sarkar, "Old Hyderabad," 523, and "Hyderabad and Golkonda in 1750," 234; Lal, *Yadgar,* particularly chapter 12, pp. 175–183; and John Malcolm's impressions of the city in 1799 in J. W. Kaye, *The Life and Correspondence of Major-General Sir John Malcolm G.C.B.,* 2 vols. (London, 1856), II, 163.

7. There are numerous examples of patron-client relations in Lal, *Yadgar,* and in a Persian court diary maintained by the Daftar-i Diwani family, recently published by APSA as *The Chronology of Modern Hyderabad, 1720–1890* (Hyderabad, 1954).

[21

Another characteristic of the Hyderabad political system was the use of *vakils,* or agents. In accordance with etiquette, members of the nobility seldom met with the Nizam or each other directly; rather, they sent their *vakils* to attend court and negotiate their affairs with other nobles. A continuous ceremonial exchange of greetings and gifts through these agents maintained friendly connections between the Nizam and leading nobles. The diplomatic ability of a *vakil* could do much to enhance his patron's position, and a *vakil's* ability to place applicants in his employer's establishment put him in a patron's role vis-à-vis those of lesser means.

The agents of such regional political powers as the Peshwa of the Marathas or the Nawab of Arcot also attended the Nizam's court and represented their employers' interests there. They, like the local agents, could act as patrons within the Hyderabad political system. These agents maintained large households in Hyderabad city and employed subordinates there. Often these *vakils* could dispense jobs and support of the same magnitude as Hyderabad nobles directly attached to the Nizam. Sometimes such an agent's position in the local political sytem became more personally advantageous to him than his position as representative of an outside power; some eventually switched their allegiance to the Nizam.[8]

The political power of these agents of external powers rested on the military success of their employers. At first the Mughal agents were prominent in Hyderabad, but in the last half of the eighteenth century those of the Peshwa, the Peshwa's nominal subordinate chiefs Scindia and Holkar, and the Nawab of Arcot became more powerful. The most important such agent by the early nineteenth century was the British Resident, who by then represented the Mughal emperor as well as the East India Company.[9]

Culturally, the city remained an outpost of the Mughal Empire in North India, despite the state's Telugu-, Marathi-, and Kannada-speaking Hindu rural population. It was an Islamic city in the sense that its builders and principal inhabitants were Muslims. A French visitor in the late eighteenth century remarked, "I have not seen the city where the manners and customs of the capital of the [Mughal] Empire are more

8. Leonard, "The Hyderabad Political System," 571–573, discusses this. For the Nizam's land grants to the *vakils* of other rulers, see "Jagirdaran o Inamdaran Subajat-i Dakan, 1198 H. [1784]," Persian manuscript no. 1015.4, IOL. Lal, *Yadgar,* 61–71, includes biographies of Hindu nobles who were originally *vakils* of outside powers.
9. See the entries in "Jagirdaran o Inamdaran," *Chronology,* and Lal, *Yadgar,* for these changes. In 1807 a *farman* (order) from the Mughal emperor to the Nizam was presented to him by the British Resident: *Chronology,* 110.

carefully followed than in this one . . ."[10] Although Shia Muslim landmarks from Qutb Shahi days were prominent features and local observances continued to center on them, Hyderabad was not a religious center for either Muslims or Hindus.

Even religious institutions reflected the philanthropy of the military men. The oldest Hindu temple in Hyderabad built by a Kayasth (Ram Bagh, constructed by a Bhatnagar noble in 1802) marked the builder's political success and integration into the nobility. The idol was a gift of the Raja of Gadwal, a tributary ruler and military leader. The Nizam attended the installation ceremony and granted a large *jagir* for the temple's support.[11] Another early Kayasth temple was constructed after its Srivastava builder's military victory; yet another had troops garrisoned on the temple grounds and guns and gunpowder stored in its basement.[12]

Development of the Administration

The military character of the state influenced the structure and development of the Hyderabad administration. In the eighteenth century, there were four general administrative areas: the land revenue collection, the military, the household establishments, and the supervision of justice and commerce. Of these, the first three were most important; the first two tended to be combined. The Nizam and his leading official, the Diwan, had authority over all of these areas but gave personal priority to the pursuit of military and diplomatic goals.

The Diwan's financial responsibilities were delegated to subordinates, *peshkars* and *daftardars*. These managerial and clerical employees handled the Diwan's correspondence and kept financial records, particularly the land revenue records.[13] By the late eighteenth century, two *daftardar* families had gradually assumed control of the land revenue records. Major officials in their own right, they presided over two central records offices that divided the state geographically. The earlier of the two was

10. Sarkar, "Old Hyderabad," 525 (the Frenchman L. L. Dolisy de Modave's visit in 1776).

11. Satguru Pershad, *Farkhundah Bunyad Hyderabad* (Hyderabad, 1964), 110-111; Manik Rao Vithal Rao, *Bustan-i Asafiyah*, 7 vols. (Hyderabad, 1909-1932), II, 749.

12. These were the Chitragupta and Kali temples in Uppaguda: Pershad, *Farkhundah Bunyad Hyderabad*, 40-41. A cannon still on the grounds of the latter has a Persian inscription giving 1783 as the date of first firing.

13. Jadunath Sarkar, *Mughal Administration*, 5th ed. (Calcutta, 1963), describes the comparable Mughal system. Leonard, "The Hyderabad Political System," 575-579, compares the Mughal and Hyderabad administrations. See also *Hyderabad Residency Records*, Political Department, Box 66, 605/92-96, "Original Constitution of Hyderabad State," prepared in 1892 (IOL).

the Daftar-i Diwani, covering the four *subahs* (provinces) of Khandesh, Aurangabad, Berar, and the Carnatic. This *daftar* became linked to a Maharashtrian Brahman family, titled the Rae Rayan family. The second, the Daftar-i Mal, covered the *subahs* of Hyderabad and Bidar; a Mathur Kayasth held this office.[14] The Mathur family was known as the Malwalas, or "those of the land revenue." By the end of the eighteenth century both of these *daftardar* families ranked in the nobility, though there were significant differences in their wealth and power.

Land revenue contracts and other financial arrangements for the Nizam were handled by these two *daftars* and their staffs. Income came from three major sources: land revenue, estimated by *taluks* or territorial divisions and farmed out to contractors; *nazranah* or tribute, presented to the Nizam in specified amounts according to purpose; and loans and deposits, received primarily from moneylenders. The land revenue financed administration in rural areas, and the tribute offerings and loans from urban financiers went towards urban expenses.[15]

Military fortune was basic to eighteenth-century finances in the rural areas. Territory changed hands frequently, and revenue was customarily collected with the help of troops. The two central *daftars* had on record only the revenue contractors, their assigned areas, and the estimated revenue; there were no records of the amounts those contractors actually collected. Assessments were based on the contract amounts for previous years; if an estimated revenue was successfully remitted, it was considered the actual revenue from that land and became the basis of the following year's estimated income. The *daftardars* awarded contracts annually and prepared official documents notifying village officials of the authorized contractors. The contractors kept their own records, or they simply used the troops and kept no records. They got two *annas* per rupee as their commission (one-eighth of the total) and whatever excess they could collect. The village and district officials took their customary share of the revenue before turning it over to higher authorities, and the troops stationed in rural areas to hold forts and collect customs and revenue were usually paid before the revenue was forwarded to the capital. Most of these shares, plus the two or three *annas* per rupee which went to the

14. The Daftar-i Diwani was connected with the Rae Rayan family from 1750: Ghulam Samdani Khan, *Tuzuk-i Mahbubiyah*, 2 vols. (Hyderabad, 1902), II (Nobles), 17; and their first recorded *jagir*, Register Asnad-i Jagir, I, no. 12, serial no. 101/12. The Mathur Kayasth is listed as *sardaftar* (head of the record office) in a 1760–1761 entry in the Register Asnad-i Jagir, I, no. 11, Bidar *subah*, serial no. 113/12.

15. A summary chart of the income and expenditure of the state according to the way the *daftardars* kept the records shows this geographic division: Rao, *Bustan*, I, 149–150.

Diwan and the quarter-*anna* per rupee which went to the appropriate *daftardar,* were supposedly paid only after the state's share had been remitted.[16] In practice, the opposite was more likely to occur. Thus, the figures which the *daftardars* recorded as the amount of land revenue were probably quite unrelated to the amounts actually collected and distributed to various employees.

Another key function of the Diwan and the *daftardars* was to negotiate and distribute the urban income from tribute and loans. The seasonal nature of the land revenue collection, the uncertainty of its remittance, and the constant expenditures at the capital led to reliance on these other sources of income for ongoing government expenses. Contracts awarded for the collection of revenue, customs, and taxes, and confirmations of succession to property, positions, and land—these and other official appointments required varying amounts of tribute from applicants. This was a steady source of cash for the Nizam's household establishment. But even more important were the loans from urban bankers and money-lenders. The Diwan and the *daftardars* negotiated the terms of loans, kept general records, and arranged for repayment when revenue was remitted. More detailed records were kept by the bankers themselves, who might therefore be likened to state treasurers.[17] There was no central treasury at the capital until the mid-nineteenth century, though there were small treasuries for household and military establishments. The *daftardars* functioned as if in a clearing house, allocating income to the smaller treasuries but apparently never commanding enough cash to make up a permanent central treasury.

The financial officials, then, did not function as careful bookkeepers and custodians of resources. They were negotiators and brokers between those who controlled or collected resources and those who needed cash for disbursement to various units of employees and dependents. Their political power grew considerably with the establishment of Hyderabad city as the capital and the increasing internal stability of the early nineteenth century.

The military was another major administrative area and a highly decentralized one. The units constituting Hyderabad's army were separately maintained by leading nobles, and there was no uniform method of training or central hierarchy of officers. Those who maintained military units

16. Rao, *Bustan,* I, 149–152, delineates the operation of the revenue system.
17. For more on the tribute and loans, see Briggs, *The Nizam,* I, 123 and Rao, *Bustan,* I, 152. See Ghulam Husain Khan, *Tarikh-i Gulzar-i Asafiyah* (Hyderabad, 1890–1891), 622–632, for the early financiers of Begum Bazar and Karwan.

received salary allotments to distribute to their troops. In some cases, for the larger and more permanent units, nobles received *jagirs* to provide income for salaries. Units were organized under dual leadership: *serrishtahdars* kept the records and disbursed the pay, and *jamadars* commanded the units in the field. In the eighteenth century, the *serrishtahdars* were the more important officials, often managing several units headed by different *jamadars*. They had the power to certify the identity of troopers and distribute the pay, and *jagirs* were sometimes given in their names to pay troops.[18] Some *serrishtahdars,* many of them Kayasths, took part in battles and earned titles and personal *jagirs*.

The third administrative area was the Nizam's household, and there were three distinct divisions within it. First was the *durbar,* whose officials were concerned with the conduct of the Nizam's relations with other nobles; this was sometimes termed the *mardanah,* the public or men's part of the household. The second division was the *mehlat* or *zenanah,* the private or women's part of the household. This included the harem, other female dependents, and close relatives of the Nizam. The *zenanah* staff was composed of females, eunuchs, and recordkeepers. The latter were usually Hindu and included many Kayasths who maintained records and distributed allowances and personal supplies. While Muslim nobles sometimes had access to the *zenanah* through marriages with the Nizam's relatives, Hindus could supervise within the household and commend themselves to the *zenanah* ladies and female staff. Through the women they could play intermediary roles in marriage arrangements and exercise political influence. The third division within the household establishment was the *karkhanahs,* the departments that produced and distributed goods and services for the court, the *zenanah,* and leading nobles. Appendix B lists the many departments and their functions. The *kharkhanahs* employed many Kayasths and other Hindus as administrative and clerical personnel.[19]

Leading nobles and close relatives of the Nizam usually had office establishments modelled on the Nizam's, with their own Diwans, recordkeepers, and treasurers. Even lesser nobles and officials needed *vakils* or agents to represent them and negotiate on their behalf with others. Nobles also had personal household establishments, though they could draw upon the Nizam's household for some goods and services.[20] In fact,

18. See Lal, *Yadgar,* 171–174, and Khan, *Gulzar,* 478–492, for the military units; A. J. Tirmizi, "Inayat Jang Collection," *Studies in Islam,* I, no. 1 (1964), 178–190, for procedures.

19. The *darogas,* supervisors of physical work or production activities, tended to be Muslims; the clerical supervisors, generally Hindus, were termed *mushrifs* and *peshkars*. See references in *Chronology* to these positions and their holders.

20. Instances in *Chronology,* 41, 50, 53, 76.

although the administrative areas have been sketched here as separate and distinct, there was considerable overlap in both functions and personnel. It was often difficult to separate employees of the Nizam from those who served leading nobles, or from any public or state administration. An individual could receive income from several payrolls,[21] but his *mansab* rank and *jagir* assignments were conferred by the Nizam.

Jagirs, mansabs, and other important indications of ranking at court were centrally determined, as in the Mughal service, though the sources of income varied. The nobles in military service held the highest *mansabs,* both personal (*zat*) and for troops (*savar*). Others who ranked high were granted *jagirs* and privileges such as a drum or band escort, a fringed carriage, or a distinctive flag for residence or procession. Special titles, jewels, and ornaments were awarded by the Nizam as well. By the late eighteenth century, when Nizam Ali Khan and leading nobles seldom left their residences in Hyderabad city, public *durbars* were held regularly. In *durbars,* nobles were seated in hierarchical order before the throne, and the Nizam received men and conferred awards. As at the Mughal court, robes of honor accompanied many appointments and distinctions. When a noble died, his rightful heir was presented with a white mourning robe by the Nizam. Such a gesture conferred legal recognition as well as condolences.[22]

In the eighteenth century, court events and ceremonies reflected the military character of the state. When angered, the reigning Nizam exiled nobles to their *jagirs,* imprisoned them in Golconda Fort, or seized their property upon their death. Ceremonial receptions and departures of nobles took place at the gates of the city, whence they were conducted to the Nizam's presence or permitted to depart. As the nineteenth century began, more ceremonies were held within the palace, in the *durbar* hall, and even in the domestic quarters. Weddings, birth celebrations, and circumcision and *bismillah* ceremonies for boys became significant court events.[23]

Hindus and Kayasths in Administrative Service

Economic and social mobility characterized the eighteenth-century political system in Hyderabad. The Nizam's nobles and administrative

21. Thus the Nizam's central payroll in both 1784 and 1820 included the courtiers of Raja Rao Rumbha, and in 1820 it included those of the former Diwan Aristo Jah and of Shams ul Umra from the Paigah noble family. See "Jagirdaran o Inamdaran" and Lal, *Yadgar,* 144 and passim.

22. Rankings are discussed in *Chronology,* vi–viii and glossary entries; the ornaments are pictured facing p. 118. For presentation of robes, see *Chronology,* 64, 165, 210, and glossary p. 18.

23. *Chronology,* 39, 40, 47, 56, 91, 93, 105.

officials show little continuity with the conquered Qutb Shahi adminis-tration.[24] Nizam ul Mulk Asaf Jah I recorded his preferences with respect to administrative personnel: like the Mughal Emperor Aurangzeb, he distrusted Deccani Brahmans, and he also opposed the employment of men from Burhanpur and Bijapur. He appointed one Puran Chand (probably a Kayasth) to be his Diwan, despite objections from some of his nobles, for the stated reason that Puran Chand had proven most efficient at revenue collection. Thus the founder of Hyderabad state, like other rulers of the Deccan before him, tried to rely on non-Deccani administrators.[25] Many Kayasths among the North Indian Hindus came south to Hyderabad and joined the Nizam's service.

Table 1 summarizes the changing origins of Hindu administrative personnel over time, listing the *jagirdars* and *mansabdars* in 1784 and 1800–1820. Despite Nizam ul Mulk's views, Deccani Hindus constituted over half the Hindu administrators in the 1780's, but by 1820 their percentage had declined. They still dominated the *jagirdar* category, but they comprised only one-third of the *mansabdars,* or salaried employees. This increase in North Indian Hindus can probably be explained by the territorial and military losses to the Marathas in the western regions of the state and by expansion of the Mughlai civil service, which utilized more salaried employees.

The opportunities for service in Hyderabad state brought Hindus into military service and into the nobility. Analysis of twenty early Hindu noble families, whose founders rose to prominence under the Nizam Ali Khan (1762–1803) and the Diwan Aristo Jah (1780–1804), shows a clear preference for military positions. Of the twenty founders, fourteen initially won recognition through civil administrative positions as *vakils, peshkars,* and lesser clerks and accountants; only six started in military positions. The founders and their immediate successors switched from one area of the administration to another or held positions in both; but seven of those who began in civil administration later achieved high positions with military units, while only one moved the other way.[26] Service with big military units like those of the Paigah family (the leading Muslim military nobles) and Sulaiman Jah (another military leader and brother of the Nizam) was more rewarding and prestigious than service with the revenue or household establishments in the late eighteenth century.

24. Leonard, "The Hyderabad Political System," 579–580.
25. Rao, *Eighteenth Century Deccan,* 64 and 68, citing Nizam ul Mulk's will. My article "The Deccani Synthesis in Old Hyderabad," in *Journal of the Pakistan Historical Society,* XXI, no. 4 (October, 1973), 205–218, reviews this tendency.
26. Lal, *Yadgar,* 61–71.

TABLE 1:
Hindus in the Hyderabad Administration, 1784–1820

	1784		1800–1820					
	Jagirdars and Inamdars[a]		Total		Jagirdars		Mansabdars	
	No.	Percent	No.	Percent	No.	Percent	No.	Percent
Deccanis	65	55	283	38	83	57	200	33
North Indians	53	45	462	62	62	43	400	67
Total	118	100	745	100	145	100	600	100

Sources: Compiled from "Jagirdaran o Inamdaran Subajat-i Dakan, 1198 H. [1784]," Persian manuscript no. 1015.4, IOL; and the lists in Makhan Lal, *Tarikh-i Yadgar-i Makhan Lal* (Hyderabad [1829]), p. 72 and passim. Indecipherable names are omitted. Hindus with the surnames of Rao, Pandit, Bhat, and Pant are assumed to be of Deccani origin. Hindus with surnames of Das, Chand, Singh, Lal, Ram, and Rae are assumed to be from northern and northwestern India, along with those designated as Gosain.

[a]*Inamdars* are salary recipients. The 1784 list did not separate the two categories of employees.

Military service was more rewarding than administration of the land revenue establishment at this time for several reasons. There were wars and skirmishes on all sides of Hyderabad, with booty and honors to be won. The military office establishments maintained important records, for military positions were hereditary and the *serrishtahdar* of each unit determined succession. Salary distribution conferred more than power upon the *serrishtahdar*: he collected a commission. Since land revenue was usually collected by troops, that revenue was largely controlled by military officials. Even though political conditions became more stable toward the end of the century, when the British East India Company became the dominant power in the subcontinent, there was no immediate decline in the power and resources of Hyderabad's military men. Treaties called for the disbanding of forces, but many forces were reallocated and retained even after their supposed reduction.[27]

The career patterns of the early Hindu nobles reveal a range of occupations and opportunities for advancement. First, men could rise rapidly if they served a powerful patron well. They could do this in military positions, through battlefield feats and the ability to control and pay

27. Of forces "disbanded" at Poona, a few thousand went to Srirangapatnam with Grant and Mir Abul Qasim Khan; 1,026 men went to Cuddapah under Raja Chandu Lal; some went into the command of Mardan Singh; 1,200 went as a bodyguard to Raja Govind Baksh; 300 became watchmen at the Nizam's palace; and the rest were assigned to customs and excise duties: Lal, *Yadgar,* 71. Briggs, *The Nizam,* I, 255–317, gives the texts of all treaties of the East India Company with the Nizams.

TABLE 2:
Kayasths in the Hyderabad Administration, 1784–1820

	1784			1800–1820					
				Jagirdars			Mansabdars		
	Number	% of all Hindus (118)	% of North Indians (53)	Number	% of all Hindus (145)	% of North Indians (62)	Number	% of all Hindus (600)	% of North Indians (400)
Kayasths[a]	6	5	11	12	8	19	60	10	15
Other probable Kayasths	25	21	47	20	14	32	215	36	54
Total: maximum possible Kayasths	31	26	59	32	22	52	275	46	69

Source: Table 1.

[a]Only those named individuals who actually can be located on a genealogy in the correct time period, and for whom there is no conflicting information to rule out the possibility, have been included as Kayasths. The other category, probable Kayasths, does not include individuals who can be positively identified as Khatris or Agarwals (the many relatives of Rajas Chandu Lal and Roshen Rai). The probable category does include men who may have been Brahmo-khatris, Khatris, Agarwals, and North Indian Brahmans.

troops, or through demonstrated ability in a patron's *jagir* or household establishment. Second, if it proved advantageous, men could change patrons or move from one kind of position to another. With the financial fortunes of the state largely dependent upon military strength, positions with the military were more desirable, though perhaps more uncertain, at the end of the eighteenth century. Such positions could be lost or diminished because of changing political boundaries or treaties, or because of internal conflicts, of course. Finally, acquired positions could be passed on to sons or designated relatives, particularly when large tributes were presented.[28] Yet individuals rose and fell according to their own abilities and those of their patrons and according to the positions to which they had access at a given time.

The familiar image of the Kayasths as writers or scribes in government service has long been fixed. One might have expected Kayasths in Hyderabad to be connected with the Mughlai civil service and to achieve prominence only in the early nineteenth century, as that administrative area became the major source of employment and patronage. But this was not the case. For eighteenth-century Hyderabad, military leadership was the surest qualification for recognition as a noble; it was the surest way to earn titles, privileges, and economic rewards such as booty, personal *jagirs,* and *jagirs* granted for troop maintenance. Many eighteenth-century Kayasth immigrants turn out to have been military men, and most of the nobles among them owed their titles and *jagirs* to military feats. There were Kayasths in the Deccan in writing occupations then, but they were not so likely to rank as nobles.[29]

It has proven possible to determine the ranking of Kayasths in eighteenth-century Hyderabad, both with respect to other Hindus and to each other. Table 2 takes the Hindu *mansabdars* and *jagirdars* of North Indian origin from Table 1 and breaks them down to measure the known and probable Kayasths. From this table, the minimum and maximum limits of Kayasth participation in the Hyderabad administration can be established. Kayasths constituted from 5 to 26 percent of all Hindu land and salary recipients in the 1780's, and from 8 to 22 percent of the Hindu *jagirdars* and 10 to 46 percent of the Hindu *mansabdars* in the 1820's. Whatever the exact percentage, their proportion among the North Indians, particularly among *mansabdars,* was always substantial.

At the level of the nobility, several indices of occupation and ranking could be constructed for 1800-1820.[30] In a contemporary book listing

28. Lal, *Yadgar,* 61-71.
29. This will be documented in Chapter 2.
30. I have relied upon Makhan Lal's detailed lists in *Yadgar*; he was employed by Raja

TABLE 3:

Hindu Nobles Ranked by Zat Mansab, 1800–1820

Zat mansab rank	Total number of Kayasths	Total number of Hindus	Percent of Kayasths to all Hindus
7000	0	2	0
5000	0	2	0
4000	0	2	0
3000	0	8	0
2000	3	16	19
1000	4	40	10
Total	7	70	10

Source: Makhan Lal, *Tarikh-i Yadgar-i Makhan Lal* (Hydera-bad [1829]), 144–156.

fifty-four leading nobles, there were eight Kayasths among the twenty Hindus. Five of these were Saksena families, with one family each of Mathurs, Srivastavas, and Bhatnagars. Most of the Saksenas were in predominantly military positions and lived in Shahalibanda, where the book's author, himself a Saksena Kayasth, lived.[31] His final chapter, on leading residents of Hyderabad city, brought the percentage of Kayasths down from 40 percent to 20 percent, with thirty-four Hindus, including seven Kayasths, among the eighty-two citizens.[32] From these two descriptive accounts, Kayasths might be thought to have constituted from 20 to 40 percent of Hyderabad's prominent Hindus at the end of the eighteenth century.

But Kayasths were not numerous among the highest-ranking Hindu nobility. The lists of *mansabdars* and *jagirdars* used to produce Table 1 can be used to rank Kayasths with respect to other Hindus and each other. Table 3 charts the Hindu nobles with *zat mansab* ranks of 1,000 or more and shows that Kayasths were concentrated in the lower ranks from 1,000 to 2,000 *zat*.

At the end of the eighteenth century, there were three other high-ranking categories in which Kayasths were not represented or were represented by only one family. First, an elite group of sixteen *jagirdars*

Chandu Lal and utilized government records in this book. While serving as the Peshkar's *vakil* to the Resident, he prepared *Yadgar* for the Resident (Metcalfe).

31. Lal, *Yadgar,* chapters 2 and 3.

32. Only three of these seven Kayasth families were included as nobles in chap. 3: the Malwalas, a Madras *vakil* Saksena family, and the Srivastava Raja Daya Bahadur.

TABLE 4.
Kayasth Jagirdars, 1800–1820

Subcaste	Name	Value of jagir	
Mathur (all Malwala)	Raja Khushal Chand	Rs. 5069	
	Rai Chatur Lal	2273	
	Rai Deepak Rai	4249	Total:
	Rai Khub Chand	750	Rs. 17,551
	Rai Ujagar Chand	3497	
	Rai Sital Das	1713	
Saksena	Raja Rup Lal	3043	
	Rai Khem Karan	1577	
	Rai Gunwanth Rai	333	
Srivastava	Raja Daya Bahadur (known as Keval Ram)	7215	
Bhatnagar	Relatives of Raja Bhavani Pershad	3243	

Source: Makhan Lal, *Tarikh-i Yadgar-i Makhan Lal* (Hyderabad [1829]), 93–123.

held major *jagirs* designated for the support of troops. Only three were Hindus, and none was Kayasth.[33] One Kayasth, head of the Malwala *daftardar* family of the Mathur subcaste, was among the seventeen Hindus to hold both personal (*zat*) and army (*savar*) *mansab* ranks.[34] (Most Hindu *mansabdars* held only a personal *mansab* rank.) The third category, that of the largest *jagirdars* in the state, is here defined as the holders of personal *jagirs* valued over 10,000 rupees a year. Only fifty-one of the five hundred fifty-two *jagirdars* fell into this category; eight were Hindus and none Kayasths.[35]

Looking at the Kayasths who did hold *jagirs* (though valued below 10,000 rupees a year), again the Malwala Mathur family was pre-eminent. The families are grouped by subcaste in Table 4.

The Malwala family stood out, with several family members listed separately as *jagirdars* and a total annual income from *jagirs* far exceeding that of other families. But the individual amounts were not too dissimilar, and they were low in comparison to those of other Hindu nobles,

33. The 16 are in the list of *jagirdars* in Lal, *Yadgar*, 93–123; the annual incomes of their *fauj jagirs* ranged from 3,659 to 1,446,881 rupees. The three Hindus were Raja Rao Rumbha, Raja Sham Raj, and Raja Sita Ram (the latter a *samasthan* ruler).
34. This was Raja Khushal Chand; Lal, *Yadgar*, 144–156 (*mansabdars*).
35. *Ibid.*, 93–123 (*jagirdars*).

TABLE 5:
Kayasth Mansabdars, 1800–1820

Mansab rank	Subcaste				
	Mathur	*Saksena*	*Srivastava*	*Bhatnagar*	*Gaur*
2000	Rai Khushal Chand	Rai Jatan Lal			
	Rai Lachman Singh				
1500				Raja Bhavani Pershad	
1000	Rai Deepak Rai	Raja Maya Ram			
		Raja Rup Lal			
700				Rai Manu Lal	
500		Rai Puran Chand			
400 or "by custom"[a]	6	19	5		8
Total men	10	23	5	2	8
Total families	3	—	—	1	5

Source: Makhan Lal, *Tarikh-i Yadgar-i Makhan Lal* (Hyderabad [1829]), 144–156.

[a]Many names were followed by the Persian notation *ba dastur* (according to custom), rather than a salary figure. These customary stipends were generally low, so I have included all such names in the lowest category here.

some of whom held individual *jagirs* ranging in value from 10,000 to 65,000 rupees per year. Particularly interesting was the relative status of the two *daftardar* families, the Rae Rayan Maharashtrian Brahman family and the Malwala Kayasth family, since they were to be constantly equated from the mid-nineteenth century. Their ranking differed markedly in the eighteenth and early nineteenth centuries. Members of the Rae Rayan family held *zat mansabs* of 5,000 to 7,000, with *jagirs* worth at least 48,000 rupees per year.[36] In the 1783–1784 manuscript listing *jagirdars* and *inamdars*, the Rae Rayan name was followed by payment entries

36. Members of the Rae Rayan and Rao Rumbha families in particular far outranked the Malwalas, with relatives of Chandu Lal and the *samasthan* rulers also well above. The 48,394-rupee *jagir* was the *zat jagir* of Raja Sham Raj (Rae Rayan); he also controlled a *fauj jagir* of 478,552 rupees: Lal, *Yadgar*, 93.

taking up two folio pages. But Bhavani Pershad, the Malwala *daftardar* of the Hyderabad province then, had only a one-line entry.[37] The difference is due to the Rae Rayan family's predominantly military service at this time.[38]

All of the *mansabdars* known to be Kayasths can be assigned to rank and subcaste in a summary of the caste as a whole (see Table 5). This distribution agrees with the family histories, confirming the prominence of particular families and roughly corresponding to later demographic data by subcaste designation. While oral tradition generally inflated the status of early Kayasths to at least equal that of other Hindus, it was essentially accurate concerning ranking within the Kayasth category. The Malwala family outranked others and was clearly rising, but its standing rested upon the number of family members holding *mansabs* and *jagirs*. The heads of families in other subcastes held *jagirs* and *mansab* ranks nearly equal to those of the head of the Malwala family. About half of the highest-ranking Kayasths at the turn of the century held positions in civil or household areas and about half were associated with military units; military service was in the background of nearly every family. These Kayasths, including the Malwalas, were rising, rather than established, members of the nobility in the late eighteenth century.

37. "Jagirdaran o Inamdaran," where the entry for the Rae Rayan family corresponds in length and type of assignment to those for Raja Rao Rumbha and other military nobles associated with the Maratha campaigns. Most identifiable Kayasths were described briefly as *munshi,* messenger, *peshkar, vakil,* and so forth.
38. *Ibid.* Specialists on Hyderabadi history may quibble about my placement of the Rae Rayan family in military service, but Raja Chimna, Raja Sham Raj, and Har Baji Pandit do belong there. See also Rao, *Bustan,* I, 145, and VII, 15, for the family's early *peshkar* positions.

CHAPTER 2

Kayasth Families
and Marriage Alliances

In the turbulent eighteenth century, Kayasths from Northern India were prominent among those who served with the Nizam and eventually settled in Hyderabad city. Like many in military and administrative occupations, they moved about with the ruler and his camp. Travel and communications were hazardous and difficult even within South India, where Kayasths served Muslim rulers in Burhanpur and Arcot, as well as in Aurangabad and Hyderabad.[1] To reach homes in North India required journeys of several weeks, through territories whose rulers might not respect the Nizam's personal "passport" sanctioning the journey.[2] The immigrants were, for all practical purposes, isolated from their former homes and relatives.

This distance and isolation presented problems when a man wished to marry or to arrange marriages for his children and dependents. Among the Chitragupta Kayasths of North India, the regulations required marriages to be arranged within the named subcaste but beyond certain degrees of relationship, usually seven degrees on the father's side and five on the mother's. For single men, adventurers in the Nizam's service in the Deccan, such problems may not have arisen initially; but once a man acquired a residence, property, and status, they did arise.

Kayasths arrived in Hyderabad as the result of individual independent migrations, and most of the immigrants were far from their previous

1. Archival records and manuscripts, and biography collections such as Muhammed Ghaus Khan, *Tazkirah-i Gulzar-i Azam* (Madras, 1855-1856), and Muhammad Sayyed Ahmed, *Umra-i Hinud* (Aligarh, 1910), testify to their presence in these places.
2. Several *dastaks* (passports), used when family members were on periodic visits to *jagirs*, have been preserved by Kayasth families.

homes and kin even though some migrations had occurred over several generations and over shorter distances. A Kayasth settling in Hyderabad had several alternatives with respect to marriage alliances: he could retain former connections, in North India or elsewhere; he could make new connections, in the South Indian region or within Hyderabad city; he could take concubines or non-Kayasth wives; he could convert to Islam. But even when others of the same subcaste were present, their background and ancestry could rarely be known with certainty. The intensive investigation of prospective relatives carried out in the North Indian homeland could not be undertaken, if indeed there had been the desire to do so. The fact of shared subcaste designation may have been sufficient for men of newly acquired or newly established position. The geographic distribution and number of fellow subcaste members in the Deccan became of major importance.

In eighteenth-century Hyderabad, dominance in a marriage network clearly rested upon an economic base. The extent to which a man could control and distribute economic resources determined his ability to build respectable marriage connections for his family. If there were few others of the same subcaste in the Deccan, wealth allowed respectable relatives to be brought from North India or from other South Indian administrative centers. Without wealth, Hyderabad Kayasths might produce a local community of doubtful ancestry, and few pure families could survive. If there were many other Kayasths of the same subcaste in Hyderabad, the problems were different. If the men held similar occupations and ranks, they might exchange children in marriage, and perhaps positions, over generations. If the internal differentiation was great, one family might dominate the others, or several different kin groups might develop among Kayasths of the same subcaste. Residential patterns, based on occupation or the establishment of a dominant family in the eighteenth century, became increasingly important as the historical development of neighborhoods in the city accentuated class and cultural differences.

The Kayasth families—*khandans,* or patrilineal descent groups—established in eighteenth-century Hyderabad illustrate these problems and alternative solutions to them. Because common subcaste membership was a necessary condition for marriages until the twentieth century, individuals and families will be grouped by subcaste for analysis here. The discussion begins with the three subcastes represented by relatively few high-ranking individuals and families: the Mathurs, Srivastavas, and Bhatnagars; it concludes with the Saksenas and Gaurs, who were more numerous and thus able to constitute local kin groups. As a total picture of Kayasths in Hyderabad in the eighteenth century, the discussion cannot be wholly accurate, because of the wealth bias in written sources and in the survival rate of families. But the findings appear to be borne out by later and more fully documented developments among Kayasth families and kin groups.

Mathur, Srivastava, and Bhatnagar Nobles

Representatives of these three Kayasth subcastes had settled in Hyderabad city by the late eighteenth century. Although they held high ranks and considerable wealth, they were apparently few in number. They followed different strategies to secure respectable marriage alliances, and the local kin groups formed by their descendants differed as a result. They controlled different kinds of economic resources, which were preserved and transmitted in different ways to their descendants.

Three Mathur Kayasth families were in the Deccan by the mid-eighteenth century, one antedating the first Nizam. According to oral tradition, the Gulab Chand family served the Mughals at Burhanpur and joined Nizam ul Mulk Asaf Jah I at Aurangabad.[3] The second family, that of Chatu Lal, began with a scribe from the Agra region who accompanied Asaf Jah I to the Deccan in the 1730's.[4] The Malwala family, the third Mathur family to arrive, is the one viewed as the founding family of the Mathur subcaste in Hyderabad. Of the three early Mathur families, certainly the Malwalas were the most powerful. The Malwala family's status has been assumed to derive entirely from its recordkeeping function as hereditary custodian of the Daftar-i Mal, revenue record office for the eastern, or Telangana, region of the state. The Malwalas held the *daftardar* position continuously from an early date, but the appearance of family members at court and their rise in the nobility probably owed something to the military services of family members as well.[5]

Despite claims of famous ancestry in North India, there is no reason to believe that the Malwala family's fortune was not entirely based upon its achievements in Hyderabad. The founder of the family in Hyderabad, Sagar Mal, was said to have been the personal protégé of the first Nizam. A composite account of the family's origin follows:

Sagar Mal's family house in Shahjahanabad [Delhi] collapsed during the reign of the Emperor Aurangzeb, and Sagar Mal was the sole survivor of the disaster.

3. Nasir ud-din Hashimi, *Dakhini Hindu aur Urdu* (Hyderabad [1958]), 33, 48; interview with Hakim Vicerai.

4. Interviews with Hind Kishore, T. R. Mathur, and Hakim Vicerai.

5. Bhavani Das, for example, is said to have proven his valor in the 1795 battle of Khardla.

38]

Since the boy was descended from Raja Raghunath, Aurangzeb's famous Diwan, he was carefully brought up as a protégé of Nizam ul Mulk. Upon reaching maturity, Sagar Mal accompanied Nizam ul Mulk to Hyderabad and was appointed to the *daftardar* position. This position was thereafter held by Sagar Mal's descendants.[6]

This traditional account does more to explain a lack of credentials than to clarify the background of the *daftardar* family.

The career of Sagar Mal and his descendants in Hyderabad depended upon continued custody of the revenue records. Sagar Mal had been appointed head of the Daftar-i Mal by 1761, for he was termed so in the official *jagir* register when his sons Bhavani Das*and Durga Das received *jagirs* in that year.[7] Under Bhavani Das, head of the *daftar* from the 1780's, family members began to receive titles and honors at court.[8] Nizam Ali Khan Asaf Jah II commended Bhavani Das for his services in 1790 with the following official letter to the Raja:

In grand appreciation of the rights, antiquity, loyalty, obeisance and faithfulness of his family, their honesty in my Rule; I, for the time being, honor him with the *sardaftari* of Deccan provinces with necessary *mansab* and *muash* and his future promotions depend upon this. He should carry out the duties entrusted to him with zeal and faithfulness; then he can expect further honor and gratis from us. Either at present or in the future, the rights of this family are established with this kingdom; and I or my successors to this kingdom will look after the interest of this family.[9]

Although the position is still termed a conditional one in this document, the family's claim to hereditary supervision of the *daftar* was soon successfully established. After 1790, the senior man in each of the two collateral lines of descent regularly received titles and *jagirs* upon the death of each successive *daftardar*.[10]

Determination of successive *daftardars* evidently did not depend upon direct lineal descent, but upon age and competency. Thus the position

---

6. Lal, *Yadgar*, 68; "Raja Rajman Maharaja Nawazwant Raja Murli Manohar Bahadur, Asaf Jahi of Hyderabad, Dn." *Kayastha*, I, no. 3 (1896), 1; and Varman, *Mukhtasir Tarikh-i Aqvam* II, 208. Two sources linked Sagar Mal to Nizam ul-Mulk's return from Delhi (after Nadir Shah's 1738 invasion): Khan, *Gulzar*, 253; Khan, *Tuzuk*, II (Nobles), 194. An earlier date of 1730–1731 was given by Saksenah, *Kayasth Sajjan Caritra*, II, pt. 3, 2.

7. Register Asnad-i Jagir, I, no. 11, serial no. 113/12.

8. "Jagirdaran o Inamdaran," fol. 70; *Chronology*, 59, 61, 76, 77, 78, 85, 87, 88, etc. (first entry dated 1779).

9. This *parvanah* was dated the first of Rabi al-akhir in the thirty-second year of "the reign," probably that of Shah Alam, the Mughal emperor, and therefore December 9, 1790. It is reprinted in Persian in Saksenah, *Kayasth Sajjan Caritra*, II, pt. 3, 3; my translation.

10. Daftar-i Mal Jagir Register, "naqul-i asnad-i Shiv Raj," file no. 66 of 1342 F. [1932–1933]. See also the *Chronology* entries in note 8 above.

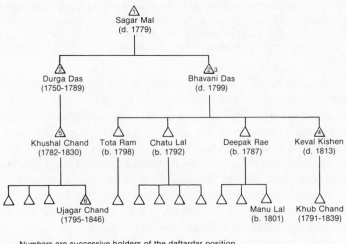

Numbers are successive holders of the daftardar position
Throughout kinship charts, eldest is on right, unless otherwise noted.

2: Genealogy of the Malwala *daftardars,* 1761–1846

passed in the eighteenth and early nineteenth centuries from the senior
to the junior line of the family, though all men received grants from the
Nizam and the *jagirs* were managed as a joint estate. The genealogy in
Figure 2 shows the successive *daftardars*. Bhavani Das and Durga Das
shared the position after Sagar Mal's death; Bhavani Das held it after
Durga Das's death; it then passed to Bhavani Das's eldest son, Keval
Kishen. Keval Kishen became ill in 1803 or 1804; his own brother and son
were very young, so the position passed to Khushal Chand, his cousin-
brother (first cousin).[11] The position stayed in the junior branch of the
family after this last transfer.

The economic resources of all three early Mathur families were considerable. The Malwala family controlled one of two major record offices
in Hyderabad. *Jagirs* were granted in the name of the *daftardar,* and other
men in the family received *inam* grants. The family income was at least
4,500 rupees per year in 1783, and in 1820 it totalled at least 17,550
rupees, distributed among six family members.[12]

11. For the genealogy, see notes 8 and 10 above. The actual head of the *daftar* for
perhaps 30 years after the death of Sagar Mal was a Saksena Kayasth, Raja Surajwant.
Surajwant had been displaced by Aristo Jah for several years, but he returned to power in
1804, apparently on recommendation of the Begum (Queen) when Khushal Chand became
daftardar: Lal, *Yadgar,* 67.
12. Lal, *Yadgar,* 33–123; and see Table 4.

In the early nineteenth century, the Malwala nobles and the other two Mathur families were also powerful military *serrishtahdars*. One of the other Mathurs was in the service of the Paigahs, the leading Muslim military noble family by 1790.[13] In fact, all five military *serrishtahs* held by Mathur Kayasths were controlled by these three early families, three by the Malwalas and one by each of the other two. And two of the three families controlled record offices, for the Chatu Lal family presided over the Daftar-i Khitabat va Manasib, which kept records of title and *mansab* grants.[14] The Malwalas maintain that they gave this smaller record office to the Chatu Lal family. All three families held *jagirs*.[15]

There is considerable ambiguity about the actual marriage connections of these three early families who were close neighbors on Chowk Maidan Khan, the major avenue running east from the Char Minar (Map 1). None of the eighteenth-century marriages are recorded or remembered; descendants today generally deny that the three were related by marriage before the late 1870's, when marriages among them are recorded. If these three families did not intermarry, they may have married with Mathur families elsewhere in southern India, or with non-Mathurs or non-Kayasths, alternatives that are generally denied. Despite the denials, it is likely that the three families were related by marriage in the eighteenth century. This can be inferred not only from the residential and occupational similarities, but from certain confusions in oral information and from knowledge of the marriage alliances made in the nineteenth century by the Malwala family.[16]

The growing wealth and status of the Malwala family by the late eighteenth century allowed it to initiate an unusual series of marriages with North Indian Mathur families. A Persian history of the late eighteenth century notes that Rai Bhavani Das, the "son of the revenue accountant for the provinces of Hyderabad and Muhaminadabad Bidar," was absent from Hyderabad for a month in 1777 because he had taken his son Keval Kishen to North India for marriage.[17] The Malwala family

13. Gulab Chand was in Paigah service: Hashimi, *Dakhini Hindu*, 33. For the military units, Khan, *Gulzar*, 489; interview with Hakim Vicerai.

14. Interview with Hind Kishore; Department of Information and Public Relations, *Some Aspects of Hyderabad 1954* (Hyderabad, 1954), 1-12.

15. For the Malwalas, Daftar-i Mal Jagir Register, "naqul-i asnad-i Shiv Raj," file no. 66 of 1342 F. [1932-1933]. For the Gulab Chand *jagirs*, see Register Asnad-i Jagir, IV, no. 15, serial no. 354/9 and supp. VI, no. 18, serial no. 21/1. For the Chatu Lal *jagirs*, see Sayyid Manzur Ali, *Anvar-i Asafiyah* (Hyderabad, 1935), 189.

16. It is likely that sons-in-law were sometimes recorded as sons in these early generations; e.g., the Chatu Lal who appears on two genealogies is probably the same man.

17. *HA*, IV, 620, in a translation of the Persian history *Hadikat-i Alam*. The quote about Bhavani Das on p. 640 refers to 1788.

KAYASTH SETTLEMENT IN THE OLD
CITY since 1780

RESIDENCY
BAZARS

To GOLCONDA FORT

SRIVASTAVAS
Dhulpet

MUSI RIVER

SRIVASTAVAS
Dabirpura

Mehbub ki
Mehndi
BHATNAGARS SRIVASTAVAS
SRIVASTAVAS CHAR
Majlis Rae MINAR MATHURS
Husaini Alam NIGAMS
SAKSENAS Chowk
Maidan Khan
BHATNAGARS
Kotla Ali Jah
Yaqutpura

Shahalibanda
SRIVASTAVAS
SAKSENAS Gowlipura
GAURS
Lal Darwaza

N

0   I KM

MAP 1

was just then becoming powerful, and while other eighteenth-century Malwala marriages are unknown, this incident provides a valuable contrast with later family practices. By the nineteenth century, emissaries might be sent north on behalf of the head of the Malwala family, but the head of the family himself never went north to arrange or attend a marriage.[18] Marriage contracts were negotiated with North Indian families, who sent several members to Hyderabad with marriageable boys and girls. Thus new Mathur families were established in Hyderabad, economically dependent upon the patron Malwala family. Aside from the first three Mathur families, almost all successive subcaste families were brought by the Malwalas in this way. These relationships will be fully traced later as they become a feature of the nineteenth century, but the first son-in-law was brought at the end of the eighteenth century.[19] The Malwala's sponsorship of new Mathur immigrants and dominance of the subcaste accompanied that family's attainment of wealth and power in Hyderabad state.

Three families of Srivastava Kayasths were in the Deccan by the mid-eighteenth century, and they ranked high in the Nizam's service by the end of the century. In contrast to the early Mathur families, none of these families has survived to the present. One Srivastava family served in the Deccan prior to the Nizam's arrival, as Mughal *vaqai-nigar,* or letter-writer, at Birh.[20] Ancestors continued to be posted as letter-writer at Birh under Nizam ul Mulk, and descendants have written confirmation of transfer of the position within the family since the late eighteenth century. Family members resided in the city of Hyderabad, and staff members at Birh compiled reports which the head of the family presented to the Nizam at *durbars.* The family was reputedly wealthy, with a large residence in Husaini Alam and its own elephants. This was a Khare Srivastava family, one of two endogamous subdivisions within that subcaste, and it neither resided near nor married with the two Dusre Srivastava families in the city.[21]

Another Srivastava family ranked high in the nobility, and its founder accompanied Nizam ul Mulk Asaf Jah I to the Deccan. In the second

18. Family Brahmans and barbers are supposed to have been sent. Hyderabad Kayasth and Brahman informants cited this tradition from printed books rather than personal knowledge, however.

19. Interview with Ramchander Narayan; Lal, *Yadgar,* 146, where Lakshmi Narayan's name appears among the Malwala names.

20. This conditional service pay ended in 1902: Ali, *Anvar-i Asafiyah,* 3. The family genealogy goes back ten generations and begins with several Singhs, a typical eighteenth-century name for Hyderabad Kayasths.

21. Financial papers with a Gaur grandson-in-law, Jagdish Pershad; interview with Mrs. Murlidhar Pershad. The Khare and Dusre divisions, according to tradition, are descended from the two sons of the subcaste founder; Khare is usually ranked above Dusre.

generation, this founder's four sons served variously as treasurers, correspondents, *zenanah* officials, and military officers. The family *jagirs* were reputedly won by Raja Dooleh Rae Asafjahi as a reward for his conquest of Jagtial Fort in 1782, and they were valued at almost 14,000 rupees a year. This Srivastava family lived in Shahalibanda in a large residence. Demography and allegations of corruption caused a downturn in the family's fortune. The four brothers had only one son between them, Raja Keval Ram, who built a large temple to Chitragupta (founding figure and patron deity of the Kayasth caste) in 1806.[22] Keval Ram's personal *jagir* was valued at 7,215 rupees per year in 1820. But, while serving as treasurer of Golconda Fort, he could not explain a shortfall in treasury funds, and he was dismissed in 1823.[23] His descendants continued to serve in treasury positions, however, and a market was named after the last representative of the line in Shahalibanda.[24] This Dusre Srivastava family left two local landmarks, the market and the Chitragupta temple, when it died out.

The third Srivastava family about which we have eighteenth-century information is best known by its later name as the Chain Rae family. Its founder also came with Asaf Jah I, and the family ranked high in the household administration, holding a major supervisory position within the Nizam's palace. Family members sometimes held other positions, including military ones. This too was a wealthy Srivastava family, with an annual income of 14,400 rupees, an elephant, and a *diwankhana* (reception hall) and library in their residence.[25] This Dusre Srivastava family lived in Dabirpura, an area of the city equidistant from Husaini Alam and Shahalibanda.

In contrast to the three early Mathur families, these Srivastava families lived in quite different parts of the city and served in different areas of the administration. Their reputed status was high and approximately equal, at least in the eighteenth century. Partly because of the Khare and Dusre distinction, there were no kinship ties between them. According to their descendants through the female line and the descendants of adopted sons

22. For titles and gifts to the Dooleh Rae family, see *Chronology*, 77, 79, 82, 90. For *jagirs*, Register Asnad-i Jagir, vol. 1, no. 12, serial nos. 174/11 and 225/11, and vol. 3, no. 14, serial nos. 360/3 and 330/26; and in Asnad-i Jagir alif-ye, I, serial no. 1288; Satguru Pershad, "Deval Sri Chitraguptaji Maharaj," *KH*, IV-V (1945), 1-2. There are apparently only two or three other Chitragupta temples in India.
23. Lal, *Yadgar*, 69, 182.
24. Interview with Roy Mahboob Narayan about Lal Pershad's market. Lal Pershad's widow received compensation for his *jagirs* in 1903-1904: Ali, *Anvar-i Asafiyah*, 253.
25. Khan, *Tuzuk*, II (Nobles) (supp.), 25-26, and interview with Ram Kumar Lal. The family is now represented by the daughter of the adopted heir's brother and her North Indian husband.

and close neighbors, even the Dusre families claimed to be unrelated. Here again is the problem of unrecorded marriages for early Kayasth immigrants. If they did not marry each other, and if there were no other respectable Srivastavas in Hyderabad, they may have maintained marriage connections with Srivastava families outside, either in North India or elsewhere in South India. Oral traditions about the three families claim that they did both, marrying with people from North India and also Madras, where there were Srivastava Kayasths in the service of the Nawab of Arcot.

There is no eighteenth-century evidence concerning specific kinship connections for the Srivastava families, but there are several clues. They did have the resources and the status necessary to contract and maintain long-distance kinship ties. And a Srivastava Kayasth in the Nawab of Arcot's service did come to Hyderabad to marry in 1783,[26] while several marriages between Hyderabad and Madras Srivastavas are documented for the nineteenth century.[27] Finally, at least one of these families, that of Chain Rae, with positions in the palace, had local in-laws.[28] Yet, in interviews, emphatic negative answers were given to questions about marriage with other Srivastavas in Hyderabad. As succeeding chapters will show, alternatives to respectable marriages were resorted to by Srivastavas (and others), producing descendants who have not been recorded on official genealogies.

There were two Bhatnagar families in Hyderabad in the eighteenth century, and both claim to have come with the first Nizam. Despite early military service, members of both families later served chiefly in the Nizam's household establishment. The higher-ranking family of Raja Bhavani Pershad was founded on *jagirs* granted to one Debi Das, *peshkar* of Diwani. The elder son Tulja Pershad was manager of the kitchens in 1783, and when he was killed on the battlefield of Pongal, the younger son Raja Bhavani Pershad succeeded him. Bhavani Pershad in 1820 was a high-ranking noble, a palace official with a *mansab* of 1,500 rupees per month and a *jagir* worth 3,244 rupees a year.[29] This family originally

26. He was Raja Makhan Lal Khirad, who wrote the chronogram for the Jama Masjid in Madras: Hashimi, *Dakhini Hindu*, 38; Khan, *Gulzar-i Azam*, 173.

27. Interview with Ram Kumar Lal, who mentioned a particular Madras Dusre Srivastava family with whom both Hyderabad Dusre Srivastava families had married. The name and title he gave appeared in the private collection of Dr. Muhammad Ghaus of Madras, "Persian Records concerning titles given by the Nawab of Arcot," tentatively numbered file 35. Other connections are given by Lala Khub Chand, *Kayasth Kul Nar Nai* (Hyderabad, 1892), 120–125.

28. Chand, *Kayasth Kul Nar Nai*, 93–94.

29. He was also a revenue contractor of eight lakhs rupees, and he had cavalry and another force of 4,000 under him. Lal, *Yadgar*, 68; Khan, *Gulzar*, 259: Khan, *Tuzuk*, II

lived in Chowk Maidan Khan next to the Mathurs, where many of the household workshops and offices were located; other Bhatnagars came and settled nearby in the nineteenth century.

The second Bhatnagar family was associated with the military and probably lived originally in Shahalibanda. In the nineteenth century, its descendants became associated with the carriage house in the household establishment.[30] Like the Srivastavas, these two Bhatnagar families lived in different localities and professed nonrelationship; unlike the Srivastavas, they recruited relatives and heirs to positions from both incoming and local Bhatnagars in the nineteenth century.[31]

The Saksena and Gaur Kayasths

The Saksena and Gaur Kayasths were the only two subcastes numerous enough to form marriage networks based in Hyderabad city in this early period. Internal differentiation among the Saksenas was greater, and there were at least two marriage networks. One dominant family characterized the Gaur network, although the family in that position changed over time.

There were many Saksenas in South India in the eighteenth century, employed by the Nizam in Aurangabad and Hyderabad and by the Nawab of Arcot in Madras. Some fifteen or twenty Saksena families had settled in Hyderabad city by the end of the century, living in two different residential areas roughly corresponding to occupational divisions. The leading Saksenas in that century were connected with the military; the others were in various household positions. The locality in which the earliest Saksena immigrants settled was Shahalibanda, but by the end of the century two or three Saksena families had moved to the new locality of Husaini Alam. The prominent military men—Raja Rup Lal, Raja Maya Ram, and Raja Buchar Mal—were not literary men, but they were high-ranking nobles and were noted in contemporary records. These military

---

(Nobles), 201. For *jagirs,* see Asnad-i Jagir alif-ye, I, serial no. 488, and for Bhavani Pershad's maternal grandsons (Manu Lal and Hanu Lal), II, serial no. 1397. Also see Register Asnad-i Jagir: for Bhavani Pershad, IV, no. 15, serial no. 223/12; for Raja Manu Lal and other dependents of Bhavani Pershad, V, no. 16, serial nos. 210/46, 291/23, 321/5.

30. Raja Inderjit from this family supervised food distribution during famine periods in the city at the end of the eighteenth century, and a central foodgrains market was named for him; he may also have collected customs. Mahender Raj Suxena, "Hyderabad aur Kayasth," 7–8; Lal, *Yadgar,* 65; *Chronology,* 97.

31. For the descendants of Raja Bhavani Pershad, interview with Brij Rani and daughters; for the descendants of Majlis Rae, interviews with Sham Karan and Balobir Prosad; for both, interview with Hakim Vicerai.

men also left behind physical landmarks and colorful oral traditions which tell a great deal about them and the times in which they lived.

In 1800, and until about 1830, it was the Saksena military leaders who commanded attention. These men were closely connected with the Diwan, Aristo Jah, with the Paigah military nobles, and with Sulaiman Jah, brother of the Nizam. Through such patrons they had access to the Nizam. Nizam Ali Khan died in 1803; his successor, Secunder Jah, was very young. Diwan Aristo Jah appointed Raja Sabha Chand, a Saksena Kayasth, as regent or co-regent responsible for the private correspondence and accounts of the Nizam. Sabha Chand's brother Jatan Lal held positions with the Paigah cavalry and in the Nizam's household. When Sabha Chand died, the regent position went to his sister's son, Raja Rup Lal, because his own son, Maya Ram, was too young. Later, Raja Maya Ram took over Jatan Lal's military duties when the latter died without an heir.[32] Thus Raja Rup Lal and Raja Maya Ram both inherited positions from their uncles; they were titled nobles and *jagirdars* in the early nineteenth century, wealthy and popular men in Shahalibanda.

Raja Buchar Mal was a military *serrishtahdar* for Sulaiman Jah and the most famous of these Saksena Kayasths. He held *jagirs,* owned and rented out large buildings in Shahalibanda, and built and patronized a Hindu temple and a Muslim shrine in the locality. The latter housed a relic for the commemoration of the Shia Muslim observance of Muharram.[33] Buchar Mal also served as a major revenue contractor and was in charge of a fortress.[34] He even appeared in the East India Company's records, since his military units were among those included in the Hyderabad Contingent in 1813.[35] (These forces were turned over to the Resident

32. Biographies appear in Lal, *Yadgar,* 67–68, 161. Maya Ram is mentioned in *Chronology,* 207. Rup Lal appears in Government of India, Foreign Department, *Nomenclature: Reports on Native Courts,* 51–52, serial no. 129 of 1814, Miscellaneous (NAI). In Register Asnad-i Jagir, the following entries: for Rup Lal, III, no. 14, serial nos. 232/4 and 243/13, and IV, no. 15, serial no. 6/6; for Maya Ram, III, no. 14, serial nos. 145/9 and 313/3, and IV, no. 15, serial nos. 245/4 and 344/22. Also for Maya Ram, Asnad-i Jagir alif-ye, II, serial nos. 1379 and 1551. The original *sanad* conferring the title Raja on Rup Lal (dated 8 Rajab 1231 H. [1816]) is with Gurucharan Das Saxena, descendant of Rup Lal's nephew.
33. Interviews with Roy Mahboob Narayan, Shakamber Raj Saxena and his mother, and Gurucharan Das Saxena.
34. For his *jagirs* see Register Asnad-i Jagir, IV, no. 15, serial no. 563/30, and V, no. 16, serial no. 108/5; Lal, *Yadgar,* 84, 91.
35. Buchar Mal appears as "Rai Barcha Mull," co-leader of the Third Cavalry, in Major E. A. W. Stotherd, *History of the 30th Lancers Gordon's Horse* (London [1912]), 17, and as "Rao Boochur Mull," assigned the district of Nirmal, in Government of India, Foreign Department, *Report on Reform in Nizam's Government,* Secret Consultation no. 8, Sept. 30, 1820 (NAI).

but were financially supported by the Nizam and included some officers from the Nizam's service.)

In addition to the military men in Shahalibanda, less prominent Saksenas in Hyderabad were clerks and *serrishtahdars.* Three of the six identifiable Kayasths listed in a manuscript of 1784 were Saksenas, two of them clerks.[36] Another early family, that of Daulat Rae, moved from Aurangabad to Hyderabad through marriage with the daughter of one of these clerks. Daulat Rae married into Hyderabad about 1770; his title placed him in a household position, but he marched with the army to seize Jagtial Fort in 1782. He had two sons, one in military service and the other, Raja Ram, in the household administration as "supervisor of thirty-six departments."[37] Raja Ram's son, Swami Pershad, married the daughter of Kumari Lal, *peshkar* of the Muslim noble Himmat Yar Khan, and he inherited from his father-in-law the *peshkari* of Asafgarh Fort, essentially a paymaster position for the forces stationed there. This family now controlled several household positions, and it moved from Shahalibanda to the developing neighborhood of Husaini Alam.[38] In 1783-1784, Raja Ram purchased a large residence and adjoining buildings there, some of which he rented out for income.[39] The turn of the century found this family linked to that of Mir Alam, a Shia Muslim family associated with many of the household departments.[40] Since Mir Alam served as Diwan of Hyderabad from 1804 to 1808, and his son-in-law Munir ul Mulk became Diwan in 1808, this Saksena family had access to the developing bureaucracy.

Another early Saksena family in Hyderabad was originally not in the Nizam's service. It was based in Madras, and a branch came to Hydera-

36. The three were Utam Chand, Rae Babu, and Todar Mal (nicknamed Chamee Lal). The latter two were clerks: "Jagirdaran o Inamdaran."

37. The genealogy of this family appears in Dwarka Pershad Ufuq, *Hiyat-i Baqi Manzum* (Lucknow, 1892-1893), 22-23. The entries are discussed in a family history, Girdhari Pershad, "Kalam-i Baqi," in *Kulliyat-i Baqi* (Hyderabad, 1887-1888), 25-28. See also Khan, *Tuzuk,* II (Nobles), 413. The latter position was *mushrif-i khansaman* (supervisor for the household administrator), wherein oral tradition credits Raja Ram with supervising thirty-six posts. This statement can be explained by the popular tradition that the Mughal *karkhanahs* numbered 36 (Sarkar, *Mughal Administration,* 165) and by the fact that most *karkhanahs* were under the *khansaman.* Thus Raja Ram's position as *mushrif-i khansaman* in Hyderabad would have included supervision of the *karkhanahs,* whatever their actual number.

38. For a summary of the accumulation of positions, Pershad, "Kalam-i Mutafarriqat," in *Kulliyat,* 25-28. They included: *mushrif-i mashalkhanah* (department of torches), *mushrif-i shadikhanah* (wedding hall), and *mushrif-i bavarchikhanah.*

39. Khan, *Tuzuk,* II (Nobles), 413.

40. This connection is noted in Swami Pershad's 1817 transcription of *Insha-i Namati* for Rae Babu, the Kayasth *munshi* of Mir Alam.

48]

bad with the *vakil* of the Wala Jahi family of the Nawab of Arcot.[41] This was probably the first Saksena family settled in Husaini Alam, and their ancestral residence was a large one. A *sati* stone near the Hindu burning *ghat* on the Musi River places members of this family in Hyderabad by the 1790's.[42] Family tradition claims that an ancestor came as chief agent of the Nawab of Arcot to supervise the *jagirs* in Hyderabad. But the earliest family member, Megh Raj, was actually in charge of the Nawab's gardens and was working under another Saksena.[43] Megh Raj's son made the family fortune by rising to the position of chief agent by 1840. This family used its kinship connections to carry out its job: the Madras branch of the family served as chief correspondent of the Nawab of Arcot, so that communications between Madras and the agents in Hyderabad often took place between brothers and, in the next generation, between cousin-brothers.[44]

There were kinship ties among these Saksenas settled in Hyderabad in the eighteenth century. Most of them lived in Shahalibanda; a few families settled in Husaini Alam. Many preserved traditions of migration to Hyderabad from North India via Aurangabad or Madras, and they married with Saksenas in both places. Marriages were recorded for this early period between the Saksenas living in Shahalibanda and those in Husaini Alam. We cannot fully reconstruct the genealogies for the earlier generations, as wives and daughters were omitted; we know least about the origins and paths of migration of the military men, as few of them left direct, legitimate, Hindu descendants. But marriage relationships existed.[45]

I use the term marriage networks for these early Saksenas and Gaurs because from the available evidence they neither limited their marriages to a small set of local families nor controlled positions as the "property"

41. Family tradition traces this family back to Delhi, then to Madras with Anwar ud-din Khan, *subahdar* of Arcot in the eighteenth century. See the private collection of the Nawab of Arcot's papers with Dr. Muhammed Ghaus of Madras, whose family served as Diwans to the Nawab, where letters ("Persian correspondence on behalf of the Nawabs of Arcot with the Hyderabad Vakils," tentatively numbered file 32) fully confirm the information obtained orally in interviews with family members in Hyderabad (Lakshmi Narayan and Shakamber Raj Saxena). The letters covered 1802 to 1857.

42. The stone has an inscription dated 1171 H. (1757–1758). Family members appear as in-laws on the genealogy mentioned for the Raja Ram family in note 37 above.

43. See the first letter, dated 1802, in the collection of Dr. Muhammad Ghaus, file 32 (note 41 above).

44. The letters between brothers were those of Megh Raj and Khusi Lal; between first cousins, Ishwar Das and Bhagwant Rae.

45. Interviews with Roy Mahboob Narayan, the mother of Shakamber Raj Saxena, and Gurucharan Das Saxena. In all recorded instances, women were given to the military men.

of such a limited group. Among these Saksenas, positions began to be inherited by kinsmen as the nineteenth century began. Maya Ram inherited his father's brother's position, Swami Pershad his father-in-law's position, and Rup Lal his mother's brother's position. In two of these cases there was no legitimate son to inherit; in the third the son was too young. Here the transition from marriage network to kin group was occurring, as marriages were made to control and consolidate positions held and shared among relatives in Hyderabad.

There were still other Saksenas in Hyderabad by 1800 who do not appear in the genealogies of those already discussed because they were not in the same marriage network. These other Saksenas were residents of Shahalibanda, often military men by profession, and supposedly were of illegitimate parentage. This *suratval* category[46] was one into which the descendants of Rup Lal, Buchar Mal, and some branches of other families would later fall. These "real" and "illegitimate" Saksenas must have known one another in the eighteenth century, as several from each category were associated with the Nizam's household or with the service of Raja Chandu Lal (the Khatri nobleman who served as *peshkar* and Diwan from 1808 to 1843). Not only must the men have worked together, several of the families were close neighbors as well.

Most Saksena Kayasths at the turn of the century, then, were settled in Shahalibanda, and the most prominent among them were associated with the military. Others occupied less conspicuous positions, usually within the Nizam's household. One of the latter families and a family serving the Nawab of Arcot had settled in Husaini Alam. But marriages occurred between the military and nonmilitary families and between the two residential areas. This outline, rough and incomplete though it might be, is clear enough; and it contrasts with the residential, occupational, and kin group patterns developed among the Saksenas in the late nineteenth century.

Finally, there were at least five families of Gaur Kayasths in Hyderabad by the end of the eighteenth century, and they were in the same marriage network. Nearly all Gaur Kayasths became dependent upon the Paigah nobles, rather than serving the Nizam directly. Like the Saksenas, there seem to have been numerous Gaurs, but in central not southern India, and migration via marriage was the characteristic pattern.

The most famous early Gaur family was that of legendary military men, the Panch Bhai Gaur (Five Gaur Brothers). The Panch Bhai lived in Shahalibanda, where all the Gaur families settled, and their fame survives in oral accounts. A composite text gives the following story:

46. The illegitimate category will be fully discussed in Chapter 6.

The family of Neelkanth came from Nizamabad via Khandesh and Aurangabad. Called the Panch Bhai, the five sons were valiant fighters and close comrades of the Nizam Ali Khan; they fought with him in Tipu Sultan's war [either that of 1792 or 1799]. They were very wealthy—their mansion was large and they kept their provisions in brass pots. The women of the family were noted for their beauty. As the Nizam's army passed the family mansion while returning to the city one day, the women were visible on the roof, drying their hair in the sun. The Nizam was smitten with one woman in particular. He secretly ordered some of his men to kill the Panch Bhai and bring the women and children into his harem. This was done. The children were raised as Shia Muslims. Some say that another set of Panch Bhai was born in the Muslim line and they again became famous military men; it is their tomb just outside of Shahalibanda which is known as Makbarah Panch Bhai.[47]

All informants agree on a dramatic end of the family, before 1820 certainly, and several agree on the likelihood of a continuing Muslim line. Some evidence points to conversion to Islam, for whatever reason and however accomplished.[48]

The origins and migration patterns of four more Gaur families in Hyderabad by 1800 show them, like the Panch Bhai family, to have moved south over several generations. Three gave Nizamabad as their place of origin. Two of them had come with the Panch Bhai family via Khandesh and Aurangabad, while the third had resided in Ujjain and Aurangabad. The fourth family gave its origin as Uchar in Gwalior state; it had resided in a small town near Bidar before moving to Hyderabad. Only one family retained traditions of service prior to that with the Nizam.[49] As with the Saksenas, generations of Mughal and other service might be postulated for the Gaur Kayasths, but evidently their ancestors were in fairly obscure positions. At any rate, their previous status was irrelevant to their careers in Hyderabad.

All five Gaur families settled in Shahalibanda and were related to each other by marriage, but dominance in the marriage network passed from one family to another according to the positions controlled. Ram Kishen, the founder of the family for which there is the earliest evidence of dominance, had married the daughter of a clerk in Aurangabad and moved to Hyderabad with the Nizam's court. Marriages brought two more families from Aurangabad to Hyderabad. Both the Panch Bhai and another

47. Interviews with Roy Mahboob Narayan and his wife, Onker Pershad and Jagdish Pershad.
48. Interviews in note 47 above, and the fact that the tomb of the Muslim five brothers is just outside the walls by the Gaur houses in Ghazibanda and on Paigah property, next to the Balmukund Gaur family temple.
49. Gaur, *Tazkirah-i Sucaru Vanshi,* 29–32, 135, 143. This Ram Kishen family served in Delhi and Ujjain.

Nizamabad-Khandesh-Aurangabad family (that of Mohan Das) first arrived as sons-in-law, and subordinates, to the Ram Kishen family.[50] Another reason for supposing the Ram Kishen family to be the dominant family among the early Gaurs comes from the fact that descendants through women in the surviving Mohan Das family named sons for men in the Ram Kishen genealogy.[51] Such naming patterns commemorated powerful ancestors.

While the Ram Kishen family held a *mansab* from the Nizam and appears to have been the earliest Gaur family in Hyderabad to dominate the others, succeeding Gaur families moved out of the Nizam's own service. The *mansab* from the Nizam continued in a son-in-law's line, but most Gaurs served in the household and military establishments of the Paigah nobles. Given the career patterns and service preferences of the late eighteenth century, it is probable that the Panch Bhai Gaur family was in Paigah service and that its wealth and prominence drew kinsmen into its expanding establishment. After the demise of the Panch Bhai and the end of the Ram Kishen male line, the Mohan Das family controlled the Paigah positions and determined marriage alliances.[52]

It is possible, then, to link the Gaur families not only to the shift of the court from Aurangabad by 1780, but also to the rise of the Paigah family to power within the state at that time.[53] The Ram Kishen family line ended; the other Gaur families, though connected by marriage with both the Ram Kishen and Panch Bhai families, moved almost entirely into Paigah household and military positions. The Paigah service expanded in the late eighteenth century, as Tegh Jung received *jagirs* and *mansabs* totalling thirty lakhs of rupees a year and his son Fakhruddin Khan married the daughter of Nizam Ali Khan and became a close advisor to succeeding Nizams.[54] The Gaur Kayasths prospered with the Paigah family. But their increased wealth and their patterns of marriage and inheritance in the nineteenth century would depend closely on the fortunes of their patrons.

50. *Ibid.*

51. The Ram Kishen family genealogy has been preserved by Jagdish Pershad.

52. Interviews with Onker Pershad, Roy Mahboob Narayan and his wife, and Mahbub Rai, and my own collation of all the Gaur genealogies.

53. Although earlier members of the family, resident in Burhanpur, had been patronized by Mughal emperors and Asaf Jah I, the first Hyderabad *jagirs* were granted for military services to Tegh Jung (d. 1786) in the 1770's and 1780's. For the Paigah family history, see Khan, *Tuzuk,* II (Nobles), 1–6; *Chronology,* 68, 226, glossary 13, 15, index 3–4; A. C. Campbell, *Glimpses of the Nizam's Dominions* (London, 1898), 307; Tej Rae, *Sahifeh-i Asman Jahi* (Hyderabad, 1904–1905).

54. *Chronology,* references cited in note 53 above, and genealogies of the Nizams and the Paigahs in the back of the *Chronology.*

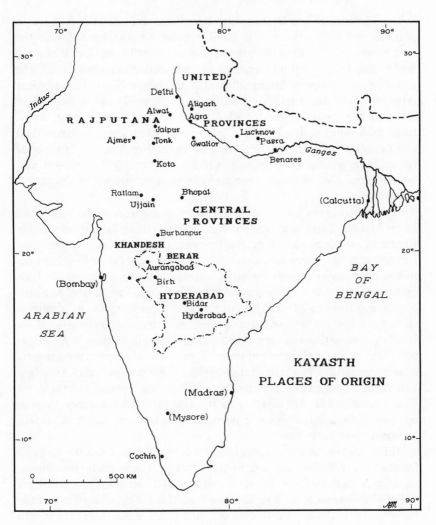

MAP 2

The evidence and oral traditions concerning these early Kayasth families in Hyderabad testify to diversity rather than uniformity. The earliest Mathur, Srivastava, and Bhatnagar families shared certain characteristics: high rank as nobles, substantial income from *jagirs* and *mansabs,* and relative isolation from others of their subcaste designation. Yet their origins and the marriage networks in which they participated differed considerably, even in the eighteenth century. (See Map 2.)

[53

The Mathurs in the Deccan were few; there were apparently none in Madras; two of the three early families came via Aurangabad with the first Nizam. All Mathurs moving to Hyderabad settled in Chowk Maidan Khan, and their early relationships are unclear. After about 1780, the power of the Malwala family allowed it to recruit North Indian client families, which accounts for the entire subsequent Mathur population in the city. Oral tradition for the early Srivastavas families is poor, as all three male lines ended by 1905; but they resided apart in Hyderabad and maintain that they married with Madras or North Indian Srivastavas rather than with each other. For the Bhatnagars, oral traditions and later evidence indicate few members of the subcaste in the Deccan or South India.

For the Saksenas and Gaurs, five or more families of each subcaste formed locally-based marriage networks incorporating families of roughly similar occupations and ranks. This meant, for the Gaurs, one marriage network and one dominant family. The Saksenas appear to have been far more numerous; they participated in two marriage networks, one of which bridged military and civil occupations and the two localities of Shahali-banda and Husaini Alam. The Gaur Kayasths have traditions of migrations from the north, and most sources refer to small groups of Gaur families moving through central India and eventually settling in Aurangabad. They moved to Hyderabad towards the end of the eighteenth century, all of them settling in Shahalibanda. While Saksenas resided in Aurangabad in sufficient numbers to be there still in the twentieth century, no Gaurs remained in Aurangabad by the late nineteenth century. And in contrast to the Srivastavas and Saksenas, no Gaurs were linked to Madras by marriage or occupation.

Differences in the kind of political and economic resources the Kayasth families controlled—recordkeeping, military, or household positions—were important to the survival of families and the transmission of resources to descendants. The Saksena and Gaur Kayasths were already beginning to make the transition from wide-ranging marriage networks to smaller local kin groups as they secured claims to certain positions in Hyderabad's expanding Mughlai administration. But legends concerning the Panch Bhai Gaur, and stories and facts about the early Saksena and other Kayasth military nobles, faithfully portray what should be regarded as "typical Kayasths" of late-eighteenth-century Hyderabad: military adventurers. These men were replaced by typical Kayasths of the nineteenth century: writers in the Mughlai administration.

Consolidation
of the Mughlai
Civil Service

CHAPTER 3

Power to the
Recordkeepers

Political and Economic Change in the Early Nineteenth Century

In the first half of the nineteenth century, the expansion and institution-alization of the Mughlai bureaucracy was accompanied by hereditary transmission of positions within family and kinship units.[1] But bureau-cratic expansion was one of several economic and political factors that contributed to the financial breakdown of the state. A major cause of financial and political instability in Hyderabad was the growing power of the British East India Company in the Indian subcontinent. Another was the increasing political role of the indigenous bankers and newly arrived mercenary troops in the governance of the state. All these develop-ments changed the opportunities for Kayasths, giving more security to those in recordkeeping positions.

In many ways the British East India Company was the catalyst for these changes, yet its responsibility can barely be indicated here.[2] British military control over increasingly large areas of the subcontinent forced Hyderabad into treaties from 1798 onwards, setting territorial boundaries and disbanding the forces of leading nobles. The establishment of a British Resident in the city forced the Diwan of Hyderabad to assume a new, more narrow role as diplomatic intermediary between the Nizam and the British; the Diwan no longer exercised the military powers typical of

1. This is shown for the nobility in Leonard, "The Hyderabad Political System," and for the Kayasths in the following chapters of this book.
2. See V. K. Bawa, "Hyderabad in Transition Under Salar Jung I, 1853-1883" (Ph.D. diss., Tulane University, 1967); Briggs, *The Nizam,* for political events and treaty texts; and Yusuf Husain Khan, "Anglo-Hyderabad Relations (1772-1818)," *Islamic Culture,* 32, no. 1 (1953), 41-57.

his predecessors in the more expansive eighteenth-century political arena. Despite British agreement to abstain from interference in Hyderabad's internal affairs, embodied in the Treaty of Subsidiary Alliance of 1800, the Resident sought access to the Nizam and offered constant advice through the Diwan. Nizam Secunder Jah, who succeeded Nizam Ali Khan in 1804, secluded himself and grew increasingly suspicious of British intentions. Forced to rely heavily on his Diwan, he distrusted the personal power of one so closely in touch with the British Resident. The Diwan's position became increasingly difficult to maintain, although Raja Chandu Lal functioned in that position for almost forty years. The nominal Diwan from 1808 to 1832 was Munir ul Mulk, but Raja Chandu Lal was *peshkar* (deputy or acting Diwan) from about 1806 and Diwan from 1832 to 1843.[3]

During this period, leading bankers functioned as chief financial advisors to Raja Chandu Lal and as treasurers and accountants of the state.[4] Disbursement of salaries in the city depended directly upon continuing loans from banking firms, whose services were valued and indispensable. When the financial dependence of the state upon bankers increased, a change occurred in the constitution of the class of revenue contractors, cutting out many of the military men.[5] Bankers were assigned *taluks* or *jagirs* as guarantees of eventual repayment of loans and even as repayment. This shift reflected the turnover of land to creditors of the state, diminishing the state's responsibilities but also its revenue base. As conditions worsened, bankers hired agents and sometimes newly arrived mercenary troops to collect the land revenue. The government began alienating state revenue land directly to military units and other employees because it was unable to meet payrolls and provide cash stipends.[6] This solution decreased the revenue base of the state further and gave territorial bases to mercenary troops who later threatened the state.

3. *Ibid.* and specific references to Chandu Lal in Sarojini Regani, "The Appointment of Diwans in Hyderabad State (1803-1887)," *Andhra Historical Research Society,* 25 (1958-1960), 12; Hastings Fraser, *Memoir and Correspondence of General J. S. Fraser of the Madras Army* (London, 1885), 35; J. D. B. Gribble, *History of the Deccan,* 2 vols. (London, 1896), II, 146-148. Chandu Lal's family was Khatri, originally from the Punjab.
4. A personal communication from Dr. Brijen Gupta emphasizes this point, which is supported by data in K. Krishnaswamy Mudiraj, *Pictorial Hyderabad,* 2 vols. (Hyderabad, 1929 and 1934), II; *Chronology,* 218, 226; and Khan, *Gulzar,* 622 and passim.
5. Revenue contractors listed by Lal, *Yadgar,* 84-90, and Khan, *Gulzar,* 157 and passim, were leading military nobles. By mid-century, the contemporary press clippings reprinted in *HA,* VI, show an overlap between contractors and leading bankers.
6. For example, an Afghan *jamadar* worked for a banker to whom Chandu Lal's *jagirs* were mortgaged: *The Englishman,* July 11, 1851, in *HA,* V, 123. And Pathans were paid in land in 1849: *Madras Spectator,"* Nov. 16, 1849, in *HA,* V, 650.

Major changes in the composition and organization of Hyderabad's military forces occurred early in the nineteenth century. The East India Company, through treaties and the creation of the Hyderabad Contingent, initiated the changes. Eager to displace the French and other European adventurers, the Company disbanded Raymond's forces in a 1799 treaty with the Nizam; most of his troops remained, however, in smaller units.[7] Another internal reorganization began in 1813 with the formation of the Russell Brigade, later called the Hyderabad Contingent. Resident Henry Russell was an intimate of the Nizam's court, and Chandu Lal made him nominal head of the new brigade, thereby obtaining European training and equipment for it. Commanded by Europeans in the East India Company service and equipped from Company stores, the Contingent troops received salaries from the Nizam's government. Major forces such as those of Salabat Khan were included in the Russell Brigade, which was initiated as a cooperative venture. But by 1829, when Nizam Secunder Jah died, the Hyderabad Contingent took orders only from the Resident, who no longer had a local role as a titled nobleman at the Nizam's court, but was an outsider in an adversary relation to the Hyderabad government. The fixed salaries of the officers and men fell due every month and constituted a major financial obligation for Hyderabad.[8] From the Nizam's point of view, the Contingent had become a financial burden and a political liability. From the British point of view, the Contingent had many advantages. The Resident controlled but did not pay it; and its existence allowed the British to argue that the Nizam did not need to employ other European officers or build up other forces because the Contingent was nominally at his disposal.

The East India Company's treaties elsewhere in India had repercussions in Hyderabad as well, when foreign mercenary troops were displaced in settlements between their employers and the Company. Some of these troops journeyed to Hyderabad in search of employment. They were initially welcomed as counters to the British military forces, since the dispersed units of Hyderabad's former army (those not included in the Hyderabad Contingent) were no longer adequately equipped or trained. The new Afghan, Arab, and other mercenaries were put on the Nizam's

7. One unit, under a Kayasth *serrishtahdar,* continued into the twentieth century as the Lines of Musa Raymun. For the military units, see "The Subsidiary and Contingent Forces of Hyderabad, 1874," correspondence of the Foreign Office, Government of India (India papers, 29653/2, SOAS); Stotherd, *History of the 30th Lancers*; W. C. Kirkwood, *The Story of the 97th Deccan Infantry* (Hyderabad, 1929).

8. Major Reginald George Burton, *A History of the Hyderabad Contingent* (Calcutta, 1905); Fraser, *Memoir,* 67–76 and passim.

payroll under command of their own leaders.[9] The older class of military men, particularly the Hindu nobles and *serrishtahdars,* fared badly during this period.

Although the mercenary forces had initially been welcomed, they were not easily combined with the existing units under Hyderabad nobles and *serrishtahdars,* and they cost much more than the Deccani soldiers.[10] As cash grew short, the mercenaries became dangerous to their *serrishtahdars,* kidnapping and imprisoning them to force payment of wages.[11] The growing problem of law and order posed by Afghan and Arab troops in the city gave the British Resident yet another weapon in his efforts to disarm the Nizam's military forces and reform the Mughlai administration. An 1851 report prepared by the Diwan for the Resident, summarized in Table 6, illustrates his argument.

According to these figures, one-fourth of Hyderabad's military expenditure was for the Contingent and almost three-fourths for "remaining troops." The remaining troops, termed by the Diwan "useless . . . and partly nominal," included some 43,000 soldiers in seventeen categories, ranging from 69 Turks to 18,326 Deccanis and including some 2,000 "respectable" *mansabdars.*[12] There were an estimated 12,000 Afghan and Arab troops at this time.[13] The Diwan proposed to eliminate the "remaining troops," thereby saving their salaries and staving off the impending financial crisis—the Nizam's government owed some three million rupees in back salaries to the Contingent in 1851. The proposal was heartily welcomed by the Resident,[14] but it was not implemented.

9. In the early nineteenth century, many Rohilla Afghans and Arabs moved from Patiala, Jaipur, and the Maratha states to Hyderabad. The three Arab leaders at mid-century were Ghalib Jung, Barak Jung, and Saifuddaula; the first two were *mawallad* (born of Deccani mothers) and the third was *asal* (real) Arab. The Arabs alone totalled 6,000 and most were recent immigrants in the 1860's, as the distinction between "real" and Deccani Arabs was still made. Sindhi and Habshi (Abbysinian) troops were also in Hyderabad. See Mudiraj, *Pictorial Hyderabad,* II, for relevant biographies; and Syed Hussain Bilgrami and C. Willmott, *Historical and Descriptive Sketch of the Nizam's Dominions,* 2 vols. (Bombay, 1883), II, 58 and passim; Richard Temple, *Report on the Administration of the Government of His Highness the Nizam in the Deccan* (Calcutta, 1868), 22–29.

10. The cost per man, according to an 1851 statement in *Nizam's Territory* (India papers, 32426, SOAS), 86–87, was as follows: ordinary Deccani *linewallas,* 5–8 rupees per month; Arabs, Sikhs, Turks, and Sindhis, 13–22 rupees; men in units with elephants, camels, and horses, 50 rupees a month.

11. See Bilgrami and Willmott, *Nizam's Dominions,* II, 58–61, for a brief coverage of these disturbances. Two specific instances, one involving intimidation of the *daftardars,* another intimidation of the Nizam in *durbar* by an Arab *jamadar,* appear in *The Englishman,* May 28, 1851, and *The Englishman,* Nov. 13, 1850, in *HA,* V, 701 and 132.

12. *Nizam's Territory,* 87.

13. Temple, *Report on the Administration,* 22–29.

14. *Nizam's Territory,* 86 (Note from Resident Davidson to the Minister, Nov. 14, 1851).

TABLE 6:
Military Expenditure, 1851

	Number of men	Rupees annually
Hyderabad Contingent	——	3,848,740
Nizam's personal troops	8,000	1,200,000
Remaining troops	45,504	10,641,676

Source: Government of India, *Nizam's Territory, Copy of all Papers relative to Territory ceded by H.H. the Nizam, in Liquidation of Debts alleged to have been due by H.H. to the British Government* (India papers, 32426, SOAS), 87.

Too many military men had become major creditors and landholders of the state.

By the late 1840's, Hyderabad's political and economic structure differed considerably from that described for the late eighteenth century. The rural areas were largely farmed out as they had been earlier, but to a new class of revenue collectors and *jagirdars* which included bankers, their agents, and Afghan and Arab military chiefs. The Resident deplored these land concessions to bankers and mercenaries, yet the East India Company, too, sought a territorial grant. British interest ostensibly lay in achieving financial stability and good government in Hyderabad, so that the Company would not have to take over the administration directly. The Resident argued that by accepting and administering a territorial grant for the debt, and using its land revenue to pay the Contingent, the Company could provide a model for administrative reform in Hyderabad.[15] But the Hyderabad government preferred to rely upon indigenous bankers who generally remained loyal and took enormous risks to continue funding it.[16]

The Rise of the Daftardars

Some men prospered in the worsening situation. Raja Chandu Lal, the Khatri officiating as Diwan, became an extremely powerful man; and the position of *peshkar* became hereditary in his family. Some bankers and other creditors, particularly certain military leaders, gained

15. Fraser, *Memoir,* 65–77, 351–402, 412–442.
16. See Fraser, *Memoir,* 289–291 for an effort by bankers to fund a government bank and the Governor-General's refusal to sanction it.

influence and land. Recordkeepers at all levels, including many Ka-yasths, became key figures because they disbursed money (when it was available) to those whom they had determined deserved priority. The two *daftardars* of the land revenue offices grew increasingly important. Their records were essential to the financial juggling, and summaries were requested by the Resident as well as the Nizam and the Diwan.[17] The *daftardars'* personal knowledge was valued, for they knew whose lands the state would benefit most from reclaiming, who could afford to make a special contribution to the state, and who could afford to take a temporary cut in stipend. They knew which revenue collectors would prove most efficient in turning over the state's share of the revenue or, if quick cash was needed, which would give the largest tribute to secure a revenue contract. They knew which *serrishtahdars* controlled their units best; that is, which payments had to be made immediately and which could be delayed. The *daftardars* had kept the records and dealt with such matters for many years: they became vital intermediaries in financial negotiations of the 1840's.[18]

Raja Chandu Lal began to lose the confidence of various parties at court, and he was forced to resign in 1843. After him a series of Diwans failed to gain the confidence of enough parties to stay in power.[19] As Chandu Lal had taken his office records with him as family property, hoping to force the appointment of his son or nephew as Diwan,[20] only the *daftardars* possessed the financial information necessary to succeeding Diwans. Cooperation between the *daftardars* and the Diwan became essential.

There were two *daftardars,* and they were often referred to in the plural; but contemporary sources tended to single out Lala Bahadur, the Malwala Kayasth. This remarkable man, Raja Ram Pershad Lala Bahadur, never actually held the title of *daftardar* himself because he was the second of four sons, and his elder brother held the official designation. Lala Bahadur had assumed supervision of the Malwala *daftar* in the 1830's. Well

17. As Salar Jung himself noted later, "the succeeding Diwans [after Chandu Lal] were compelled to seek from the Dufterdars information and assistance. This circumstance gave them real power," Salar Jung, *Hyderabad State. Miscellaneous Notes on Administration* (Hyderabad [1856]), 6–7 (SJL).

18. *Ibid.,* and Moulavi Cheragh Ali, *Hyderabad Under Sir Salar Jung,* 4 vols. (Bombay, 1884–1886), I, 73–75.

19. Fraser, *Memoir,* 190, 200, 205, 223–224, 302, 308–309, 332–334; H. P. McAuliffe, *The Nizam* (London, 1904), 39.

20. Chandu Lal had established his own office, bypassing the record office of former Diwans, and when he resigned in 1843 he took almost 40 years of records with him. His nephew, Ram Baksh, was made *peshkar* in 1843 chiefly because he had access to that *daftar*: Fraser, *Memoir,* 192.

before Chandu Lal's 1843 resignation he had assumed control of some of the Diwan's financial functions. After 1843 he emerged as the most powerful figure in the state, rivalling successive Diwans for control of state finances in the 1840's and early 1850's.[21]

It was Lala Bahadur who authorized payments and loan arrangements for the state during the three-year period 1843-1846, when the Nizam refused to appoint another Diwan to succeed Chandu Lal. The Nizam tried to assert his independence by temporizing and appointing only *peshkars* or *vakils* to represent him to the British. When the Nizam finally accepted Siraj ul Mulk, the candidate supported by the Resident, as Diwan in 1846, those who traditionally dealt with the Diwan had become accustomed to dealing with the *daftardars*. This was particularly true of the Malwala *daftardar,* one of the few people trusted by the Nizam at this time.[22] Lala Bahadur became the representative of all those in the Mughlai administration who feared the reforms being proposed by the Resident and successive Diwans, reforms which included dismissal of troops, resumption of lands, cuts in the revenue percentages retained by various officials, and checks on the authenticity of *jagirs* and other grants.

The Diwans (Siraj ul Mulk and, next, Shams ul Umra of the Paigah family) found Lala Bahadur to be their chief opponent within the Nizam's government.[23] Shams ul Umra began by rejecting the *daftardars'* revenue statements as false; he subsequently discovered that revenue contractors accepted contracts only from the *daftardars,* and that sources of credit were available only through the intermediacy of the *daftardars.*[24] Declaring himself unable to obtain a satisfactory revenue statement from "the

21. The relative insignificance of the Daftar-i Diwani lay partly in its diminished responsibilities (much territory in its jurisdiction had been lost to the Marathas and British as early as the 1770's), but the misfortunes of the *daftardar* family also diminished its influence significantly. A long series of early childless deaths in the male line meant that distant cousins became heirs and that *daftar* management was almost always in the hands of employees and not family members. Sonaji Pandit, acting head of the *daftar* at this time, lacked the prestige accorded to members of hereditary noble families. Lal, *Yadgar,* 62; Khan, *Tuzuk,* II (Nobles), 17-22.

22. Lala Bahadur is supposed to have served twice as Diwan in the 1840's: Saksenah, *Kayasth Sajjan Caritra,* II, 8-9. This biography states that Lala Bahadur once presented the Basant offering to the Nizam—a prerogative reserved for a Hindu Diwan. It would be more correct to regard this offering as the prerogative of the highest Hindu nobleman, and Chandu Lal's long tenure as acting Diwan caused the association with that position.

23. Fraser, *Memoir,* 210-282, covers Siraj ul Mulk's first diwanship. The author's father, General Fraser, was Resident in Hyderabad 1838-1852.

24. *The Englishman,* April 20, 1849, in *HA,* V, 97-98. Shams ul Umra told General Fraser: "Unless all the revenues formerly apportioned for the general expenditure of the government were restored to the charge and control of the Minister, and he were really invested with full powers, he would tender his resignation . . ." Fraser, *Memoir,* 297.

[63

principal Dufturdar," he reportedly confiscated the Malwala's customary revenue fees and *jagirs*.[25] But a month later Shams ul Umra had resigned, and no such confiscation had occurred.[26] The next Diwan also attacked the *daftardars*, charging that they had drawn fifteen lakhs of rupees secretly in addition to their legitimate fees. The Nizam ordered an investigation, but four months later there was a new Diwan and the *daftardars* remained in power.[27] By 1850, rather than appoint another Diwan and produce another stalemate, the Nizam determined to direct the administration himself with the advice of the *daftardars*, but nothing came of it.[28]

Siraj ul Mulk became Diwan again in 1851. He tried to circumvent the *daftardars* and to establish direct connections with the revenue contractors and moneylenders, but the former declared they would discuss the budget with no one but Lala Bahadur[29] and the latter, at least one of whom would still lend money on the pledge of Lala Bahadur, would not lend money to Siraj ul Mulk.[30] The hopelessness of Siraj ul Mulk's position brought about a partial acceptance of the idea that Lala Bahadur should actually run the government; and one critic attacked the Diwan's damaging interference with the *dafta·dar*.[31]

At this point, the British intervened decisively. In 1852 the Governor-General, Lord Dalhousie, lost patience with his Resident's continuing efforts to assist the Diwan with reforms, and he sent an ultimatum. Repayment of the Company loan had fallen due in 1850, and Dalhousie demanded that land be turned over to British management so that the Nizam's alleged debt would be paid and the Contingent would have a source of regular income. The Nizam still trusted Lala Bahadur to discover sources of extensive funds;[32] but when the Treaty of 1853 was concluded in May of that year, the *daftardars* were present only to provide statistical tables concerning the areas being ceded to the Company.[33] Lala

25. *The Englishman,* May 1, 1849, in *HA,* V, 101.
26. *The Englishman,* June 12, 1849, in *HA,* V, 105–107.
27. *The Englishman,* July 11, July 15, 1850, in *HA,* V, 122–123, 126; Fraser, *Memoir,* 313–314.
28. *Madras Spectator,* Nov. 11, 1850, in *HA,* V, 131, and *The Englishman,* Nov. 13, Oct. 3, 1850, in *HA,* IV, 63–65, 71–72.
29. *The Englishman,* Aug. 5, 1852, Oct. 27, 1851, in *HA,* V, 159, 164.
30. *The Englishman,* Oct. 4, Nov. 26, 1851, in *HA,* V, 163, 166.
31. *The Englishman,* Aug. 5, 1852, in *HA,* V, 160. "The government of a country in the hands of Lala Bahadur, judging in the abstract, cannot be good, but brought in contrast with the government of Suraj-ool-Moolk [Siraj ul Mulk] there could be no question as to an improved condition."
32. Dalhousie's impatience was clear as early as 1849: Fraser, *Memoir,* 229. For the Nizam's trust in Lala Bahadur, *The Englishman,* May 18, 1853, in *HA,* V, 189.
33. *Madras Spectator,* June 17, 1853, in *HA,* V, 189; text of the treaty, Briggs, *The Nizam,* I, 312–316.

Bahadur's influence was still great nevertheless, and he was able to determine the choice of the next Diwan, for Siraj ul Mulk died soon after concluding this controversial treaty. With Lala Bahadur's backing, Siraj ul Mulk's twenty-four-year-old nephew, Salar Jung, was chosen to succeed him.

Salar Jung and the Mughlai Officials

Salar Jung's thirty-year Diwanship established a new political and economic direction for Hyderabad. The Kayasth Malwala *daftardar,* Lala Bahadur, represented the leading Mughlai nobles and officials of Hyderabad in their last stand against the inauguration of administrative reforms. In retrospect, Lala Bahadur's contest with the young Diwan Salar Jung in 1853 and 1854 was a decisive turning point in Hyderabad's history, although the changes following Salar Jung's victory occurred far more gradually than many have thought.[34]

Not considered the strongest candidate for Diwan, Salar Jung was selected precisely because he was a weak candidate. It was thought he would make an ideal puppet, easily manipulated by his backers, principally Lala Bahadur.[35] The argument that is supposed to have been conclusive with the Nizam was: "It is not a Minister, but your prestige which governs . . . Lala Bahadoor, who did everything, will, as before, conduct the affairs of the administration for Salar Jung . . ."[36] According to rumor, Lala Bahadur promised the Nizam thirteen lakhs of rupees within two months of Salar Jung's appointment, and the Nizam obtained a pledge from Lala Bahadur for the young Diwan's good conduct before presenting Salar Jung with the robe of office.[37] Lala Bahadur sponsored Salar Jung's candidacy, and few doubt that he meant to control the young Diwan.

But Salar Jung declined the role of puppet and won enough support to re-establish the authority of Diwan. His victory in the contest for power

---

34. Popular accounts, such as M. Fathufla Khan, *A History of Administrative Reforms in Hyderabad State* (Secunderabad, 1935), considerably overstate the implementation of reforms under Salar Jung I.

35. *The Englishman* and the *Madras Spectator,* June 8, 1853; *United Service Gazette,* June 10, 1853, and *Madras Spectator,* June 8, 1853, in *HA,* III, 2–4. Oral tradition maintains that Lala Bahadur was responsible for Salar Jung's appointment, and that Salar Jung requested frequent guidance from his patron afterward. Some say that Lala Bahadur himself wanted to be Diwan, but, heeding his wife's remark that "Diwan means *diwani* [crazy]," he recommended Salar Jung instead. Interviews with Sri Rang Pershad, Hakim Vicerai, and Raja Mahbub Karan.

36. *The Englishman,* June 11, 1853, in *HA,* III, 3.

37. *Madras Spectator,* June 8, and *The Englishman,* June 1, 1853, in *HA,* III, 3, 5.

with Lala Bahadur accomplished, he could initiate or delay administrative procedures, and he did both. Appointed Diwan in June 1853, within two weeks he had refused to sign papers presented by Lala Bahadur, saying that "he could not sign papers till he had satisfied himself by a knowledge of their contents of the propriety of doing so . . . Lala Bahadoor was taken aback by it, and is said to be somewhat sore."[38] By early August the relations between the two showed serious strain:

> The young minister and his principal Dufturdar divide the authority of the State and do not pull together . . . The Minister had charged the Dufturdar, Lala Bahadoor, to his Sovereign with perversion of facts, falsifying accounts and gross frauds . . . This division between the two leading members of Government calls peremptorily for the removal of one or the other from office. If it be left to the Nizam . . . he has a strong leaning towards Lala Bahadoor . . . The Minister declines sanctioning the accounts brought to him by the Dufturdar by refusing his signature to them, and the whole Government is necessarily paralyzed. None of its functions in connection with its receipts and disbursements is discharged.

> [The dissension between Salar Jung and Lala Bahadur] is universally known . . . Lala Bahadoor appears at a shadee [wedding], now celebrating at his house, unadorned, whilst the rest of the family are decked out . . . in their richest ornaments. He was solicited to do honour to the occasion and to join happily in the celebration; his reply was that there had been no peace for him since Chundoo Lal's resignation of office.[39]

The two challenged one another directly at the end of August. Lala Bahadur presented Salar Jung with a financial statement of the state's predicament and "requested his direction as to the way and means for the supply of money." Salar Jung responded by submitting a petition for specific administrative reforms to the Nizam and threatening to resign if it was not endorsed.[40] The Nizam endorsed the petition, awarding victory to the Diwan, who then proceeded to eliminate the *daftardars* as intermediaries between himself and the moneylenders and revenue contractors:

> [After the failure of the *daftardars* to improve their administrative practices was evident] I gradually . . . made arrangements with certain sahookars [bankers] quite unconnected with the Dufterdars to make advances to meet the exigencies of the Government, and in consequence of the period of the revenue collections being yet eight months distant, I deprived the Duftardars of the power to appoint Talooqdars, a privilege which they had hitherto arrogated to themselves . . . I obtained His Highness the Nizam's guarantee for the first advances from the

38. *The Englishman*, June 20, 1853, in *HA*, III, 7.
39. The first quotation is from the *Madras Spectator*, July 25, 1853, the second from *The Englishman*, Aug. 6, 1853, in *HA*, V, 194, 196.
40. *The Englishman*, Aug. 29, 1853, in *HA*, III, 7–8.

sahookars . . . he . . . accepted and signed at two different times the sahookars papers of requisitions, and the two Wajib ool Urzis I submitted to him.[41]

Why had Lala Bahadur lost the backing of the Nizam at this crucial point? There are indications that he, like Chandu Lal before him, was losing the support of key groups in the state. The bankers and money-lenders attempted to found a government bank in the late 1840's. Such a bank would probably have displaced the *daftardars* had it succeeded. Just after Salar Jung's appointment, one major banker refused to loan money to Lala Bahadur.[42] Some of the military were turning against him: the Pathans threatened to kidnap him in an effort to collect their pay, so he was unable to leave his house. Following Salar Jung's appointment, a revenue contractor complained that Lala Bahadur had favored Arabs at the expense of other contractors.[43] Above all, Lala Bahadur's direction of the state's finances had failed to halt the financial crisis, as the forced cession of Berar province dramatized.

Many in Hyderabad looked for alternatives to the deadlock between the Diwan and the *daftardars* that had characterized the state since 1843, when Chandu Lal resigned. Salar Jung, unlike earlier Diwans, succeeded in winning significant allies. He himself stressed, in the quotation above, the initial backing of bankers "quite unconnected with the Dufterdars." His financial measures won him "the confidence of his Sovereign, of the financial community, and the British Government."[44] Salar Jung also secured the backing of certain Arabs, particularly Ghalib Jung, one of the three most powerful mercenary leaders, by a combination of personal diplomacy and political concessions. Ghalib Jung's father had originally been employed by Mir Alam, Salar Jung's maternal great-grandfather. Salar Jung approached Ghalib Jung and other Arab leaders personally, emphasizing his Arab ancestry. Probably more important, he recognized their authority by establishing a special Arab Court in his own palace, conceding to the leaders the power to arrest and punish their own people.[45] Then Salar Jung began to resume the state lands held by Arab and other military forces, making small initial payments and giving security on

41. Jung, *Hyderabad State,* 7. The second petition (*Hyderabad State,* app. I, p. 64), provided that the Nizam would sanction the Diwan's proposals in relevant matters, including the appointment and removal of *talukdars.*
42. *United Service Gazette,* June 10, 1853, in *HA,* III, 3.
43. *Madras Spectator,* June 17, 1853, in *HA,* V, 190-191.
44. Fraser, *Memoir,* 393. Ali, *Hyderabad Under Sir Salar Jung,* I, 78, 83, shows that district and *taluk* treasuries had been established by 1864 to reduce reliance on bankers.
45. Mohamed Abdul Muttalib, "The Administration of Justice under the Nizams, 1724-1947," (Ph.D. diss., Osmania University, 1957), 68, 87, 189; Campbell, *Glimpses,* 37; Bilgrami and Willmott, *Nizam's Dominions,* II, 116.

certain bankers for the remainder.[46] These steps were sufficiently promising to command the support of the Nizam.

Thus Lala Bahadur was displaced by Salar Jung as key financial figure in the Hyderabad government. But the new Diwani administration developed slowly and in many cases did not fully supersede the Mughlai bureaucracy until after Salar Jung's death in 1883. One historian has broken his thirty-year Diwanship into three decades: the Dark Ages, plagued by problems from the former administration; the Middle Ages, characterized by experimentation with new structures and methods; and finally, a decade of steady improvement under the momentum of earlier reforms.[47] My own analysis would emphasize two important turning points. The first was in 1869, when Nizam Afzaluddaula died and Salar Jung ruled as co-regent for the young Nizam, Mahbub Ali Khan. The second came in 1877, when the co-regent, Shams ul Umra of the Paigah family, died. The Paigah noble had been imposed as co-regent by the British Resident and had been a conservative and restraining influence on Salar Jung.[48] Both these deaths allowed the Diwan to centralize the evolving administration more firmly under himself, and both freed him somewhat from the need to conciliate the Mughlai nobles. By either reckoning, most of the significant changes initiated by Salar Jung began in the 1870's. But perception of these changes was slowed by his successful preservation of the traditional structures and personnel, particularly those departments and officials close to the Nizam. His protective policies helped conceal the passing of political power to the new administrative structures centralized under the Diwan.

The nineteenth century began with the consolidation and decentralization of Hyderabad's Mughlai administration, processes that allowed Kayasth and other kin groups to control positions through the practice of bilateral inheritance. Despite the new administration begun by Salar Jung at mid-century, the Mughlai administration continued to function and Kayasth families developed a variety of strategies to retain their hereditary positions.

46. Campbell, *Glimpses,* 37.
47. Manik Rao Vithal Rao, *Bustan-i Asafiyah,* 7 vols. (Hyderabad, 1909–1932).
48. Two major sources for this period are Bawa, "Hyderabad in Transition," and Thomas H. Thornton, *General Sir Richard Meade and the Feudatory States of Central and Southern India* (New York, 1898).

CHAPTER **4**

Building a
Mathur Subcaste

The rise to power of Lala Bahadur, the Malwala *daftardar,* had important consequences for the Mathur Kayasths in Hyderabad. At the beginning of the nineteenth century, the Malwala family had been rising in the *mansabdari* ranks and was represented there by family members from two collateral branches as well. By mid-century, the junior branch of the Malwalas had secured firm hold on the *daftardar* position and was using its political and economic resources to constitute a subcaste in the city. All Hyderabad Mathurs were eventually related by marriage, and they shared the resources and reputation of the Malwala family.

The *daftardar* position had passed in 1804 to Khushal Chand of the junior branch of the family because eligible heirs in the senior branch were too young. When he died in 1830, there were adult men in the senior branch who could have assumed the position, but it passed to Khushal Chand's son, Ujagar Chand. From this point on, the *daftardar* position, higher titles, and larger *jagirs* were awarded to members of the junior branch.[1]

Ujagar Chand may have been the titled *daftardar,* but his younger brother Lala Bahadur actually functioned in that capacity from about 1830, as established in Chapter III; it was he who consolidated the dominance of the junior branch within the Malwala family. Ujagar Chand died in 1846 and was officially succeeded by Budh Karan, his eldest son. Raja Budh Karan was deaf—one of the few physical afflictions which in strict Mitakshara law disqualified men from marriage or inheritance; in any case, Lala Bahadur continued to head the *daftar.* In fact, from the

1. When Ujagar Chand became *daftardar,* Khub Chand of the senior branch got a *jagir.* Both men received titles: *Chronology,* 193; Register Asnad-i Jagir, IV, no. 15, Hyderabad *subah,* no. 381/ 51B, for Khub Chand's *zat jagir* award.

time Budh Karan died in 1854 no successor was named until after Lala Bahadur's death in 1858. Neither Budh Karan nor Lala Bahadur left a son, but the succession remained in the junior branch with Raja Inderjit, the younger brother of Budh Karan. This arrangement was made by Lala Bahadur shortly before his death.[2]

The Malwala family's growing wealth and influence enabled it to acquire additional property in Chowk Maidan Khan. Raja Budh Karan purchased a large residence near the original family home in 1834. That acquisition and others changed the demography of the neighborhood. Earlier house deeds, dated 1776 and 1817, show Muslim-owned residences on all three sides of the 1834 purchase; later these all became Mathur Kayasth properties.[3] Lala Bahadur also acquired extensive garden lands just beyond the city limits, where he developed a pleasure garden and constructed a temple.[4] The acquisition of pleasure gardens and the patronage of temples were typical signs of prosperity for Kayasths and others in the first half of the nineteenth century.

The economic resources commanded by the Malwalas were now quite impressive. As *daftardar,* Lala Bahadur received $\frac{1}{64}$ of every rupee of the land revenue contracted through his office for the provinces of Hyderabad and Bidar. By the 1830's, two family members were earning commissions as *serrishtahdars* of *mansabdars.* They paid monthly stipends to some three hundred fifty or four hundred *mansabdars* and received $\frac{1}{16}$ of the amount they distributed. Two other family members were *serrishtahdars* of military units, earning the same commission. In 1836, Lala Bahadur was awarded the post of *qanungo* of Hyderabad (a position that empowered him to record and make legal decisions in land revenue cases); this earned him a commission of one of every hundred rupees involved in the cases.[5] From the 1820's to 1850, members of both branches of the Malwala family were awarded a total of seventeen *inam* grants and six *jagirs.*[6] Attempts to calculate a rupee income produce varying results, but the family was certainly wealthy.[7]

2. Saksenah, *Kayasth Sajjan Caritra,* II, chap. 3, p. 10: giving less time to the position after his son's death, Lala Bahadur "appointed Raja Inderjit to assist at this time."
3. These documents are still with the family of Hakim Vicerai (recruited from Jaipur in the 1840's), to whom the house was given.
4. Pershad, *Farkhundah Bunyad Hyderabad,* 96; Leonard Munn, *Hyderabad Municipal Survey 1911* (Hyderabad, n.d.).
5. The *qanungo* position may have been awarded to Ujagar Chand in 1811–1812: Saksenah, *Kayasth Sajjan Caritra,* II, ch. 3, p. 7. Khan, *Gulzar,* 489, for Ujagar Chand as *serrishtahdar* of a Sindhi unit; *The Englishman,* Nov. 8, 1949, in *HA,* V, for Rajas Tej Rae and Chiman Lal as *serrishtahdars* of *mansabdars.*
6. Entries in Register Asnad-i Jagir for those years.
7. An 1850 estimate put the Malwalas' annual share of revenue at 1,500,000 rupees; the

The number of sons in both branches of the family who survived to marry is good evidence in itself of prosperity. Sagar Mal's two sons produced five more, who produced thirteen, who produced nineteen. All of these men obtained government grants, either *jagirs* or *inams*. In the course of the nineteenth century it became customary for members of the *daftardar* line to receive personal *jagirs*, while members of other lines of descent got *inams*.[8] Since all men received income awards from the Nizam, the joint family resources were increased rather than diminished by the number of sons.

The Recruitment of Relatives

A major indication of the family's increasing wealth and status was its initiation of marriage alliances with Mathur families from northern and western India. These marriages were based upon economic contracts, and a pattern of systematic recruitment of Mathur families to provide brides and grooms for marriageable children can be reconstructed. The head of the *daftar* held authority in the joint family and arranged for the importation of most families. Even when a newcomer's initial marriage was with another branch of the Malwala family or another Mathur, the ultimate sponsorship of the head of the Malwalas was recognized: "their first marriages were with the children of Pratap Bahadur and Keerat Bahadur, but Ujagar Chand called them."[9]

Well might this sponsorship be emphasized, since financial support of the Malwala family was the basic condition upon which most of these marriages depended. Table 7 delineates the growth of the Mathur subcaste and will be referred to in discussions of financial arrangements and kin groups. It correlates the periods of Malwala political power in the state with the importation of new Mathur families. Lala Bahadur, rather than earlier *daftardars*, appears to have been the first really powerful Malwala and the initiator of these marriages. After him, Raja Inderjit brought almost as many families, although a difference in the extent to which they were supported will be noted below. And even later, some of the few families to arrive during Raja Shiv Raj's fifty-year leadership of the family were brought by branches rebelling against his authority.

family was one of six thought able to loan the state 200,000 rupees in the same year: *Madras Spectator*, July 24, Nov. 11, 1850, in *HA*, V, 126.

8. See entries in Register Asnad-i Jagir and the Daftar-i mal Jagir Register, "naqul-i asnad-i Shiv Raj," file no. 66 of 1932–1933 (APSA, Section R2).

9. Urdu summary prepared by Hakim Vicerai in January, 1966.

TABLE 7:

Chronological Summary of Mathur Families

Successive Mahwala daftardars (family 2)	Family number[a]	Arrival date	Founder in Hyderabad	Place of origin		Brought by family number
				Lucknow area	Rajasthan	
Sagar Mal	1	1720–1750	Gulab Chand			
Durga Das	16		Kanval Nain			
Bhavani Das	2		Sagar Mal			
Keval Kishen, 1799–1803	3	1800	Baxtawar Singh	x		2
Khushal Chand, 1803–1840						
[Lala Bahadur, 1830–1858]	4	1830	Gur Pershad	x		4
	5	1830	Dhunyapet	x		4
	17	1830	Naval Karan	x		4
	8	1830	Mehtab Rae, Aftab Rae		x	2
	7	1830	Chiman Lal		x	2
	21	1833	Mul Chand		x	2
	9	1842	Chaturbhuj		x	2
	6	1842	Khwaja Baksh		x	2
Ujagar Chand, 1830–1846	14	1845	Prem Chand, Lal Chand	x		2
	28	1850	Shanta Pershad	x		2

No.[a]	Date	Name			
Budh Karan, 1846–1854					
24	1855	Deen Dayal	x		2
25	1855	Bije Narayan	x		24
15	1855[b]	Brij Lal		x	14
Raja Inderjit, 1858–1875					
10	1858	Sham Bali	x		2
11	1860	Durga Pershad	x		2
26	1862	Kalyan Baksh	x		?
23	1870	Ayodhya Pershad	x		?
12	1870	Chahu Lal		x	2
29	1872	Sail Chand		x	6
13	1875[c]	Jag Mohan Lal	x		10
Raja Shiv Raj, 1875–1925					
27	1875	Narayan Pershad	x		?
18	1892	Surajwunt	x		2
22	1905	Rup Kishore	x		?
19	1908	Kanvar Bahadur	x		2
20	1910	Anand Bihari Lal		x	2

Source: Compiled from interviews and other materials. Three of the 29 male lines have ended. The table fails to account for only 20 to 25 of 420 named men about whom information was collected.

[a] Field note numbers.
[b] A second branch of this family came in 1890.
[c] A second branch of this family came in 1885.

Two contrasting patterns of recruitment and marriage in this early expansive period appear when the arriving Mathur families are differentiated by geographic origin. The first documented Malwala marriage, that of Keval Kishen in 1777, was with North Indian Mathurs, and his bride came to Hyderabad.[10] Next came a father and son, then three more families, all from Lucknow in northern India. They were followed after 1830 by a series of families from the Rajputana states in western India. There was a change, then, in the area of recruitment around 1830. The way in which families were recruited also differed. According to oral tradition and the genealogies, the first immigrant family from Lucknow called the next three, who provided marriage partners primarily for it, although subsequent marriages took place with Malwala family members. This was not the case for the earliest Rajputana families, for all six were recruited separately and directly by Lala Bahadur's emissaries.[11] Again, the timing here points to Lala Bahadur as the first Malwala to dominate and control the Mathur marriages. By the time descendants of these Rajputana families were growing up in Hyderabad, there was a pool of Mathur Kayasths large enough to provide marriage partners without reference back to their former homes.

Reconstruction of the initial marriages of the first four families from Lucknow illustrates the complexities of the prevailing marriage practices and the closeness of kinship ties. The first family from the north was that of Baxtawar Singh, whose son Lakshmi Narayan married the daughter of either Bhavani Das or Durga Das and received *jagirs* as a Malwala son-in-law. The marriages of Lakshmi Narayan's four sons and five daughters show the effects of an early age of marriage, a relatively high rate of female mortality, and serial monogamy for men. They demonstrate the continued arrangement of marriages between families already related by marriage. The brides of two sons are unknown; the other two married daughters of Mehtab Rae, one of the first Rajputana sons-in-law of Raja Budh Karan. The first daughter was married locally, to Raja Chatu Lal, whose family (number 16 in Table 7) had been long established in the city, but bridegrooms from North India came for the other daughters. The second daughter married Gur Pershad, founder of family 4, but she soon

10. No oral information has come down concerning this marriage; the reference is in an eighteenth-century Persian history, *The Hadikat-i Alam,* which appears translated in *HA,* IV, 620.
11. Several of the Rajputana families have preserved tne correspondence arranging the alliances; the first representatives of all six married Malwalas before making alliances with other Mathurs.

died. Gur Pershad then married a daughter of the Malwala Raja Ujagar Chand; later, his eldest son by this second wife married the fifth daughter of Lakshmi Narayan. (Gur Pershad's second son by his second wife married a daughter of Raja Chatu Lal's, who could have been either a granddaughter of Lakshmi Narayan or a daughter by Chatu Lal's second wife.) For the third and fourth daughters of Lakshmi Narayan, the bridegrooms Dhunyapet and Anandi Lal were brought (families 5 and 17).[12]

The cases above show that kinship ties became close and complicated as men produced children and arranged their marriages over long periods of time, often through successive wives. They also provide examples of marriages of both daughters and sons to local Mathurs, although more bridegrooms than brides were brought from outside. Finally, it is clear that the three bridegrooms (families 4, 5, and 17) were initially called to marry the daughters of the first Lucknow son-in-law; but either they or their children subsequently married with the Malwalas and other Mathurs in Hyderabad.

Evidence for the families brought from Rajputana is different. The Malwala family directly called all of the first six families from Rajputana to come between 1830 and 1845, and marriage contracts were negotiated separately between each founder and the head of the Malwala family. These Rajputana Kayasths were, like the Malwalas, already removed from their original homeland in North India: they too were in the service of princely states. In Lala Bahadur's time, the six Rajputana families all provided sons-in-law to the major (junior) branch of the family.[13] During the same time, six Mathur families arrived from the Lucknow area; at least three and perhaps all of them came through connection with the first Lucknow family, and most provided marriage partners to Malwalas only in the second generation if at all. By 1875, Lucknow families outnumbered those from Rajputana thirteen to nine. But three of the Lucknow families had not married with Malwalas, compared to only one of the Rajputana families; and two of the Lucknow families had died out, compared to none of the Rajputana ones.[14] These differences can be attributed directly to the importance of Malwala patronage.

12. Interviews with Ramchander Narayan and Hakim Vicerai.
13. These sons-in-law were Mehtab Rae and Aftab Rae (family 8 in Table 7); Kalyan Baksh (7); Fateh Chand (21); Shadi Lal and Har Lal (9); Baktawar Lal and Ram Deen (6); and Prem Chand (14).
14. The two Lucknow families that died out were those of Deen Dayal (24) and Bije Narayan (25); the three without marriages to Malwalas were 25, 26, and 23. The Rajputana family of Sail Chand (29) was called by family 6 and has no recorded marriages with the Malwalas.

Ranking Among the Mathurs

Status and wealth within the growing Mathur community derived from close relationship by marriage to the Malwala *daftardar*. Most Mathurs were related in some way to the Malwalas. Twenty-four of the twenty-eight other Mathur family genealogies recorded marriages with Malwala family members.[15] In at least fourteen of these twenty-four families, the first marriages into Hyderabad were with Malwala family members and were the reason for migration. But the marriage patterns changed over time, as did the ranking of families with respect to one another.

The economic advantages accompanying initial alliances with the most powerful and wealthy family among the Mathurs were quite explicit. Several families have preserved the original Persian letters with the signatures of the heads of both contracting families. The descendants of Chaturbhuj (family 9 in Table 7) have such a contract, signed by Raja Ujagar Chand after two preliminary exchanges of letters. A translation of the Persian document appears in Table 8; Chaturbhuj's demands are on the left and the comments and signature of Ujagar Chand on the right.[16]

This final document was taken back to Rae Chaturbhuj in Ajmer; he then brought at least three children to Hyderabad. His sons, Shadi Lal and Har Lal, married two daughters of Raja Budh Karan, and his daughter married the future *daftardar* Raja Inderjit. Chaturbhuj's two sons both secured *jagirs* within the Malwala estate as "sons-in-law to Lala Bahadur." The Malwalas provided the family with a residence in Chowk Maidan Khan. Shadi Lal was awarded an *inam* grant in about 1850 to support the family's temple and garden establishment just outside the city wall beyond the Chowk. Shadi Lal was a famous *hakim* (doctor) in Hyderabad, an occupation traditional in this Rajasthan family prior to its move to Hyderabad, but his immediate descendants did not practice that or any other occupation. They became *jagirdars*, dependent upon the Malwala family.[17]

In the case of this Ajmer family, some status derived from its contribution to the Malwala line of succession: Chaturbhuj's daughter married

15. The fifth family (which came after 1875) not to marry with the Malwalas was family 22.
16. This letter was approved with Ujagar Chand's seal, dated 1245 H. [1830] when he became official *daftardar*; the contract was made in 1842: interview with Anjani Shanker Lal.
17. Interview with Anjani Shanker Lal; Register Asnad-i Jagir, XVII, no. 6, Hyderabad *subah*, serial nos. 116/34 and 188/17, and XVIII, supp., no. 6, Hyderabad *subah*, serial no. 109/1. (Shadi Lal and Har Lal were actually sons-in-law to the titled *daftardar*, Raja Budh Karan.) After an interval of *jagirdars*, the present adult generation has taken up professions related to medicine: doctors, medical representatives, life insurance representatives, and medical students.

TABLE 8:
A Malwala Marriage Contract

200 rupees a month, income in former home	accepted
basic food provisions, cloth, and clothing	accepted
conveyance	maybe[a]
residence	accepted
all things given to all the others[b]	accepted
expenses of the marriage	accepted

Source: Persian letter of 1842, approved with the seal of Ujagar Chand, in possession of Anjani Shanker Lal.

[a]A conveyance meant status in Hyderabad, and the rights to different kinds were awarded to nobles by the Nizam.

[b]This clause shows awareness of the way Mathur families were being recruited and supported by the Malwalas; the precise content or meaning is no longer clear.

Raja Inderjit and was the mother of Shiv Raj. Although this woman died and Raja Inderjit took two more wives, her family was noted within the subcaste because she produced the heir to the *daftardar* position. But the family's income derived from its provision of sons-in-law to the current *daftardar*.

The same results are seen when the three Lucknow families who were brought by the first one are followed into the next generation. All had come as sons-in-law of the first Lucknow family. One subsequently became a son-in-law of the Malwala *daftardar* as well. Five (three sons and two daughters) of the second's seven children married Malwalas, four of them from the *daftardar* branch. These sons-in-law all received land grants (families 4 and 5 in Table 7). But among the children of the third newcomer (17), only one son married a Malwala, and she was from the declining senior branch of the family. This third family did not achieve so-called *jagirdar* status within the Mathur subcaste, but the other two did.[18]

An attempt to delineate the other Mathur families noted as *jagirdars* within the subcaste over time confirmed that ranking among Mathurs depended upon close kin ties with the Malwala *daftardar,* through marriage relationships which changed from generation to generation. The sons-in-law recruited earliest were given sub-*jagirs* from the Malwala

18. *Jagirdar* status became relevant in the early twentieth century, and an organization formed then included the first two families: interview with Hakim Vicerai.

estate and large residences with *diwankhanahs.*[19] Families who arrived later, after the high point of Malwala political power and after distribution of the larger residences on the Chowk, received cash stipends and quarters whose ownership remained with the Malwala family. But more important than the timing of their arrival were the marriage relationships a family maintained with the Malwala family. Families who initially provided sons-in-law to the current *daftardar* were well established, but this initial standing was not always retained. Subsequent generations of other families could provide sons-in-law to later heads of the Malwala family, and then these men and their families gained access to greater resources. Through provision of economic support and the arrangement of marriages for its sons and daughters, the Malwala family controlled members of the Mathur subcaste and determined their social and economic status. Thus the Mathur *jagirdar* families were not originally given permanent and hereditary allocations of land from the Malwala estate, as some outsiders wrongly believed.[20] The families were allotted stipends and properties that could be redistributed by the head of the Malwala family, and the allotments depended upon the changing marriage patterns.

The Mathurs recruited from northern and western India probably accepted the marriage proposals conveyed by Malwala emissaries from distant Hyderabad for economic reasons. The Malwala family did not conform to traditional Hindu concepts of family purity, for its ancestry and the marriage alliances of its first members in Hyderabad were somewhat ambiguous. Yet it had much to offer in terms of political status and economic security. In addition, since the Malwalas ranked as noblemen in the state, Mathur relatives could share in the prestige and style of life characteristic of the nobility.

An interesting aspect of this marriage pattern was the recruitment, not simply of bridegrooms or brides, but of families. Entire households were brought and established in Hyderabad. According to most oral tradition, sometimes a whole lineage would dispose of its properties and move; in most cases, one branch of a lineage moved to Hyderabad.[21] The Malwalas

19. Eight households had *diwankhanahs,* and *jagirs* were given to the ancestors of Ramchander Narayan, Somnath Pershad, Hakim Vicerai, Anjani Shanker Lal, and Jivan Pershad (families 3, 4, 6, 9, and 11 in Table 7). All of the above men were titled *jagirdar* in a list of Mathur Kayasths in K. C. Roy Saksena, *Kul Hind Kayasth Conference* (Hyderabad, 1938), 10; also, interviews with them.

20. Interviews with men from other subcastes elicited statements of this sort, such as that the Pedapalli *jagir* had been set aside for all dependent Mathur families. Some Mathur families later attempted to convert the provisions of their marriage contracts into permanent and hereditary holdings; their partial success contributed to the idea of a fixed *jagirdar* group.

21. I did not go to North India to verify the information given about home villages and antecedents, but the informants assumed that I intended to do so and I did not correct

were willing and able to support many dependents, and in all cases, Mathurs who moved to Hyderabad did not retain property or kinship ties in their former homes. Most families claim to have lost touch completely with former relatives. Genealogies simply show no further lines of descent in the branches left behind, while the Hyderabad branch continues to expand and be recorded. Unlike other Kayasth immigrants to Hyderabad, most Mathurs maintain that their families had wealth and status in their former homes. Yet even the most recent immigrants did not retain property interests. Almost no one I spoke with could recall an instance of a family member returning to visit his former home. Brides brought from outside did not return to their natal homes for the birth of children, since their parents had also moved to Hyderabad.[22] Mathur Kayasths were born and brought up exclusively in Hyderabad city.

As population of the subcaste increased, social relations among members remained narrowly focused. The controlling position of the Malwalas through marriage alliances and the distribution of economic resources had been established. Since all families were supported financially by the Malwalas, there was no reason to leave the city; Mathurs proudly stated that life was so comfortable in Hyderabad that no Mathur had ever left. Acceptance of the marriage contracts and the economic support of the Malwala family did mean a loss of independence, however. Some incoming Mathur families had been noted for producing famous occupational specialists, but as *jagirdars* in Hyderabad they no longer followed professions.

Only Malwala family members held positions in the Hyderabad administration. Other Mathurs were discouraged from seeking positions of their own.[23] Other Mathur families did build alliances with each other, sometimes arranging multiple marriages over several generations. The formation of smaller kin groups within the subcaste became significant in the late nineteenth century, when occupational diversification began.

Chowk Maidan Khan: The Mathur Neighborhood

Analysis of the Mathur neighborhood culture shows the extent to which the Mathurs functioned as a unit. Like the marriage alliances, development of this kind of joint activity occurred under Lala Bahadur. The

---

them. Several families gave information which could easily have been verified or contradicted; for example, that their ancestors were *talukdars* of Oudh, certified by the British Government.

22. Hakim Vicerai was the only Mathur I met who had visited his place of origin: Hindon, Jaipur, in 1912.

23. Interviews with Maharaj Karan and Hakim Vicerai.

Mathurs all settled in Chowk Maidan Khan, a locality named after the broad street running east from the Char Minar to the city wall (see Map 1). In early Asaf Jahi times, the Muslim Shia nobles settled in Mir Alam Mandi, to the north, and the Chowk was also settled by Muslims. Qutb Shahi mosques, *ashurkhanahs,* and tombs were interspersed throughout the residences on both sides of the Chowk. Next to the Char Minar, at the western end of the Chowk, stood government and private shops, while residences lined the street up to the Yaqutpura gate. That gate separated the Chowk from the less prosperous and more heterogeneous neighborhood of Yaqutpura outside the wall.

In the nineteenth century the Malwala family acquired most of the residential property adjacent to the Chowk, dominating the eastern end, and Mathur residences pushed up the small side streets as well. The Malwala palace, constructed in mid-century, was the most impressive residence in the area. Across from its huge and elaborate gateway was the *naubatkhanah,* the place for ceremonial beating of the drums that signalled the arrival and departure of nobles. High walls surrounded the private household apartments, the *diwankhanah,* buildings for storage and production, and servants' quarters. The Malwala palace was eventually flanked by stables for elephants and horses, a distillery, a central provisions storehouse, and a wedding hall for the use of all Mathurs.[24]

Much of the activity in the neighborhood consisted of entertainments held within the walls, in *diwankhanahs* and the Malwala wedding hall. For the men, favorite events were poetry recitations and musical performances, with dancing girls and musicians. Guests at such events included men of other communities. The women were in *purdah*, and for them domestic Hindu ceremonies and weddings were the major social events. Celebration of Hindu life-cycle ceremonies, such as hair-cutting, name-giving, and birthdays, involved close relatives and occurred frequently. Weddings were the most elaborate ceremonies, and though non-Kayasths attended, the women associated only with other women in separate apartments and ceremonies. Because of the Malwala's position in Hyderabad state, many eminent noblemen were invited to Malwala weddings, sometimes even the Nizam, and these were festive and lengthy occasions. The Malwala family prided itself on serving guests fine Mughlai cuisine and special wine, privately produced by the family. The host served the wine in an elaborate ceremony involving many toasts. At Mathur weddings, the head of the Malwala family placed the headdress

24. The description is based on the detailed series of maps in Munn, *Hyderabad Municipal Survey 1911,* maps 45–48, 52–56, 60–64; interviews with Hakim Vicerai, Kishen Raj, Mahbub Karan, and Sri Rang Pershad.

on the bridegroom's head before the customary horseback ride to the home of the bride, symbolizing ultimate Malwala approval and control of Mathur marriages.[25]

The most significant demonstration of Mathur dependency on the Malwala family occurred on the annual festival of Dasserah, when Hindus traditionally worship the tools used in their hereditary occupations. Ordinarily this consisted of a private domestic ceremony for members of separate families or households, but it was the occasion for the major annual assembly of all Mathur men in Hyderabad. They attended a *durbar* in the Malwala palace reception hall in full court dress, including *dastars,* the unique headdress worn in the Nizam's *durbar.* They all presented *nazrs,* professing their loyalty to the head of the Malwala family. Then they jointly offered homage to the tools of the Kayasth profession, a pen and an inkpot.[26] In this ceremony, Mathur Kayasths formally acknowledged their economic dependence on the Malwalas in a *durbar* modelled on the Nizam's court.

There was a public life in Chowk Maidan Khan as well, centered on institutions and historical events associated with Muslim rule in Hyderabad. As one of the wealthiest families in the locality, the Malwala family was a leading patron of neighborhood institutions and events. The wealthier families on the Chowk jointly supported the neighborhood mosques (the Kotla Ali Jah mosque, the Maidan Khan mosque, and the two Lodhi Khan mosques) and the *ashurkhanahs,* where religious relics were kept for Muharram. The Malwala family furnished floor matting and lamp oil for the mosques and donated money in *Ramzan,* the Islamic month of fasting. Three Muslim families paid the mosque attendants and financed repairs to the buildings. Another Mathur family, whose house adjoined a small *dargah,* or tomb of a Muslim saint, assumed responsibility for its annual commemoration ceremony.[27] On Muslim holidays, large households had certain obligations to the public. The Malwala family gave out alms and illuminated the palace on the Prophet Muhammad's birthday and for Abdul Qadir Gilani's annual commemoration ceremony.[28]

25. On weddings, literary, and other entertainments, see Saksenah, *Kayasth Sajjan Caritra,* II, 10, 12, 32, 74, and Hakim Vicerai, *Ramayan Manzum* (Hyderabad [1960]), the foreword by Balobir Prosad. For the wine, interviews with Mahbub Karan, Raj Pershad, and many non-Kayasths; letter from Dr. Brij Mohan Lal of Sept. 26, 1965. Called *seh atish* (3 fires) and produced with the special permission of the Nizam, the wine was made from coarse brown sugar and flavored with cardamom, anise, jasmine, sweet lime, or rose petals.
26. Interviews with Hind Kishore (who included swords and horses among the objects of homage), Hakim Vicerai, Sri Rang Pershad, and Mahbub Karan.
27. This was family number 4 in Table 7; interview with Hakim Vicerai.
28. Abdul Qadir Gilani was the founder of the Sufi Qadiri order in India. The two

The grandest public occasion for Chowk Maidan Khan came during Muharram. Then the local Shia religious relic, the Bik Alam, was taken out in procession on an elephant. The procession passed through the city streets, pausing in the gateways of noble residences for the customary cash offerings. The Malwala palace was the traditional halting place on Chowk Maidan Khan, and the head of the family presented the family offering with great ceremony. Other Mathur families presented offerings along the route. Some Mathur households kept replicas of the shrine of Hasan and Husain, and these *taziyahs* were also taken out in Muharram processions. During Muharram the Malwala family displayed its *taziyah*, set up an *abdarkhanah* or shelter to serve sherbet to the public, and distributed alms.[29] Thus the Malwala family assumed the role expected of a wealthy noble family of Hyderabad, and the Mathur families were integrated into the major events of neighborhood and city.

The Malwalas and Salar Jung after 1853

Lala Bahadur achieved a great deal of political power and formed a subcaste in Hyderabad, but he lost power in 1853 to Salar Jung. Despite popular predictions that Lala Bahadur would be deprived of his office at once, Salar Jung's victory had no immediate impact upon the fortunes of the Malwala family.[30] The *daftardars* were not replaced, nor were their hereditary positions abolished. Instead, Salar Jung worked indirectly and slowly to set up new financial offices and install new personnel. He appointed two Marathi-speaking Brahmans from his own *jagirs* as heads of new "accountancy" and "treasury" offices.[31] Initially called the *munshikhanah* (clerical office), the former duplicated the work of the *daftardars,* but its ambiguous title was selected to disguise that fact:

. . . to name it the Accounts Office was not thought advisable as the accounts work was entirely connected with the Daftars of Mal and Diwani, and it was difficult to allow any other office to share their work or to ask them to do other work than theirs. The members of the old offices would not have tolerated the

---

holidays are called *Dvazdahum* (the twelfth) and *Yazdahum* (the eleventh) because they occur on the twelfth of *Rabi al aval* and the eleventh of *Rabi al akhir,* months of the Hijri calendar year. For the Malwala observance of them, see Saksenah, *Kayasth Sajjan Caritra,* II, 14.

29. Khan, *Gulzar,* 579; Saksenah, *Kayasth Sajjan Caritra,* II, 8, 14; numerous interviews. The Bik Alam, or *bibi ka alam,* is an inscribed metal standard that was placed in the shrine by the famous Qutb Shahi queen, Hayat Bakshi Begum: Rao, *Bustan,* II, 743. The procession and the Malwala role in it are still carried out, as observed in 1965 and 1971.

30. *The Englishman,* Oct. 26, 1853, in *HA,* V, 202, predicted Lala Bahadur's dismissal.

31. Rao, *Bustan,* I, 153, and VII, 307–308.

accounts work done by the new offices. The late Diwan did not want to hurt their feelings, therefore . . . the [new] accounts office was said to be maintaining the Diwani accounts.[32]

Salar Jung managed to secure his own set of revenue and financial records through this new office; while the *daftardars* continued to store the original state revenue documents, they no longer had exclusive control of the records.[33] This was not so much an administrative reform as installation of a new set of officials and records under the Diwan's control.

Salar Jung did try in 1854 to reduce the *daftardars'* emoluments, and he is supposed to have secured the Nizam's consent to confiscation of the Malwala *jagirs*. He planned to pay the Malwala family a salary of fifteen thousand rupees a month in place of the *jagirs*. The proposed salary was equal to his own, indicating that Lala Bahadur's influence with the Nizam was still great. In fact, Salar Jung's proposal did not succeed. He made no further attempts to change the payments made to the two *daftardars*; in the case of the Malwalas, the proposed rupee salary may actually have been added to their existing income.[34]

The Daftar-i-Mal continued to carry out its increasingly minor and old-fashioned functions, though Salar Jung had created alternatives to the old administrative offices. The record offices continued to be the sole repositories of documents from pre-Salar Jung days; but all later documents had copies filed elsewhere. The *daftardars* became known as "custodians of the state records," and their political power in Hyderabad was much reduced. Their chief function came to be archival—verifying *jagir* and *inam* claims by reference to the original documents.[35]

This function of verification became more important with commencement of the Inam Investigations in 1876. In that year, twenty-three years after Salar Jung's appointment, a commission was appointed to discover invalid claims on the government's finances. Government grants made from 1840 to 1853 were particularly suspect. The Mal and Diwani *daftars* furnished most of the materials for the investigation, and the volume of

---

32. Rao, *Bustan*, I, 153. The establishment of a treasury presented no difficulties, as none had existed earlier. Even after a treasury had been established in the city, Salar Jung relied on bankers to conduct financial transactions in the districts; district treasuries were said to be established in 1864: Ali, *Hyderabad Under Sir Salar Jung*, I, 78.

33. Rao, *Bustan*, I, 153–156, discusses the ways in which this was done.

34. *The Englishman*, July 6, 1854, in *HA*, V, 209; J. F. Gorst, "The Kingdom of the Nizam," *Fortnightly Review*, 35, n.s., January-June 1884, 526. In 1901 the Malwala family received a salary of 11,797 rupees a month (the Diwan's was 12,000 rupees), an honorarium of 54,516 rupees a year, a *qanungo* fee of 87,000 rupees a year, and *jagirs* worth 5 lakhs rupees: Elahi Buksh (Hyderabad correspondent) in *The Hindu*, July 20, 1901 (CC).

35. Rao, *Bustan*, I, 153–156, tells how they kept original documents and prepared certified copies upon demand.

cases investigated was enormous. From 1876 to 1884, some fourteen thousand cases were decided. During the Inam Investigations the *daftardars* once again assumed some political importance. Intermittently, charges were made against them for possible connivance with the holders of invalid *sanads* (documents conferring titles or rights). On such occasions, the *daftars* themselves were investigated, bringing criticism of the lack of precautions taken for the storage of *sanads* and the old-fashioned methods still prevailing in both *daftars*.[36] But the offices and their incumbents were retained.

The Malwalas benefitted from Salar Jung's conciliatory policies towards the Hyderabad nobility. At first, the Diwan viewed powerful nobles as rivals and believed that their exercise of political power was detrimental to efficient administration.[37] As Salar Jung began to establish the new Diwani bureaucracy, modelled on the Anglo-Indian administration and staffed largely with British-trained Indians from outside Hyderabad, he sought to isolate the new personnel and structure from the Mughlai nobles and structures. But Salar Jung also valued the nobles and the Hyderabad court culture. By enforcing strict adherence to the Mughlai etiquette of the Nizam's court and denying the new administrators access to that arena, he hoped to preserve the dignity of the Nizam and the traditions of Mughlai Hyderabad.[38]

Until Salar Jung's death, the Malwala family and other Mughlai nobles were honored much as before, but in an increasingly limited sphere of ceremonial activities within the old city walls of Hyderabad. Lala Bahadur retired soon after the conflict with the new Diwan, apparently because of the death of his elder son, and he himself died in 1858.[39] The Diwan honored Lala Bahadur's successor, Raja Inderjit, by personally attending

36. Of the 800,351 rupees involved in the 14,000 some cases decided from 1876 to 1884, 412,888 rupees' worth of claims were decided in favor of the holders, and 387,463 rupees' worth of land and allowances were confiscated by the government: Ali, *Hyderabad Under Sir Salar Jung*, II, 241–253. For complaints about the *daftardars*, letter to Mehdi Ali, chief secretary, June 4, 1885, installment 39, Mal and Mulki div., list 5, serial no. 52, file H6/fl of the APSA; and letter to the political and financial secretary, June 17, 1885, installment 14, list 1, serial no. 56, file H8, G50 of the APSA.

37. Nawab Bahadur Server-el-Mulk, *My Life*, trans. Jivan Yar Yung Bahadur (London, 1932), 271.

38. *Ibid.*, 100. For fuller discussion, see my "Cultural Change and Bureaucratic Modernization in Nineteenth Century Hyderabad: Mulkis, non-Mulkis, and the English," in P. M. Joshi, ed. *Studies in the Foreign Relations of India* (Hyderabad, 1975).

39. Saksenah, *Kayasth Sajjan Caritra*, II, 10. Lala Bahadur's sharp conflict with Salar Jung has been repressed; he is now remembered as the patron and lifelong friend of the young Diwan. He was even named as one who assisted in framing Hyderabad's new system of government: "Original Constitution of Hyderabad State," prepared in 1892, Government of India, Political Department, *Hyderabad Residency Records*, Box 66, p. 2 (IOL).

the marriage of his son, Raja Shiv Raj, in 1868. Salar Jung appointed Raja Inderjit to arbitrate disputes among nobles and within the old Mughlai administrative units. Several disputes occurred within the Mathur community, just before and after the death of Raja Inderjit, and Salar Jung's personal arbitration on these occasions was viewed as a sign of his special regard for the family.[40]

Another aspect of Salar Jung's evolving policies towards the old nobility actually reinforced the Malwalas' status in the state. The Diwan's initial attempts to keep members of the nobility disassociated from the new Diwani administration jeopardized public acceptance of Diwani functions, particularly acceptance by the nobility. Salar Jung soon found that nominal association of selected nobles with some of the new departments as "ministers" helped win the support of influential nobles and the public in general. Since competent Secretaries actually carried out departmental work,[41] such appointments did not hamper administrative operations. Further, they served the related goal of educating and enlightening the younger nobility.

Salar Jung established a private school emphasizing Western education in his palace for his own sons and a few other noble youths.[42] He gave personal encouragement to some promising young nobles and encouraged them to undertake Diwani administrative careers. In the case of the Malwala family, Salar Jung advised Raja Inderjit (Lala Bahadur's successor) to study English and acquaint himself with the new administration. There is little evidence that either Inderjit or his son and successor Raja Shiv Raj followed this advice, but Salar Jung was more successful with Shiv Raj's younger brother Murli Manohar, who studied in Salar Jung's school and later served in financial branches of the Diwani administration. He and other Malwalas and Mathurs, when they entered the new administration at the end of the nineteenth century, were associated with the revenue and accounts departments.[43] This association lent a somewhat deceptive continuity to the old public image of this noble family as recordkeepers.

40. Interviews with Mahbub Karan and Maharaj Karan, Hakim Vicerai, and Sri Rang Pershad; Saksenah, *Kayasth Sajjan Caritra*, II, 10, 12. For arbitration of Sarf-i Khas disputes, see paper no. 11, bundle for 1280 H. [1856], in the records of the Arbab-i Nishat (Sarf-i Khas files, APSA).
41. Ali, *Hyderabad Under Sir Salar Jung*, I, 90; Server-el-Mulk, *My Life*, 95.
42. Server-el-Mulk, *My Life*, 271; Syed Hossain Belgrami Motaman Jung, *History of the Operations of His Highness the Nizam's Educational Department for the last 30 years together with a detailed Report and Returns for 1883–85* (Hyderabad, 1886), 17.
43. For Salar Jung's personal interest and supervision, Saksenah, *Kayasth Sajjan Caritra*, II, 10-11, 71-72; *Kayastha*, I, no. 3 (1895), p. 1; Campbell, *Glimpses*, 74.

Internal Change and Conflict

During the second half of the nineteenth century, shifts in Mathur migration and marriage patterns gave ascendancy to new families from Lucknow. As Table 7 shows, during Raja Inderjit's tenure as *daftardar*, more families migrated from Lucknow than from Rajputana. Several families moved from Lucknow right after the Mutiny of 1857 in northern India and formed advantageous marriage alliances with the Malwala family, putting them in a better position than the Rajputana families already established in Hyderabad.

Two Lucknow families who arrived after 1857 illustrate again the importance of close affinal ties to the Malwalas for income and status within the Mathur subcaste. After 1857, one Durga Pershad, called by Inderjit, brought two daughters and three sons to Hyderabad. This family's initial connections with the Malwala family were highly advantageous, as shown in Figure 3.[44] The three sons married three daughters of Raja Inderjit, and the two daughters also married into the major branch of the Malwala family. The family was known thenceforward as a *jagirdar* family among the Mathurs, and its residence had a *diwankhanah*. The three sons were sons-in-law to the head of the *daftar*; they were also *hamzulf* to one another (the Persian term for those married to sisters). Through their own sisters, they were linked to both other surviving collateral lines in the *daftardar* branch of the Malwala family.

Another Lucknow man, Sham Bali, brought his children to marry in Hyderabad after the Mutiny.[45] One of his three daughters married Raja Shiv Raj in 1868, becoming the first of his five wives, and one of his three sons married into the senior branch of the Malwala family. A few years later, Sham Bali's brother's daughter was brought from Lucknow to marry Shiv Raj's younger brother, Murli Manohar. This strengthened Sham Bali's ties to the leading branch of the Malwalas by providing Raja Inderjit with a second daughter-in-law.

Around 1880, Sham Bali called his *hamzulf*, the husband of his wife's sister, to bring his children for marriage in Hyderabad; Jag Mohan Lal brought his brother's two sons along with his own children. One of Jag Mohan Lal's daughters married into the senior branch of the Malwalas, and the two sons of his brother married daughters of Raja Inderjit and Raja Shiv Raj, becoming sons-in-law to successive Malwala *daftardars*.

44. For Durga Pershad's family, interview with Jivan Pershad and Khan, *Tuzuk*, II (Nobles), 366. Figure 2 includes only genealogical information relevant to the discussion here.
45. Interview with Hakim Vicerai; Mahender Raj Suxena, "Chand Kayasth Shora," *KH*, VII–VIII (1948), 13–14.

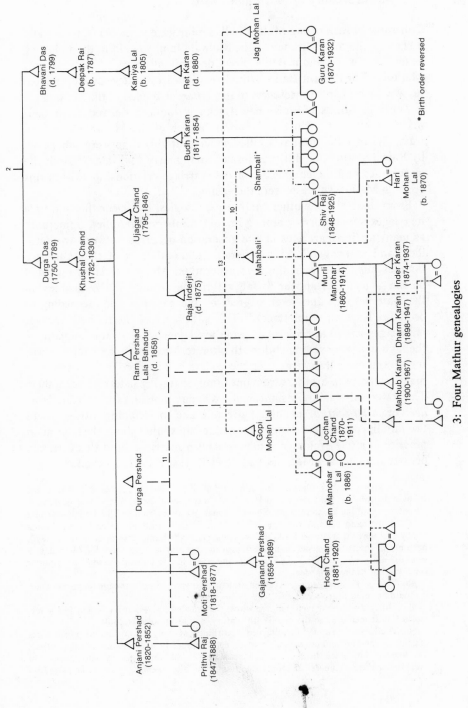

3: Four Mathur genealogies

*Birth order reversed

This same branch of Jag Mohan Lal's family gave three bridegrooms and a bride to the major branch of the Malwala family again in the following generation, while Sham Bali's direct descendants married non-Malwala Mathurs. Thus Sham Bali's affinal relatives from Lucknow supplanted his own descendants in closeness to the *daftardar* branch of the Malwalas.[46]

The high status of these new Lucknow families derived from their marriage alliances with the *daftardar* branch of the Malwalas. In contrast, the two Rajputana families arriving at this time were not called by Raja Inderjit, nor did they immediately marry Malwalas.[47] Both the importance and the complexity of the marriage relationships within this growing Mathur subcaste were increasing.

From these and the other Mathur genealogies, it is clear that multiple marriages were occurring among limited numbers of families. Sometimes as many as five marriages in one generation occurred between two families, and marriages linking different collateral lines of the same two families might follow in the next generation. Many marriages recorded on the genealogies appear to fall within the prohibited five degrees on the maternal side and seven degrees on the paternal side (according to orthodox Kayasth regulations).[48] This is because of the limited number of lineages settled in Hyderabad and the frequency of serial monogamy— the high mortality rate in childbirth often resulted in a man's taking two, three, and even five wives over the course of his lifetime.[49] There were many instances of brothers from one family marrying sisters from another. There were also many instances of exchange marriages (in Urdu, *leen-deen* or *aatha-saatha,* meaning "give and take" or "coming with"), where two families exchanged daughters. As kinship studies show, the continued practice of sister exchange results in cousin marriage, and this certainly occurred among the Mathurs and other Kayasths in Hyderabad.[50]

46. Interview with Professor Shiv Mohan Lal. The *hamzulf* relationship which had brought Jag Mohan Lal's lineage to Hyderabad was re-established in the next generation when the sons of Jag Mohan Lal and Sham Bali married sisters from another Lucknow family

47. Sail Chand's family (number 29 in Table 7) came through an earlier Rajputana family and never married with Malwalas. Tulja Pershad's family also arrived about 1870, but only in the second generation did it provide two marriage partners for Malwalas: a second, short-lived wife for Raja Shiv Raj, and a son-in-law to Moti Pershad, in a junior collateral line of the *daftardar* branch.

48. This is the most widely accepted statement of prohibition, though some maintain it should be seven degrees on both sides.

49. Thirty-six Mathur men had two wives, six had three wives, and one had five wives; most of these men lived in the nineteenth century, and seven were Malwalas.

50. The Kayasths supposedly followed a patrilineal system, and of the four possible sets of cousins—parallel and cross—only one set, ego's father's brother's children, falls in ego's own lineage. The other three sets of cousins belong to different lineages, and these could provide marriage alliances. The only rigorous prohibition seems to have been placed on

Anthropologists have pointed to the economic advantages offered by such marriage patterns. The Mathur Kayasths, with a limited number of their families in Hyderabad dependent upon the Malwala family, exemplify that situation well. Exchange marriages eliminated the need for a dowry, and multiple marriages performed at the same or nearly the same time lessen expenditures. The practice of multiple marriages among Mathur families was basic to the maintenance and control of economic resources within a limited population group. When conflict developed over economic resources, the marriage alliances reflected it.

There is no evidence of dispute over succession to the *daftardar* position from the late eighteenth century to the appointment of Raja Inderjit in 1858. This is so despite movement of the position from the senior to the junior branch of a family or from a man to his cousin-brother or brother, and despite the occasional coexistence of a nominal titleholder and an actual performer of the office. Furthermore, the *daftardar* was also recognized as head of the joint family, the *karta* or manager of the family property. Under Mitakshara law this was a coparcenary estate, in which all males held shares by birth; the shares remained jointly owned and managed.[51] Up to this point in the history of the Malwala family, the *daftardar* and the *karta* functions were performed by the same person; but upon the death of Raja Inderjit in 1875 the situation changed.

In 1875, succession to the *karta* and *daftardar* positions was disputed, and the two functions came to be recognized as separate. This dispute provides the first evidence of conflict within the community, conflict that occurred on two levels. One dispute, over which individual would inherit the *karta* and *daftardar* positions, was within the Malwala family. Another occurred among the Malwalas and certain of the "client" Mathur families, specifically those most recently brought, whose marriage contracts appeared to grant them sub-*jagirs*, legal rights to part of the Malwala estate.

The dispute within the Malwala family divided collateral lines in the junior branch. Raja Inderjit left three sons, the eldest, Shiv Raj, born in 1849. Raja Inderjit's first cousin, Prithvi Raj, was born in 1848 and was therefore elder to Shiv Raj, both in generation and by birth. The estate was claimed by Raja Shiv Raj and the claim challenged by Raja Prithvi Raj. The dispute was ultimately adjudicated by the Diwan Salar Jung, to

unions between direct descendants within two generations. I am aware that many Hyderabad Kayasth marriage practices deviate from alleged regulations and preferences, as described by Sylvia Vatuk ("A Structural Analysis of the Hindi Kinship Terminology," *CIS*, n.s., III [1969], 94–115) and others.

51. D. F. Mulla, *Principles of Hindu Law* (Bombay, 1959), 18 and passim.

whom Raja Inderjit's widow appealed personally on behalf of her son. Salar Jung's award specified that both men should share equally in the income and in the work of supervision of the estate and the position of *daftardar*. He observed that, had it been Raja Inderjit's intention to transfer his legacy only to the eldest, it would have gone to Prithvi Raj, but that ability as well as age and relationship had to be assessed. But Shiv Raj won the title of *daftardar*,[52] a victory over the collateral line of Prithvi Raj that caused a lasting split within the Malwala family.

This decision was important for several reasons. First, it marked the first dispute within the family and publicly enunciated a principle of succession combining ability with seniority. (However, seniority had not been the sole determinant of succession in the past.) Second, it re-invoked the concept of shared responsibility for the properties and office, as performed by the brothers Durga Das and Bhavani Das. Since their time the family had grown, and political events had halted its expanding wealth and influence. Sharing supervision of the office did not work out in practice, and Raja Shiv Raj as titled *daftardar* controlled the position.

Most important, Salar Jung's decision confirmed the increased potential for conflict between collateral lines of the enlarged joint family. Resources controlled by the Malwalas were now allocated according to membership in collateral lines. Earlier, all male family members had received grants and had been listed individually, as members of a single family. By the time of this 1875 decision, and certainly after it, awards were made to the senior member of each collateral branch, or to these members' dependents and descendants collectively.[53] Perhaps this was a natural development, as the number of adult male members had increased to nineteen in the fourth generation after Sagar Mal. It can be attributed also to the pressures on land grants dating from the mid-century. The Inam Investigation was only one manifestation of the government's policy to examine and retract, rather than expand, such grants. The effect on the Malwala family, as on others by the end of the nineteenth century, was to produce competition among collateral lines. In this particular case, Prithvi Raj died in 1888, leaving a sixteen-year-old son who died shortly after marriage without an heir. Shiv Raj assumed control without further challenge, but those families allied to Prithvi Raj by marriage continued to feud with the *daftardar* branch.[54]

52. This Persian *sanad*, dated 1875, is preserved by Hakim Vicerai.
53. Register Asnad-i Jagir for these years, and Daftar-i Mal Jagir Register, "naqul-i asnad-i Shiv Raj," in file no. 66 of 1932–1933 (both in section R2, APSA).
54. Interviews with Hakim Vicerai and Sri Rang Pershad.

The death of Inderjit, the succession dispute, and the Inam Investigation caused anxiety among the Mathur client families. Evidently fearing that the sub-*jagirs* granted by Raja Inderjit in their marriage contracts might not be recognized by his successors, some of the sons-in-law petitioned Salar Jung at this time for state recognition of their right to portions of the Malwala estate. The petition stated that they had come for marriage and given up all contracts and property elsewhere, trusting in the awards from Raja Inderjit; they now sought government sanction of the Raja's sub-*jagir* awards. Those who petitioned had come from Lucknow after 1857 and were powerful men among the Mathurs. Salar Jung did grant them official recognition of their holdings, setting a precedent which encouraged further litigation when drastic changes in the state administration took place later.[55]

Little evidence exists concerning the marriage alliances of the few Mathur families in Hyderabad in the eighteenth century—as is true for most Kayasths then. In one instance, the head of the highest-ranked Mathur family, the Malwala recordkeepers, did take his son to North India for his marriage. As the nineteenth century began, the powerful Malwala family initiated an unusual series of marriages, bringing Mathurs from outside and creating a subcaste whose inclusiveness and solidarity contrasted with the social structures formed by Kayasths of other subcastes in Hyderabad city. This subcaste was larger than the kin groups characteristically formed by other Kayasths at that time. It was based upon patrilineally inherited wealth and centrally distributed resources, rather than upon continuing performance of jobs allocated to kinsmen of both male and female lines. Income and status within the Mathur subcaste depended upon the kind and closeness of marriage alliances that each family had with the dominant Malwala family. Despite the Malwalas' relative loss of political power after 1853 and the beginnings of internal conflict, the Mathur families maintained their subcaste cohesiveness.

55. The original draft of the application and the *sanad* sanctioning the grant, dated 1874 and 1876, are with Hakim Vicerai.

CHAPTER 5

Saksenas and Bhatnagars: Kin Groups and Positions

The Kayasths who prospered in the early nineteenth century were those who, like the Malwalas, held positions central to the expanding Mughlai bureaucracy in Hyderabad city. Positions in the Nizam's household service provided the economic base for many Kayasths, particularly Saksenas and Bhatnagars. These administrators and recordkeepers, most of them below the level of the nobility, secured and retained control of positions through patrons and relatives. The bilateral inheritance of positions, through affinal as well as consanguineous relatives, encouraged the formation of local kin groups. Patron-client relations, still significant at higher levels, were supplemented or replaced by these groups, which transmitted and distributed positions at lower levels. When household managerial and clerical positions were plentiful, relatives were employed, and at times recruited, to retain them. When an area of administrative service was contracting or being abolished, relatives could be rivals for positions; even one's own sons might be too numerous for economic health. Neighborhood boundaries also became increasingly important. Since the records were kept in each official's residence, and many office functions were carried out there, the relative prosperity and security of the Mughlai bureaucrats helped develop Husaini Alam as a residential area for Hindu civil servants. Many Bhatnagars and Saksenas moved there and shared a neighborhood culture which contrasted with that of the Mathur Kayasths in Chowk Maidan Khan.

Bhatnagar Nobles and Clerks

The highest-ranking Kayasth in the Nizam's household service in the early nineteenth century was the Bhatnagar noble Raja Bhavani Pershad,

92]

who successfully moved from a primarily military career to one of super-vising household positions. But he and his descendants had difficulty retaining control of those positions. The relation of other Bhatnagars to this noble family and to the positions controlled by the family initially shows only partial development of a Bhatnagar kin group in the city. Despite Raja Bhavani Pershad's performance as a patron for local Kayasths and immigrant Bhatnagars, he and his heirs were supplanted by the Saksena and Bhatnagar men who actually worked in the positions.

Raja Bhavani Pershad had acquired noble status through both military achievements and household services. He had confirmed his high status in 1802 by constructing the oldest Kayasth temple in Hyderabad (see Chapter I). But Bhavani Pershad died in 1836 without a son. His positions, which included supervision of the kitchens, of the royal ceremonies, and of the *serrishtah* (unit) of court musicians and dancing girls, passed to his daughter's sons, Raja Hanu Lal and Raja Manu Lal. The younger, Raja Manu Lal, held the posts first, and it was he who was granted land and built a large new residence on the edge of Husaini Alam. He earned high titles, honors, and *jagirs* but was dismissed for inefficiency and confined to his residence. The elder brother, Raja Hanu Lal, was then honored with the positions and reputedly became a close confidant of the Nizam Nasiruddaula. Manu Lal died, still in disgrace, in 1847; his son held a *mansab* of one hundred fifty-five rupees per month in the customs office and died without heirs.[1] Hanu Lal's successor in 1858, Raja Durga Pershad, continued to hold key household positions.[2]

Another early and high-ranking Bhatnagar family moved from Sha-halibanda to Husaini Alam around 1800, but there were no recorded marriages between it and Bhavani Pershad's Bhatnagar family.[3] Though its forebears were known for military feats, nineteenth-century members of this second family served as *serrishtahdar* of the carriage house. They were associated with Raja Bhavani Pershad in the household administra-tion. Majlis Rae, head of the family in the early part of the century, had five sons, and *jagirs* were awarded to the three elder ones from 1825 to 1830. The marriages of the two younger sons are the only ones recalled or recorded, however; Bhatnagar wives were brought from North India for them. The three elder sons are recorded as never having married.[4]

---

1. Khan, *Tuzuk*, II (Nobles), 201.
2. "Salary receipts of Durga Pershad's *serrishtah* for 1286 H. [1862]," paper no. 15, bundle for 1280 H. [1856], records of the Arbab-i Nishat (Sarf-i Khas files, APSA).
3. They built a double-storied residence in a new locality, called Majlis Rae after the head of the family: interviews with Brij Rani and daughters and Sham Karan.
4. Register Asnad-i Jagir: for Majlis Rae's son Ramchander, IV, no. 15; serial no. 271b/5; for Majlis Rae's son Kishen Chand, V, no. 16, serial no. 18/18; for Majlis Rae's

Bringing brides from the north for the younger sons meant that there was sufficient wealth to overcome the difficulties and expenses of such alliances. These marriages may have indicated rising wealth and prestige, and possibly competition between the two Bhatnagar families, following the Malwala example. In any case, the elder brothers may have left descendants by concubines or unacknowledged local wives, for the purity of marriage alliances made locally did become an issue for some Bhatnagars.

During the first half of the nineteenth century, other Bhatnagar Kayasths came to Hyderabad, secured positions in the household administration through Raja Bhavani Pershad, and settled down in Chowk Maidan Khan near their patron's residence. Thus their immigration can be placed between 1820 and 1836, before Bhavani Pershad's death and Manu Lal's move to Husaini Alam. Two of these families, unlike other Kayasths moving to Hyderabad, retained ties with their places of origin in North India. This strikingly different pattern can be attributed to the wealth of their North Indian families and the management of the Hyderabad positions as part of the joint family's assets. The position-holders in Hyderabad were invariably the younger sons,[5] who avoided local or Hyderabad marriages.

Both of these immigrant Bhatnagar families, from the United Provinces, were known in Hyderabad as "U.P." families because of their continued ties with the Provinces and their avoidance of local marriage alliances. In one family, younger sons were sent to Hyderabad to obtain household and military *serrishtahdari* positions, which they did through the patronage of Raja Bhavani Pershad Bhatnagar.[6] Their ancestral home in Hyderabad is near Bhavani Pershad's original residence. Members of this family never received titles or *jagirs* in Hyderabad, but they retained their *serrishtahdari* positions. They also retained an interest in the ancestral property in Mangalore, Saharanpur district, U.P. Men frequently journeyed north to confer about management of the property, to take their sons and daughters for marriage with North Indian Bhatnagars, and to take the brides back to their natal homes for confinements and visits.

---

sons Kishen Chand and Murlidhar, V, no. 16, serial no. 182/19 and VI, no. 17, serial no. 152/7. Also, interviews with Sham Karan; Dr. R. C. Bhatnagar and his mother and Harish Chandra; and Balobir Prosad and his wife.

5. Genealogies, and interviews with Balobir Prosad and Mahabir Pershad.

6. As evidence of this patronage a descendant, Mahabir Pershad, has an illustrated Urdu manuscript of the *Srimat Bhagvat* which gives as authors of the Urdu version Hira Lal and Ram Dayal, sons of Kunji Lal, formerly of Mangalore, Saharanpur district. The manuscript is dated 1841; it is dedicated to the "late Raja Bhavani Pershad and Manu Lal Pershad."

Children often stayed in North India for several years before being sent down to Hyderabad.[7]

The second U.P. Bhatnagar family also managed its Hyderabad positions as part of a larger economic unit controlled by the North Indian joint family. But this family had early difficulties controlling its Hyderabad position. Sohan Lal, the first member to come down (before mid-century), secured a position as *serrishtahdar* of religious affairs for the Nizam's immediate family, probably through the aid of fellow Bhatnagars. In this capacity he supervised and paid one hundred seventy *moulvis*, pundits, and astrologers to perform prayers and other rituals on behalf of the Nizam. He and other employees were given the house in which they rented quarters in 1855, and both U.P. Bhatnagar families have resided there ever since.[8] Sohan Lal's son Satnarayan Pershad inherited the *serrishtahdari* position, but he "fell into bad company," drinking heavily and marrying a woman from Hyderabad; their daughter married a Bhatnagar who came from Aurangabad. When Satnarayan Pershad died, his widow tried to give the position to her local son-in-law. To forestall this, the North Indian family sent down Hira Lal, second son of Satnarayan Pershad's younger cousin-brother, who secured the Diwan Salar Jung's help and successfully reclaimed the position.[9] Here an early instance of local marriage threatened the North Indian family's control of the Hyderabad income and provided a rationale for the avoidance of local alliances.

There were other Bhatnagars in Hyderabad by the 1830's, employed as clerks and accountants and residing near the household establishments on Chowk Maidan Khan. They and later immigrants eventually moved into the Husaini Alam area, and most were employed under the four Bhatnagar families above (the two nobles and the two U.P. families). All these families shared a subcaste designation and occupational specialization, and most were settled in Husaini Alam. But they were members of several different kin groups.

The two early Bhatnagar noble families married with other Bhatnagars in Hyderabad and Aurangabad; in some instances, North Indian brides were imported. But the two U.P. Bhatnagar families retained their joint

7. Mahabir Pershad, late head of one Hyderabad branch of this family and a member of the fifth generation in the city, named the employees who managed the family property in the north until its sale in 1943. Interviews with Mahabir Pershad and Mrs. Jag Mohan Lal.
8. The Nizam became angry at a close relative who owned the residence, imprisoned him, confiscated the house, and gave it to the renters. The gift was orally conveyed by a Palace *mama*, or serving lady. Interviews with Balobir Prosad and Roy Mahboob Narayan and with Balobir Prosad and his wife.
9. Interview with Balobir Prosad and his wife.

family residences and marriage networks in North India and did not move to Husaini Alam when Raja Manu Lal did. Perhaps this was because they had been given property in Chowk Maidan Khan; but, just as important, there were no kinship ties with the Hyderabad families. For despite the noble status and wealth of the two Hyderabad Bhatnagar families and their patronage of the newer immigrants, marriage alliances were never made between these families and the U.P. families.[10] The prohibition of local marriages may have been based upon concepts of purity and pollution or upon the threatened loss of the Hyderabad positions. Certainly, local marriages threatened the successful integration of the Hyderabad positions with the U.P. joint family enterprises; while the Hyderabad positions of both these families were relatively minor ones, they were hereditary and available for younger sons.

The Bhatnagar Kayasths did not constitute a single effective kin group in the city, although initially there was some use of the highest-ranked Bhatnagar to secure jobs. There was one kin group associated with transmission of positions in the Nizam's household. The two families who retained major economic holdings elsewhere neither resided nor married with the other Bhatnagars. One of these families received title to property directly from the Nizam and had a disputed inheritance settled by appeal to the Diwan Salar Jung, demonstrating its lack of dependence upon Raja Bhavani Pershad. Within Hyderabad, Bhavani Pershad's descendants retained their noble status, but the men working below them were the ones who actually controlled the transmission and distribution of the positions. The well-developed local kin group of the Saksena Kayasth Bansi Raja eventually presided over the Nizam's household, displacing the descendants of Raja Bhavani Pershad and other Bhatnagars.

Saksena Kin Groups

At the beginning of the nineteenth century, the military men in Shahalibanda were the most prominent and powerful Saksenas. As noted in Chapter II, two Saksena families in relatively minor clerical and managerial positions with the Nizam and the Nawab of Arcot settled in the locality of Husaini Alam. One of these families was that of Bansi Raja, who gained supremacy in the Nizam's household after 1850. The other, more powerful in the 1830's and 1840's, utilized patronage and kinship

10. This was allegedly because of the small number of Bhatnagars in Hyderabad and the U.P. concern for "pure" marriage alliances: "local" was used to mean "impure" in the dispute over Satnarayan Pershad's marriage and position. Interviews with Balobir Prosad and his wife, and Mahabir Pershad and Mrs. Jag Mohan Lal.

ties to rise in the Mughlai bureaucracy of the Nawab of Arcot in Madras; its members then began marrying with Hyderabad Saksenas. The downfall of this family came simultaneously with the rise of Bansi Raja's, and a comparison of the two families during this time shows the ways in which local kin groups adapted to changing political and economic circumstances.

The Wala Jahi Saksena family (in the service of Nawab Wala Jah of Arcot) had its senior branch in Madras and a junior branch with the Nawab's establishment in Hyderabad. Megh Raj, head of this junior branch, wrote letters in his official capacity to his older brother, the Nawab's chief correspondent in Madras, from 1803 to 1819.[11] Megh Raj's son, Ishwar Das, succeeded his father and did well. When the Nawab's *vakil* in Hyderabad resigned in 1840, Ishwar Das threatened to resign unless he was promoted. He was strongly recommended by his Muslim superior, who stressed that his local connections were good: he was "well liked by every talukdar, zamindar, and rais [respectable man]" in Hyderabad. The Nawab accordingly appointed him deputy agent, and within two years he had become the Nawab's chief agent. By this time, the correspondence between Madras and Hyderabad was between cousin-brothers.[12]

As the Nawab of Arcot's agent in Hyderabad, Raja Ishwar Das Wala Jahi was an important political figure. He negotiated on behalf of the Nawab with the Nizam's Diwan, Raja Chandu Lal, and with the British Resident.[13] He presided over the disbursement of thousands of rupees to employees and contractors in Hyderabad: in 1854 the annual income of the Hyderabad *jagirs* was Rs. 55,000 and expenditures in Hyderabad totalled Rs. 22,401.[14] Other matters called for supervision. Travelling employees and guests of the Nawab were accommodated in his Hyderabad buildings, and intelligence reports were filed upon them as they were upon

11. Papers of the Nawab of Arcot, with Dr. Muhammad Ghaus of Madras: file tentatively numbered 32, "Persian Correspondence."

12. *Ibid.*: letters to Husein Ahmed Khan from Daya Bahadur, *Rabi aval* 21, 1256 H. and *Rabi duvum,* 29, 1256 H. [July and August, 1840], and final appointment, undated, but according to sequence about 1842. His salary was 135 rupees per month, with a bonus of one anna for each rupee of back revenue collected from the Nawab's Hyderabad *jagirs.* He also received stipends to maintain eight *bhoyan* and one torchbearer, and when he became chief agent 15 rupees more per month for a horse and transport. For the cousin-brother evidence, see Chapter 2, note 44.

13. Papers of the Nawab of Arcot, file tentatively numbered 32, "Persian Correspondence," letters of 19 *Rajab* 1250 H., 6 *Ramzan* 1254 H., and 7 *Rabi duvum* H. [1834, 1838, and 1839]. Sometimes Madras advised Ishwar Das to go to the Resident first, so that Chandu Lal would take more notice, and generally the Resident was considered more reliable and friendly. The Wala Jahi title was being used in the letters by 1848.

14. Papers of the Nawab of Arcot, file tentatively numbered 32, "Persian Correspondence," accounts statements for July 1854 to July 1855.

the Nizam and members of his court. Luxury items unavailable in Madras —fine cloth and crafts, special fruits and condiments, even dancing girls—were sent from Hyderabad. The Nawab had ongoing expenses in Hyderabad, such as the upkeep of carpets and provisions of lights for the Mecca Masjid (mosque), sponsorship of funeral observances for relatives and well-known saints buried there, and the support of religious charities for *Ramzan.* Raja Ishwar Das supervised all these activities.[15]

Raja Ishwar Das utilized both political and social connections in Hyderabad. Raja Chandu Lal was Diwan until 1843, and in 1839 and 1840 Ishwar Das attempted to gain access to him in two ways, through Chandu Lal's relatives and through his own relatives. First, he offered the contract for revenue collection in the Nawab of Arcot's *jagirs* to Chandu Lal's nephew, Raja Ram Baksh, at a time when the "restoration," or resettlement, of the Nawab's *jagir* boundaries was being negotiated.[16] Second, he suggested that the Nawab's family affairs might best be settled with the help of Alam Chand, an agent of Raja Chandu Lal's son. This chosen intermediary was a Saksena Kayasth and a relative by marriage of Ishwar Das. The wording used by Ishwar Das's superior shows unawareness of any kinship tie between Ishwar Das and the "one Alam Chand" being recommended for this delicate negotiation.[17] Thus kinsmen, employed at lower levels, negotiated the affairs of their noble employers.

By 1850 Raja Ishwar Das had built the large family residence in Husaini Alam, and under his leadership several marriages were made with other Saksenas in Hyderabad. But the prosperity of this Wala Jahi family depended directly upon the Nawab of Arcot, and when the English refused to recognize an heir in 1855 and terminated the Carnatic Nawabship, Raja Ishwar Das suddenly found himself in difficult circumstances. Among the papers terminating Ghulam Ghaus Khan's estate in Madras was one noting that Raja Ishwar Das Bahadur had successfully transferred to the service of the Nizam of Hyderabad.[18] But the positions he obtained in the Hyderabad service were much lesser ones, though the Nizam appointed the Saksena Wala Jahi family to manage the Arcot *jagirs*

15. *Ibid.*: accounts statements and other letters concerning these matters. Ishwar Das was favored by the Nawab, who sent 500 rupees on the occasion of his daughter's marriage in 1848; they exchanged the customary personal congratulations, condolences, and gifts upon occasions of marriage, birth, and death. By 1854 his title was Maharajwant Bahadur.

16. *Ibid.,* letter from Husein Ahmed Khan to the Nawab in Madras, n.d. but about 1840 according to sequence.

17. *Ibid.,* letter from Husein Ahmed Khan to the Nawab, 1 *Ramzan* 1255 H. [1839]. (This son of Chandu Lal was Raja Dhiraj Bala Pershad.)

18. Papers of the Nawab of Arcot, with Dr. Muhammad Ghaus, "Persian Records concerning titles given by the Nawab of Arcot," file tentatively numbered 35, entry of 1857.

(which passed under Hyderabad's control).[19] The loss of status and income experienced by the Wala Jahi Saksena family with the downfall of the Nawab of Arcot was partially overcome through kinship ties developed in Hyderabad. Megh Raj's first four sons had married into Madras families, but the last son and two daughters married into Hyderabad families. These first three marriages with Hyderabad Saksenas were with the families of Ram Pershad and Raja Maya Ram, military *serrishtahdars,* and Swami Pershad, who was in household service.[20]

These Saksena families' marital and occupational patterns emphasize the strength of ties between men through their mothers, wives, and sisters, and also the practice of bilateral inheritance. Two kin categories were particularly significant: *samdhi,* or co-fathers-in-law; and *hamzulf,* "of the same hair," or men married to sisters.[21] (See Chapter IV for *hamzulf* among the Mathur Kayasths.) Three Saksena families were closely linked in both ways. Megh Raj and Alam Chand gave daughters to the sons of Swami Pershad, making the three fathers *samdhi,* or co-fathers-in-law.[22] This relationship stressed the common generational standing of the men and their common interest in the welfare of their children. The three families intermarried in the next two generations as well. Grandsons of Swami Pershad and Megh Raj married sisters, the granddaughters of Alam Chand. These marriages made the men (Bansi Raja and Balkishen) *hamzulf.*

The functional aspects of these complex marriage patterns are delineated in Figures 4 and 5. Figure 4 shows the transition of the Wala Jahi family to positions in Hyderabad.[23] When Megh Raj first married his children with Hyderabad Saksenas, Raja Maya Ram was a leading military noble and the Swami Pershad family was beginning to accumulate positions. With the downfall of Raja Maya Ram, and Raja Ishwar Das's loss of the Arcot connection in 1855, the kinship ties with Swami Pershad and Ram Pershad proved most useful.

Because they had access to resources of their wives' families, descendants of Megh Raj who had Hyderabad in-laws fared better than those married with Madras families. Balmukund, earlier in the shadow of his

19. Rao, *Bustan,* I, 317.
20. Interviews with Satguru Pershad and Mahender Raj Suxena, and Lakshmi Narayan.
21. In Sanskrit, Persian, and Urdu literature, hair has special connotations with respect to love, marriage, and inheritance. Expression through the Persian term *hamzulf* charged the relationship with special meaning, marking not only intimacy but close involvement in determination of inheritance and occupation among the Saksenas and other Kayasths in Hyderabad.
22. See Appendix C for these and the *hamzulf* relationships in detail.
23. It includes all males who married and for whom there was occupational information.

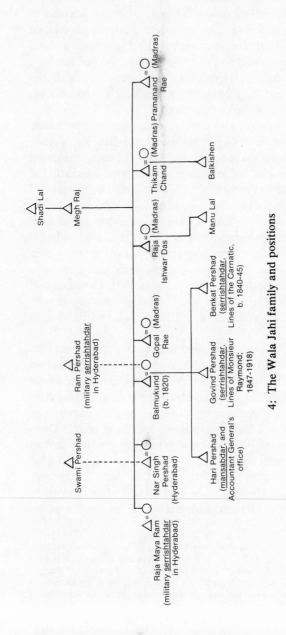

4: The Wala Jahi family and positions

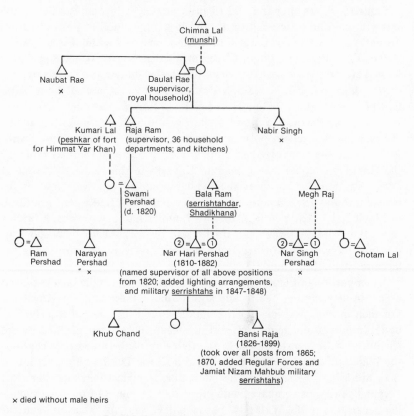

x died without male heirs

5: The Bansi Raja family and positions

elder brother, Ishwar Das, married the daughter of a military *serrishtah-dar* who died without a male heir. Thus Balmukund's first two sons obtained positions as military *serrishtahdars* for the Lines of the Carnatic and the Lines of Monsieur Raymond.[24] These *linewalla* troops, trained in the European fashion as part of Raymond's forces at the end of the eighteenth century, were chosen by Bansi Raja to become part of the Regular, or modernized military forces of Hyderabad after mid-century.[25] In contrast, Ishwar Das and Gopal Rae and their sons had wives from Madras families; their lines lapsed into obscurity.[26]

24. Interview with Lakshmi Narayan.
25. Bansi Raja was charged with organizing the Regular Forces in 1862 by the Diwan Salar Jung I: Girdhari Pershad, "Kunuz-i Tavarikh," in *Kulliyat,* 64.
26. Interviews with Lakshmi Narayan and Maheshwar Raj Saxena. One son of Ishwar Das died unmarried, the other produced no sons. One of Gopal Rae's grandsons married

[101

Figure 5 shows that the rise to prominence of Swami Pershad's line was gradual and proceeded partly through acquisition of positions from affines, notably Kumari Lal and Bala Ram, who died without sons. Swami Pershad's young sons, under fifteen at his death in 1820, were probably looked after for some years by Megh Raj, father-in-law and close neighbor of the elder son. But Nar Singh Pershad died young and without heirs, leaving the positions to Nar Hari Pershad. Nar Hari Pershad's first son was Girdhari Pershad or Bansi Raja, born in 1826; he inherited all the military and household positions accumulated by his father and grandfather.[27] By the time of Bansi Raja's second marriage, he had replaced the Bhatnagar noble as the leading Kayasth in the Nizam's household administration.[28] This marriage, which occurred relatively late in his career, around 1875, made Bansi Raja *hamzulf* to Balkishen, grandson of Megh Raj.[29] The power of the two families had been reversed by this time: Bansi Raja's father and uncles had been cared for by Megh Raj, but now Bansi Raja provided Balkishen with housing and support in his large residential complex.[30]

A comparison of Figures 4 and 5 shows that demographic factors played a part in determining wealth and status among these Saksena Kayasths. For men in their positions, at the middle and lower levels of the Hyderabad administration, more sons did not mean more *jagirs* granted by the Nizam, as with the Malwalas. In the first half of the nineteenth century, the Wala Jahi family under Megh Raj and Ishwar Das had more resources than did Swami Pershad and his successor, Nar Hari Pershad. Nar Hari Pershad's two sons compared with more male members of the corresponding generation in the Wala Jahi household: it was this Wala Jahi generation that faced the loss of the Arcot connection. Then Bansi Raja's younger brother died, leaving him with all the positions accumulated from paternal and maternal lines over the previous three generations. The Bansi Raja

Maya Ram's granddaughter (a marriage of second cousins) and died young; the other came under the aegis of Bansi Raja, who arranged his marriage in the 1890's to the sister of his own son's wife.

27. Raja Ram and Swami Pershad died within a year of each other, in 1810. Their successor, Nar Hari Pershad, was about 12 years old, probably just barely married to the daughter of Bala Ram, whose household position of *serrishtahdar* of the wedding hall was later added to those of the Swami Pershad family. Figure 5 is compiled from Khan, *Tuzuk,* II (Nobles), 413; and Pershad, "Kalam-i Mutafarriqat," in *Kulliyat,* 25–28.

28. The duties attributed to Bansi Raja at that time, in Server-el-Mulk, *My Life,* 136–137, included many attributed earlier in the century to Raja Bhavani Pershad and his heirs Manu Lal and Hanu Lal.

29. Nar Singh Raj, *Dard-i Baqi o Durd-i Saqi* (Hyderabad, 1933), 13–14, says that the *peshkar* Narinder Bahadur insisted he remarry.

30. Interview with Ghoshal Raj.

family prospered for four generations through the acquisition of positions by only one surviving son; the Wala Jahi family divided into several branches, and the family's resource base declined drastically.

Bilateral inheritance, utilization of kinship connections, and movement to Husaini Alam characterized upwardly mobile Saksenas during this period. The security and prosperity experienced by the Saksenas and Bhatnagars, most of whom resided in the Husaini Alam area, in the Nizam's household administration contrasted with the fates of most Shahalibanda military men and the increasing poverty and dubious reputation of that locality. Many Saksena families moved from Shahalibanda to Husaini Alam. In the family of Raja Rup Lal, a leading Hindu noble of the 1820's whose direct descendants were Muslim,[31] collateral branches moved to Husaini Alam about 1840, leaving the original residence in Shahalibanda to a son-in-law. The reason for this move was the family's transition to household rather than military positions, through a marriage and subsequent inheritance from a father-in-law in Husaini Alam.[32] Other Shahalibanda Saksena military men left behind Muslim descendants or no descendants and colorful stories of poverty and decadence.[33]

In the nineteenth century, the Shahalibanda locality developed a reputation for unorthodox ways of life. It continued to provide disproportionate shares of Muslim and illegitimate children by Kayasth fathers and converts to Islam.[34] Distinctions began to be made between Kayasths from Shahalibanda and other Kayasths, evidenced in marriage arrangements and in the settlement patterns of new immigrants. This division became apparent in Saksena genealogies about 1840, as families began marrying within and not between each locality. Locally born illegitimate Kayasths and newcomers of unknown parentage or low economic status settled in Shahalibanda.[35] Whether or not the newcomers were originally of uncertain ancestry, once they had married with Shahalibanda Kayasths their status in Hyderabad was fixed. What had been the residential area

31. Lal, *Yadgar*, 67–68, where Rustam Ali Khan is alleged to be Rup Lal's son.

32. Interview with Gurucharan Das Saxena; Mahender Raj Suxena, "Chand Kayasth Shora," 8, 11–12.

33. See Appendix D for two such accounts.

34. In this period, in addition to Raja Rup Lal's Muslim son, there were the conversions of the Saksena Raja Makhan Lal and (probably) Raja Buchar Mal's son Ghansur Mal. See Appendix D. In the Saksena family of Kapu Lal, a Muslim branch began with Kapu Lal's brother, who converted in the 1850's. Interviews with Dr. Eshwar Raj Saxena, Benkat Prasad, and Roy Mahboob Narayan.

35. Among these newcomers were Kapu Lal, a Saksena from Madras (interview with Dr. Eshwar Raj Saxena), and Hira Lal, a Saksena from Ellichpur (interview with Manohar Raj Saxena).

for wealthy nobles and military *serrishtahdars* fell into disfavor in the nineteenth century. Shahalibanda became known as the locality for poor and disreputable Kayasths; at least, that was the view from Chowk Maidan Khan and Husaini Alam.

Bansi Raja and the Recruitment of Kinsmen to Control Positions

Bansi Raja consolidated his control of positions after Salar Jung became Diwan in 1853. The Diwan utilized and supported him as a reformer in his military capacities and as the chief enforcer of Mughlai traditions in his household capacities. Bansi Raja was able to confirm his status in Husaini Alam and build a Saksena kin group that compared in some ways to the Mathur subcaste in Chowk Maidan Khan.

Bansi Raja's modern career rested on Salar Jung's efforts to implement military reforms. One of the new Diwan's immediate concerns was the unreliability of the Hyderabad military forces. Few troops could be relied upon: their pay was in arrears; mercenary units held large areas of the countryside; all units were decentralized and ill-trained. The British Resident urged extensive reductions of the Nizam's forces, but such reductions would have increased Hyderabad's dependence on the British and the British-controlled Hyderabad Contingent. To avoid this, Salar Jung determined to establish a modern army for Hyderabad state, and from 1854 he tried to organize a Regular Force.[36]

In 1862, Salar Jung gave the responsibility of organizing the Regular Forces to Bansi Raja, a *serrishtahdar* of proven competence.[37] Bansi Raja's grandfather had been employed by both Salar Jung's maternal great-grandfather and his grandfather.[38] Bansi Raja and his father had demonstrated their ability to bring unruly troops under control in 1847, 1849, and 1850.[39] And Bansi Raja had probably helped Salar Jung put

---

36. *Nizam's Territory* (Government of India), letter of Nov. 19, 1851, Resident David-son to the Minister; Pershad, "Kunuz-i Tavarikh," in *Kulliyat,* 64, citing British pressure on Salar Jung.

37. *Ibid.*; Raj, *Dard-i Baqi,* 15; M. Soobaraya Moodellear, *Hyderabad Almanac and Directory, 1874* (Madras, 1873), 190.

38. See Swami Pershad's 1817 transcription of *Insha-i Namati,* done for Mir Alam's *munshi,* Rae Babu.

39. Bansi Raja successfully reorganized the mutinous troops of Nawab Raunaq Ali Khan in 1850 and became their *serrishtahdar* at 500 rupees per month. He and his father had taken over the units of a dismissed *serrishtahdar* in 1847 and troops from a *jagir* confiscated by the government in 1849. Interview with Nar Har Raj; Raj, *Dard-i Baqi,* 15.

down an Afghan insurrection in Hyderabad during the Mutiny of 1857, gaining residential and temple properties as a reward.[40]

Charged with constitution of the Regular Forces, Bansi Raja first formed an infantry battalion and gave the command to a European officer in the Nizam's service. He then secured the trained troops and cavalry of the Raja of Wanparty, a tributary ruler with great enthusiasm for European military practices. Other units were recruited from existing Hyderabad forces. (Units left out of the Regular Forces became known as the Irregular Forces.) In 1864, when a military secretary was appointed to the Regular Forces, they consisted of six infantry battalions, five cavalry regiments, and an artillery unit. Bansi Raja was named head *serrishtahdar* and charged with establishing a munitions and gun factory. According to his own testimony, he was entrusted with the management of two million rupees of annual military expenditures.[41] Somewhat later, in 1870, he organized a special European-trained Arab force to quell disturbances caused by members of the Irregular Forces, particularly other Arabs and Afghans. Called the Jamiat Nizam Mahbub, or the Maiseram Regiment (for the locality in which it was stationed), its *serrishtahdar* was Bansi Raja.[42]

This military reorganization was accomplished without British assistance, utilizing resources indigenous to Hyderabad: *serrishtahdars,* Europeans in the Nizam's service, and a tributary ruler. The legendary French eighteenth-century commander of Hyderabad's first European-trained forces, Monsieur Raymond, was invoked as a symbol; Raymond's old sword was presented to the commander of the Regular Forces. In the British view, "old memories of Raymond's Corps were not very tactfully

40. The Afghan commander's *serrishtahdar,* Mehtab Rae, a Saksena Kayasth from Husaini Alam, was hunted down and seized. The Saksena family of Mehtab Rae came to a sudden end (possibly continued by an "impure" branch in Shahalibanda). Its properties were deeded to Bansi Raja, whose first wife was probably from Mehtab Rae's family. The properties included the Chandranaraingutta temple and lands south of the city. In 1857–1858, Salar Jung authorized the temple's transfer to Bansi Raja, stipulating that the area be made free of bandits and put to productive use. Bansi Raja renamed the temple Keshavgiri after his only surviving son by his first wife, Keshav Pershad. Whatever their specific relationship or Bansi Raja's actual role in the events of 1857, he benefited from Mehtab Rae's misfortune in 1857. Pershad, *Farkhundah Bunyad Hyderabad,* 88; "Judgment of Original Suit No. 32 of 1959 (Keshovgiri temple case)," II Additional Judge, file in the Endowment Office of Andhra Pradesh state; Pershad, "Keshav Namah," in *Kulliyat,* 1–21; Raj, *Dard-i Baqi,* 21; Rao, *Bustan,* II, 749; and interviews with Nar Har Raj and Vinayak Pershad.

41. Pershad, "Kunuz-i Tavarikh," in *Kulliyat,* 64–66. See also McAuliffe, *The Nizam,* 54, Rao, *Bustan,* II, 727–728.

42. Raj, *Dard-i Baqi,* 17. Later, Afghans were included in this unit: Rao, *Bustan,* I, 404.

[105

revived. . . ."[43] But Salar Jung had achieved his objective, a European-trained army developed by unquestionably loyal servants of the Nizam, which would permit attempts to reduce the remaining Irregular Forces.

Bansi Raja, a key figure in the military transition, was able to move some relatives from Irregular positions into the Regular Forces. Since he had direct contact with not only the Diwan, but the *peshkar* as well, Bansi Raja also helped relatives establish themselves in that service.[44] Two more Saksena families, mid-century immigrants, found places in the *peshkar*'s service and in the new Regular Forces units, and both settled in Husaini Alam.[45]

Bansi Raja's most influential role was as supervisor within the Nizam's household. Here is a description of his many responsibilities written by a tutor of the Nizam in about 1880:

In accordance with the old established customs of the Kings of Delhi, in the month of Safar . . . gold and silver rings were distributed . . . Bansi Raja sent me seven . . . In the month of Rajab . . . I received an invitation through the Bansi Raja to attend the "Koonday" feast . . . in honour of one of the Imams. [At this feast] Bansi Raja, in Court dress, with his family head-dress . . . would be busy entertaining the guests . . . The Raja was very active . . . The management of the palace rested on his shoulders, without anyone else to share his responsibility. He . . . looked after all the "Zenana" [internal] and the "Mardena" [external] affairs of the palace on festive occasions. He . . . also made arrangements for the Durbars, both Moglai and English . . . the Raja also tried to enforce the old customs and regulations in vogue at the Court of the Kings of Delhi and handed down from the times of the First Asaf Jah, and would not permit deviation from them . . . In Shab-e-Barat I received fireworks . . . in Bakr-Fed, camel flesh; in

43. The quote is from McAuliffe, *The Nizam,* 52–53; see also Thornton, *General Sir Richard Meade,* 383.

44. Govind Pershad of the Wala Jahi Saksena family secured positions in the "Reformed military," probably through his *hamzulf* Bansi Raja. His successful cutting of military expenses brought him to the attention of the Diwan, who appointed him to several committees mediating between old and new bureaucracies. Lakshmi Narayan, ed., *Vinay Govind* (Hyderabad, 1937), 1–3; *Advocate of India,* Sept. 2, 1897 (CC). For the family of Hira Lal, who inherited his father-in-law Alam Chand's position with the *peshkar,* see Khan, *Tuzuk,* II 417–418.

45. One, from Madras, married with the Wala Jahi family and that of Bansi Raja and found employment with the *peshkar*: the family of Thakur Pershad. Interview with Gurucharan Das Saxena; Mahender Raj Suxena, "Chand Kayasth Shora," 13. The other moved from Aurangabad, and its founder served as military *serrishtahdar* of a special cavalry force which helped Salar Jung defeat the Afghan insurrection in 1857. Perhaps more crucially, the family head helped arrange financial transactions with leading bankers in the 1860's. He then built a small temple in his residence and sponsored a major annual festival to commemorate Krishna's birthday; both were supported by a government grant. This was the family of Raja Isri Pershad Bahadur: Khan, *Tuzuk,* II (Nobles), 75.

Nowaz eggs; and during the mango season, mangoes. The distribution on such occasions was made by the aforesaid Raja.[46]

The same writer recalled Bansi Raja joking about his many jobs and terming himself the "elder daughter-in-law of the State," a phrase which conveys exactly the right sense of devoted, demanding, and often little-publicized service.[47]

Bansi Raja had considerable patronage power with respect to appointments within his areas, but his own positions did not bring to the family wealth or rank comparable to that of the Malwalas. And retention of the positions depended upon the ability and performance of their holder or holders. Bansi Raja was entrusted with essentially private and personal tasks, such as mediating between Salar Jung and his co-regent, Shams ul Umra of the Paigah family, at a time when they were extremely hostile to one another.[48] Most of his functions were carried out within the court and household circles, and his influence there was recognized through personal letters and visits from the Nizam.[49] He held properties, which he had purchased himself, bringing an income of forty to fifty thousand rupees per year, and he retained a clerical staff of ten to fifteen employees.[50] His titles and honors came later, when his real power was waning.[51]

Bansi Raja functioned in the neighborhood culture of Husaini Alam somewhat as the Malwala nobles did in Chowk Maidan Khan, but on a lesser scale. The locality was bordered on the north by the main road from Char Minar to Golconda, on the south by the properties of the Paigah nobles, and on the east by the Nizam's Chowmohalla palace. The major landmarks, like the Shia *alam* for which the locality was named, were Muslim and dated from Qutb Shahi days.[52] There were seasonal occasions upon which Bansi Raja served as host or donor for both Hindus and Muslims.[53] The annual great event in the neighborhood came during

46. Server-el-Mulk, *My Life,* 136–137.

47. *Ibid.,* 269.

48. In this capacity, he met Salar Jung daily from 1880 to 1882; *ibid.,* 19.

49. *Ibid.,* 19–22, 35–38.

50. Interview with Nar Har Raj.

51. Raj, *Dard-i Baqi,* 22: he was titled Raja Bahadur in 1884 and given a guardhouse, band, and palanquin; the title Mahbub Nawazwunt came in 1895.

52. Munn, *Hyderabad Municipal Survey 1911,* maps 41–44, 49–52. The Husaini Alam mosque took its name from the *langar* or chain installed as an *alam* by the Qutb Shahi queen Hayat Bakshi Begum. Details of the story in Rao, *Bustan,* II, 744–745.

53. Raj, *Dard-i Baqi,* 31; interviews with the mother of Shakamber Raj Saxena, and Prithvi Raj.

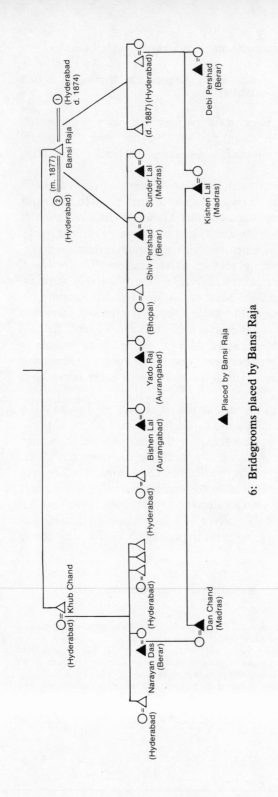

6: **Bridegrooms placed by Bansi Raja**

Muharram, when the Husaini Alam procession was held. The *alam* housed in the neighborhood mosque was taken out on the fifth of Muharram amidst the famous Langar procession of the military forces. This was a much rowdier procession than that of the Bik Alam in Chowk Maidan Khan. Bansi Raja, seated on an elephant as head *serrishtahdar* of the Regular Forces, led the procession of both Regular and Irregular troops.[54]

Having achieved a certain eminence and control of economic resources, Bansi Raja became the dominant figure in a Saksena kin group in the second half of the nineteenth century that in some ways resembled the Mathur subcaste. He began to arrange marriages with bridegrooms from outside Hyderabad—a distinct departure from the practice of arranging marriages only among the Hyderabad Saksenas.

Figure 6 shows Bansi Raja's genealogy and the initial marriages of the eight bridegrooms he sponsored from 1860–1890.[55] Bansi Raja placed the earliest of these sons- and grandsons-in-law in positions under his control. Narayan Das, from Berar, who married the daughter of Bansi Raja's brother in about 1865, worked in Bansi Raja's private estate; so did Kishen Lal, from Madras, who married a daughter of Bansi Raja's eldest daughter. These two couples lived at first in Bansi Raja's residence.[56] The bridegroom of another daughter of Bansi Raja's eldest daughter, Debi Pershad, from Berar, took a place in the *bavarchikhanah* (kitchen) and later in the *serrishtah* of Raja Durga Pershad Bhatnagar.[57] These three came before 1880. The four who came in the 1880's as Bansi Raja's own sons-in-law were settled into the house and maintained there (as *khanah-damads*); one received some land as a dowry.[58]

Oral tradition concerning the initiation of these marriages with new-comers states that this departure from customary practice among the Hyderabad Saksenas was caused by demographic factors. There was a need for boys: more girls than boys were being born and surviving to marriage age among the Saksenas, therefore sons-in-law had to be brought to the city. The explanation cannot be adequately tested, although it is true that in the Saksena genealogies the overwhelming majority

54. Interview with Nar Har Raj. This procession was described by many European writers in the late nineteenth century.
55. Compiled from the printed genealogy of Bansi Raja in Dwarka Pershad, *Hiyat-i Baqi Manzum* (Lucknow [1892–1893]), and interviews with Satguru Pershad and Mahender Raj Suxena, Prithvi Raj, Vinayak Pershad, and Gurucharan Das Saxena.
56. Interviews with Nar Har Raj and Dr. Mahender Raj Suxena.
57. Interview with Vinayak Pershad and documents concerning Debi Pershad's jobs from 1878 to 1886.
58. Interviews with Prithvi Raj and Gurucharan Das Saxena. But, as will be shown, Bansi Raja lost power after the death of Salar Jung I, and even the first three bridegrooms moved from the positions in which he had placed them.

of newcomers arrived as sons-in-law.[59] But the explanation may simply be that there were fewer *eligible* Saksena boys than girls, and this is verifiable. Comparing the genealogies, residence patterns, and fuller kinship information of the late nineteenth century, it is evident that the differing circumstances of Saksenas living in Husaini Alam and Shahalibanda led to a shortage of eligible Saksena men. In Shahalibanda, men moved steadily out of the category of respectable Saksena Kayasths. There were several instances of conversion to Islam, at least two for love of a Muslim woman;[60] several married across subcaste or caste lines; others formed informal liaisons with non-Kayasth women of the locality. A large proportion of the respectable Saksena families in Shahalibanda terminated for lack of legitimate Hindu heirs.

There was also the lower status ascribed to families residing in the Shahalibanda locality, which for both Saksenas and Srivastavas had become an area of families usually termed *suratval*—although such families could be found elsewhere as well. The "need for boys" among Husaini Alam Saksenas in the late nineteenth century may have owed more to status considerations than to actual numbers. Sons could evidently take concubines or even brides from another subcaste or caste, or any locality, without incurring severe social sanctions; but respectable alliances were required for daughters. This may have impelled acceptance of sons-in-law from outside Hyderabad in preference to local Saksenas of doubtful reputation.

Aside from these demographic trends and status differentiations, the appearance of bridegrooms from outside the city at this time can be explained, first, on economic grounds. It was the Saksena families with more resources who took such sons-in-law, thus it could have been a display of patronage power perhaps modelled upon the Malwalas' sponsorship of client Mathur families. Yet in most cases there was no tradition of "calling," no search or sending of emissaries, by Bansi Raja or others. In some cases, Saksena men seem to have come to Hyderabad in search of employment; once there, they found both jobs and marriage alliances.

This points to the second reason: for the Saksenas, these alliances seem to have been necessary to retain and consolidate their positions.

59. Both oral and written genealogies consistently omitted daughters. Only daughters who survived to be married were sometimes represented by their husbands' names. Unless specifically questioned, informants failed to mention children of both sexes who did not survive to marriage age. Furthermore, the mortality rate of women was high, and informants sometimes omitted marriages that had produced no children or had been superseded by a more productive marriage.

60. See note 34 above.

While the Malwalas brought both brides and bridegrooms and discouraged the bridegrooms from taking positions in Hyderabad, the Saksenas recruited bridegrooms and placed them in positions that contributed to the income of the kin groups. The frequency of inheritance of positions by sons-in-law, and the late-nineteenth-century incorporation of sons-in-law from outside, supports the hypothesis that continued control of economic resources depended upon a continuing supply of heirs.[61]

Kin groups controlled and transmitted positions at middle levels of the Mughlai bureaucracy, particularly within the Nizam's household. Despite the nominal adherence of all Kayasths to Mitakshara patrilineal inheritance law, positions and property among the Bhatnagar and Saksena Kayasths were customarily transmitted bilaterally. When major economic changes occurred, such as termination of the Arcot Nawabship or the military reorganization begun by Salar Jung, kinship connections could be as important as noble patronage. Conversely, a noble without an effective local kin group could suddenly find his administrative responsibilities effectively controlled by others.

The nature of the offices in this Mughlai bureaucracy is clear from the material in this chapter and in Chapters III and IV. Just as Raja Chandu Lal and Lala Bahadur kept their own set of records in their palaces, *serrishtahdars* and clerks at lower levels kept their records in their residences. Pay disbursement and other job functions also occurred there. Bansi Raja paid the troops at his gateway; one of the U.P. Bhatnagar families paid religious specialists at his doorway; and so on.

In this respect, neighborhood settlement patterns were directly relevant to control of the records and functions connected with various positions. The military reforms, for example, involved stationing some of the Irregular Forces outside the city walls and taking their pay there for disbursement; no longer was Shahalibanda dominated by large residences of the military *serrishtahdars,* where the troops gathered regularly for their pay. When the Bhatnagar Raja Bhavani Pershad moved to a new suburb, away from the *karkhanahs* he controlled, he lost them to Bhatnagars who had arrived more recently and who would not marry with Hyderabad people. Bansi Raja's residence was closer to the Nizam's palace and household apartments; he supplanted Raja Bhavani Pershad's heirs in other areas of the household administration.

61. This motivation is particularly relevant in Bansi Raja's case, for he needed sons and heirs. By the end of the century, the demographic factors that led to the accumulation of resources by only one or two sons for several generations began to operate to his disadvantage, as Chapter 10 shows.

Bilateral inheritance practices helped kin groups keep positions, but the number and status of local subcaste members proved crucial to the formation of kin groups. Within both the Bhatnagar and Saksena subcaste categories, several mutually exclusive marriage networks developed. There was increasing differentiation with respect to eligible marriage partners, occupations, and residential localities in the city. As economic and social boundaries became more elaborate and more closely correlated, control of these boundaries by kin groups became essential.

CHAPTER 6

Gaurs and Srivastavas:
Other Adaptations

The Gaur and most of the Srivastava Kayasths were not centrally located in the Hyderabad Mughlai bureaucracy. The Gaurs' isolation resulted from the employment of all families but one in a single noble establishment, that of the Paigahs. Thus they did not have direct access to other, more central areas of the Nizam's bureaucracy. Analysis of marriage and inheritance among the Gaurs illustrates the advantages and dangers of a small kin group dependent upon a single powerful patron.

In the case of the Srivastavas, a major disadvantage was the fact that many were latecomers, arriving only in the second half of the nineteenth century. The Mughlai administration was no longer expanding, and the better positions were already controlled by others. In addition, many Srivastavas were *suratval*, the offspring of marriages or liaisons unsanctioned by the few Srivastava families with economic and social resources. A few Bhatnagars and Saksenas fell into these latecomer and illegitimate categories, but the majority were Srivastavas. Analysis of the Srivastavas shows the vulnerability of those who held insecure lower-level positions and who were unable to gain admittance to established kin groups in the old city. While the newcomers' marriage networks were ultimately broader than any others among the Kayasths, they had access only to insufficient and unstable economic resources.

The Gaurs and Their Patrons: Inheritance Problems

The Gaur Kayasths, residents of Shahalibanda and members of a single kin group, were almost all employed by the Muslim Paigah noble family, which had consolidated the largest bodies of troops under it at

[113

the beginning of the nineteenth century. Many Kayasths connected with the military forces lost power and positions in the financial crisis of the mid-nineteenth century. Some adapted by moving into recordkeeping and household positions, and others became associated with incoming units of mercenary troops or Hyderabad's Regular Forces. Gaur Kayasths continued to function as military *serrishtahdars* for the Paigahs, but their security and prosperity during this period were clearly due to their attainment of positions in the household departments as well. One other Gaur family, that of Bala Pershad, rose in the service of the Arab military chief Ghalib Jung, perhaps the most powerful of the mercenary leaders in mid-nineteenth-century Hyderabad. Here too, although his patron was noted for the military threat he posed, Bala Pershad's responsibilities included recordkeeping and general supervision in addition to disbursement of pay to the troops.[1]

For the Gaur Kayasths and their Paigah patrons, the period from 1820 to 1880 was one of expansion and prosperity. The head of the Paigah family, Fakhruddin Khan, was married to the daughter of the former Nizam and was a close advisor to the reigning Nizam, Nasiruddaula. In 1838 he received confirmation of the Paigah *jagirs* and grants to his descendants in perpetuity, so the position of the Paigahs and of their servants the Gaur Kayasths appeared very secure. Even the gradual bureaucratic centralization begun by Salar Jung, and the Paigah nobles' antagonism to the Diwan, did not endanger the power of the Paigah family.[2]

The experience of the Paigahs and the Gaurs shows that those who were powerful enemies, as well as allies, of the Diwan continued to hold high status in Hyderabad; those who worked for them could continue to be protected from basic economic changes in the state.

At the end of the eighteenth century the leading Gaur families had been those of Ram Kishen and the Panch Bhai Gaur; by 1830, a third family had assumed leadership (see the end of Chapter II). The family of Mohan Das, a son-in-law of the Ram Kishen family, was now the central one in terms of allocation of positions and arrangement of marriages. Mohan Das's three grandsons, Dal Chand, Balmukund, and Jaswant

1. Gaur, *Tazkirah-i Sucaru Vanshi*, 32: "The Hyderabad brotherhood is connected only with service, and here with the Paigah estate only. There is this peculiarity, that whether it is unconditional or service with conditions, after a man's death the place and emolument is transferred to his real heirs. Therefore this service is called "jagir" or hereditary [*jaedad murusi*]. Most of the Gaurs here serve in the estate of Nawab Muhammad Moinuddin Khan Bahadur." For the Bala Pershad family, interview with Roy Mahboob Narayan and wife.

2. Their continued political power is documented by such histories of the period as V. K. Bawa's thesis; Server-el-Mulk, *My Life*; and Thornton, *General Sir Richard Meade*.

Rae, consolidated the family fortune. Balmukund headed the dominant Gaur family from the 1830's to the 1870's, building a palatial residence, dispensing positions, and sponsoring marriages which brought more Gaurs to Hyderabad. At mid-century, this grandson of Mohan Das presided over one of the largest establishments in the Shahalibanda area.[3]

The positions controlled by Balmukund were actually eleven separate jobs. He and his brothers served as accountants in the Paigah workshops and treasury offices and as *serrishtahdars* of the military units, elephant stables, bullock carts, and other units. Men in the Mohan Das family held positions bringing in at least five hundred rupees per month; as these positions involved supervision of other employees and distribution of household and military salaries, there was undoubtedly some additional income. Supervision of the elephant stables and conveyances entitled the family to utilize such status symbols as bullock carts and elephants to some extent themselves, and some of the Paigah household servants were delegated to serve Balmukund's family.[4]

From mid-century, Balmukund's control of the Paigah positions resulted in changed marriage patterns in the Gaur kin group. Earlier marriages among the Gaurs had drawn upon Central Indian and Deccani Gaurs and then narrowed to the four families settled in Hyderabad. But between 1850 and 1865, Balmukund called four new Gaur men from North India, directly from Nizamabad, U.P., the traditional place of origin of his own family. Three of these men became his own sons-in-law and the fourth his brother-in-law.[5] The comparison with the Malwala family's recruitment of marriage partners is obvious, but there was one major difference. The long-distance recruitment of relatives required resources. For the Malwalas, resources were so abundant that whole households were brought and the men became dependents of the *daftardar* family. Gaur sons-in-law brought to Hyderabad were themselves additional resources, needed to retain and carry out the positions accumulated under Balmukund.

In 1863, the first division of the Paigah estate between two collateral branches of that family worked out to the advantage of Balmukund,

3. Why Balmukund rather than his elder brother Dal Chand headed the family is not certain, but Dal Chand was a colorful character and conformed more to the military style of life characteristic of Shahalibanda at the turn of the century. He had a Kayasth wife and daughter but no son, and a Telugu concubine and a daughter by her.
4. Interviews and written material with Jagdish Pershad; interviews with Onker Pershad and Roy Mahboob Narayan.
5. These were Subhan Roy, Bishen Chand, Bala Pershad, and Deepak Rae. Communication from Jagdish Pershad, and see Gaur, *Tazkirah-i Sucaru Vanshi,* 30–31. At this time also, Jaswant Rae built a small temple and Balmukund built the large family residence: interviews with Onker Pershad.

[115

increasing the Paigah positions over which he had control. He was able to consolidate the two sets of positions which he and his father had handled separately, and he appointed his younger brother and his own son to be companions and servants to the two young Paigahs next in line to inherit the larger estate (see Figure 7).[6] Thus, from 1863, Balmukund managed the affairs of the leading Paigah nobles, allocating positions and arranging marriages within the whole Gaur kin group. At this time he constructed the palatial family residence.

Despite the prosperity, the importation of bridegrooms, and the favorable circumstances at this first division, Balmukund presided over an increasingly insecure livelihood. Divisions were developing within the Paigah family, and it mattered a great deal which Gaur was connected to which Paigah. Demographic circumstances at the succession of 1863 had favored Balmukund, but in the 1870's his lineage was without heirs. He had assigned his son Manik Chand to the service of the younger Paigah brother, Asman Jah, the likely heir to the estate. But Manik Chand never married, and he died in 1876.[7] This death placed the leading Gaur family in a predicament, for Manik Chand's position with the future heir was the key to all the other positions. Balmukund's younger brother, Jaswant Rae, was newly widowed at fifty years of age and appeared unlikely to produce heirs.[8] The key position with Asman Jah had to be filled, and Balmukund allocated it to Devi Pershad, his maternal grandnephew, a young man in his teens. Balmukund also arranged the marriage of Devi Pershad, bringing a bride from the Ujjain branch of his own lineage and drawing him closer into the kin group.[9] Balmukund's employer died in 1877. Balmukund died in 1879, and Devi Pershad was left in sole charge of the estate inherited by Asman Jah. When Asman Jah's childless elder

6. When Fakhruddin Khan, head of the family, died in 1863, three of his five sons had predeceased him. The Paigah estate was divided between the two living sons, Rafiuddin Khan and Rashiduddin Khan. A third son had left two young heirs; as Rafiuddin Khan, inheritor of the title and the larger share of the estate, had no heirs, he adopted them and raised them as his own sons. (Balmukund's father had been in the service of Bashir ul Mulk, deceased father of the two young boys, and Balmukund was in the service of Rafiuddin Khan.) Khan, *Tuzuk,* II (Nobles), 1-6; the Paigah genealogy is in the back of *Chronology.*

7. Balmukund's elder brother Dal Chand died in 1872 and left no heir; Manik Chand kept a Muslim woman and left only a daughter by her. Of Balmukund's three sons-in-law, one was well placed with the Arab Ghalib Jung; one died without heirs; the third died leaving a son, Tota Ram. Balmukund had already allocated Dal Chand's position to Tota Ram, claiming he had adopted him. Interviews with Roy Mahboob Narayan and Jagdish Pershad.

8. His wife died in 1872: communication from Jagdish Pershad; interview with Onker Pershad.

9. See Gaur, *Tazkirah-i Sucaru Vanshi,* 117, 135 (genealogies 1, 3), 115, 160.

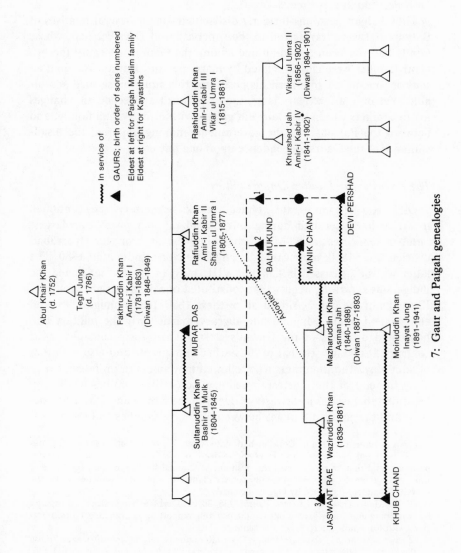

7: **Gaur and Paigah genealogies**

brother, holder of another portion of the estate, died in 1881 without an heir, his servant Jaswant Rae, also childless, became dependent upon Devi Pershad. In fact, Jaswant Rae transferred his duties officially to Devi Pershad at this time.[10]

Thus Paigah positions formerly distributed among several relatives of Balmukund were transferred to the supervision of Devi Pershad, whose family had not been a leading one among the Gaurs.[11] Because the two Gaur families were closely related by marriage, and Jaswant Rae had no sons or sons-in-law to inherit his positions, this situation seemed acceptable. Yet only a few years later, major political and economic changes led to conflicts within the Gaur kin group, within the Paigah family, and between the Paigahs and the government, making apparent the disadvantages of the Gaurs' dependence upon one patron.

The Srivastavas: Limited Opportunities

Other Kayasth immigrants, typically clerks or military men, continued to arrive in Hyderabad during this period on their own. The largest number were Srivastavas. Many moved into the city from the Hyderabad districts after 1850; more came directly from North India after 1880. The latter will be discussed in Chapter VIII; most of the former joined the indigenous *suratval* category that constituted one of the largest groups of Kayasths in the city.[12] Almost all of these 1850–1880 immigrants found employment in the Mughlai bureaucracy, particularly the military and household divisions of the Nizam's estate. Their socioeconomic status contrasted starkly with that of the earlier immigrants and also with that of later Kayasth immigrants who followed more modern professions.

By the end of the nineteenth century, some fifty families in the city identified themselves as Srivastava. Despite the Khare and Dusre distinctions and the status difference between old noble families and the others,

10. A document written by Devi Pershad, dated Sept. 22, 1881, confirms this. He states that Balmukund had cared for him after the death of his father and given him service positions, and that he now accepts the positions sanctioned for him by Jaswant Rae and will return them to Balmukund's future descendants, if any, when sanctioned by the Nawab. Document furnished by Jagdish Pershad.

11. See Gaur, *Tazkirah-i Sucaru Vanshi*, 135, 30–31. Devi Pershad evidenced prosperity by developing a pleasure garden outside the city and supporting several concubines: interviews with Roy Mahboob Narayan and Mahbub Rai.

12. *Suratval* means "those resembling"; an alternate spelling *sarhadval*, means "those on the border." Other terms for this group in Hyderabad were *hul hul bacce* (mixed children), *adhe Kayasth* (half-Kayasth), and *khijri* (name of a mixed rice and pulses dish). The children of Kayasths by Muslim concubines were given Muslim names and joined the Muslim community.

these Srivastavas cannot be analyzed without difficulty. There is no sense of a single subcaste, or even of kin groups well defined and ranked with respect to one another. There were few kin groups associated with hereditary positions or property, and there was no residential core. But these Srivastavas can be traced back to several originally separate marriage networks, some of which were associated with specific localities. The old noble households in Shahalibanda, Dabirpura, and Husaini Alam were centers for locally born *suratvals,* while most newcomers arriving before 1880 settled in two areas, one adjacent to Husaini Alam and the other in Dhulpet. (See Map 1.)

These incoming Srivastava families were of respectable ancestry, with genealogies tracing their ancestors back to North India over several generations of movement south. But they were not accepted for marriage purposes by the few Srivastavas in Hyderabad who ranked as nobility at the end of the eighteenth century. Many of the new Srivastavas moving into the city continued to participate in marriage networks based in the Hyderabad districts. One group of some fifteen Dusre families, originally from Benares, Allahabad, and Bareilly, had relatives in Bidar, Berar, Amaravati, Gangakher, Nagpur, Hingoli, Marathwari, Aurangabad, Kalyani, and Udgir, district towns and places to the northwest of Hyderabad. Intermarrying before and after moving to Hyderabad, they established themselves in the city as military *serrishtahdars* in the Irregular Forces and as administrators and clerks in the Nizam's personal estate.[13] Their coming coincided with the Diwan's successful separation of the Nizam's personal budget and treasury from the state budget and treasury in the 1860's and 1870's; so from arrival they were associated with that smaller and more traditional Mughlai administration.

The Nizam's personal estate, including private troops, *jagirs,* and household departments, was formed after the death of the fifth Nizam in 1869. Then the Diwan Salar Jung was made regent to the minor heir, and he placed the Nizam's personal *jagir* under the management of the modern administration, designating it, like the Nizam's personal troops, Sarf-i Khas.[14] He formed the Nizam's scattered *jagir* holdings into districts and appointed *talukdars* (revenue contractors) to collect the revenue. Kayasths already in Hyderabad, particularly Bansi Raja and some of the

13. The North Indian references, given orally, appeared also in Chand, *Kayasth Kul Nar Nai,* 95–96; interviews with Dharminder Pershad and Manohar Lal.
14. The term Sarf-i Khas originally designated the small division of troops maintained by the Paigah nobles for the Nizam's personal protection. Under Raja Chandu Lal, scattered areas of land were set aside under personal control of the Nizam; later Nizams added to these initial *jagirs.*

Bhatnagars, held good positions in the Nizam's estate. Immigrants seeking employment in Mughlai departments were placed at lower levels. These families, of modest income and resources despite proud traditions of literary, artistic, and medical achievements in North India and elsewhere, settled predominantly on the outskirts of Husaini Alam, in lower-class housing behind the Saksena and Bhatnagar families already living there.[15]

A second marriage network of Srivastavas moving into Hyderabad city after 1857 centered on a single *jagir,* Mulkir, in the districts, that was held by a Shia *jagirdar.* Some eight Khare families were employed here in relatively minor clerical positions.[16] On moving into the city, these Srivastavas tended to work in the postal system or as policemen or soldiers, taking positions which put them in the lowest levels of the modern bureaucracy. Most of them settled in the rough lower-class neighborhood of Dhulpet, across the river from the old city. Dhulpet had been settled largely by low-caste North Indian soldiers and illicit liquor distillers; it was a heterogeneous locality.[17] While some intermarriages and residential exchanges occurred later between these two originally separate networks of Srivastava immigrants, members of the second group tended to marry more with a third group of Srivastavas that already existed in the city.

This third group, consisting by the late nineteenth century of at least twenty nominally Srivastava families, has already been referred to as the indigenous *suratval* population. These people were born in the city and their parentage was known. They were settled mostly in lower-class neighborhoods near the homes of the two earliest Srivastava noble families, those of Raja Dooleh Rae and Raja Chain Rae, in Dabirpura and Shahalibanda.[18] Many families in this group were linked by common ancestry and by marriage; most men followed nonadministrative careers of a nonhereditary and uncertain nature. Many were soldiers and policemen.[19] The lower educational attainments and economic insecurity of

15. Interviews with Dharminder Pershad and Manohar Lal.
16. This *jagir* was near Gulbarga, west of Hyderabad city. Genealogies and interview with Dr. Manik Pershad, now the representative of several of the families; interview and correspondence with Sohan Lal Arya.
17. Interviews with Sohan Lal Arya and Roy Mahboob Narayan.
18. Of undoubted wealth and status early in their Hyderabad careers, the two families had declined by the late nineteenth century. Their marriage patterns cannot be satisfactorily reconstructed; they apparently tried to marry only with respectable families from outside. As with the Bhatnagars, families anxious to maintain a pure genealogy but dependent upon connections outside Hyderabad sometimes recorded male family members as unmarried. It is often admitted that such men had "keeps" and *suratval* descendants.
19. Interviews with Manohar Lal, Sohan Lal Arya, Captain Surya Pratap, Chander Srivastava, N. Inder Lal, and Bala Pershad.

these *suratvals* were in marked contrast to most of the Kayasths in Hyderabad. The ambiguity of the origins and marriage patterns within the group also contrasted with the claims and carefully kept records of most other Kayasths in the city.

These indigenous *suratvals,* and many of the mid-nineteenth-century immigrants categorized as *suratvals* by Srivastavas and other Kayasths well established in Hyderabad, constituted the bottom levels of the Kayasth caste in the city, although there were exceptions to this generalization. Most of them held insecure, nonhereditary, lower-paid Mughlai positions; those who joined the modern administration did so at its lowest levels. The group as a whole offered marriage alliances to others, Kayasth or not, who did not have the economic resources to retain long-distance marriage networks or to command acceptance from those of their own subcaste already in the city. Thus a few families of incoming Saksenas and Bhatnagars married with Srivastavas in their initial matches in Hyderabad; and once this had been done, their *suratval* status was set. Like the Saksenas and Srivastavas, Bhatnagars who had arrived earlier, held higher positions, and perhaps retained ties to marriage networks outside of Hyderabad were in a position to accept or reject newcomers. The few "pure" Srivastava families had not even married with each other, much less with the indigenous Srivastava *suratvals*; there was no reason for them to accept immigrants from the districts after 1850, men of unknown background and lower economic standing.

Among the poorer Kayasths, marriage networks formed that crossed subcaste lines.[20] Many of the immigrant Srivastavas had as much in common with their similarly classified Saksena or other neighbors in Shahalibanda as with other Srivastavas. For the *suratval* category of Kayasths, the social boundaries were not tightly maintained; class, unqualified by subcaste designation, was the basis of marriage alliances. The employment and marriage patterns of this poorer and relatively large group of Kayasths attest to the contraction of opportunities for newcomers after 1850. They also point to the control of positions exercised by the Kayasths already in Hyderabad, a control essential to the formation of effective kin groups.

Comparisons and Contrasts Among the Kayasths

In the early and mid-nineteenth century, power in the state passed from the old military aristocracy to recordkeepers at all levels of the Mughlai

20. See Appendix E for several generations of *suratval* marriages across subcaste and caste lines.

bureaucracy. The *daftardars,* leading officials of the land revenue system, achieved considerable political power by mid-century. They and other Mughlai officials consolidated hereditary claims to their positions. When Salar Jung I became Diwan in 1853, his efforts to centralize power and authority in his position meant wresting control from such kin groups, as well as from bankers and units of mercenary soldiers. But Salar Jung's efforts took effect only gradually, and for many Kayasths a period of expansion and prosperity continued.

The Mathur Kayasths retained their economic and social status because of the Malwalas' standing in the old nobility of Hyderabad. Some Saksenas and Bhatnagars prospered in the household administration. Other Kayasths prospered because of the patrons to which they were attached—patrons whose political power allowed them to participate in or to withstand the gradual bureaucratic centralization. This principle was seen at work in the cases of Lala Bahadur, Salar Jung's chief opponent, and Bansi Raja, his close ally in military reform and the household administration. It worked for the Gaur Kayasths, who were in the service of the Paigah nobles. But most of the newer Srivastava immigrants were unable to secure patrons or good positions. They filled in the lower levels of the Nizam's personal estate, which was being set aside at this time, and the developing modern administration.

The social structures formed by Kayasths during this period varied a great deal. Only the Mathurs formed a subcaste, an endogamous unit including all Mathurs in Hyderabad. The tight control of economic resources and social status by the Malwala patron family was the basis of that unity. Bhatnagar, Gaur, and Saksena families also formed kin groups based upon their control of economic resources. The control of economic and social resources during this period could be measured by the recruitment of relatives from outside the city, by construction of residences and temples, and by the sponsorship of religious and cultural events.

The extent of control exercised over marriage alliances and residential boundaries was also a measure of prosperity. The Malwala *jagirs* and grants continued to provide for dependent families, and the Malwala family continued to dominate the growing number of Mathur families. The new Mathurs settled in Chowk Maidan Khan and formed a homogeneous neighborhood, following the style of life set by the nobility. Their high position in the state enabled them to exercise substantial control over social and residential boundaries.[21]

21. All Mathurs married with other Mathurs, with only two instances of conversion to Islam (Dooleh Rae and Kashinath converted over 100 years ago) and no confirmed instances of irregular descent: interviews with Hakim Vicerai.

The Saksenas and Gaurs also took in new men as sons-in-law in Hyderabad; these periods of expansion coincided with the height of political power for Bansi Raja and the Paigah family. These men were able to support others, not because they possessed large hereditary sources of income, but because they controlled positions in Mughlai bureaucracies, in the Nizam's household, and in the Paigah estate. In these cases, demographic factors—the ending of male lines and the sex and age structure of particular families—played a major role in determining dominance of the kin groups. This was true not only for the Kayasths, but for the Gaurs' patron Paigah family as well.

Just as the non-Mathur Kayasths exercised less complete control of their economic resources than did the Mathurs, their social and residential boundaries were less rigid as well. Husaini Alam had a population markedly more heterogeneous than Chowk Maidan Khan. It included Maharashtrians, Muslims, and Kayasths from three different subcastes, and it ranged in income from the well-off to poorer and more recent immigrants. Fewer families had reception halls. The Langar procession, the Muharram festival that was peculiar to this neighborhood, was popular, even riotous and disorderly, in contrast to the stately procession of the Bik Alam in Chowk Maidan Khan. Shahalibanda continued to be diverse in population, styles of life, and income levels while the influx of *suratval* immigrants and continuing instances of conversion to Islam added to its unorthodox reputation. Other localities, generally poorer ones on the margins of the city, received some of these latest Kayasth immigrants, too. The new immigrants, often despite proud traditions of origin and service, found established residential and social boundaries to their disadvantage.

Thus far, the study has concentrated on the Kayasths in the old city of Hyderabad—men predominantly associated with the old style of military and household administration. But the city and state changed greatly during the second half of the nineteenth century, presenting even old city residents with new opportunities and new constraints.

PART THREE

Establishment
of the Modern
Administration

CHAPTER 7

The Changing Environment of the Late Nineteenth Century

From the 1880's to the second decade of the twentieth century, the economic, political, and social conditions in Hyderabad changed drastically. Those Kayasths whose control over economic resources was secure maintained stable kin groups, but those whose positions and incomes were threatened adapted their marriage alliances to the new circumstances, as succeeding chapters will show.

When Salar Jung I became Diwan in 1853, he presided over a Mughlai court and city. The palatial British Residency, built across the river in 1806, was becoming the center of a growing commercial and residential area, but it did not rival the Nizam's court as a cultural center. The language of government was Persian; Muslim law or Hindu customary law prevailed in urban centers; education was acquired in mosque schools or through private tutors. There was no indigenous class of men who knew English or had studied Western subjects. There was a modern medical school, but it was Urdu-medium, and its graduates were in private practice or in the service of nobles. At mid-century, Hyderabad state was still poorly integrated with British India. The Nizam's government had its own currency and a separate postal system, and there was no link with the British Indian railway system.

Some of these circumstances changed before Salar Jung's sudden death in 1883, but the major changes came after his death. By the turn of the century the language of government was Urdu, with considerable use of English. New educational and judicial systems had been instituted in the city and state, and a new class of Western-educated men dominated political and social life in the capital. Most of these men were immigrants imported to staff the modernizing administration begun under Salar

Jung. They started many new educational and social institutions in Hyderabad city. They brought their relatives to Hyderabad and monopolized the higher levels of the modern civil service. Change came rapidly, but its impact upon residents of the old city was uneven. Relatively few Kayasths were able to adapt to the new conditions.

A New Administrative Elite

The Diwan Salar Jung's efforts to modernize the state required the recruitment of men trained in British India to establish an Anglo-Indian or modern bureaucracy. Most were Muslims from northern India, and Aligarh, the Muslim college founded by Syed Ahmed Khan, was a major source of recruitment.[1] The newcomers formed a new social category, non-*mulkis* or "foreigners," in the city. The Diwan's deliberate attempts to separate the old and new groups of employees into two administrative and social groups in the city largely succeeded; thus he prevented the new men from attaining political power. Direct conflict between these two social groups was avoided by maintenance of a dual system of administration.

With Salar Jung's death, the modern administrators became politically dominant. The new Diwan, the young Salar Jung II, became their ally and puppet—a development made possible by Salar Jung I's gradual centralization of power in the Diwan and the modern bureaucracy. The bureaucracy became largely autonomous, its administrators maintaining an elite and generating their own behavioral norms. They could no longer be checked by the Nizam, the Diwan, or powerful nobles, and they made decisions affecting the structure of Hyderabad society. The old Mughlai bureaucracy was effectively dismantled and its personnel disinherited at all levels. The educational and professional differences between old and new administrators were maintained as the modern officials devised regulations that would perpetuate their dominance of the new administration through their descendants.[2]

The expansion of the modern bureaucracy after 1883 provided opportunities for employment and promotion, but Western-educated newcomers monopolized the positions. Their statistical domination, particularly of the highest and most lucrative positions, became the central political issue in Hyderabad in the 1880's and 1890's. The dominance of "outsiders" was not only true in the earliest civil lists, but it increased as the

1. See Server-el-Mulk, *My Life,* for numerous instances of such recruitment; for the Aligarh connection, Gorst, "Kingdom of the Nizam," 524.
2. For a full discussion, see my article "The Mulki—non-Mulki Conflict in Hyderabad State," in Robin Jeffrey, ed., *People, Princes and Paramount Power* (Delhi, 1978).

administration expanded. Lists of those appointed from 1884 to 1886 revealed that men from Hyderabad received approximately one-fourth the salary of men from outside the state. Salar Jung II attributed this pattern to the large number of high-ranking appointments being made to the Judicial, Survey, and Education departments, for which local talent was not available. Despite explicit instructions from the Nizam, expansion of the modern bureaucracy continued to favor the outsiders. The gazetted civil service posts (those at the highest level) increased by one-half from 1886 to 1894, and the percentage of outsiders in them rose from 48 to 66.[3]

It proved difficult for men from Hyderabad to move from the Mughlai to the modern bureaucracy. This was, first, because of the deliberate introduction of measures designed to continue the newcomers' control. By promulgating a new definition of resident or citizenship status and devising new regulations governing recruitment and government employment, the newcomers and their sons could monopolize the modern administrative positions.[4] Secondly, other government regulations explicitly discouraged traditional employees from moving into new educational and career patterns. One required *mansabdars* to forfeit a percentage of the family's *mansab* payments if they entered government schools (1877); another cut a family's hereditary *mansab* according to an employee's salary level in the modern administration (1896).[5]

As the dual system of administration was superseded by the modern bureaucracy, new policies and practices adversely affected Kayasths and other traditional employees. The replacement of Persian by Urdu as the language of administration and the courts worked against local men like the Kayasths: their specialized knowledge of Persian had been a valued skill in the old administration. Persian was no longer a spoken language in most of India, and the old Hyderabad officials, both Hindu and Muslim, had held a certain advantage so long as it remained the state's official

3. Salar Jung II, *Confidential Memorandum* (n.p. [1886]), 60–61 (SJL), for the 1880's; *The Deccan Budget,* June 1, 1894 (CC).

4. See Nawab Aziz Jung, *Khazina-i Finance va Hisab* (Hyderabad, 1909–1910), 35–37. The earliest preferential order was in 1869; but orders specifying definitions and conditions of employment came in the mid-1880's from the Finance Secretary. A *mulki,* or resident, was defined as one who had resided in Hyderabad state for 15 years, or one continuously in government service for at least 12 years, or a male descendant of such persons. A non-*mulki* could be employed by proving that his knowledge and experience were not yet available in Hyderabad; he then received a certificate of domicile, known as a *mulki* certificate. For an English version (first printed in 1919), see (Government of Hyderabad) *Regulations Relating to Salary, Leave, Pension, and Travelling Allowances* (Hyderabad, 1938), 10–12.

5. Two percent of the monthly income was forfeited if a *mansabdar* joined a government school, according to the first order: Rao, *Bustan,* I, 341. For the second cut, see the *Deccan Mail,* September 23, 1896 (CC).

language. Even though Urdu was the Kayasths' mother tongue, they and other local Urdu scholars found the North Indian Urdu-speakers contemptuous of the Hyderabad dialect.[6] The change of language, then, did not help indigenous speakers of Urdu gain entry to the new administration.

Administrative Change and the Jagirdars, Mansabdars, and Serrishtahdars

Other administrative changes of the late nineteenth and early twentieth centuries, first implemented in areas of the state under the modern administration, undercut the old administrative system and its personnel.[7] Many obsolete but still honored hereditary positions were reduced or abolished. As the result of thirty years of reorganization, almost all *mansabdars* and similar traditional employees had become concentrated in such old-fashioned Mughlai units as the Nizam's personal estate and the Irregular Forces. From 1883 to 1885, the Mansab Department was merged into the Accountant General's office; a Managing Board was established for the Nizam's personal estate; the Irregular Forces were merged with the Regular Forces; and a Court of Wards was established to supervise transmission of the estates of nobles and *jagirdars*.

These general organizational changes had important economic and social consequences for the Kayasths and other traditional employees. Despite certain difficulties, three categories of Mughlai employees can be singled out to assess the impact of administrative change. First the general policies affecting all *jagirdars* and *mansabdars* will be given, then the *serrishtahdars* will be considered in more detail.[8]

Few Kayasths held large *jagirs*, and the Malwala family was the only major *jagirdari* family among them. Many held small *jagirs*, however, either as permanent recognition for an individual service or as conditional upon service in a specific capacity. Military *serrishtahdars* often held the latter kind of *jagir*, termed *tankhah* or salary *jagirs*, which they administered to pay themselves and their troops. Salar Jung I had begun resuming these *jagirs*; he had also changed the method of reimbursement of

---

6. Interviews with Roy Mahboob Narayan and Balobir Prosad.

7. Sizeable geographic areas remained outside the jurisdiction of the modern administration well into the twentieth century. Only half the land in Hyderabad state was *khalsa* (public); the other half was privately administered by *jagirdars, samasthan* or tributary rulers, and the Nizam's personal estate, the Sarf-i Khas.

8. The terms used for categories of employees were imprecise and overlapped. *Jagirdars* and *mansabdars* referred not to mutually exclusive sets of employees, but to methods of payment of employees; *serrishtahdars* were recordkeepers and paymasters for specific administrative units.

these and other *serrishtahdars* by substituting *mansabs* or salary payments. These men continued as *serrishtahdars,* but the substitution of *mansabs* or salaries distributed from the Central Treasury meant considerable loss of autonomy and possibly personal income for them. Few of these *serrishtahdars* losing *jagirs* were compensated; the few who were usually turned out to be Malwalas.[9]

Many of the *jagirdars* who retained their *jagirs* went into debt or tried to sell their hereditary holdings in the late nineteenth century. When the Nizam enforced a rule prohibiting the sale or transfer of *jagirs* without his or the Diwan's permission, many *jagirdars* were obliged to mortgage their holdings instead. Since the *jagirs* could not be taken over directly, bankers became permanent "employees" of *jagirdars,*[10] although they actually controlled the estates.

Conflicts arose often between the modern officials and the *jagirdars* as the new Revenue Department became more efficient in rural Hyderabad. Delineation of *jagir* boundaries and the internal administration of *jagirs* received critical attention; the Paigahs and other large *jagirdars* were subjected to critical reviews and reorganizations by government officials.[11] The new Judicial Department also put pressure on *jagirdars,* the largest of whom exercised judicial and police powers in their *jagirs.* The department repeatedly asked for definitions of their jurisdiction and lists of *jagirdars* entitled to exercise such powers. In 1897, most *jagirdars* still had not set up judicial systems; the Malwala Kayasth family did submit reports to the Judicial Department and was one of the few to do so.[12] The department pressed for clarification and conformity in yet another area, that of personal immunity from state jurisdiction. Some nobles and *jagirdars* were not subject to appearance before the established tribunals in cases involving themselves or others, and the department opposed continuation of these privileges.[13]

9. For the kinds of grants and the investigation, see Ali, *Hyderabad Under Sir Salar Jung,* II, 241–253; (Government of Hyderabad) *Report on the Administration of His Highness the Nizam's Dominions for the four years 1304 to 1307 Fasli* [1894–1898] (Madras, 1899), 53; and Rao, *Bustan,* I, 381–384. The lists of grants resumed in Ali, *Hyderabad Under Sir Salar Jung,* I, 14, 15, 17, and app. B, xi, xxxv, and xlii, include several non-Mathur Kayasths. But two Malwalas, Rajas Bhum Raj and Inderjit, were granted *jagirs: ibid.,* app. C, lviii and xlvi.
10. Elahi Buksh in *The Hindu.* Aug. 8, 1901 (CC).
11. Ali, *Hyderabad Under Sir Salar Jung,* II, 198–200; A. J. Dunlop, *Report on the Districts belonging to the Nawab Vikar ul Umra, for the year 1293 Fasli* [1884] (Bombay, 1885), 13, 54–55; and Salar Jung II, *Confidential Memorandum,* app. I.
12. Salar Jung II, *Confidential Memorandum,* app. I, 73; Nawab Emad Jang, *Report on the Administration of Justice in H. H. the Nizam's Dominions for 1299 F.* [1899–1900], (Secunderabad, 1891); *Report on the Administration . . . 1304 to 1307 Fasli,* 94–95.
13. *The Hindu,* April 28, 1898 (CC); *The Muhammadan,* Feb. 24, 1896 (CC).

After 1883, *jagirdars* were supervised by a Court of Wards. During an heir's minority, his estate went under the direct supervision of the court or its special appointee. Some entrusted estates were eventually merged into the Nizam's estate or the public domain. In other cases, a portion of the estate's assets was retained by the government when the inheritance was released to the heir. Even the marriages of heirs were subject to approval by the Court of Wards.[14]

More Kayasths fell into the category of *mansabdar* than of *jagirdar.* Here, too, Salar Jung I and his successors implemented measures to reduce state expenditures. Salar Jung tried to end these hereditary awards by a regulation phasing them out gradually. All *mansabs* were to cease four generations from the date of the original grant, by decreasing the amount at each succession by a quarter of the sum first granted. The regulation was not enforced, however, for the Nizam inquired about it in 1901.[15] Documents show that by the twentieth century a "customary reduction" was occurring with each succession, but the reduction was one-fourth of the previous, not the original, grant.[16] Thus *mansabs* were not entirely cut off, despite the passage of four generations or the reduction of the amount to almost nothing. There is also little or no evidence of a decrease in state spending on *mansabdars* by the end of the nineteenth century.[17] But there can be no doubt about the general tightening of supervision and control over them.

Beyond these two rather general categories of Mughlai officials, many *serrishtahdars,* men of established power and resources in the old administration, can be traced in the state records at this time. Holdovers from eighteenth-century military forces in many cases, a large proportion of them were Kayasths. They were not grouped consistently under one or another administrative structure. Some were recordkeepers and paymasters under the modern administration and some in the Nizam's estate, and some were moved back and forth from one department to another.[18]

14. For details about the Court of Wards, see Rao, *Bustan,* I, 381; *Report on the Administration . . . 1304 to 1307 Fasli,* 87–88. Rao, *Bustan,* IV, 204, mentions that the marriages of heirs required approval.

15. Column by Elahi Buksh in *The Hindu,* Aug. 8, 1901 (CC).

16. See the Muntakhab Mansabdaran files in section R1, APSA.

17. In one statement, Salar Jung claimed considerable savings on *mansabdars* ("Financial Statement of 1288 F.," repr. in *HA,* VI, 86–87), but other sources showed no savings.

18. Even in cases where the lines of Diwani, Sarf-i Khas, and departmental jurisdiction were clear, the extent of internal change in the unit cannot be judged from the fact of jurisdiction alone. Some Mughlai units fell only nominally under the modern jurisdiction while their nobleman served there. Other Mughlai units, particularly military ones, were reorganized but left in the Irregular Forces or the Sarf-i Khas for political reasons (to avoid notice of the Resident).

There was a particularly high proportion of Kayasths in three areas: among the *serrishtahdars* of *mansabdars* (for both the modern administration and the Nizam's estate); among all other *serrishtahdars* in the Nizam's estate; and among *serrishtahdars* of the Irregular Forces under the modern military administration.

It is difficult to generalize about those Mughlai units that were put under the modern administration. This was usually only a nominal affiliation; their structure and function had not changed, as modern administrators discovered after Salar Jung's death. For example, even in 1894 no one in the English Kitchen knew English, and the *serrishtahdar* requested that government officials correspond with him in Urdu.[19] In the same year, the Financial Department tried to audit the accounts of its Mughlai units. Such discrepancies were found that it was determined to pre-audit them before allowing the Nizam to sanction them in the future.[20] Soon after this, some Mughlai units under the modern administration were reduced or abolished. In 1896, nine *serrishtahs* (including five of *mansabdars*) were put under the Central Treasury, itself now firmly supervised by the Revenue and Finance Department. In 1897, the *bandikhanah* (unit providing bullock carts for transport) was abolished; its Bhatnagar Kayasth *serrishtahdar* lost his position. In 1901, the staff of the old-style kitchens was reduced; its *serrishtahdar* was a Saksena Kayasth.[21]

Some of the Paigah units employing Gaur Kayasths were put under central government supervision while two Paigah nobles, Asman Jah and Vikar ul Umra, served as successive prime ministers of Hyderabad state in the 1890's. These units stayed on as part of the Prime Minister's staff, with the men evidently posted as guards at various palaces and offices. When the Accountant General and Minister of Finance inquired about their numbers and salaries in 1906, it was discovered that some were paid by the Irregular Forces office, some directly by the Prime Minister, and some from the Nizam's estate.[22]

19. Letter from Mirza Sadiq Ali Beg, *serrishtahdar* of the English Kitchen, to the Minister's Private Secretary (Faridunji Jamshedji, from 1884 to 1914), dated 12 Ardebehisht, 1303 F. [March 17, 1894]: FCS, installment no. 39, list 10, serial no. 37, file L8/d2.

20. Letter no. 216, Jan. 15, 1894, Faridunji to C. E. Crawley of the Finance Department: FCS, installment 24, list 2, serial no. 83.

21. For the nine *serrishtahs,* Rao, *Bustan,* I, 189. For the *bandikhanah,* letter from Faridunji to Mr. Seaborne of the English Kitchen: FCS, installment 24, list 2, serial no. 115. The Bhatnagar Nageshri Pershad was its last *serrishtahdar*: interview with Balobir Prosad. The Saksena *serrishtahdar* of kitchens was Manik Pershad: Order of the Nizam, under signature of Faridunji, 24 Aban, 1310 F. [Sept. 30, 1901], FCS, installment 39, list 10, serial no. 149, file L9/J6.

22. FCS, installment 39, list 10, serial no. 149, file L9/J6, concerning the *serrishtahs*

Social History of an Indian Caste

The group of *serrishtahs* of *mansabdars* under the modern admin-istration was treated somewhat similarly. There were eight units of *man-sabdars,* five under Kayasth *serrishtahdars.* In 1869 Salar Jung had established a separate office under the Revenue Secretary for distributing *mansabs.* In 1877 this office went under the Military Secretary of the Irregular Forces, only two years after the Irregular Forces office had been established and one year after the appointment of its Military Secretary. Then, in 1884, the Mansab Department of eight *serrishtahs* went under the Accountant General's office. This was done on the suggestion of Salar Jung II, as part of his reorganization of the administration; the Regular and Irregular Forces were merged at the same time.[23] In 1895, five of the eight *serrishtahs* were "merged" with the Treasury. What the merging process meant for *serrishtahdars* then in office was that they, like their *mansabdars,* now received funds directly from the Treasury under the Finance and Revenue Department, not via the Irregular Forces or the Accountant General.[24] By 1902, only two *serrishtahdars* of *mansabdars* retained control of their *serrishtahs.* Not surprisingly, they were Mal-walas: Raja Shiv Raj and Raja Murli Manohar.[25] Again, the noble status of the Malwala family helped it retain hereditary positions while other Kayasths were losing theirs.

---

of Khub Chand. The object of the investigation was reduction, and a 1906 decree pro-vided that vacancies by death were not to be filled save by son, real brother, or real brother's son (copying a 1904 order to the Irregular Forces).

23. Ali, *Hyderabad Under Sir Salar Jung,* I, 106; Salar Jung II, *Confidential Memo-randum,* app. I, p. 38. Direct access of the *serrishtahdars* to the Diwan probably ceased in 1885: the earlier changes of supervision apparently interfered little with their internal procedures. For example, Salar Jung stated in 1878, in "Financial Statement for 1288 F. [1878]," *HA,* VI, 1: "Departmental officers, especially the sheristedars [sic] or paymasters of troops and others, were not accustomed to collect and prepare the materials . . . required for compiling a financial statement such as the one now submitted."

24. Rao, *Bustan,* I, 189; VI, 452. The merged *serrishtahs* were those of the Kayasths Lal Pershad, Suraj Pratab, and Ranchor Rai (Srivastava, Mathur, and Saksena), and the Brahmans Raja Rae Rayan and Ram Rao. In 1902, a sixth one (of Sunder Lal) also went under the Treasury. At some point, five other *serrishtahs* of *mansabdars,* all under Kayasth *serrishtahdars,* were put under the Nizam's estate administration.

25. Murli Manohar had succeeded to one of the family *serrishtahs* in 1884-1885, after personal negotiation to have his succession confirmed by the Nizam. Since he was Accoun-tant General when the other *serrishtahs* of *mansabdars* were removed from the Accountant General's supervision and put under the Treasury, he may simply have refused to relinquish the two held by his own family. At any rate, in 1897 and 1898 a commission from the Judicial Department was obliged to visit the Malwala palace several times to meet the Malwala *serrishtahdar* and examine documents relevant to disputed *mansab* inheritances. The recordkeeping functions, if not the pay distribution, continued to reside with the Malwala palace until after Raja Shiv Raj's death. FCS, installment 14, list 2, serial no. 669, file p2/6331; and installment 14, list 1, serial nos. 217, file H17/b15, and 234, file H17/b15.

Major administrative changes within the military forces were particularly important for Kayasths. While few military positions were completely lost before the end of the nineteenth century, the resources and independence of the *serrishtahdars* decreased drastically. The Irregular Forces were brought more and more into conformity with the Regular Forces and had been placed under the same administrative structure by the end of the century.

The process of centralization of the military administration had begun in 1864, when a Regular Forces Military Secretary was appointed. But *serrishtahdars* of the Irregular Forces continued to send petitions and enlistment rolls directly to the Diwan Salar Jung through their own messengers. In 1875 an office was set up to supervise salary distribution in the Irregular Forces (the Daftar-i Nazm-i Jamiat). In 1876 a Military Secretary for the Irregular Forces was appointed, who was charged with reducing costs through administrative reforms and troop reduction. In 1878 he tried to introduce new methods of recordkeeping and financing modelled on those introduced in the Regular Forces the year before. But the real changes came after the death of Salar Jung, with the merging of the Regular and Irregular Forces in 1884. They were separated again in 1885, remerged in 1893 under the *peshkar,* and finally put under the army minister in 1898. In 1899, salaries began to be distributed directly from the Central Treasury to troopers, commanders, and *serrishtahdars.* [26] This last change struck directly at the autonomy and authority of the *serrishtahdars* and left them with only recordkeeping functions. [27]

Other efforts centered on reduction of the troops. The numbers and costs of the Hyderabad Irregular Forces provoked frequent criticism from many, including the British Resident. Salar Jung had planned that when a trooper died the vacancy would simply be left unfilled, but the hereditary principle was too strongly established to enforce this. He had also planned to transfer some of the Irregular Forces into the Police Department, first organized in 1874, but few units were actually transferred. Another plan was to retrain men and transfer them into the Regular Forces. [28] In 1878, the Regular Forces consisted of 6,528 men

26. The centralization process is described by Rao, *Bustan,* I, 393–408; Ali, *Hyderabad Under Sir Salar Jung,* I, 106; Salar Jung II, *Confidential Memorandum,* app. I, 38, 45, 53.

27. As late as 1895, nobles and Arab *jamadars* were exempted, and their Irregular Forces *serrishtahs* had not submitted to this change: FCS, installment 24, list 4, serial no. 55.

28. In 1907 there was a plan to cut the Irregular Forces to 12,000 men, putting retrenched men in the Regular Forces, city and district police, or on pension: Rao, *Bustan,* I, 392. In 1902, the Resident made reduction of the Hyderabad Contingent forces dependent on reduction of the Irregular Forces: proposed in Jan., 1902, and May 7, 1902, in letters to Diwan Kishen Pershad: Political Department, *Hyderabad Residency Records,* box 66,

and the Irregular Forces of 24,173. Twenty years later the Irregular Forces had decreased by less than 1,000. In 1901, the Irregular Forces still cost nearly twice as much as the Regular Forces.[29] Successful reduction was defeated "because there are many and varied interests concerned, and hereditary rights of succession have been admitted for so long, and their continuance is so confidently relied on, that any sudden change in the organization of the force would be unpopular."[30]

An Irregular Forces committee appointed in 1893 involved *jamadars* and *serrishtahdars* in an effort to suggest methods of reduction. The results were evidently unsatisfactory, since another committee reported in 1896–1897. But this committee's proposals concerned only the forces in the districts, about a quarter of the Irregular Forces. Since most of the troops were stationed in the city, and they were perhaps the least usefully employed, yet another report was requested.[31] A description of the Irregular Troops at the end of the century illustrates the problem: "The Irregular Troops are chiefly on escort and guard-mounting duties. They generally furnish escorts for the palaces of His Highness and chief nobles . . . Not the least of their duties, however, is to lend additional pomp and importance to weddings and other social or religious processions . . ."[32] Finally, in 1904, an order decreed that future vacancies caused by death in the Irregular Forces were not to be filled save by the previous holder's son, real brother, or real brother's son.[33]

Other changes that inevitably affected the Irregular Forces *serrishtahdars* accompanied the rise to power of a young officer, Colonel Afsar ul Mulk, who became army commander in 1893. He incorporated many miscellaneous units into the Regular Forces and put others under his personal command, displacing at least three Kayasth *serrishtahdars*.[34]

serial no. 49 of 603/92–93 (IOL). For Salar Jung's own statements and plans, see Salar Jung, "Financial Statement for 1288 F.," in *HA*, VI, 9.

29. For 1878, Salar Jung, "Financial Statement for 1288," *HA*, VI, 11. For 1898, *Report on the Administration . . . 1304 to 1307 Fasli*, xxi, 160. For relative costs, *The Hindu*, July 27, 1901 (CC).

30. *Report on the Administration . . . 1304 to 1307 Fasli*, 157.

31. *Ibid.*, 157–159, xxi.

32. Campbell, *Glimpses*, 109–110.

33. FCS, installment 39, list 10, serial no. 149, file L9/56.

34. Asfar ul Mulk took over the Golconda Brigade in 1884, displacing its Bhatnagar *serrishtahdar* of the artillery unit, Raja Durga Pershad. Also in that year he took over the Maiseram Regiment of Arabs and Afghans, which had been organized by Bansi Raja, and Bansi Raja's arms factory. He formed the Raja Paltan, including the forces of the Saksena *serrishtahdar* Govind Pershad (Wala Jahi). After becoming army commander of the Nizam's Regular Forces, he took men from the Irregular Forces to form two cavalry regiments as the Imperial Service Troops of the British Emperor. In 1895, he took over another body of African cavalrymen from the Irregular Forces and reorganized it as the Prince Body

While most of the units he formed were of Irregular Forces personnel and were nominally left in that category or put into the Nizam's estate for political purposes,[35] their de facto association with the Regular Forces and its commander changed the nature of the remaining *serrishtahdars'* positions.

By the end of the nineteenth century, the direction of change in the Irregular Forces was quite clear, and the actual loss of jobs for *serrishtadars* began. The first official order, put out by the Legislative Council in 1894, decreed that no one was to be appointed to vacant *serrishtahdar* positions in the future and no new positions were to be created.[36] As the *serrishtahdars* died, their *serrishtahs* were to be taken under direct control of the Irregular Forces office, and in most cases this did happen.

These reductions affected many Kayasths, who constituted nearly two-thirds of the Irregular Forces *serrishtahdars* in 1898. Of the twenty-seven to thirty *serrishtahs* in the Irregular Forces from 1898 to 1925, at least sixteen and probably nineteen had Kayasth *serrishtahdars*.[37] In 1898, only four of these thirty *serrishtahs* had been taken under direct control by the Irregular Forces office.[38] The Administration Report of 1910 stated that the thirty-four *serrishtahs* had been reduced to fourteen.[39] By 1918, only seven Kayasth *serrishtahs* were still independent. Three of their remaining *serrishtahdars* were Mathurs, all Malwala family members.[40]

Guard (African Lancers). *The Deccan Times,* Sept. 4, 16, 1884, in *HA,* IX, 159–160; Campbell, *Glimpses,* 115; Rao, *Bustan,* I, 400–403.

35. For example, the Golconda Brigade continued to be termed part of the Irregular Forces, although the Resident charged that it was really part of the Regular Forces, which had supposedly been frozen by a treaty in 1878. See enclosures of the Minister's letter no. 636, Sept. 14, 1892, Salar Jung II to Sir Oliver St. John, the Resident: Political Department, *Hyderabad Residency Records,* box 66, serial no. 49 of 603/92–93 (IOL).

36. Order of the Diwan in Council dated 17 *Khurdad* 1304 F. [April 22, 1895], cited in Rao, *Bustan,* VI, 453.

37. Government of Hyderabad, Office of the Accountant General, *The List of Officers H. H. the Nizam's Government: 1898, Military List,* 29 and passim. The Regular Forces, Imperial Service Troops, and Golconda Brigade are included in this list. According to some informants, there are only 16 Kayasths; disagreement hinges on the units classified as Irregular, since the government lists are inconsistent in classification of the Sikh *serrishtah,* the Hazir Guard, the Jamiat Nizam Mehbub, and the Golconda Brigade. The Kayasth *serrishtahdars* included four Mathurs, eight Saksenas, three Srivastavas, one Bhatnagar, and possibly three more Saksenas; the others were one Khatri, three Brahmo-khatris, and seven Brahmans.

38. These included those of two newly deceased Kayasths, Isri Pershad (Saksena) and Lal Pershad (Srivastava): *Ibid.*

39. *Report on the Administration of H.H. the Nizam's Dominions, for the four years 1316–1319 Fasli* [1906–1910] (Madras, 1913), 52.

40. The Malwalas were Shiv Raj, Hosh Chand, and Girdhar Raj; the other four were Saksenas: the son of Bansi Raja; Mohan Lal Peshkari; Benkat Prasad of Shahalibanda;

Centralization and administrative reform was slowest for employees in the Nizam's pivate estate. From 1869, this administrative area began to change, largely through the addition of new sections like those in the modern administration. The older sections—the household, service and production departments and the military—were slow to be subjected to supervision. The Kayasths and other *serrishtahdars* who had been placed in these administrative divisions in 1869 were the last affected by modernization.

Nonetheless, changes did occur. New accounting and bookkeeping methods, introduced into the modern administration in 1877, were introduced in the corresponding departments of the Nizam's estate in 1878. The older sections were more directly affected when the Nizam's estate began to prepare a budget in 1881–1882, soon after the first modern administrative budget was published.[41] Until the death of Salar Jung I, the Nizam's estate office supervised the estate with the aid of the Diwan and two leading members of the Paigah family. After that, when Mahbub Ali Khan was installed as Nizam in 1884, a Managing Board was set up consisting of six members. The Nizam himself assumed personal control of the estate for a short while, then he returned supervision to the Board.[42]

After the Managing Board took over again in 1884–1885, practices began to change throughout that administration. Until then, most of the Nizam's orders had been issued verbally to employees, leading to misunderstandings. In 1884, papers began to be submitted through the Secretary of the Nizam's estate. The two offices which had formerly kept records and validated documents were abolished, and a new record office was established under the Board's control. A treasury had been established, subordinated to the Accountant General's office, in 1885. But a separate office continued to handle the finances of the military forces. Even though, in 1886, the Central Treasury took over payment of pensions and compensations to military personnel, *serrishtahdars* still continued to pay the troops from the Nizam's own military office.[43]

By the twentieth century, the newer sections of the Nizam's estate administration were not only modeled after the modern administration, they were often directly administered by it or by its officials on loan to the Nizam's estate.[44] Those older sections which continued their Mughlai

and Govind Pershad Wala Jahi. Government of Hyderabad, *The Classified List of Officers of the Military Department of H.E.H. the Nizam's Government* (Hyderabad, 1918).

41. Rao, *Bustan*, I, 133.
42. *Ibid.*, 128, 131–132.
43. *Ibid.*, 133, 129.
44. Allegations of corruption and mismanagement were frequent, and there was confusion and controversy over the division of resources between the Diwani and Sarf-i Khas

practices became noted as a refuge for traditional or backward personnel drawn almost entirely from within Hyderabad. The Nizam's own military forces, for example, consisted of some 8,000 troops, including *serrishtahs* of *mansabdars,* bodyguards, palace attendants, and porters. Only one of these battalions, led by a European whose family had long been in the Nizam's service, had military training.[45]

Those military *serrishtahdars* who had been put under the Nizam's estate numbered seventeen, and while few lost their positions, they became isolated. Seven were Kayasths, five Bhatnagars, and two Saksenas, and at least ten other Bhatnagar Kayasths held lesser positions in other divisions of the Nizam's estate.[46] Most of these Kayasth *serrishtahdars* continued their hereditary duties, supervising and paying units of Arab and other troops, musicians and dancing girls, reciters of the Quran and pandits, the ceremonial clock-strikers, palace dependents and African bodyguards. In contrast to the Irregular Forces, directly under the modern administration, policies of reduction were not implemented here even in the early twentieth century, and the Nizam's estate civil and military lists continued to list Mughlai positions and position-holders with few changes until the 1940's.[47]

Even though relatively few changes occurred within these Mughlai sections of the Nizam's estate, it should be clear that this was not necessarily advantageous for the Kayasths and others employed there. By the twentieth century, new departments and new personnel outnumbered the Mughlai ones. The new employees received salaries rather than *mansabs* or customary payments, and they were charged with reorganization

---

administrations. Revenues were mistakenly transferred from one account to the other, and the Nizam continued to draw money from either treasury. See the *Evening Mail,* March 10, 1903, XVIII, no. 29 (SCL), and R. I. R. Glancy, *Report on the Claims of the Sarf-i Khas Department* (Hyderabad, 1913) (APSA).

45. Rao, *Bustan,* I, 129.

46. The non-Kayasths of the 17 military *serrishtahdars* included 6 Brahmans, 3 Khatris, and 1 Muslim. Nine of the 17 handled 39 separate units, with 10 to 500 employees each. Five Kayasth *serrishtahdars* had units of *mansabdars* under them. See the two lists prepared for me in 1965 by the Sarf-i Khas office: "Fehrist-i Mansabdaran muratib khizanah Private Estate H.E.H. the Nizam," and an untitled list of military *serrishtahdars.* Some of the *serrishtahdars* received pay from two or three different sources within the Sarf-i Khas, and several held additional *mansabs* in Diwani *serrishtahs.* The five Bhatnagar Kayasths had the largest numbers of employees in their *serrishtahs*: two were from the U.P. families who retained their joint family identity and properties in North India, and the third and fourth were from the Hyderabad noble families of Durga Pershad and Majlis Rae.

47. The first printed Sarf-i Khas civil list I have seen is *Fehrist-i Ohadahdaran o Mulaziman Sarf-i Khas Mubarak: 1325 F.* [1915] (Hyderabad, n.d.), and they continue into the 1940's. Also, interview with Mohamed ul Husaini (retired manager of the Sarf-i Khas).

and modernization. Many reform measures, such as implementing restrictions on loans and purchases by inmates of the royal palace, chiefly affected the Mughlai sections. The Kayasths in the Nizam's estate were not only part of the most traditional administrative structure in Hyderabad, they served in the most old-fashioned divisions of that structure.

The Urban Environment

By the end of the nineteenth century, the modern administration had achieved considerable administrative integration of rural and urban areas in Hyderabad state. At the same time, the taking of the census and the compilation of statistical and other information emphasized the many contrasts between the capital city of Hyderabad and the rest of the state. In the capital city, changes during this period underlined the political and social dominance of the new class of Western-educated administrators and the gradual incorporation of men from the districts into urban life. Factors particularly significant for the Kayasths were the growth of the new suburbs, newly critical perceptions of the old city and of Urdu-speaking Hindus, and the slow progress of Western education in the old city. (See Map 3.)

The population trends for the state and city show that the urban population of the state as a whole increased by 42 percent from 1881 to 1911, though the rate of urbanization was slow.[48] Hyderabad city grew from 365,962 in 1881 to 500,623 in 1911. It was the only town with over 100,000 residents; even in 1911, its two nearest competitors had some 30,000 residents each.[49]

Characteristics of the population of Hyderabad city differed from those of the state, and there were sharp differences as well between the old city and the new suburbs. In the two decades before the first state census was taken in 1881, estimates of the population within the old city walls ranged between 45,000 and 150,000 and of the suburban population between 100,000 and 130,000. In 1860, it was estimated that Hindus comprised about one-third of the walled city population and two-thirds of the suburban population.[50] These various estimates were not far wrong: the first census showed that the city (defined as the walled city) included 123,657 people, 63 percent Muslims and 67 percent Urdu-speakers.

48. The percent of urban residents to the population ranged between nine and ten in these decades: *Census of India1 1921, XXI, Hyderabad State* (Hyderabad, 1923), pt. I, 38.
49. The number of towns (over 5,000 residents) increased from about 70 to only 85 from 1881 to 1911. *Census of India, 1911, XIX, Hyderabad State* (Bombay, 1913), pt. I, 10.
50. Briggs, *The Nizam*, II, 238; E. Balfour, *On the Ethnology of Hyderabad in the Dekhan* (Madras, 1871), 5-6.

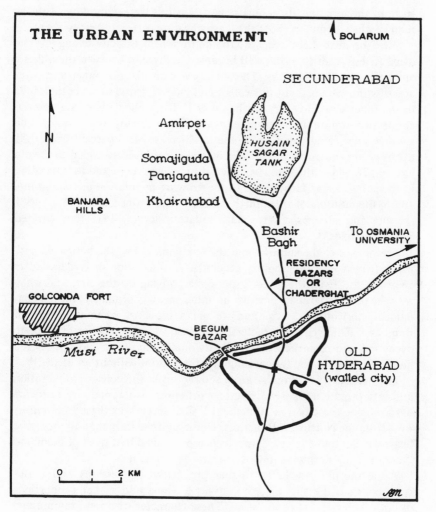

MAP 3

Telugu-speakers made up 22 percent of the city population and speakers of other languages under 5 percent each. But in the suburbs, then defined as Residency Bazar, Secunderabad, and areas adjacent to the old city walls, there were 231,287 people; 32 percent were Muslim and 40 percent Urdu-speakers, 63 percent were Hindus and 43 percent Telugu-speakers.[51]

51. Ali, *Hyderabad Under Sir Salar Jung,* I, 455–457, and Bilgrami and Willmott, *Nizam's Dominions,* II, 571 (both citing the 1881 census).

[141

In both the city and its suburbs, non-Muslims were recording Urdu as their mother tongue in 1881; the Kayasths were certainly among them.

Over the next three decades, the definition of the city changed. The Musi River rather than the wall became the division between the old city and the expanding suburbs. The old city was divided into inner and outer areas (within and without the walls), and in 1901 wards were created, four in the inner city and three in the outer.[52] The walled inner city covered about two square miles, where density was already quite high. The suburbs grew rapidly, with a population increase of 19 percent from 1881 to 1891.[53] In the same decade, 858 occupied houses were added to the old city and 28,843 to the suburbs. The census report remarked that building in the suburbs was largely due to the growing population of immigrants and to the building of villas further out by "the better classes."[54] In 1881 the city and suburbs covered 23.5 square miles; by 1911 they covered 51 square miles.[55]

The growth of the suburbs and their settlement by "the better classes" was reflected in contemporary accounts. A description of Hyderabad in 1899 noted: "Even the minor grandees are giving up the city, and when we speak of Hyderabad now we no more mean the place to which that name historically belongs than we mean the Fort when we speak of Bombay." The writer characterized the old city as "a favorite place to decay in" and remarked that while its quaint character had not altered much, Europeans could now safely venture into it without an escort.[56]

The new class of administrators showed up in the census enumeration and interpretation. In 1891, the proportion of Hyderabad city residents born outside the city was 20 percent.[57] One-seventh of these immigrants were from the Northwest Provinces, Oudh, and the Punjab, and they were heavily male (four to one). The census report noted that most of them had "lucrative appointments in Government departments."[58]

While the old city had a higher proportion of Muslims and Urdu-speakers than the suburbs, the city as a whole had higher proportions of both than the rest of the state. These characteristics were maintained

---

52. Shah Manzoor Alam, *Hyderabad-Secunderabad* (Bombay, 1965), 84–85, discusses the wards over time.

53. *Census of India, 1891, XXIII, Hyderabad State* (Hyderabad, 1893), pt. I, 118; the city population grew only .3 percent during the same time.

54. *Ibid.,* 53–54.

55. *Census, 1911,* pt. I, 10.

56. *Times of India,* Jan. 11, 1899 (CC).

57. *Census, 1891,* pt. I, 108. An 1871 estimate classified one-third of the city population as foreign born. Balfour, *Ethnology,* 6.

58. *Census, 1891,* pt. I, 109, quote on 111.

TABLE 9:
Religions, 1881–1911

	City				State			
	1881	1891	1901	1911	1881	1891	1901	1911
Muslim	43%	42%	42%	44%	9%	10%	10%	10%
Hindu	54%	55%	54%	52%	90%	89%	89%	87%

Source: *Census of India, 1921, XXI, Hyderabad State* (Hyderabad, 1923), pt. I, 74, 192.

or heightened by the immigrant population, as Tables 9 and 10 show. Muslims comprised almost half the population of the entire city and over half of the inner city, but only 10 percent of the total population of Hyderabad state. Urdu, the dominant language in the capital city, ranked only fourth in the state.

Changing perceptions of culture and society were reflected in the census treatment of Urdu and Urdu-speakers at the end of the nineteenth century. In 1881 Urdu was classified as a dialect of Hindi and included Hindustani; in 1891, Urdu included Hindustani, but Urdu and Hindi were listed separately. In 1901, Urdu, Hindi, and Hindustani were listed separately. In 1911, for the first time, the number of Urdu speakers fell below the number of Muslims in the state, showing that non-Muslims were no longer returning themselves as Urdu-speakers in the census.[59]

The Kayasths can be examined in detail here, since the Hyderabad census, like that of British India, utilized caste categories in its enumeration. This was done somewhat erratically, however, and the Kayasths were only listed separately twice, in 1881 and 1891. (See Table 11.)

Most Kayasths lived in the old city, but there were many in the new city and the districts. Most of the latter were probably members of a Kayasth subcaste new to the state, the Asthana subcaste, and newly arrived Srivastavas. Men from these groups accounted for most Kayasth literacy in English in 1891.[60] (See Table 12.)

Taken in conjunction with Table 11, which gives the total Kayasth population, these figures attest that 44 percent of all Kayasth males were literate in Urdu and 2 percent in English; none returned themselves as literate in Hindi in 1891. Less than 2 percent of Kayasth women were literate; again, Urdu was the language listed. This measure of Kayasths

59. *Census, 1891*, pt. II, 81–82; *Census, 1911*, pt. I, 117–118.
60. See Chapter 8 for a discussion of these men in modern occupations.

TABLE 10:
Languages, 1881–1911

Mother tongue	City (including suburbs)				State			
	1881	1891	1901	1911	1881	1891	1901	1911
Urdu	49%	47%	48%	49%	11%	10%	10%	10%
Telugu	36%	38%	38%	37%	43%	43%	46%	48%
Marathi	5%	4%	4%	3%	32%	30%	26%	26%
Kannada	——	——	——	——	13%	13%	14%	13%

Source: *Census of India, 1921, XXI, Hyderabad State* (Hyderabad, 1923), pt. I, 74, 192.

was not taken again. The only later statistic of relevance indicated that there were 1,845 Hindu men in Hyderabad city literate in Urdu in 1901. It is risky to postulate how the Kayasths chose to describe themselves in that year, given the choice between Urdu, Hindustani, and Hindi. But it is likely that they continued to designate Urdu, and that Kayasths constituted nearly half of that specialized minority in the city.[61]

Education and Social Change

At the end of the nineteenth century, the English language and British Indian administrative and social practices were gaining influence in Hyderabad. This was true despite the choice of Urdu as the official state language and reinforcement of it by a sizeable and important element of the urban immigrant population. A welcome result of the 1884 installation of the young Nizam and almost equally young Diwan was the dropping of restrictions on social intercourse enforced by Salar Jung I. Modern officials and the younger generation of Hyderabad nobles began to participate together in the English-oriented society of the new city and Secunderabad. Some members of the nobility, both Muslim and Hindu, began to acquire Western education and participate in that society, too. The free mingling of Europeans, Hyderabad officials, and nobles contrasted with the past, as a newspaper correspondent stated in 1895:

61. In Hyderabad city, 10,857 people were literate in English in 1901 and 18,997 in 1911 (almost all males); the figures for the rest of the state were 3,862 in 1901 and 7,529 in 1911. *Census of India, 1901, XXII, Hyderabad State* (Hyderabad, 1903), pt. II, 42–43; *Census, 1911*, pt. II, 74.

TABLE 11:

Kayasths in the Census, 1881–1891

	1881			1891		
	Men	*Women*	*Total*	*Men*	*Women*	*Total*
Hyderabad city	1,057	1,020	2,077	1,196	1,081	2,277
Suburbs including Secunderabad	225	196	421			
Rest of the Atraf-i Balda[a]	57	24	81	13	13	26
Districts	441	407	848	488	442	930
Total	1,780	1,647	3,427	1,697	1,536	3,233

Sources: *Census of H. H. the Nizam's Dominions, 1881* (Bombay, 1884), statement VIII, p. 20; *Census of India, 1891, XXIII, Hyderabad State* (Hyderabad, 1893), pt. III, sect. XXXIV. In 1901, Kayasths were put into a larger Kshatriya category. In 1911, only castes contributing one-thousandth of the total population were listed separately.

[a]The rural areas in the Nizam's Sarf-i Khas administrative unit encompassing Hyderabad and Secunderabad.

In those days [of Salar Jung I] the relationship between the city and the Residency was extremely formal . . . Within the course of a very few years, things have changed . . . No one would certainly like to revert to the old state of affairs. Suspicion is gradually wearing away on both sides and with advanced education and enlightened views, mutual friendship and confidence is courted . . . His Highness the Nizam himself is not slow to recognize this merit . . . and is the first to avail himself of the opportunity.[62]

For a brief time at the close of the nineteenth century, a vigorous and eclectic Hyderabadi society seemed to be developing in which all men of some wealth and standing could participate.

There had been a gradual increase in Western education and English language instruction in the state. This had occurred without much assistance from Salar Jung I and had run counter to the pioneering Urdu-medium Hyderabad Medical School begun in conjunction with the British Residency in 1839.[63] By the end of the century, English appeared to be

62. *The Hindu*, July 23, 1895 (CC); and see my article "Cultural Change and Bureaucratic Modernization," in Joshi, *Studies*.

63. The Hyderabad Medical School was started by the Resident in Bolarum and moved to the Residency in 1846. It was funded by the Nizam. The resident surgeon served as superintendent, and examinations were administered in Urdu by the residency surgeons in Madras. The six-year course had produced 17 graduates by 1859, almost all Muslims. Of the 28 students on the rolls in 1859, 26 were Muslims, one was Eurasian and one was a South Indian Hindu. Since there was no government medical service then, most graduates

TABLE 12:
Kayasth Literacy, 1891

	Men			Women	
	In Urdu	In English	Total Population[a]	In Urdu	Total Population[a]
Hyderabad city	596	25	1,196	16	1,081
Rest of state	147	12	501	6	455
Total	743	37	1,697	22	1,536

Source: *Census of India, 1891, XXIII, Hyderabad State* (Hyderabad, 1893), pt. III, 23–29.

[a]See Table 11.

gaining at the expense of the vernacular languages. Although Hyderabad city was still far behind urban areas in British India in both English and vernacular literacy, the census reports indicate that English education was progressing more rapidly than vernacular education, both in 1901 and in 1911.[64]

The complex history of the founding and amalgamation of educational institutions helps to explain the educational choices made by Kayasths at this time. Western education in Hyderabad began under private sponsorship and was very limited until the 1880's, especially in the old city. Salar Jung I started an Oriental school (Dar ul Ulum College) in 1856; its English branch, the City High School, was added in 1870. He also started a school for young nobles, the Madrasa-i Aliya, which offered Western education, in his own palace in 1873; it moved across the river close to the Residency in 1877. Salar Jung founded the Civil Engineering College, with an English middle school attached, in the new city in 1870. This Anglo-vernacular English middle school in the Chaderghat area of the new city merged with the City High School, and in about 1880 they were approved by Madras University as the Hyderabad College. Other early English-medium schools were begun in the new city. Protestant mission-

entered private practice or the service of nobles. From 1855 the school published an Urdu journal to keep its graduates in touch with medical developments. This emphasis on education in Urdu was a matter of pride to the English superintendents as much as to Salar Jung, but about 1859 the Medical School students began to take English lessons in the Madrasa-i Aliya (see next paragraph in text). See *Report on the Hyderabad Medical School, for the year 1858–1859* (Government of India, 1861), selected records, India, no. 34 (BM); also the *Deccan Post,* Oct. 9, 1896 (CC).

64. *Census, 1901,* pt. II, 147; *Census, 1911,* pt. I, 106–107. These literacy statistics are not quite comparable for the 1881, 1891, and 1901 censuses, and they are incomplete for the vernaculars in 1911.

aries had founded St. George's Grammar School in 1845, and Dr. Aghornath Chattopadhyya, a Bengali educator (Sarojini Naidu's father) hired by the Nizam's government founded the Hindu Anglo-Vernacular School (also known as Chaderghat School or Gloria High School) in 1877. But the old city had only the Dar ul Ulum until 1878, when the Madrasa-i Aizza was founded to serve the sons of nobles there. (Nearly half the all-Muslim student body of the latter consisted of young relatives of the Nizam). Both old city schools were much stronger in Oriental than in English subjects.[65]

The first two private schools offering Western education and English instruction in the old city were begun in 1880 and 1882, by the Malwala Kayasth family and leaders of the Khatri caste, respectively. Both schools received government aid as the government system expanded after 1883. Both were backed by high-ranking noble patrons and served predominantly members of their own Hindustani-speaking communities. Each had enrolled about one hundred pupils in the mid-1890's, according to the *Reports on Public Instruction,* but the Khatri school had doubled in size and added a section for girls by the end of the century. In the 1890's, two Marathi-medium schools in Shahalibanda offered some English, but Shahalibanda Kayasths went to the Mathur or Khatri school instead because they were Urdu-medium institutions.[66]

In 1883-1884, one of the new Western-educated administrators became Secretary of Education and persuaded the government to inaugurate a hierarchical school system based on vernacular-medium primary schools. Until then the Education Department, which had been initiated in 1860 as a subdivision of the Revenue Department, had done little. The new Secretary threatened that, without an adequate primary and secondary school system, the state could have no institution of English-medium higher education.[67] Once the lower levels had been started, the system was topped by amalgamation of the Madrasa-i Aliya and the recently founded Hyderabad College into Nizam College in 1886. Nizam College was affiliated to Madras University in 1886-1887, becoming part of the

65. See Rao, *Bustan,* I, 340-362, for the development of schools and the government system and regulations. For the Madrasa-i Aliya, see Server-ul-Mulk, *My Life,* 271. For the Madrasa-i Aizza, see Syed Hossain Motaman Jung Belgrami, *History of the Operations of His Highness the Nizam's Educational Department for the last 30 years together with a detailed Report and Returns for 1883–84–85* (Hyderabad, 1886), 17.

66. Rao, *Bustan,* I, 349-350; *Report on Public Instruction in H.E.H., the Nizam's Dominions, 1306 F.* [1896-1897] (Hyderabad, 1899), APSA, and successive years. See also Begum Lateefunisa, "Private Enterprise in Education and the contributions of some famous private High Schools to the Advancement of Education in the cities of Hyderabad and Secunderabad," (Masters in Ed. diss., Osmania University, 1956), OUL.

67. See Belgrami, *History of the Nizam's Educational Department,* 1-16.

British Indian educational system. This small English-medium college had enrolled some forty students, mostly Eurasians and "foreign" Hindus and Muslims, at the turn of the century.[68]

Those old city residents interested in preparing their sons for English-medium higher education sent them to St. George's Grammar School or the Gloria High School in the new city of Hyderabad. Vacancies for non-Christian boys in the former were eagerly competed for.[69] But members of the nobility and *mansabdari* classes in the old city showed relatively little interest in Western education. The meagre attendance of sons of the nobility at Madrasa-i Aliya was frequently noted, and there was talk of compulsory education for *jagirdars*.[70] A government report for 1894–1897 gave statistics for children in school, classified by their parents' occupations: the three categories into which most Kayasths then fit—noble, *mansabdar, jagirdar*—had the lowest attendance figures of all occupations. In contrast, the children of "government officials," clearly the modern officials, constituted a disproportionately large group.[71] Using the same table to measure the percentage of daughters among the school-children by parental occupation, undoubtedly a more valid indication of the value placed upon education, again those most closely associated with the Mughlai bureaucracy and the old city were low. Almost 8 percent of the children in school at that time were girls, and 20 percent of them were daughters of government officials (879 of 4,414). The daughters of *mansabdars, jagirdars,* and nobles combined constituted only 2 percent (83) of that total.[72]

One of two published opinions at the turn of the century about the progress of Western education in Hyderabad was that of the new Director of Public Instruction, who stated in 1898: "Twenty years ago, there were scarcely six persons in the city who could read an English letter or draft an English telegram, and now there are scarcely six houses in which there is not some one who can do both."[73] The other was that of a Hyderabad

68. "The Nizam College and Madras-i Aliya," in the *Deccan Mail,* No. 18, 1896 (CC). The small Arts College at Aurangabad, also affiliated to Madras University, and the Oriental Dar ul Ulum College, affiliated to Punjab University, completed the governmental institutions at that level in the 1890's: *Report on the Administration . . . 1304 to 1307 Fasli,* 345–346.

69. *Deccan Budget,* Aug. 31, 1894 (CC).

70. *Deccan Mail,* July 15, 1896; *Deccan Budget,* July 13, 1894 (CC).

71. *Report on the Administration . . . 1304 to 1307 Fasli,* 231. I have discussed this statistical data more fully in my article "The Mulki—non-Mulki Conflict," in Jeffrey, *People, Princes.*

72. *Ibid.,* and see my article "Women and Social Change in Modern India," *Feminist Studies,* III, no. 2 (Spring/Summer, 1976).

73. *The Pioneer,* Sept. 28, 1898 (CC).

correspondent of *The Muhammadan,* who objected to the Director's "uttering such nonsense . . . I can safely say that for every hundred or even thousand houses in the city there is none who could interpret an English letter or at least telegram correctly." He went on to relate the difficulty his father had had on receiving an English wire from relatives in northern India. The old gentleman walked about for three or four hours, covering all places within half a mile, and finally went to the business office of a major local firm, where the one man who knew English was absent.[74] *The Muhammadan* correspondent lived in the old city, the Director in the new suburbs.

As elsewhere in India, the development of voluntary associations accompanied the expansion of education and marked the changing social boundaries. In Hyderabad this organizational activity began in the Chaderghat area with the Resident, English military officers, modern officials, and some nobles leading the way. At least thirty-seven voluntary associations were started between 1879 and 1920, and a breakdown into ten-year periods shows changes in terms of locality and membership. From 1879 to 1890, the associations were largely social clubs (including military men and leading officials and nobles in the Nizam's government) and British or missionary-inspired social reform groups. All were located in Chaderghat or other new areas of Hyderabad city. But in the 1890's, neighborhood societies and societies sponsored by leading noblemen began forming in the old city. Some emphasized sporting activities. Others focused on education, setting up reading rooms and libraries with English and vernacular publications. Another popular activity in the 1890's in both the old and new sections of the city was public lectures, sponsored by local lawyers and journalists but often delivered by orators from outside Hyderabad.[75]

Hyderabad city at the start of the twentieth century included several different groups of Western-educated men. There was the new class of "foreign" administrators. Then, as Western education became available in the old city (many new caste and community schools were begun between 1900 and 1915), some local men acquired the skills necessary to compete for modern positions.[76] This younger generation of urban residents was augmented by an incoming group of district-born men, also

74. *The Muhammadan,* Nov. 28, 1898 (CC).
75. Rao, *Bustan,* lists voluntary associations and societies of various kinds: II, 673 and passim; IV, 83 and passim; V, 275.
76. See Rao, *Bustan,* I, 340–364; Begum Lateefunisa, "Private Enterprise in Education"; successive Hyderabad Government *Reports on Public Instruction* in the twentieth century (APSA); and Syed Ali Akbar, ed. *Education under Asaf Jah VII: A Retrospect* (Hyderabad, 1936–1937).

Western-educated, who represented the majority of the Nizam's subjects: the Telugu-, Marathi-, and Kannada-speaking Hindus of the Hyderabad districts. Drawn by the expanding educational system, the modern bureaucracy, and professional opportunities, they sought careers in Hyderabad city and other administrative centers.[77] Many of the district-born men had studied in British India, and their place in Hyderabad politics and society was ambiguous. They did not share the urban background, the fondness for Mughlai culture, and the deep loyalty to the Nizam characteristic of longtime residents of Hyderabad city. They knew Urdu and/or English for professional purposes, but they also founded vernacular libraries and cultural associations, strengthening these indigenous traditions in the capital city. With their residences in the newer sections of Hyderabad and Secunderabad, and their social and political interests, they shared characteristics with the "foreign" administrators. Like the old city residents, however, they were confronted by "foreign" domination of social and administrative life.

Residents of the old city suffered many disadvantages and had many competitors as they sought to adapt to the rapidly changing environment during this historical period. The new class of administrators had undercut most of the Mughlai positions, yet they made it difficult for members of the older bureaucracy to transfer to the modern administration. Part of the difficulty lay in the monopoly exercised by the outsiders; part was caused by lack of Western education in the old city. The extension of the new and relatively efficient administration throughout the state had drawn in new groups and created new tensions, both economic and cultural, in the capital. The only Kayasths clearly equipped to benefit from the changing circumstances were those brought in by Salar Jung I as modern administrators.

77. See biographical information in Mudiraj, *Pictorial Hyderabad*, II; Swami Ramanand Tirtha, *Memoirs of the Hyderabad Freedom Struggle* (Bombay, 1971); Department of Information and Public Relations, *Our MLA's* [members of the Legislative Assembly] (Hyderabad, 1952).

CHAPTER 8

Asthana and
Srivastava Immigrants in
Modern Professions

The first Kayasth to enter modern administrative service in Hyderabad was not a native of Hyderabad state. Rae Manu Lal was a member of a subcaste new to the city and state, the Asthana Kayasths. Recruited from Agra, in the United Provinces of British India, he arrived in 1872 and immediately established a powerful kin group in Hyderabad. He and his Asthana kinsmen shared the characteristics of the Western-educated administrators recruited for the modern administration by Salar Jung. They differed in many ways from the Kayasths already settled in Hyderabad, and they ranked above most of them in the new political, economic, and social environment. Beginning in 1880, another new wave of immigrants, Srivastavas, came to Hyderabad. Like the Asthanas, they were from North India and associated with the modern administration; but few of them joined or formed kin groups in the city.

The Asthana Kin Group

All of the Asthana Kayasths in Hyderabad in the twentieth century, some ten to fifteen families, trace their migration to that of Manu Lal.[1] His career began in North India, where the family had served with the Mughal emperors. When Delhi fell to the English in the early nineteenth century, Manu Lal's father, Sohan Lal, moved from Delhi to Agra and from Mughal to British service. Sohan Lal was placed in charge of the excise tax for Agra city. During the Mutiny of 1857, he toured the area maintaining order for the British and was rewarded with three villages in

1. Brij Mohan Lal, "Our Asthana Family Ancestry," 1953, copy with Kunj Behari Lal and microfilm with me: interviews with Dr. Brij Mohan Lal and Lokendra Bahadur.

Bulandshaher, augmenting the family properties in the Gokalpura section of Agra. He sent Manu Lal to an English-medium school in Agra and then to Roorkee Engineering College. Though he entered British service before finishing his degree, Manu Lal was made assistant engineer on the Ganges Canal and given a teaching post at Roorkee Engineering College.[2]

In 1870, Salar Jung wrote to Roorkee College asking that a capable engineer be recommended for Hyderabad service. Manu Lal was recommended, and in 1871 he accepted a position as assistant to Principal Wilkinson of the Hyderabad Engineering College (established in 1870). The British Resident in Hyderabad helped obtain Manu Lal's transfer from the government of the Northwest Provinces.[3]

When Manu Lal arrived in Hyderabad, he rented houses in Troop Bazar, near the Residency in the new city, for his family and those families of his elder brother and sister's husband. These two men did not enter the Hyderabad service, but their sons[4] joined the modern administration along with Manu Lal's sons. The subsequent growth of the Asthana community in Hyderabad is summarized well by one of Manu Lal's descendants:

The Asthanas who arrived in Hyderabad with Rai Munnu Lal and later, were closely related to each other being first and second cousins or the husband and children of their daughters. Thus according to Hindu law, inter-marriage between them was impossible. Therefore they had to seek brides for their sons, and husbands for their daughters from their own community in Northern India and the marriages were mostly performed there. Many of these husbands of the daughters settled in Hyderabad and found employment, thus increasing the numbers of Asthanas.[5]

Table 13, of Asthana families established in Hyderabad and their relationships to each other, confirms this statement.

The organization of the Asthana kin group somewhat resembled that of the Mathurs, with one dominant family (that of Manu Lal). Of the fifteen families subsequently represented in the city, all were related by marriage to Manu Lal's family or to those of his two affines, who followed him to Hyderabad. Sometimes, because of serial monogamy and earlier

2. "Halat-i Khandan Rajah Rae Murlidhar," Persian obituary (preserved by Gurucharan Das Saxena).
3. FCS, installment 14, list 2, serial no. 262, file b2/b164, letter from Wilkinson of Aug. 17, 1871.
4. These were Bhagwat Pershad and Kalyan Rae, sons of Chironji Lal, and Jyoti Pershad and Hemchander, sons of Munshi Ganga Pershad: interviews with Dr. Brij Mohan Lal.
5. Letter to me from Dr. Brij Mohan Lal, Sept. 26, 1965.

TABLE 13:
Asthana Families

Family number[a]	Approximate arrival date	First man to arrive	Relation to others[b]
1 A	1872	Rae Manu Lal	
B	1882	Prabhu Lal	Manu Lal's FBSS; a student friend of Manu Lal's S
C	1912	Gaya Pershad	Manu Lal's FFBSS
2	1872	Ganga Pershad	Manu Lal's ZH
3 A	1898	Yudhistr Bahadur	Manu Lal's BSDH
B	1899	Jung Bahadur	5th cousin of Yudhistr Bahadur; *hamzulf* to Manu Lal's SS
4	1890's	Ragubir Dayal	Prabhu Lal's (family 1C) ZH
5	1900	Uma Shanker	son of Prabhu Lal's *hamzulf*
6	1905	Ragubir Sahae	Manu Lal's SDH
7	1910	Jogeshwar Narayan	Ganga Pershad's (family 2) SDH
8	1920	Mahendra Kishore	Manu Lal's SDH
9	1923	Lalta Pershad	Murlidhar's[c] DDH; Yudhistr Bahadur's (3) BDDH; Murlidhar's DDH (3 wives)
10	1925	Lalta Pershad	Gaya Pershad's (IC) SDH; later, became Muslim
11	1930	Lalta Pershad	Gaya Pershad's (1C) WBS
12	1933	Kalicharan	Ganga Pershad's (2) SDH
13	1935	Sons of Sham Sunder Lal	Sham Sunder Lal was Yudhistr Bahadur's (3) BDH
14	1945	Purshottam Asthana	Yudhistr Bahadur's (3) SWBS
15	1945	Shiv Shanker Lal	Purshottam Asthana's (14) ZH

Sources: Interviews with Lokendra Bahadur, Kunj Behari Lal, Dr. Brij Mohan Lal; letters from Dr. Brij Mohan Lal of Sept. 26, Nov. 26, 1965.

[a]Chronological order of arrival in Hyderabad.

[b]Customary usage here as follows: F = father; B = brother; S = son; Z = sister; H = husband; D = daughter; W = wife.

[c]Murlidhar was the son of Manu Lal.

marriages between members of collateral branches in North India, Hyderabad Asthanas were related to each other in two or three different ways.[6]

6. For example, Dr. Brij Mohan Lal and Lokendra Bahadur of families 1 and 3 in Table 13; Brij Mohan Lal's mother and Lokendra Bahadur were sixth cousins, while Brij Mohan Lal and Lokendra Bahadur's mother were third cousins; Brij Mohan Lal himself, according to generational reckoning in Hyderabad, was thought of as uncle to Lokendra Bahadur.

All those men who moved to Hyderabad were younger sons of the junior branches of their lineages, indicating parental control of their marriages, educations, and careers. And despite fairly distant and complex consanguineal ties between many Asthana men who eventually settled in Hyderabad, it was usually affinal ties or school friendships that brought immigrants to the city. Thus when the first member of family 3 in Table 13 married with Manu Lal's family and moved to Hyderabad, his fifth cousin, Jung Bahadur, followed shortly. But Jung Bahadur and Manu Lal's grandson Jag Mohan Lal were married to sisters, and it was this *hamzulf* relationship which drew Jung Bahadur to Hyderabad. In another instance, Manu Lal's son Murlidhar went north to Mayo Central College in Allahabad; his fellow student and good friend Prabhu Lal (also his second cousin) returned to Hyderabad with him.[7]

The number of Asthana kinsmen who took positions in the Hyderabad service increased, but the Asthanas did not at first consider Hyderabad their home. For Manu Lal's family the residence in Agra continued to be home. Cousin-brothers descended from Sohan Lal's grandfather continued joint ownership of that compound and the houses attached to it. Daughters of Manu Lal's family were married in the Agra home, to which large wedding parties went up from Hyderabad. The last daughter from Hyderabad taken to Agra for her wedding was Manu Lal's grandniece in 1917. Sons' marriages also took place in North India, in the homes of their brides' parents. After such a marriage, the new bride was "taken into the family fold" by worship at one particular temple of the goddess Durga in Agra—the family's chosen temple. Similarly, children were taken to that temple for an initiation ceremony into Manu Lal's lineage: "On that occasion the servant took each of us in his arms to where a sweeper sacrificed a piglet for each child and put a mark on the forehead of the child . . . with a broomstick."[8] Even after marriages of daughters began to be performed in Hyderabad and the temple initiation for children ceased to be customary, property and kinship responsibilities continued to link Hyderabad Asthanas to their ancestral home. Their continuing ties to North India helped set them apart from almost all Kayasths settled earlier in Hyderabad.

As career members of the modern administration, Asthana young men participated in an occupational and social life which contrasted greatly with that of Kayasths in Mughlai positions in the old city. Manu Lal

7. Lal, "Our Ancestry," 13; Dr. Brij Mohan Lal's written comment on my Dec. 19, 1966 summary.
8. Letters from Dr. Brij Mohan Lal, Sept. 26, 1965 and Dec. 13, 1965 (quote from the latter), and his "Our Ancestry," 1, 2, 19.

established an English-medium school near the family's first rented houses in Troop Bazar[9] and sent his sons north to British India to school. His son Murlidhar studied at Mayo Central College in Allahabad, but Salar Jung brought him back and made him a third-class *talukdar* in the late 1870's, before he finished the F.A. (First Arts, or intermediate) course. Murlidhar spent his early years of service in the districts and was promoted to second, then first *talukdar*.[10] Promotion through district service was a typical pattern for those in the Revenue Department. Life in the districts meant hard work and a social milieu that was confined to those few men of similar background and rank posted in the area. Officers frequently entertained one another at official and unofficial dinners and parties, and drinking was a major part of their social life. Some Asthana homes had bars after the English fashion, stocked mostly with port, whiskey, and other European-style drinks. Friends were usually drawn from among others in modern administrative and professional occupations.[11]

As more Asthanas settled in Hyderabad, their residential preferences confirmed their membership in the modern administrative elite. At times only one man—first Manu Lal and then, after his death in 1888, Prabhu Lal in the Finance Department—was actually resident in the city. As kinsmen were promoted or transferred back into the city, the original rented houses in Troop Bazar were supplemented by new residences constructed further out in the popular suburbs developing to the northwest, Khairatabad and Panjaguta (see Map 3). The large residence built by Murlidhar in Khairatabad became the central one.[12]

As head of the family from 1888 to 1929, Murlidhar helped place even more Asthanas than his father had in the Hyderabad services. By 1900 there were four Asthana lineages established in Hyderabad, two represented by several collateral branches. Almost every man in the kin group was well placed in the modern administration. Some twelve men were in service in Hyderabad, seven from Murlidhar's family.[13] Rae Murlidhar,

9. Belgrami, *History of the Nizam's Educational Department.* This Hindu Anglo-vernacular girls' school had been started by Dr. Aghornath Chattopadhyya in 1881, and Rai Manu Lal headed the committee that continued it. It moved to the Residency Bazars and enrolled some 50 Hindu and 26 Muslim girls in 1885.

10. For Murlidhar's career, see Campbell, *Glimpses,* 73–74; Khan, *Tuzuk,* II (Officeholders), 20; and Rao, *Bustan,* VII, 210–211. He became a first-class *talukdar* in 1883.

11. Lal, "Our Ancestry," 55–56; and his "Story of My Life," 1953, with Kunj Behari Lal, 43–44; also, his letter to me of Sept. 26, 1965. He lists friends of his father and uncles in "Our Ancestry," 3, 15, 33–35.

12. Lal, "Our Ancestry," 8, 28; Lal, "My Life," 3, 58; Lal, letter of Sept. 26, 1965.

13. Murlidhar himself, Jag Mohan Lal, Kanhya Lal, Lakshmi Kant, Chail Bihari Lal, Ram Kumar, and Prabhu Lal (family 1); Jyoti Pershad and Hemchander (2); Yudhistr Bahadur and Jung Bahadur (3); and Ragubir Dayal (9) (all family numbers from Table 13).

promoted through appointments to the Inam Commission and then the Revenue Board, had become one of the highest-ranking officials in Hyderabad, earning 1,700 rupees a month.[14] His position made him a patron in Agra as well, where he supported widowed relatives and helped sponsor the education of nephews and other young men. He was also active in Kayasth affairs in Allahabad, his old college town, where the Kayasth Pathshala (school) had been established in 1873; Murlidhar was a member of the board of trustees.[15]

The first generation of sons went north for college. The next generation attended Nizam College in Hyderabad, which at the turn of the century offered a good English-medium education under European professors.[16] Yet Asthana men continued their orientation to institutions and events outside Hyderabad, a trend reflected by the reading matter in their homes. Murlidhar took the following newspapers in 1900, in addition to the three local papers: *The Hindu, The Advocate of India, The Leader, The Paisa Akhbar, The Modern Review, Review of Reviews, Indian Review, Punch, Tidbits,* and *The Spectator.*[17]

Another outside influence on the Hyderabad Asthanas was the Arya Samaj, then making converts among North Indian Kayasths.[18] As many Hyderabad daughters married into northern Arya Samajist families, they "brought back to their maternal homes new ideas . . . Thus the Asthanas became more broadminded in their outlook on religious or social matters and relatively more open to western influence in education."[19] The medical doctor who made this remark said of the period 1895-1900:

In those days I have found the home of Arya Samajist Hindus in Northern India more hygenic and clean and the members of the house, both men and women, lived better lives. Though Purda system prevailed, the women were less restricted in their movement . . . There was no illiteracy amongst these women of the Arya Samaj families. I have personal experience in this matter. The elder of my sisters was married into a well to do Arya Samaj family of Lucknow and she was very happy there and became more refined in her manners and social association. During confinement . . . a lady doctor or trained mid-wife was invited to conduct

---

14. Khan, *Tuzuk,* II (Officeholders), 20.
15. Lal, letter of Sept. 26, 1965, for the family assistance; Kayasth Pathshala, *Golden Jubilee, 1873-1923* (Allahabad [1924]).
16. Lal, "Our Ancestry," 9, 12, 17, 39, 42; and Lal, letter of Sept. 26, 1965, for the first generation.
17. Lal, "Our Ancestry," 33.
18. The Arya Samaj, an interesting combination of Vedic revivalism and reforms such as girls' education and the abolition of caste, was gaining popularity in the Punjab and United Provinces. The founder, Dayanand, first published his basic beliefs in 1874: *Satyarth Prakash,* in Urdu. See J. N. Farquhar, *Modern Religious Movements in India* (New York, 1918), 101-129.
19. Lal, letter of Sept. 26, 1965.

TABLE 14:

Occupations of Hyderabad Kayasths, 1892

Subcaste	Named men with occupational information given		Total named men	Total overlap with my records
	Mughlai administration	Modern administration or profession		
Asthana	0	5	5	5
Bhatnagar	3	1 (*vakil*)	4	2
Gaur	0	0	0	0
Mathur	14	1 (Lalta Pershad)	15	15
Nigam	0	0	0	0
Saksena	17	1 (clerk)	105[a]	91
Srivastava	8	20	62	27

Source: Lala Khub Chand, *Kayasth Kul Nar Nai* (Hyderabad, 1892), 92–97, 107–112, 118–119, 125.

[a]Khub Chand probably took his Saksena list from a Saksena publication in the same year, since the two lists are nearly identical. The difference is that the Saksena publication gives no occupational references but gives kinship terms, with Bansi Raja as point of reference: Pershad, *Hiyat-i Baqi Manzum.*

the case. The Arya Samajists of those days had many schools for children and colleges of their own. The younger of my sisters, a few years later, was married into an orthodox, rich zamindar family of Bareilly. I have found in her husband's place, the home dirty, women ignorant and superstitious . . . My sister was confined by the barber's wife and died of septic fever due to infection carried by the barber's wife.[20]

Asthana contacts with Kayasths in the old city of Hyderabad were practically nonexistent in the nineteenth century. In occupations, residences, and social life, most Asthanas moved in a different world, one with which only a few old-city Kayasths were familiar. In one man's opinion, "the Kayasths of the old city, who had arrived much earlier and were larger in numbers, remained isolated in the midst of alien communities and continued to be more orthodox in their views on religious, social and political matters and were influenced to a large extent, by the traditions and habits of the surrounding state neighbours."[21]

Srivastava Immigrants

Table 14, compiled from an 1892 publication on the Kayasths, gives the occupational distribution of Hyderabad Kayasths at that time. The Asthanas' position vis-à-vis the old-city Kayasths is confirmed; but the

20. *Ibid.*, Nov. 12, 1965.   21. *Ibid.*, Sept. 26, 1965.

presence of so many Srivastavas in the modern administration is surprising. A closer look at the Srivastavas in the table, possible because the
author of the source was a Srivastava and gave fuller information about
them than about the Asthanas, shows that most were newcomers and few
stayed to establish families in Hyderabad.

Table 15 presents the Srivastava data as organized by the same author,
Khub Chand, an employee of Mr. Thomas Palmer, a barrister who had
arrived from Benares in 1880. What stands out here is the relative smallness of the Khare group, outnumbered in Hyderabad in all time periods
and concentrated in the western localities of the city (see Map 1). Because
they were fewer, and because marriages occurred between the older families and some of the more recent immigrants, Khub Chand put all Khares
into a single category. But in fact, among the Khares there were two
distinct kin groups: families related to the titled letter-writer of Birh, and
families moving in from Mulkir *jagir*. There was also a growing *suratval*
group, often increased by men arriving in British military service, which
by some definitions included the kin group coming from Mulkir.[22]

The Dusre Srivastavas, at least twice as numerous, were listed separately according to their status as longstanding or recent immigrants. The
two eighteenth-century Dusre noble families and the kinsmen they recruited from Madras account for most of the former group. These older
families resided in Dabirpura or Shahalibanda. They constituted two kin
groups, since there were three or four male lines in each, and a single
inherited position supported each group. In each group, the in-laws and
adopted sons were used to assure the social and economic continuity of
the family originally granted the position.[23]

The newcomer Dusre families differed from the older ones in many
respects. In almost all cases their occupations were associated with the
modern administration; and they neither settled nor married with the
other Dusres. Most striking is the fact that, according to my records, only
five families settled in Hyderabad. Dusre Srivastava men (like Khub
Chand) who came directly from North India in the 1880's did not form ties
with the local Srivastavas but returned to North India. This is an interesting contrast with the Asthanas, also newcomers to Hyderabad, who imported kinsmen and established a kin group of high status in the city. The
Srivastava newcomers found large numbers of local Srivastavas in several

22. The families from Mulkir actually came soon after 1857 (see Chapter 6); those who
settled in Dhulpet frequently married with *suratval* Kayasths.
23. These were the noble families dependent on a Treasury position and *jagirs* (Dooleh
Rae) and a supervisory palace position (Chain Rae).

TABLE 15:
Srivastavas in Hyderabad, 1892

Designation	Number of men named	Number of families	Traceable families	Occupations	Number of families in Hyderabad localities	Number of families by place of origin
Khare	16	14	8[a]	1 letter-writer, Birh[a] 2 in Revenue and Finance	Husaini Alam: 6[a] Dhulpet: 2[a]	Faizabad: 1 (1[a]) Lucknow: 4 (1 via Mulkir *jagir*[a]) Bhopal: 2 U.P.: 2
Dusre Srivastava (old residents)	14	9	8[a]	1 *jagirdar* 1 Palace superintendent	Dabirpura: 6 Shahalibanda: 3	Allahabad: 1 Jaunpur: 1 Benares: 1[a]
Dusre Srivastava (newcomers)	32	24[b]	5[a]	6 *vakils* (lawyers) 7 in Revenue and Finance 3 clerks to English barrister 5 clerks to Bansi Raja 1 clerk to Shiv Raj 2 clerks to Iqbaluddaula[c]	Husaini Alam: 2[a] New City: 3[a]	Allahabad: 1 Barabanki: 3 Benares: 3 Fatehpur: 3 Gaya: 2 Lucknow: 10 (1 via Aurangabad[a]) Mirzapur: 3 Oudh: 1 Rae Bareilly: 2 Unao: 4

Source: Lala Khub Chand, *Kayasth Kul Nar Nai* (Hyderabad, 1892), 5, 92–97.

[a]Information added from my records.

[b]Khub Chand remarked on relationships and listed related men in the same numbered line; I assume his numbered lines represent different families.

[c]A Paigah nobleman who travelled in Europe and became Prime Minister in 1893. These two are listed under modern occupation in Table 14.

mutually exclusive kin groups. Some of these groups had doubtful reputations and all suffered from declining political and economic circumstances in the late nineteenth century (see Chapter X). Few of the newcomers elected to pursue careers and establish families in Hyderabad. Many were *vakils,* in any case, and they could practice their profession wherever Anglo-Indian judicial systems were operative. They went elsewhere as easily as they had come to Hyderabad.

Those five who did stay, whose families are remembered or continue today, were not typical Srivastava newcomers. Three worked for Bansi Raja, and two of those settled in Husaini Alam.[24] A fourth, a *vakil,* lived at first in Chowk Maidan Khan with the Mathurs and became a leader of the Hyderabad Arya Samaj.[25] All four of these families had come to the city from the Hyderabad districts and Central India, not directly from North India; the first three represent two kin groups with at least six families in each.[26] The fifth was also a *vakil,* a close friend of the leading Asthana family; he and his son, who did not marry locally, died without heirs.[27]

It is certain that most of the new Srivastavas shared the perceptions of the old-city Kayasths expressed by the Asthanas. Few of those who came after 1870 and 1880 mingled socially or married with their subcaste-fellows already in Hyderabad. The only Srivastava kin group that did move in after 1880 settled in the new city and avoided marriages with old-city Srivastavas.[28] The local reputation of Hyderabad Srivastavas was clearly a negative incentive to the establishment of families there, despite the opportunities open to Urdu-speaking immigrants with modern occupational skills. Thus, most of these Srivastavas returned to North India. The Asthanas, in contrast, stayed and prospered, and they did not face the problem of relationships with old-city Kayasths until the twentieth century.

24. Listed by Khub Chand as newcomers, the families of Dwarka Pershad and Sital Pershad had moved into the city from the districts from about 1860 (Chapter 6).
25. This was Kunwar Bahadur, who will be discussed in Chapter 11.
26. See note 24 above for one kin group; the other, of Lachpat Rae, settled in the new city and the men followed modern occupations. (Shiv Kumar Lal, commissioner of police in the 1940's and 1950's, is probably the best-known figure in the latter group.)
27. This was Pratab Narayan, referred to in Dr. Brij Mohan Lal's writings.
28. This is the second kin group in note 26 above. These men came mostly from Hingoli, Aurangabad, and Gulbarga districts, and their positions were in the Police, Public Works, Agriculture, and Public Health departments: interviews with Shiv Lal and Pyari Mohan Lal.

CHAPTER **9**

Diversification
Among the Mathurs

During the last decades of the nineteenth century, the rapid political and social changes brought differentiation and division to the Malwala family and the Mathur Kayasth subcaste. Raja Inderjit's successor as *daftardar*, Raja Shiv Raj, the embodiment of all the old Hyderabadi virtues of a loyal noble, stayed in that position for fifty long years, from 1875 until his death in 1925. But under him, his younger brothers and other Mathurs broke away from the Malwala family and embarked upon new social and economic ventures.

The first to break away was Lalta Pershad, who obtained a modern education and a high position in the new administration. He encouraged other young men, family members and relatives, to follow his example, thus forming a distinctive kin group. From within the Malwala family, Murli Manohar, the younger brother of Shiv Raj, also took a position in the modern administration. Later, Shiv Raj's youngest brother and others attempted to force legal division of the estate. Finally, as the nineteenth century ended with threats to the Malwala retention of the *daftar,* some other Mathur families began moving men into the modern administration.

Lalta Pershad and His Kinsmen:
Education and New Occupations

Salar Jung had selected promising young nobles to train for the modern administration, among them Lalta Pershad. Lalta Pershad came from one of the Rajputana families; born about 1855, he was a maternal grandson of Lala Bahadur.[1] In 1870 he was recommended by Salar Jung to the

1. Khan, *Tuzuk,* II (Nobles), 361.

newly established Hyderabad Engineering College, where he was taught by the Asthana immigrant Rae Manu Lal. Salar Jung's letter of introduction said: "Permit me to introduce to you Lulta Pershad, a native gentleman of high family connections here . . . regarding whom I spoke to you personally . . . this is the first gentleman of high family who seeks entrance from no mercenary motives."[2] Lalta Pershad was graduated with high praise, entered the Revenue Department in 1877, and became a first-class *talukdar* in 1885.[3]

In 1894, Lalta Pershad was chosen for a prestigious appointment to replace a European as manager of the debt-ridden Salar Jung estates.[4] The Government of India pressed for another European, but the astute choice of Lalta Pershad forestalled most criticism: "Rae Lalta Pershad is one of the best Revenue officials in the Nizam's service. He is a connection of the well known Malwallah house, one of the chief Hindoo Noble families in Hyderabad . . . by birth, position and training fitted."[5] Lalta Pershad held this high position for about twenty years and repaid his deceased benefactor by setting straight the tangled finances of the estate. His salary in 1896 was high, a little over 1,000 rupees a month.[6]

Lalta Pershad's influence within his own family and the Mathur subcaste can be measured in several ways. First, he is still remembered as a rebel and as an example to Mathur youth; we have an account, for example, of his being called before Raja Shiv Raj for a public rebuke when he entered Diwani service in 1877.[7] It had been a boast of the Malwalas that no Mathurs in Hyderabad needed to enter service, and Lalta Pershad was the first to establish himself as independent of the patron family. His defiance of Raja Shiv Raj was manifested by his departure from the Mathur enclave in Chowk Maidan Khan; he was the

2. FCS, letter from Salar Jung's private secretary to Wilkinson of Aug. 1, 1870, installment 14, list 2, serial no. 54, file p2/b165. For the Hyderabad Engineering College, see Rao, *Bustan,* I, 345.
3. "Liaqatnamajat Rai Lalta Pershad," a privately published volume of the certificates and letters of commendation awarded up until 1893, is in SJL, accession no. 2884, Persian. For an English summary of his career, see Campbell, *Glimpses,* 371.
4. Salar Jung II died young in 1889, leaving an infant son and many contestants for management of the estate. First, an Englishman headed a committee of management consisting of himself, a relative of Salar Jung, and Raja Shiv Raj. This proved unsatisfactory, the committee was abolished, and an interim commission of Diwani administrators sought a manager. See the *Deccan Budget,* Aug. 24, 1894, *The Pioneer,* Nov. 2, 1894, *The Hyderabadee,* Aug. 22, 1894, and *The Hindu,* Sept. 25, 1894 (CC).
5. *Advocate of India,* Nov. 29, 1894 (CC): see also *The Pioneer,* Nov. 21, 1894 (CC).
6. Government of Hyderabad, *Report on the Administration of the Salar Jung Estate for 1905–06* (APSA), 5; for the salary, *Report . . . for 1896–97,* 91.
7. Interviews with Hakim Vicerai, Sham Raj, and Ragukul Pershad.

first Mathur to move out of the old city. By 1911 he had built a large residence in the new suburbs, far from the Malwala palace and close to the Asthana residences.[8]

Second, the educational and career patterns of his younger brothers, cousin-brothers, and sons differed from those of most other Mathurs of their generation. They learned English and made their careers in the modern administration. Some of these young men served in the Salar Jung estates and the Revenue Department, while others worked in the Accountant General's office.[9] Lalta Pershad sent his own sons through the Dharmvant Anglo-Vernacular School to the Madrasa-i Aliya and the English-medium Nizam College. His first son, Bala Pershad, whom he tried to have trained for revenue service in the British-Indian Madras Presidency at his own expense, eventually became superintendent of the Telephone Department.[10] His second son, Sitaram Pershad, was sent to England to the Liverpool Agricultural College and became director of the Agriculture Department. Here again Lalta Pershad showed his independence, refusing to put Sitaram under the protection of Mr. Seaton, retired principal of Nizam College and the Nizam's special guardian for young Hyderabadis studying in England at the turn of the century.[11] Lalta Pershad's third son earned an LL.B. degree and became a lawyer.[12]

Finally, the marriage alliances of Lalta Pershad's dependents and the occupational placement of his younger kinsmen clearly reflect his guidance. The following figures show the genealogical relationships of the first Mathurs to enter the modern administration. Figure 8, Lalta Pershad's genealogy, shows his placement of family members. At the end of the nineteenth century, the men of his generation had some English education

8. This building, a palatial one, is now used as an orthopedic hospital.
9. Lalta Pershad's younger brothers, Ganesh Pershad and Tulja Pershad, were judicial assistant (100 rupees per month) and revenue *tehsildar* (40 rupees per month) in the Salar Jung estate: *Report . . . for 1896–97,* 92; *Report . . . for 1901–02,* 16. Two cousins (Janki-pat Pershad and Rukmini Pershad) and a son-in-law (A. S. Lal) worked in the Accountant General's office.
10. Lalta Pershad's attempt to send his son to Madras for training in the British Indian administration at his own expense was turned down by the Nizam in 1906: FCS, installment 14, list 2, serial no. 952, file p2/122 (letters between Lalta Pershad, Faridunji Jamshedji, and Mr. Dunlop, November, 1905 to October, 1906). Nicknamed Bala Pershad Telephonewalla Pershad, that son presided over the major expansion of the telephone service outside the city and conversion from magneto to a central battery system: Mudiraj, *Pictorial Hyderabad,* II, 544–545.
11. FCS, Department of Mal and Mulki, installment 39, list 3, serial no. 109, file c1/c321. Since the boy was going at his own expense, his father would have had to request this protection and pay £10 annually; he declined the offer (letter to the Resident, April 4, 1911).
12. Interview with Hakim Vicerai.

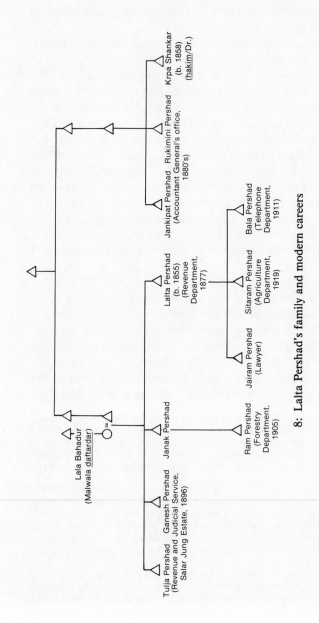

8: Lalta Pershad's family and modern careers

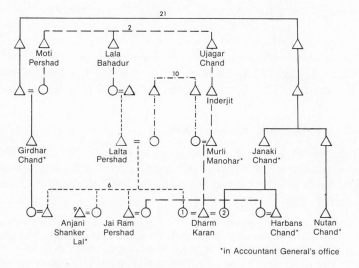

9: Kinsmen in the Accountant General's office

but no degrees; the educational level of his nephew and sons, in the next generation, was higher.[13]

Figure 9 shows Lalta Pershad's close relationship to Murli Manohar, Raja Shiv Raj's younger brother, and their placement of kinsmen in the Accountant General's office.[14] He and Murli Manohar were not only contemporaries and fellow protégés of Salar Jung, they were *samdhi* (exchange marriages occurred between their children) and *hamzulf* (through cousin-sisters). Lalta Pershad's cousins (Figure 8) had preceded Murli Manohar in the Accountant General's office. After Murli Manohar's 1893 appointment as Accountant General, Nutan Chand, Janaki Chand, and Girdhar Chand of family 21 (Table 7) gained employment there. In terms of kinship, the fathers of Lalta Pershad and Girdhar Chand were *hamzulf* (their wives were first cousins), and Lalta Pershad and Girdhar Chand were *samdhi*. Later on, Janaki Chand's son married Murli Manohar's daughter and also secured a position in the Accountant General's office,

13. Interviews with Ragukul Pershad and Hakim Vicerai; (Government of Hyderabad, Offices of the Accountant General or of Finance), *Classified Lists of Officers of the Civil Departments of H.E.H. the Nizam's Government,* relevant years from 1887–1948 (APSA). After 1907, civil and military lists were printed separately.
14. Interviews with Hakim Vicerai, Mahbub Karan, Dr. Benkat Chandra; relevant *Classified Civil Lists.*

[165

and a son-in-law of Lalta Pershad's was placed there in the early twentieth century.[15]

Finally, and perhaps most significant, Figure 10 shows that all of the earliest Mathur modern administrators were related by marriage through the family of Lalta Pershad's first wife (family 10). It points definitively to Lalta Pershad as the innovator and decision-maker in the kin group.[16]

Differences Within the Malwala Family

To outside observers, the Malwala family continued to appear united, prosperous, and secure. A Kayasth recently arrived from northern India, writing about the Hyderabad Kayasths in 1892, depicted the Mathur community thus:

Raja Shiv Raj is the only patron of his family, which consists of 300 persons of his community. It is well known throughout India and Hyderabad. According to the customs of his family the eldest son is the owner of the samasthan or jagir and all other relatives have their shares . . . There is no custom of division of inheritable property . . . I could not find a kindhearted and great person who supports such a large family and other brothers of the community, though I have visited cities and met other Kayasths.[17]

In fact, there were differences among the brothers and cousin-brothers, and some of them sought legal division of the estate at the end of the century.

Among the brothers, the contrast was strongest between Raja Shiv Raj and Murli Manohar. Shiv Raj, born in 1848, was educated in Persian and Urdu. His two younger brothers, Murli Manohar and Lochan Chand, born of Raja Inderjit's second wife in 1860 and 1870, were Western-educated men who differed from Raja Shiv Raj in their social attitudes

15. Interviews with Dr. Benkat Chandra, Maharaj Karan, and Anjani Shanker Lal; relevant *Classified Civil Lists.*

16. Interviews with Hakim Vicerai and Professor Shiv Mohan Lal. Note that Rameshwar Pratab (family 5), the second Mathur to take up a modern career, was *hamzulf* to Lalta Pershad. Guru Karan, a lawyer, came from the dissident senior branch of the Malwala family. Families 13 and 17, represented at the turn of the century in the Customs and Police departments, were also in Lalta Pershad's kin group. Lalta Pershad clearly arranged the marriages of his first wife's nieces and nephews with members of his own family (6) and that of his second wife (16). Of his first wife's three nephews, one married the sister of his second wife, one married the daughter of his second cousin, and one married the daughter of his second wife's first cousin. Of his first wife's four nieces, one married his own brother's son, two married brothers who were first cousins of his second wife, and the fourth married another first cousin of his second wife. Looking at this series of marriages from the point of view of family 10, Sham Bali's and Maha Bali's seven children married members of five different families; three brothers in the next generation produced another seven children, but all married members of only two families (6 and 16).

17. Chand, *Kayasth Kul Nar Nai,* 117 (translation).

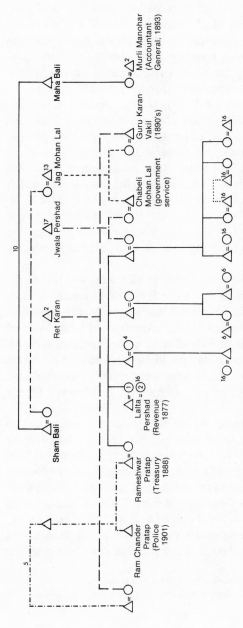

10: Lalta Pershad's kin group in the modern administration

and actions.[18] Although Shiv Raj was invariably portrayed as the patron of various actions toward modernization in the late nineteenth and early twentieth centuries, it was really Murli Manohar who initiated them.

Raja Shiv Raj was a leading courtier of Mahbub Ali Khan, who was Nizam from 1883 to 1911. Both privately and publicly, Shiv Raj symbolized the virtues of that popular reign, eulogized as a time of Hindu-Muslim harmony. He was honored at court throughout his life with jewels, titles, and other awards. When the Diwan set up special commissions involving members of the nobility, Shiv Raj was often chosen to head them. He served as the Nizam's official host for visiting Hindu princes, and it was he, as representative of the Hyderabad nobility, who met the Viceroy, Lord Curzon, on his 1907 visit.[19] Like his ancestors, Raja Shiv Raj participated in local festivals of Islamic origin; and he was widely praised for his generosity and public service. An account of 1899 remarked that "his personality is an asset to the state." It also mentioned that "for some time his vision has been defective, for which he is getting treatment."[20] Despite this problem, he continued to rule the family and *daftar* until 1925.

Raja Murli Manohar, twelve years junior to Shiv Raj, was one of the young noblemen selected by the Diwan Salar Jung and groomed for modern administrative service. He attended Salar Jung's Madrasa-i Aliya, where he learned English as well as Persian, Arabic, and Urdu. As part of his training, he served short periods of time in the Revenue, Judicial, and Settlement departments, attaining his highest position, Accountant General, in the 1890's.[21] But his official career was less distinguished than his patron might have hoped, for he was more of a dilettante than a serious career administrator.

Murli Manohar's major impact within the Mathur subcaste and in Hyderabad came through his social activities. In 1886 he founded the Malwala Sabha, a "social" club featuring weekly lectures on social reform and education. He was a member of a group, including Western-educated Hindus from the city, that came to be called the Chaderghat Social Club because of its location in that Residency locality.[22] The Malwala family sponsored the local cricket club, organized by Lochan Chand, the youngest brother, and a more general sports club known as the Dharmvant Club. Here young nobles from the old city engaged in polo, tent-pegging,

18. Khan, *Tuzuk,* II (Nobles), 194; interview with Mahbub Karan.
19. *The Hindu,* Feb. 5, 1895, (CC); Saksenah, *Kayasth Sajjan Caritra,* II, 11–32.
20. Khan, *Tuzuk,* II (Nobles), 194.
21. Saksenah, *Kayasth Sajjan Caritra,* I, 70–83.
22. *Ibid.,* 80; [P. V. Naidoo], *Hyderabad in 1890 and 1891* (Bangalore, 1892), 9.

cricket, lawn tennis and marksmanship. This club, whose members included officers from the Nizam's forces and the Secunderabad British garrison, met at the Malwala palace.[23] The family also sponsored the Malwala Plate at the horse races in Secunderabad.[24] The Malwala palace in the old city became the setting for parties that included representatives of the modern administration, military men, and nobles. Raja Shiv Raj usually presided over such occasions, but his younger brothers organized them.[25]

The younger Malwalas and a few other Mathurs joined other new clubs and voluntary associations springing up throughout the city. One was the Nizam Volunteers, a corps of nobles who received military training and provided an honorary escort for the Nizam.[26] Murli Manohar and others belonged to the exclusive Hyderabad Club and the Freemasons, organizations with British military officers, modern administrative officials, and a few nobles among their members. The Masonic lodges began in the cantonment with British military men as members, and English was the language used initially. As Muslims joined the chapters, Urdu began to be used in ceremonies. Finally, an Urdu-medium Lodge Hyderabad was started, and Murli Manohar and other men from the old city joined it.[27]

Murli Manohar's first educational effort was the establishment of a school in the Malwala palace in 1880 that offered some English and Western education for Mathur boys. It was soon named the Dharmvant Anglo-Vernacular School.[28] He founded a Sanskrit school for Brahmans, as an act of religious charity, in 1890.[29] He then learned of the North Indian Kayasth educational and organizational efforts and organized a Mathur Kayasth club and a Hyderabad Kayasth Sadr Sabha affiliated with the northern organization.[30] (These activities will be discussed further

23. *Hyderabad Chronicle,* July 23, 1898 (CC); FCS, installment 20, list 1, serial no. 124, file c2/d7.
24. Rao, *Bustan,* I, 404-405.
25. *The Madras Mail,* July 26, 1894 (CC); Khan, *Tuzuk,* II (nobles), 194.
26. Rao, *Bustan,* I, 404-405.
27. *Ibid.,* II, 685, 675; J. D. B. Gribble, *History of Freemasonry in Hyderabad (Deccan)* (Madras, 1910), 222. Murli Manohar was installed as Right Worshipful Master of the Lodge Hyderabad in 1898; he remarked that "in Hyderabad . . . the fraternity is therefore an important factor in combining the heterogeneous elements of society which would not otherwise meet," *The Pioneer* [November, 1898] (CC).
28. Khan, *Tuzuk,* II (Nobles), 194; Saksenah, *Kayasth Sajjan Caritra,* I, 79. (Raja Shiv Raj was awarded the title of Dharmvant in 1888.)
29. Saksenah, *Kayasth Sajjan Caritra,* I, 79. This was the Dharm Pracharik Manohar Pathshala, attended chiefly by Maharashtrians.
30. *Ibid.,* 77-78. He accompanied the young Nizam Mahbub Ali Khan to the Delhi *durbar* in 1877 and to Calcutta in 1884 and probably made contact with North Indian Kayasths on those trips.

later.) He also had an interest in social reform and published an article in English on the need to raise the marriage age and make other reforms.[31] But his Urdu writings on caste reform for Kayasth publications expressed reservations about the actual implementation of reform until caste members had been properly educated.[32] In these activities of writing and organization, Murli Manohar conformed to the expectations that the modernizing elements of Hyderabad may have had of him—so much so that he was accused of striving for a British title.[33]

Whatever the motives and outcome of these activities, Murli Manohar was genuinely interested in the mechanical aspects of modernization in the late nineteenth century. In 1881 he wrote to the government Workshop and Stores Department requesting a rain gauge "for Raja Shiv Raj," a matter requiring the Diwan's sanction. He requested a government concession to electrify the Chaderghat area and establish an electric tramway in the new city. Finding coal deposits on one of his *jagirs,* he wanted to lease the mining rights to an English firm.[34] But few of these ambitious projects proceeded beyond plans on paper.

Murli Manohar's one major successful project brought him into direct conflict with his elder brother, and the incident reveals their different approaches to change. In 1896, Murli Manohar secured government permission to establish a special private connection for the Malwala palace to the expanding municipal water supply system. When the pipes were laid, he dismissed many of the family *bhois* (water carriers), since their services were no longer necessary. The dismissed servants immediately petitioned Raja Shiv Raj, who sent an order through his secretary to cut the pipes and re-employ the family's hereditary servants. As a compromise, the pipes were left intact but the water carriers were taken back on the payroll.[35]

Murli Manohar was the first man from the Malwala family to take a modern administrative position, and his status as a noble secured him

31. "Harimaitism and How to Prevent it," in Murli Manohar, *The Industries of Ancient India etc.* (Madras, 1897).

32. Pershad, *Ittehad al Akhwan,* II, letter in appendix.

33. It was rumored that Murli Manohar offered Rs. 25,000 to Mr. J. D. B. Gribble, while the latter was still in the Madras Civil Service, to secure a title: *Advocate,* Jan. 14, 1896 (CC).

34. FCS, installment 13, list 1, serial no. 108, file R8/b1, letters of July 1881, wherein the Diwan sanctioned selling a rain gauge for 4 rupees, 3 annas, and 2 pice; FCS, installment 22, list 4, serial no. 72, file L5/a84, for the electricity proposal; and Muhammad Ali Varsi, *Makatib Yamin-us Sultanat Kishen Pershad Bahadur* (Hyderabad, 1952), repr. of letter from Murli Manohar to Varsi of June 2, 1913, regarding the coal deposits.

35. Interview with Syed Mohiuddin Pasha; letters of 1896 in FCS, installment 15, list 3, serial no. 222, file S6/a20.

regular advancement. As Accountant General from 1893,[36] he was personally liked and credited with sincere attempts to learn his job and do it well. But he "did not overhaul the absurd Moglai system which failed to give accurate results . . . perhaps, his orthodox notions would not allow him to do away with an old system on sentimental grounds."[37] This position was the high point of Murli Manohar's career.[38] He became a Secretary to the Finance Department after 1902 and finally moved into the Nizam's estate administration in 1910. He died in 1914, having furthered his sons' careers as best he could.[39]

Murli Manohar did not encourage his sons or relatives to seek careers other than in government service, and he always utilized his family and official connections rather than sever or defy them in any way. In these matters, his behavior contrasted with the more independent example set by Lalta Pershad.

There were men in the Malwala family who sought more independence, and two of them took steps to achieve legal title to shares of the Malwala estate. In the 1880's, the youngest brother of Raja Shiv Raj, Raja Lochan Chand, requested legal division of the estate with separate titles for Shiv Raj, Murli Manohar, and himself. The separate titles were given, but with unfortunate consequences. Lochan Chand was so heavily in debt that he mortgaged his share, arousing strong opposition from other members of the Malwala family and the entire Mathur community.[40] Murli Manohar appears to have become indebted.[41] Many other *jagirdars* at the turn of

36. Khan, *Tuzuk,* II (Nobles), 23, incorrectly says 1887. Rao, *Bustan,* I, 161, gives 1893.

37. *Deccan Post,* July 10, 1896 (CC). It is hardly fair to blame him for the persistence of practices assumed to have been done away with by Salar Jung between 1853 and 1883. Salar Jung had asserted personal control over the accounts, but his newly appointed accountants continued to maintain them in the old way. He introduced an intermediary step, translating the Mughlai accounts into a British form for the perusal of the Resident, but the old system still prevailed in the 1890's. A newcomer then termed Salar Jung's appointees "hereditary accountants," in contrast to Raja Shiv Raj, whom he termed a noble: Server-el-Mulk, *My Life,* 99, 101, 110.

38. He did successfully arrange for surplus cash balances in the district treasuries to be remitted to the city, so that the central treasury could avoid borrowing during the rainy season when communication with the districts was cut: *Deccan Budget,* June 8, 1894 (CC).

39. Rao, *Bustan,* VII, 26 40–41, 123, 310, for Murli Manohar's career; and 323, 48 for his son Inder Karan's career. Inder Karan began well, passing his F. A. (intermediate) exam in 1897 (*The Pioneer,* Feb. 11, 1897, CC), but he preferred leisure pastimes to official duties.

40. Interview with Syed Mohiuddin Pasha.

41. Salar Jung appointed Girdhari Pershad (Bansi Raja), the Saksena Kayasth, to work on the "settlement of accounts" of Murli Manohar for two years. Bansi Raja states that this was a mark of Salar Jung's appreciation of his abilities, and by explicitly identifying Murli Manohar as the brother of Raja Shiv Raj of the Daftar-i Mal, he indicates that he was settling personal, not office, accounts: Pershad, "Kalam-i Mutifarriqat," in *Kulliyat,* 28.

the century had similar debts and were in danger of losing their estates, but the Malwala case was of such major significance that the Nizam's government decided that estates would be awarded to one family member only and that *jagirdars* would not be allowed to mortgage their *jagirs*. A High Court decision returned control of these estate divisions to Raja Shiv Raj as eldest brother in about 1906. This reassertion of control caused another lasting split within the Malwala family.[42]

Another permanent major division came at the turn of the century when Nim Chand, a young member of the senior branch of the lineage, had his share legally separated from the Malwala estate. Unsuccessful in his attempts to get a second cousin (representative of the only other collateral line descended from Bhavani Das) to join him, he secured the settlement on his own.[43] Unable or unwilling to marry locally, Nim Chand went north to find himself a bride. His descendants and those of Lochan Chand intermarried with a third family (family 21 in Table 7), in what might be called an informal alliance against the dominant branch of the Malwala family. This kin group produced some outstanding professional men in the twentieth century, following the example of occupational diversification set by Lalta Pershad's kin group.[44]

Threats to the Malwala Daftar

When the Malwala resources appeared endangered, a few other Mathur families began to place members in the modern administration. The late-nineteenth-century press attacked Hyderabad's two *daftardar* families, the Malwalas and the Rae Rayans, as conspicuous examples of the old "feudal nobility" of the state. As the Inam Commission continued investigations of hereditary claims on the state, the *daftardars* were intermittently accused of conniving with holders of invalid *inams*. In 1885, the Inspector General of the Revenue Branch asserted that some documents offered to substantiate claims were false, and he carried out a simultaneous investigation of the Mal, Diwani, and Inam Investigation offices. A few forgers were caught, and the Inspector General criticized the inadequate precautions taken for the preservation of documents.[45] Other

42. Interviews with Syed Mohiuddin Pasha and Hakim Vicerai. The date is tentative, during the time Kishen Pershad was Diwan (1902–1912).
43. Interview with Sunder Karan; Khan, *Tuzuk*, II (Nobles), 454.
44. Nim Chand's bride was accompanied by her brother, who established almost the last Mathur *khandan* to arrive in the city in about 1908. Nim Chand died very soon after, leaving a son and daughter. When his son died in 1911 and the estate went under the Court of Wards its annual income was 40,000 rupees per year. The daughter married a member of family 21, who formed a "doctor" marriage network (Chapter 15).
45. See letters regarding this investigation in FCS, Mal and Mulki division, installment 39, list 5, serial no. 52, file H6/f1, and installment 14, list 1, serial no. 56, file H8/G50.

criticisms centered upon the old-fashioned methods prevailing in the two offices and the inaccessibility of records to the public.[46] Yet the old offices continued to function.

In 1896, the Hyderabad government confiscated the Daftar-i Diwani, an action viewed as a threat to all traditional administrators, particularly the Malwalas. The records kept by the Rae Rayan family were moved to the State Archives: "Many a heart in the city, throbbed and sighed . . . when the State Records were being removed in loads on many and many a wagon from the sacred precincts where they had been so long kept . . ."[47] It was predicted that "the next Estate to be dealt with similarly will be that of Shiva Raj Bahadur . . . who also enjoys the same kind of Jagir and Revenue as Raja Raya Rayan Bahadur . . ."[48] But the Daftar-i Mal was not confiscated at this time. It continued to be singled out in a series of articles in *The Hindu* in 1901 on administrative abuses. The hereditary position of *qanungo* (legal advisor on revenue matters) held by the Malwala family also drew comment. One critic pointed out that "a Hindu has the jagir, a Muslim fills the office, and a European performs the functions."[49] As *qanungo,* Raja Shiv Raj received 41,613 rupees in 1892, an amount considerable enough to warrant continuing criticism.[50]

Those Mathur families who feared the possible result of such criticisms and moved several members into the modern administration shared certain characteristics. Four of the families (numbers 1, 5, 16, and 17 in Figure 7) had means of support independent of the Malwala family, access to the modern administration through incorporation of their military *serrishtahs* into the Regular Forces, and strong support from relatives (chiefly Lalta Pershad). Family 5, whose *serrishtah* was merged into the Treasury in 1895, had close affinal ties with both Lalta Pershad and Murli Manohar.[51]

Families 16 and 1 had preceded the Malwalas in the Deccan and held separate positions. Family 16, with its own hereditary record office and *jagirs,* held a military *serrishtahdar* position with Arab troops that came under the supervision of the modern administration in the 1890's.[52] The

46. *The Hindu,* July 3, 1895 (CC).

47. *Deccan Mail,* Sept. 23, 1896 (CC).

48. This comment from the Urdu paper *Shaukat ul-Islam* was reprinted in the *Deccan Mail,* Oct. 7, 1896 (CC).

49. Elahi Buksh in *The Hindu,* July 20, 1901 (CC). The references are to Mr. Eardley Norton, appointed standing counsel to the Nizam's government in 1899 (*The Pioneer,* April 29, 1899, CC), and the Muslim official Nawab Imad Jung.

50. *H.H. The Nizam's Government Budget Estimate for 1304 Fasli* [1894–1895] (Hyderabad, 1894), 88, with 70,000 rupees estimated for 1894. He received an additional 33,384 rupees as honorarium in 1892, with 40,000 rupees estimated for 1894; *ibid.,* 32.

51. See Chapter 7 and Figure 10; Murli Manohar's mother was from family 5.

52. Interview with Hind Kishore: Swami Pershad was last to function as *serrishtahdar.*

head of family 1 was also receiving his military salary from the modern administration by the 1890's, since the family's service was with the Paigah noble Asman Jah, Diwan of Hyderabad from 1887 to 1893. Through the Diwan, one of this Mathur family's military *serrishtahs* became attached to the modern administration. Two men of the family, as *peshkars* to Asman Jah and Khurshed Jah (heads of the two halves of the Paigah estate, divided in 1882), were brought into contact with the rapidly Westernizing social world of the late nineteenth century.[53] The family began marrying with other Mathurs who were learning English and taking modern positions.[54] Members of family 17 also served a leading Muslim noble who figured in the modern administration, Nawab Shamsher Jung, minister of the Police Department from 1870 and in the Cabinet Council from 1883 to 1887. Members of this Mathur family served as military *serrishtahdars* and as the Nawab's personal secretary, and some men eventually joined the Police Department.[55]

An additional common factor in families 1 and 17 was the early death of the *jagirdar* head of each family. This forced or enabled younger members to rely upon slightly older brothers or brothers-in-law for educational and marriage arrangements.[56] Conservative elders in their own families did not hold them to more traditional resources. With independent economic support, the men from families 1, 16, and 17 were not strongly controlled by the Malwalas, either.

As the twentieth century began, the Malwala estate looked less and less secure; but it was not until 1915 that the Hyderabad government made the first move to incorporate the *daftar* into the Finance Department. Raja Shiv Raj, then sixty-seven years old, was nearly blind, and false certificates were being issued under his signature. The prime minister, Sir Akbar Hydari, pressed to complete the administrative reorganization begun so long ago. Finally, in 1915, the Nizam ordered the Daftar-i Mal placed under the Finance Department.[57]

53. Chand, *Kayasth Kul Nar Nai,* 118, names Thakur Pershad and Vithal Pershad as the *peshkars.*

54. Families 6, 5, 21, and 15 (the latter a Rajputana family providing three sons-in-law to the Malwalas): interview with Hakim Vicerai.

55. Chand, *Kayasth Kul Nar Nai,* 118, names Gansham and Jaganath Pershad in these positions. The first in police service was Narinder Pershad, their brother's son, who left Hyderabad to take B.A. and M.A. degrees from Benares University: interview with Anand Sagar.

56. In family 1, Girdhar Pershad died young and his children were raised by his sons-in-law, of family 15; in family 17, Shiv Karan and Chander Karan both died young, and their four sons included a lawyer, a doctor, and the man in police service (see preceding note).

57. Rao, *Bustan,* III, 422.

The timing was related to two deaths, those of Nizam Mahbub Ali Khan in 1911 and Raja Murli Manohar in 1914; that of Raja Shiv Raj would have to have occurred before final action could be taken. Nizam Mahbub Ali Khan had protected the *daftar* and its family. The new young Nizam who came to the throne in 1911, Osman Ali Khan, was less favorably inclined towards the Malwala family. Raja Murli Manohar had retired to serve in the Nizam's personal estate, and just after his death[58] the order taking the *daftar* into the Finance Department (based on Raja Shiv Raj's defective vision) was issued. Indicating some distrust of the recordkeepers, the *daftar* was locked in preparation for its transfer.[59] When the Malwala family appealed the decision, the Nizam ordered that a superintendent be appointed to run the *daftar* under Malwala supervision until the death of Raja Shiv Raj.

The superintendent, or "assistant," thus apointed to Raja Shiv Raj was Rae Prabhu Lal, a member of the Asthana Kayasth family of Manu Lal and Murlidhar. Prabhu Lal was also ordered to investigate the *daftar* because it had, by personal order of the Nizam, earlier been exempted from inclusion in the state Administration Reports.[60] His comprehensive report suggested specific new procedures to replace old ones, and although he emphasized the *daftar*'s continuing function as part of the government, he evidently met opposition from the Malwala family. A long letter of protest by Raja Shiv Raj was appended to the final report to the Nizam, and the following phrases from it illustrate his insular attitude:

although this office continues in its old fashion and has been carrying on excellent work in its own way, still the mode of keeping records and other arrangements connected with the office will be brought up to date as suggested . . . all are aware that my family has had this job for 200 years and when the entire management is left to the discretion of the said family . . . it is in no way improper that the details of the internal management of the same should be left entirely to those that are responsible for it . . . The constitution of the Daftar-i-Mal is under the old scheme and leaves nothing to be desired . . . these men [staff] being hereditary servants, I have perfect faith in them . . . [it is] unnecessary that any new appointments should be made.[61]

Rae Prabhu Lal died shortly after sending in his report; since Raja Shiv Raj was still living, the Finance Department asked for a capable man

58. Rao, *Bustan*, VII, 41, gives the death date.
59. Rao, *Bustan*, III, 422, mentions the locking. The incorporation order is in FCS, installment 79, list 3, file 575, serial no. 109, Finance Dept., enclosure no. 1 (APSA).
60. *Ibid.*, enclosure no. 2 (the order after the appeal) and enclosure no. 6 (the exemption order of 1908).
61. *Ibid.*, enclosure no. 7 (appointment of Prabhu Lal); and Daftar-i-Mal "Report of Rae Prabhu Lal, Daftar-i Mal," 36/E/Mal 1326 F., no. 36 (Urdu, APSA); the protest letter from Shiv Raj to Glancy (in English), appendage no. 4 to the "Report," pp. 8–13.

from the Malwala family to act as superintendent until Shiv Raj's death. The son of Shiv Raj, Shanker Raj, was appointed, but he died suddenly. Then a committee, chaired by Raja Inder Karan, Murli Manohar's eldest son and an official in the Revenue Department, was set up to supervise the *daftar* and its *jagirs*.[62] Once again the government had hesitated to seize the *daftar* directly; but there was little doubt that the death of the aged Shiv Raj would be an important turning point.

By the early twentieth century several Mathurs had succeeded in establishing themselves and their relatives independent of Malwala support. They followed Lalta Pershad's example of work and achievement, and they often had his active assistance. Some young men were aided by Murli Manohar from his modern administrative position. At least one "modern" kin group was developing, and both marriages and occupational choices promoted increasing diversification within the subcaste.

62. FCS, installment 79, list 3, file 575, serial no. 109, enclosures 10, 11, 12 for the death of Shiv Raj and the appointment of Shanker Raj; Rao, *Bustan,* IV, 210, for the death of Shanker Raj, and V, 291, for the constitution of the committee.

CHAPTER **10**

Kayasths in Decline

For most old-city Kayasths, poverty had set in by the end of the nineteenth
century. The cumulative effect of the administrative changes for *jagirdars,*
mansabdars, and *serrishtahdars* was economic decline, accompanied by
changing patterns of inheritance and marriage. The Asthanas had entered
Hyderabad as leading members of the modern administrative elite. The
Malwala family had largely retained its wealth and status, and a few
family members and other Mathurs were transferring to the modern administration. But most of the Kayasth nobles and *serrishtahdars* whose
families had served the Nizam since the eighteenth century tried to retain
control of their traditional resources and failed. The official efforts at
reduction of Mughlai positions and the application of more stringent
criteria for legal succession led to competition between kinsmen for
resources, and the marriage patterns of established kin groups changed.

Reduction and Disinheritance among Srivastavas,
Bhatnagars, and Nigams

Srivastavas, Bhatnagars, and Nigams who were tradionally employees
of the Nizam shared common problems in the late nineteenth and early
twentieth centuries. (Since few Nigams were in Hyderabad in the early
nineteenth century, they have not yet been discussed.) These Mughlai
employees sought to ensure legitimate heirs and the continuation of adequately funded positions for their families. Their difficulties resulted
partially from the relative smallness of their kin groups and the attempts
of a few noble and well-placed families to restrict or prohibit local marriage alliances. When the imposition of Anglo-Indian judicial codes in

[177

Hyderabad state defined legitimate heirs more narrowly, these families had fewer choices for the succession. In other cases, administrative inspection and curtailment of Mughlai positions reduced family resources, or too many heirs reduced the amount available to each.

The three Srivastava noble families dating from the late eighteenth century exemplify these developments. One family was highly placed in the Nizam's household, but the last of the male line died in the 1870's. The deceased's father-in-law, Manu Lal, retained and carried on the position, and the widow adopted Manu Lal's daughter's son, Chain Rae. Chain Rae was recognized as legal heir in 1884, but the monthly income dropped from 1,000 to 400 rupees at this point; since Chain Rae was only five years old, Manu Lal continued to perform the duties. Chain Rae married twice, his first wife from Madras and his second from Lucknow, but he produced no heirs and died in 1905. Chain Rae's widow designated as heir his real brother, who also died without issue; the designation then went to the youngest real brother, Ganesh Pershad, who also died without an heir. Ganesh Pershad had a son-in-law, but he did not get the position; it simply lapsed.[1]

The Dooleh Rae Srivastava family, who constructed the Chitragupta Kayasth temple, also ended. The last member of this family, Lal Pershad, was a *serrishtahdar* in the treasury of the Nizam's estate. He lived in Shahalibanda and died just before the end of the nineteenth century, leaving no legitimate male heir. The family had held *jagirs* worth some 14,000 rupees per year, but the government gave his widow a pension of 50 rupees a month.[2] Lal Pershad left a son, referred to as "adopted," who functioned as manager of the Chitragupta temple but was not accepted as legitimate heir.[3]

The Srivastava family of the letter-writer in Birh had heirs, but it

1. Khan, *Tuzuk,* II (Nobles), 1st supp., 25–26 (Manu Lal also had no male heir); interviews with Ram Kumar Lal and Miss Pushpa Srivastava.

2. The *serrishtah* records in the APSA cover expenses for 1854–1863: Persian bundle, "Ikharajat ilaqa Khizanah-i zat Lal Pershad." For the pension, sanctioned in 1903–1904, Ali, *Anvar-i Asafiyah,* 253.

3. Interviews with Roy Mahboob Narayan and his wife and Jagdish Pershad. The reason for his non-acceptance may be that an illegitimate son could inherit only among Sudras, and such a legal claim would have risked severe sanctions from other Kayasths. While the temple was allegedly taken by the government, along with the *jagirs,* upon Lal Pershad's death, a map (with me) accompanying an application to the municipality for sponsorship of repairs in 1919 names the "adopted" son (Brij Mohan Lal) as manager. When Brij Mohan Lal, despite four successive wives and a concubine, died childless, the Malwala family received the temple *jagir* grant. Whether they held it on behalf of the "Kayasth community" or whether the temple had become part of the family's private estate was disputed later.

suffered from administrative changes made after Salar Jung's death. Appointment papers and correspondence confirm the earlier routine transfers of the position from father to son: from Balaji Sahae to Gopal Singh in 1852, to Girdhari Lal in 1859, to Murari Lal in 1871. But in 1884, just after the death of Salar Jung, inquiries concerning the salary and duties of the letter-writer began. Murari Lal lost his direct access to the Diwan and was subordinated to the modern Accounts Office. His reports, once sent to the Diwan, were relegated to an old Mughlai department in the Nizam's estate.[4] After the death of Murari Lal in 1902, the position ended. A small allowance was dispensed to his heirs, and that only after considerable effort and constant negotiations on their part.[5]

Among the Bhatnagar Kayasths, the eighteenth-century noble families of Raja Bhavani Pershad and Raja Majlis Rae experienced the same problems in the late nineteenth century. Inheritance of the Mughlai household and military positions had proceeded in Raja Bhavani Pershad's family from him to his daughter's sons and then, from 1858 to 1907, to Raja Durga Pershad.[6] The family *jagirs* and positions had been worth at least 50,000 rupees per year. Salar Jung I's military reforms cut the *jagir* to 15,000 rupees a year, and the military pay was dispensed directly by the government. In 1884, Durga Pershad's artillery unit was merged into the newly formed Golconda Brigade.[7] The Raja retained some hereditary income and privileges, including 8,093 rupees per year for his Sri Ram Bagh temple festival and the exercise of judicial powers within his *jagir*.[8] He also retained one of the most colorful units in the Nizam's household, the Arbab-i Nishat or Department of Enjoyment. This unit employed dancing girls, musicians, singers, and buffoons who performed for the Nizam and nobles. Durga Pershad managed this *serrishtah* with the assistance of a Nigam Kayasth and a *mama* (female servant) from the

4. The family's Persian documents were given me by Jagdish Pershad (Gaur), who married a daughter of this Srivastava family. They include several originals and three "fair copies" (prepared by the Daftar-i Mal in 1884 for the investigation) as follows: Salar Jung's 1871 order to the first *talukdar* of Birh to pay Murari Lal 2,156 rupees per year directly; an inquiry from the Daftar-i Muhasib (1884); a letter from Murari Lal (1889); the reply from the Madr ul Moham's adjutant (1889); and the receipt for seven reports from Murari Lal from the Daftar-i Mulki (1890).

5. Ali, *Anvar-i Asafiyah,* 3, for the Prime Minister's ending of the position. Jagdish Pershad has the records of fifteen appeals and decisions to and from appropriate government bodies, as well as the stamped receipt books of his mother-in-law down to 1936.

6. Khan, *Tuzuk,* II (Nobles), 201.

7. *Ibid.,* for the *jagir* cut; Rao, *Bustan,* I, 400–401, and *Deccan Times,* Sept. 16, 1884 (CC), for the Brigade.

8. Khan, *Tuzuk,* II (Nobles), 201. He had the powers of a class II magistrate and civil judge for criminal and civil suits.

palace to communicate with the women.[9] While this was a fascinating relic of Mughlai court culture, it represented a reduction in responsibility since the days of Raja Bhavani Pershad, who had performed major managerial tasks within the Nizam's household in the early nineteenth century.

Like others, Raja Durga Pershad approached the end of the nineteenth century with no legitimate son to inherit his positions. He adopted a Bhatnagar boy from northern India around 1900, an adoption ultimately sanctioned by the Nizam's government after supervision by a Court of Wards managing committee. But the adopted son, named Bhavani Pershad for that famous ancestor, inherited a substantially reduced estate. For one thing, Durga Pershad owed at least 35,000 rupees to bankers in the city.[10] The adopted boy lived long enough to marry (a bride was brought from Delhi with her mother and father) and to sire two daughters. But his inheritance of the estate was disputed by other descendants of Durga Pershad—a son and grandsons by a local concubine—and the law suit continued until 1933.[11]

The other high-ranking Bhatnagar family, that of Majlis Rae, lost resources rapidly in the 1870's. Raja Majlis Rae had four sons, at least two of them *jagirdars*;[12] only one, Chandi Pershad, produced a child who survived, a daughter. She was married to a newcomer to Hyderabad, a Srivastava Arya Samajist neighbor whose father had come from Bhopal. This unusual marriage occurred in the 1880's.[13] As Chandi Pershad was without a son and legal heir, he adopted Bansidhar, the son of a recent Bhatnagar immigrant from northern India. The Majlis Rae position (*serrishtahdar* of the buggies) now went to Bansidhar, who inherited it at the age of seventeen in about 1892; the salary was 300 rupees per month.[14] In this last instance, family holdings of several personal *jagirs* and *mansabs*

9. The Persian bundle of Durga Pershad's Arbab-i Nishat records (APSA) includes salary receipts for 1862 for the singers and musicians; and interviews with Dwarka Pershad Nigam and Roy Mahboob Narayan.

10. Khan, *Tuzuk*, II (Nobles), 201; Ali, *Anvar-i Asafiyah*, 31–32. For the debt, see FCS, installment 22, list 2, serial no. 222, file H4/a9.

11. Interview with Brij Rani (wife of the adopted heir). This local son is mentioned in Khan, *Tuzuk*, II (Nobles), 202/1; his sons lost the lawsuit to Brij Rani in 1343 F. [1933–1934]: Urdu copy of the court proceedings with Brij Rani, "Mahkamah-i Judicial Committee, Mahbub Rae aur Brij Rani, numbers 1 aur 2 inheritance, 1343 F."

12. Register Asnad-i Jagir, IV, no. 15, serial no. 271b/5, and V, no. 15, serial nos. 18/18 and 183/19 (all Hyderabad *subah*).

13. Interviews with Benkat Prasad and Dr. Kanval Chandra. Such a marriage, between two Kayasth subcastes and according to Arya Samaj ritual, might have been acclaimed as a social reform; but in those days it was more likely to be the result of poverty or of inability to secure a proper alliance for some other reason.

14. Interviews with Dr. R. C. Bhatnagar and Balobir Prosad.

were reduced within one generation to a single position, *serrishtahdar* of a minor department in the Nizam's estate.

The Nigam Kayasths in Hyderabad also suffered economic decline at the end of the century. Members of the leading Nigam family, said to have served as specialists in medicinal herbs and intoxicants, ranked high within the palace.[15] The family *jagir* was worth more than 1,800 rupees per year in 1830. But the head of the family had four sons, and upon his death in the 1860's the *jagir* was split four ways. The large family residence in Kotla Ali Jah was built in the 1830's; the builder's grandsons fought over it, sold it, and sued one another at the end of the century.[16] Because the divided *jagir* was not sufficient to support all later descendents, some of the men born after 1870 took minor clerical positions in the office of their Malwala neighbor Raja Shiv Raj. Members of the younger branch of the family continued in palace service and managed the Department of Enjoyment for the Bhatnagar Raja Durga Pershad.[17]

Nigam marriage patterns also changed, though the highest-ranked Nigam family tried to maintain its tradition of importing brides from the north. In fact, from at least the 1880's, many of its brides were taken locally from poorer Nigam families who had just moved into Hyderabad from northern India. These newcomers held minor posts in the Nizam's estate or the modern administration; some had kinship ties with similarly placed Kayasths from other subcastes.[18]

In most of these cases, the Srivastava, Bhatnagar, and Nigam families tried to adapt to declining circumstances by arranging adoptions, appealing to the judicial system to retain positions and income, and changing their marriage patterns. This last could mean reducing rivalry for resources by bringing marriage partners from outside who would be less likely to claim shares according to earlier bilateral inheritance practices. It could also mean, for even poorer families, arranging marriages locally across subcaste boundaries to reduce expenditures.

Inheritance Problems Among Saksenas

Although the Saksena kin groups were somewhat larger, and the family of Bansi Raja appeared to maintain its high status, the Saksena Kayasths

15. Interviews with Roy Mahboob Narayan, Balobir Prosad and Dwarka Pershad Nigam.
16. Interviews with Dwarka Pershad Nigam and his sons and Somnath Pershad; Ali, *Anvar-i Asaifyah*, 152, for the inheritance divisions.
17. Interviews with Somnath Pershad and Dwarka Pershad Nigam. Another sign of the family's decline was inability to continue sponsoring a nearby temple.
18. Interviews with Somnath Pershad and Sham Kishori Nigam.

were also experiencing major economic difficulties by the late nineteenth century. The same problems occurred—loss of positions, reduced incomes, too few legitimate heirs, too many kinsmen competing for dwindling resources. Even in Bansi Raja's case, members of his kin group experienced the difficulties characteristic of the time and adopted strategies to counter them.

Bansi Raja, that colorful representative of the old Mughlai bureaucracy, retained much of his influence by mediating between the old and new administrations. Yet his duties and relation to the Diwan changed towards the end of the nineteenth century, decreasing his power considerably. Salar Jung's establishment in 1869 of a separate administrative division for the Nizam's personal estate (the *jagirs*, the household departments, and the troops) did not at first alter Bansi Raja's power; he continued to report directly to Salar Jung. In 1884, after Salar Jung's death, the Managing Board was set up for the Nizam's estate, and at that time Bansi Raja lost much of his autonomy. There was an inquiry in 1886 into Bansi Raja's expenditures for the palace and an attempt to control them; this was instigated by Salar Jung II as part of his reform efforts.[19]

Bansi Raja had organized the Regular Forces and remained head *serrishtahdar,* but later changes rendered his role largely ceremonial. He (or his son Keshav Pershad or nephew Sri Pershad) continued to distribute the troops' salaries from his Husaini Alam gateway and to lead the military forces in the Muharram Langar procession.[20] But when the Central Treasury was established in 1888, *serrishtahdars,* commanders, and troopers were paid directly from it, cutting out the *serrishtahdar's* major source of power. In the 1890's, reorganizations placed the Regular Forces firmly under the modern administration.[21]

The death of Salar Jung I marked a turning point in Bansi Raja's career. He himself wrote of the changed regime in 1884 as though his career were over. In a brief poem commemorating the accession of Nizam Mahbub Ali Khan and Diwan Salar Jung II, he poignantly contrasted the young Nizam and Diwan with their faithful servant the writer, who was about to die.[22] Bansi Raja, however, had been titled Raja in 1883, and Mahbub Nawazwant (beloved of the Nizam Mahbub Ali Khan) not until 1885 or 1886.[23] He was a literary figure and a favorite of the young Nizam. To outside observers, his status appeared equal to that of Raja Shiv Raj,

19. Salar Jung II, *Confidential Memorandum,* repr. of memorandum to the Resident, Sept. 18, 1886, App. I, 87 (SJL).
20. Interviews with Nar Har Raj and Mahender Raj Suxena and Satguru Pershad.
21. See Chapter 7.
22. Girdhari Pershad, "Maktubat-i Muazzamah," in *Kulliyat,* 28–30.
23. Khan, *Tuzuk,* II (Nobles), 413–414.

and he functioned similarly on public occasions in the city, often named by the government to represent the Hindus of Hyderabad on matters of public controversy.[24]

But Bansi Raja's private affairs in the last two decades of the century were marked by conflict. Some of his nearest relatives contended for his positions and property; the situation was aggravated by the deaths of his sons, leaving him without a son several times near the end of his life. The rivalry was so great that some attribute the death of his first son to it. Bansi Raja had only two surviving children from his first wife: a son, Keshav Pershad, and a daughter. The daughter married into an old Hyderabad family (descended from Sabha Chand), and her son, Durga Pershad, became a bitter enemy of Keshav Pershad. The popular tale of their enmity begins with a beautiful dancing girl and ends with murder: when Keshav Pershad rode out on the lead elephant in the Muharram Langar procession in 1887, as head *serrishtahdar* of the Regular Forces, Durga Pershad had him pushed off and he died. He did fall from the elephant and die that day, though other stories attribute his death to love or sunstroke.[25] Whatever the cause, Bansi Raja's only son was dead and bad feelings within the family were so intense that his daughter's son could be suspected of murder.

Although Bansi Raja's second wife was bearing him sons, the first two died in infancy and the third and fourth were sickly children. The genealogy in Figure 11 illustrates his predicament.[26] In about 1890, after he

24. For example, the committee to consider whether state scholarships to England might properly be awarded to Hindus, on which Raja Shiv Raj and Bansi Raja were the two Hindu members: [Naidoo], *Hyderabad in 1890 and 1891*, 6, 9, and Rao, *Bustan*, III, 561. Along with Malwalas, Bansi Raja was on the managing committee for the Ripon Memorial Meeting (*Hyderabad Ripon Memorial Meeting* [Hyderabad, 1884?], 10), and he had personal immunity from the judicial system (*The Muhammadan*, Feb. 24, 1896, CC).

25. A fuller version is this. The dancing girl arrived in Hyderabad and offered her services to the highest bidder. Durga Pershad put up 90,000 rupees; the young Nizam put up 90,500 rupees; but Keshav Pershad won her with 100,000 (one lakh) rupees, giving her the name Lakhi. He celebrated his victory with a splendid party at Keshav Bagh in 1882, and Lakhi danced at it. Having successfully outbid the Nizam, Keshav Pershad aspired to the vacant Diwanship after the death of Salar Jung I in 1883. Here his rival was the Khatri noble Kishen Pershad, grandson of Chandu Lal. Although his uncle Maharajah Narinder Bahadur was also a leading contender for the Diwanship, Kishen Pershad believed he could become Diwan. He conspired with Durga Pershad, suggesting that if Keshav Pershad were to die, Durga Pershad would inherit all of Bansi Raja's possessions; they would both benefit. For these reasons. Durga Pershad had Keshav Pershad pushed off the elephant. Some say that the Nizam took Lakhi away, and just as the elephant passed the residence in which she was being kept, Keshav Pershad gazed into her eyes longingly and died. Others say that it was, after all, a time of fasting and a very hot day, so that the most probable cause of his fall and death was sunstroke. Interviews with Vinayak Pershad, Mahender Raj Suxena and Satguru Pershad.

26. Only two of Bansi Raja's 13 siblings survived to marry, a brother and a sister. His

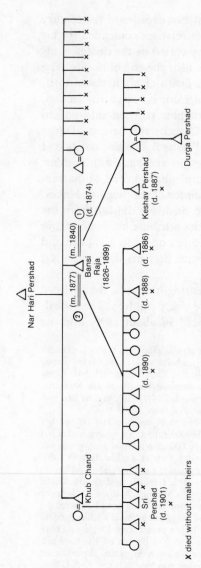

11: The genealogy of Bansi Raja

x died without male heirs

had lost the first two sons by his second wife, Bansi Raja took his third and fourth sons by her (aged six and five) on a pilgrimage to Puri and Benares to ensure their protection and survival. The elder boy became ill and died on the way to Puri; Bansi Raja took his surviving son, also ailing, to his guru in Benares, Swami Bhaskaranand Saraswati. The Swami urged him to find a suitable bride for the boy immediately, so that he himself could perform the marriage and *bismillah* ceremonies. A Saksena family there from Bhopal with an infant daughter was found and the marriage performed; the young bride and her parents accompanied the pilgrimage party back to Hyderabad.[27] The young bridegroom survived; and Bansi Raja sired one more son before his death in 1896. By 1893 Bansi Raja had two living sons again, and two contemporary publications eulogized him as leader of the Saksenas and the central figure in terms of kinship.[28]

The significance of this story lies in the fact that when Bansi Raja sought a bride for his young son he chose to bring a Saksena girl from Bhopal—the "first bride from outside." This was a marked departure from prevailing marriage patterns among the Hyderabad Saksenas.[29] In the story as told above, the idea of the Benares marriage is attributed to Bansi Raja's guru, after their arrival there. But an official document from Bansi Raja to the Diwan had requested that arrangements be made for his trip to Benares for his son's marriage, so his intention was fixed beforehand.[30] The old man must have much distrusted his Hyderabad affines and determined to bring in an outside family, without sons, in order to acquire relatives completely under his control.

Yet the positions Bansi Raja had commanded were no longer essential to the state or bountiful. In his *serrishtahs,* problems were evident by the 1890's: men were being dismissed and disinherited.[31] Bansi Raja's

---

younger brother Khub Chand sired five children, but all four sons died without heirs. Bansi Raja first married in about 1840, when he was 14 and his bride five. From the 1850's to the 1890's he sired 16 children, only seven of whom lived to marry. Raj, *Dard-i Baqi,* 12–15; Pershad, *Hiyat-i Baqi Manzum,* gives a genealogy.

27. Raj, *Dard-i Baqi,* 32–33.

28. Pershad, *Hiyat-i Baqi Manzum,* and Chand, *Kul Kayasth Nar Nai,* 107–112.

29. Interviews with Nar Har Raj, Prithvi Raj, and Gurucharan Das Saxena.

30. See the letters to and from Girdhari Pershad, starting Dec. 26, 1895, to make arrangements with the Hyderabad government and the Resident. He traveled in grand style, taking some 200 persons to Benares for the wedding; the Diwan's private secretary described him to the Resident as "a very old and respected citizen of Hyderabad." FCS, installment 32, list 6, serial no. 108.

31. A petitioner in 1895 stated that the places of his deceased uncle and brother as accountants in the *serrishtahs* of Bansi Raja had been left vacant and that he had not been given either place; he asked for a position in the Regular or Irregular Forces in Bansi Raja's *serrishtah.* The reply was that vacancies were not being filled. Another petition from

positions were transferred to his son Narsing Raj after his death, but they were transferred "as a mark of patronage to old families" and "in compensation for Baqi's [Bansi Raja's] work."[32] They had become largely ceremonial, though they were still salaried positions. Bansi Raja's sons were minors, and evidently there were continuing internal disputes between members of his family and with his affines.[33] Bansi Raja's sons-in-law and grandsons-in-law were moving from the positions in which he had placed them and embarking upon new careers, another indication of the diminished resources.[34] The sons-in-law who had come after 1860 were not involved in contention for the Mughlai positions Bansi Raja had accumulated.

Others in the Husaini Alam Saksena kin group lost positions entirely or became indebted. The Wala Jahi family, transferred to the Nizam's service after 1857, was headed in the late nineteenth century by Govind Pershad. One of the traditional Mughlai *serrishtahdars* picked by Salar Jung to mediate within the military administration, Govind Pershad was also a noted Urdu poet and participant in the literary activities sponsored by Bansi Raja and others.[35] But as with Bansi Raja, literary prominence did not mean economic security. The military *serrishtah* which Govind Pershad held, the Lines of Monsieur Raymond, was part of the Irregular Forces and subject to increasing regulation in the 1890's. The family also lost its *jagir* in the 1890's; lapsed to the Nizam in 1856, it had been put under the Nizam's personal estate sometime after 1869. Later, it went successively to the Accountant-General, the Secretary of the Army and Mansabs, and the Private Secretary of the Prime Minister. In 1892 the

---

three artisans (a painter, a coppersmith, and an ironsmith) once employed in Raja Girdhari Pershad's workshops stated that after Bansi Raja's death the workshops were broken up and put under the Grants Department and then into the miscellaneous *serrishtah*; they had been dismissed and sought reinstatement. FCS, installment 22, list 3, serial no. 11, file L5/a168, and installment 39, list 10, serial no. 137, file L5/a48.

32. Raj, *Dard-i Baqi,* 39.

33. Bansi Raja's brother's son Sri Pershad managed the properties and positions after Bansi Raja's death in 1896 until his own death in 1901: Khan, *Tuzuk,* II (Nobles), 222. Sri Pershad was cousin-brother to the young sons of Bansi Raja, but the relationship appears to have been a bad one. There are references to Nar Singh Raj and Mahbub Raj, Bansi Raja's young sons, as "real brothers," in contrast to "brother-enemies, like some": Nar Singh Raj, *Armaghan-i Mahbub* (Hyderabad, 1932), 60. One source states that after Bansi Raja's death, the estate was managed by "incapable and unworthy" persons: Mahender Raj Suxena, "Chand Kayasth Shora," 14. These references may be to Sri Pershad or to continuing problems with affines.

34. See Chapter 5. Narayan Das became an advisor to Muslim *jagirdars* and placed his son in the Accountant General's office. Kishen Lal and Dan Chand became associated with the Paigah service and the Accountant General's office respectively, and Debi Pershad also moved into the Accountant General's office. Chapter 13 will discuss this trend.

35. Narayan, *Vinay Govind,* 1–3; Hashimi, *Dakhini Hindu,* 67.

Wala Jahi *jagir*, still managed by the Saksena family, went under the new Ecclesiastical Department (presumably because the major annual expenditure was for the death commemoration of the first Nawab of Arcot). The Ecclesiastical Department took the administrative position away from the Hindu Wala Jahi family and confiscated its small personal *jagir*, granted as payment. Govind Pershad appealed this decision from 1895 on, evidently without success.[36]

Another Husaini Alam Saksena family, that of Isri Pershad, earned some 1,258 rupees a month as a modernizing military *serrishtahdar* in the 1870's. This family had established a temple in its residence and received an income from the state for that, too. Before the death of Isri Pershad in 1894, the duties had passed down twice within the family. But Isri Pershad left no son (he had adopted one, but the boy predeceased him). Despite the presence of two sons-in-law, the Prime Minister reclaimed the positions for the state and auctioned almost all the property to pay outstanding debts. Isri Pershad's two daughters were given 100 and 125 rupees per month. And "thus the name of a family whose ancestors served the State faithfully . . . was erased from history."[37] That was not quite true, for at least one branch of the family continued in an illegitimate line, through a son who was apparently unable to establish legal claim to the family positions.

Raja Mohan Lal, another Husaini Alam Saksena and holder of both household and military positions in the Nizam's estate, had become indebted by the end of the century.[38] Conflict occurred within this family in the 1890's as Mohan Lal's elder son, Jwala Pershad, left his Saksena wife and family for a Muslim woman and became a Muslim. The younger son, Raja Bala Pershad, inherited the positions, the debts, and Jwala Pershad's Hindu children to bring up in the Husaini Alam residence.[39]

In Shahalibanda, the loss of positions and indebtedness marked the

36. For the *jagir's* transfer among Diwani departments, see Rao, *Bustan*, I, 316–317. The decision to take the *jagir* and Govind Pershad's appeal of the decision are in FCS, installment 30, list 3, serial no. 15, letters covering 1895–1899.

37. Khan, *Tuzuk*, II (Nobles), 75–76. When one of Isri Pershad's daughter's husbands died in the early twentieth century, his *mansab* was released to his brother but only after the customary reduction had taken effect, decreasing the income to 92 rupees per month with half of it committed to the widow's maintenance for the rest of her life: interview with Banarsi Das Pilibhit Saxena.

38. Interview with Gurucharan Das Saxena, and the Debt Commission case file with him.

39. Jwala Pershad was a brilliant scholar of Persian and Arabic and a noted poet whose knowledge was proverbial among the Saksenas. His Muslim son also became a poet and was known to the Saksenas. For Jwala Pershad: interviews with Shakamber Raj Saxena and Gurucharan Das Saxena; Mahender Raj Suxena, "Chand Kayasth Shora," 11. For the inheritance, Muntakhab Mansabdaran, 1345 F. no. 128, Persian section R1 (APSA), where Bala Pershad's *mansab* of 75 rupees a month went to his son in 1935.

noble family of Hira Lal at this time. Married with Husaini Alam Saksenas, Hira Lal had inherited a *jagir* and *serrishtahdar* positions (in the
Irregular Forces and with the Chandu Lal *peshkari* family) from his
father-in-law. At his death during the Diwanship of Salar Jung I, his *jagir*
was changed into a *mansab,* though the military and *peshkari* duties were
transferred to Sohan Lal, eldest of his three sons. Hira Lal's other two
sons held military *serrishtahdar* positions. Despite special favors because
of their close relationship to the *peshkari* family,[40] the brothers became
heavily indebted. In 1898, they appealed to the Prime Minister (then
Vikar ul Umra II of the Paigah family) to prevent execution of a warrant
against them, pleading insolvency and pledging half of Sohan Lal's salary
to their creditors. Their debt was 15,000 rupees, and the family's only
asset was its residence. Orders staying execution of the warrant were
issued to the Judicial Department,[41] but the family had lost resources
and status. When the youngest son died in 1898 without sons, his position
was merged into the Irregular Forces office. When Sohan Lal died in
1899, a much-reduced *mansab* payment continued to his two sons, but
the duties went under supervision of the Accountant General and the
Irregular Forces office.[42]

Other Saksenas in Shahalibanda, once among the respectable families
for purposes of marriage, died out or disappeared from the genealogies
and histories of the Husaini Alam Saksena kin group. Khazanchi Tulja
Ram, Sital Pershad Khurram, and Bichu Lal Tamkin and their descendants were not included on either of two lists of Saksena men published
in the 1890's; neither list included any of the *suratval* Saksenas.[43] Yet
Tulja Ram was a *jagirdar*; Sital Pershad and Bichu Lal, contemporaries
of Bansi Raja and famous poets, both held good positions.[44] These three
men (or their sons) are supposed to have married or left children by
non-Saksenas, and from the late nineteenth century their families began
intermarrying with those in the "other" or *suratval* marriage network in
Shahalibanda.

40. Khan, *Tuzuk,* II (Nobles), 417–418. They had been exempted from some administrative changes on special orders of Maharajah Narinder Bahadur: FCS, installment 11,
list 1, serial no. 42, file n4/c1.
41. FCS, installment 22, list 3, serial no. 14, file L5/a29.
42. Khan, *Tuzuk,* II (Nobles), 418.
43. Pershad, *Hiyat-i Baqi Manzum*; Chand, *Kul Kayasth Nar Nai.*
44. Sital Pershad earned 40 rupees a month in 1900 as *serrishtahdar* of the tambulkhana,
the Sarf-i Khas department of perfumes and pan (betel leaf) that fell in Bansi Raja's area:
Khan, *Tuzuk,* II (Poets), 58. Bichu Lal was a well-known *hakim* and tutor to Maharajah
Kishen Pershad: Hashimi, *Dakhini Hindu,* 40. For Khazanchi Tulja Ram, see Ali, *Hyderabad Under Sir Salar Jung,* I, app. B, xlii; and Muntakhab Mansabdaran, Register 2,
no. 831, *muntakhab* (award) no. 1, *serrishtah* of Shiv Raj (APSA).

Among the lower-status Shahalibanda Saksenas, those who came in the nineteenth century, there were similar signs of decreasing economic resources. One man had come at mid-century and managed a stable of forty horses for a new military unit of the Paigahs. Although he was able to pass the position on to his son, the horses were reduced to twenty-two. Two men in the same family had secured *mansabs* upon arrival, while kinsmen who came slightly later became shareholders in a single *mansab* from the Paigahs.[45] Among the Kayasths in Shahalibanda, marriages beyond orthodox boundaries (and conversion to Islam) increased in the late nineteenth and early twentieth centuries as the poverty there deepened.[46]

It was at this time (1899) that an account of the Kayasths included a definition of illegitimacy explicitly focused on the right to inherit. The writer, a local Saksena, said: "And the ruling of religion is thus, if he takes a non-Kayasth girl, the offspring is called 'suratval' and there is no legal definition for such a one [he cannot inherit]."[47]

In case after case, Saksena families in both Husaini Alam and Shahalibanda lost some or all of their hereditary positions and incomes. Appeals to the government and efforts to have sons-in-law or other kinsmen recognized as successors did not succeed. Despite Bansi Raja's partial association with the modern administration, neither he nor others in his kin group made the transition directly to Western education and a modern administrative position before the twentieth century. Most Saksena families focused their efforts upon attempts to retain Mughlai positions, and they avoided marriage alliances which threatened inheritances. Thus Bansi Raja sought an outside bride, without brothers, for his young son, and lines of allegedly impure descent were relegated to the *suratval* category.

Downfall of the Paigah Nobles and the Gaurs

The Gaur Kayasths of Shahalibanda had prospered because the Paigah nobles protected them from Salar Jung I's tentative reforms. The Gaurs had formed a single kin group; the allocation of positions within the Paigah estate had been controlled by Balmukund, head of the dominant family. These decisions had been confirmed by the head of the Paigah

---

45. Interviews with Manohar Raj Saxena and Roy Mahboob Narayan.

46. Cases in the family of Roshen Chand, a colorful *serrishtahdar* who named his sons Munir Chand and Iqbal Chand, and the conversion of Jaganath Pershad to Islam (he was so like a Muslim in his learning and manners that he became a *moulvi*) are well known instances: interviews with Roy Mahboob Narayan and Benkat Prasad.

47. Fateh Chand, "Kaifiyat Ibtida-i Kayast," in *Dabdabah-i Asafi,* II, no. 7 (1899), 37 (translated from the Urdu).

family without apparent difficulty. But at the end of the nineteenth century, bitter disputes between Paigah brothers and cousin-brothers produced economic strain and conflicts among the Gaurs that split the kin group.

When the Paigah noble Rafiuddin Khan died without heirs in 1877, relations between Gaurs and Paigahs became complex and uncertain. Rafiuddin Khan's will awarded his share of the estate to the two sons of his brother Bashir ul Mulk, boys he had apparently adopted (see Chapter VI). But his surviving brother, Rashiduddin Khan, bitterly disputed the will and the adoptions, claiming all the properties for himself and his descendants. Salar Jung attempted to arbitrate, but before he could reach a decision, both Rashiduddin Khan and the elder adopted son of Rafiuddin Khan, Waziruddin Khan, died (in 1881). Salar Jung divided the Paigah estate in 1882, awarding most of Rafiuddin Khan's share to the surviving adopted son, Asman Jah.[48] In effect, this settlement split the total Paigah holdings roughly into thirds, between Asman Jah and the two sons of Rashiuddin Khan, Khurshed Jah and Vikar ul Umra.

These events caused Balmukund's family to lose its pre-eminent position in the Gaur kin group. Balmukund had died in 1879, after the death of Rafiuddin Khan but before Salar Jung had made any decision. He left his own younger brother, Jaswant Rae, appointed to serve Waziruddin Khan (the elder of the adopted sons) and Devi Pershad to serve Asman Jah (the younger). But Waziruddin Khan was childless, and after his death in 1881, Jaswant Rae served his widow, who came under the care of Asman Jah and received funds from him. Thus Devi Pershad's patron, Asman Jah, headed this branch of the Paigah family; Devi Pershad, then in his early twenties, acquired control of the Paigah positions.[49] Asman Jah, however, had inherited one-third rather than half of the estate, reducing the resource base somewhat for the Gaur Kayasths.

Conflict arose between Jaswant Rae and Devi Pershad in 1881, as their respective positions became clear; they attempted to resolve it by a legal compromise. An official document stated that Asman Jah confirmed Devi Pershad in all the positions formerly held by himself and Balmukund's line; but at the same time, Devi Pershad promised to return the positions and income derived from Balmukund to Balmukund's legal heirs, should

48. *Statement of the Claims of Koorshed Jah* . . . (SJL). Another source is R. I. R. Glancy, *Report on the Paigah Estates* (APSA), 79–83. Salar Jung was not on good terms with Rashiduddin Khan's branch of the family: references in Server-ul-Mulk, *My Life,* and Richard Temple, *Journals Kept in Hyderabad, Kashmir, Sikkim, and Nepal,* 2 vols. (London, 1887) I, 71 and passim.

49. Interviews with Onker Pershad and Jagdish Pershad; also, handwritten Persian petition by Jagdish Pershad, reciting the history of men and jobs.

there be any.[50] In 1881, Jaswant Rae had no heirs and had recently become a widower.

At this juncture, the widowed daughters of Balmukund acted decisively to secure heirs for Balmukund's lineage. They determined to find a second wife for their uncle, Jaswant Rae, so that male heirs might be produced. One, the widow of Bala Pershad (*serrishtahdar* of the Arab Ghalib Jung), also needed bridegrooms for her daughters, sons-in-law to hold that position with Ghalib Jung. The widowed daughters themselves journeyed to North India to recruit new relatives. They succeeded, bringing back a bride for Jaswant Rae and three bridegrooms. Jaswant Rae fathered two sons, born in 1884 and 1887, who contended with Devi Pershad for control of the Paigah positions in the early twentieth century.[51]

Devi Pershad, now the dominant figure among the Gaurs, attributed his rise to ability rather than to circumstances within the kin group. According to his own account, he first gained a small position in the Paigah household in 1872 and "spent 38 years being promoted," eventually being put in charge of all household arrangements by Asman Jah. Asman Jah's political stature grew, and he was appointed Diwan of Hyderabad state from 1887 to 1893. He died in 1898, orally entrusting his estate to his widow, and Devi Pershad became her personal secretary. This position was a strong one, for Asman Jah's widow was sister to the reigning Nizam, and there was a minor heir (Moinuddaula), on whose behalf she managed the estate. She died in 1904 or 1905; Moinuddaula inherited the estate and entrusted Devi Pershad with many duties. Devi Pershad was now an eminent figure in Shahalibanda, sponsoring local events and financing the construction of a water pipe for his neighborhood. He was also active in contacting North Indian Gaur Kayasth organizations.[52]

But Devi Pershad's leadership of the Gaur community and his claim to Asman Jah and Moinuddaula as patrons were disputed by Balmukund's lineage. Jaswant Rae did succeed in having Asman Jah appoint his elder son, Khub Chand, as servant to the young heir Moinuddaula.[53] (Devi Pershad had no legitimate sons whom he could assign to Moinuddaula, and he held the more powerful position with the widow of Asman Jah during Moinuddaula's minority.) Even in 1911, a budget of the Asman Jahi Paigah listed Devi Pershad as head treasurer, head of the household, and an army *serrishtahdar,* while Khub Chand appeared as an assistant

50. Persian document given me by Jagdish Pershad.
51. Interviews with Ram Mohan Roy and Jagdish Pershad.
52. Account of Devi Pershad in "Gaur Hitkari," vols. 4 and 5 (a North Indian journal) repr. in Gaur, *Tazkirah-i Sucaru Vanshi,* 30.
53. Letter from Jagdish Pershad, 1972; interview with Onker Pershad.

accountant, *serrishtahdar* of the cart and elephant departments, and, with his younger brother Kubir Chand, military *serrishtahdar*.[54] While both families held positions then, at the turn of the century, Devi Pershad continued to hold higher ones. But as Khub Chand and Kubir Chand came of age and Devi Pershad produced no heirs, the balance began to shift again.

Alliances at the end of the nineteenth century reflected these conflicts within the Gaur kin group. From the 1850's to the 1880's, new families had been brought by the Balmukund family. But after 1881, Devi Pershad became the sponsor of new families as well, and two separate kin groups developed. Devi Pershad formed one with the sons-in-law recruited by Balmukund's widowed daughters—a circumstance that owed much to economics. Originally, these three brothers had been brought by the Balmukund family to hold on to the position with the Arab commander, Ghalib Jung. But after Ghalib Jung died in 1881, the declining political power of his successor and other Arab military men became evident. It was Devi Pershad who helped the newcomers obtain jobs in the Irregular Forces and in the Paigah estate, through his patron, Asman Jah.[55]

The two kin groups drew new relatives from different places outside Hyderabad. Devi Pershad and the three brothers allied with him recruited most of their brides and grooms from Gaur families settled in Gwalior and Ujjain, bringing seven girls and five boys to Hyderabad between 1881 and 1915. The Balmukund family and its two allied families continued to draw upon the United Provinces directly, bringing five girls and two boys to Hyderabad during that same period.[56] After 1881, no marriages occurred in Hyderabad between members of the two kin groups, although before that time all Gaurs in Hyderabad had intermarried, even within prohibited degrees of relationship. This cleavage was sudden, and it was clearly based upon the competition for economic resources between Devi Pershad and Jaswant Rae's sons, Khub Chand and Kubir Chand.[57]

54. See the printed annual Paigah budgets: Muhammad Najmuddin, ed., *Taqvim 1329 H.* [1911] (Hyderabad, n.d.), 1–8, in the final list of officials.

55. Interviews with Roy Mahboob Narayan, Mahbub Rai, and Ram Mohan Roy.

56. Gaur, *Tazkirah-i Sucaru Vanshi*, 30, 67–70, 115, 117, 125, 135, 137, 143, 151, 156 and 160.

57. At least two of the three brothers brought by Balmukund's widowed daughters worked directly under Devi Pershad in the Paigah Accounts and Treasury Department, and Devi Pershad gave positions to three more newcomers with whom his group arranged marriages. Devi Pershad's second wife was brought by her brother, Kunj Bihari Lal, in about 1906, and the brother married a girl from the family of the three brothers (above). Two years later, Kunj Bihari Lal brought one of his cousin-sisters for the brother of Devi Pershad's first wife. After Devi Pershad's death in 1915, his widow secured a groom for his only daughter from a non-Hyderabad family which had married with the family of the three brothers (above) in the 1890's.

The cleavage into two kin groups was reinforced by demographic trends during the second half of the nineteenth century. There was a high rate of mortality of Gaur lineages, approaching fifty percent from 1820 to 1882. And four of the six Gaur lineages present in 1882 had died out by 1910, leaving only two families, those of Devi Pershad and the brothers Khub Chand and Kubir Chand.[58] New marriage partners had to be recruited from outside, and, given the conflict between the two families, they constructed two separate kin groups. By this time, improved systems of communications and transport in India meant a decrease in cost and time of travel between Hyderabad and other parts of India; so, from the 1880's, competition between the two families could be expressed in a broader geographic framework.

The pattern of marriages with Gaur families elsewhere shows that Hyderabad served as an outlet for younger sons. Gaur families in central and northern India sent only younger, not first sons, to Hyderabad, and they secured positions there. In the case of the marriages arranged by the widowed daughters of Balmukund in the 1880's, three younger brothers married into Hyderabad while the eldest brother remained as "zamindar [land holder] and patwari [recordkeeper]."[59] Similarly, Jaswant Rae's young bride's eldest brother remained in U.P., but another brother accompanied her to Hyderabad and married there. There is no evidence of a Hyderabad Gaur being sent outside for marriage, but some twelve brides and seven grooms came to Hyderabad between 1882 and 1915. Even in 1911, some of these men were described as "in Hyderabad temporarily for service."[60]

But the Mughlai positions in the Paigah estates for which members of the two Gaur kin groups competed at the end of the nineteenth century were changing in nature. Two processes drastically curtailed their political and economic importance. First, the Paigah nobles themselves were carrying out some administrative reforms and some degree of Westernization. Second, pressures exerted by the modern administration encouraged further modernization within the Paigah estates and also reduced the influence of the nobles within the state.

Rafiuddin Khan and Rashiuddin Khan had been noblemen in the old Mughlai tradition, but their sons and nephews acquired varying degrees of Western education and participated in the Westernizing society of late-nineteenth-century Hyderabad. Waziruddin Khan served as Salar Jung's co-regent after 1869; Salar Jung selected Asman Jah for a position in the modern administration in the same year, starting him on a career

58. Gaur, *Tazkirah-i Sucaru Vanshi*, 30–31.   59. *Ibid.*, 69.
60. *Ibid.*, 31.

which culminated in the Diwanship. Khurshed Jah had a close relationship with the British Resident in the 1870's and 1880's, using that relationship to continue the dispute between the two branches of the Paigahs.
Asman Jah was Diwan from 1887 to 1893, then Vikar ul Umra II served
as Diwan until 1901. All three Paigah nobles presided over palatial new
residences constructed in the new city and suburbs and became patrons
of Western education and hosts of lavish entertainments. As with other
nobles at this time, there were indications of financial difficulties.[61]

To the misfortune of their Gaur employees, all three Paigah estates
began to reorganize and reduce their Mughlai departments. Educational
and medical services were instituted in the *jagirs,* and Western-educated
administrators were appointed to manage each estate. Some of these administrators were from groups new to Hyderabad: for example, all three
estates employed Parsis by the 1880's. Others were from groups traditionally in Paigah service but they adapted to Western education earlier than
the Gaurs. Thus Brahmo-khatris and Maharashtrians became prominent
in the Asman Jahi and Khurshed Jahi estates, respectively.[62]

Even stronger pressures from outside the Paigah estates culminated in
actual state takeover of all three estates after the deaths of Asman Jah
(1898) and Khurshed Jah and Vikar ul Umra (1902). No family members
were put in complete charge of any Paigah estate for over twenty-five
years after.[63] Following the death of Nizam Mahbub Ali Khan and the
accession of Osman Ali Khan in 1911, all three heavily-indebted Paigah
estates went under the Court of Wards. In 1912, a special Board of
Administration under a Controller General was created to administer
them. The modern administration and the Nizam's personal estate claimed
some of the Paigah land; disputes between the three estates continued
as well.[64]

61. See the CC for Paigah entertainments and new residences at this time; one new
palace, Falaknuma, had to be given to the Nizam to pay debts.
62. For the Parsis, see Server-el-Mulk, *My Life,* 147–148, 201. For the Asman Jahi estate
(Tej Rae and Vithal Rao), see the consecutive budgets cited in notes 54 above and 66 below.
For the Khurshed Jahi estate, see *Paigah Committee Report, 1347 H.* [1929], 22–23 (APSA).
For the Brahmo-khatri and Maharashtrian earlier adaptation to Western education and
modern administrative professions, I rely on their earlier founding of schools and production of Western-style lawyers.
63. Asman Jah's widow was allowed some supervisory power until her death in 1905:
Paigah Committee Report, 36–38.
64. By this time Asman Jah's estate owed 34 lakhs rupees, Khurshed Jah's 19 lakhs,
and Vikar ul Umra's 18.5 lakhs. A series of inquiries was held to establish the rights of
the contending parties, but they had to reconcile eighteenth-century documents with the
desires of Nizam Osman Ali Khan and with Muslim inheritance law. In the meantime, the
number of wives, concubines, and resulting claimants to shares of the Paigah estate
increased. See Y. K. Sovani, *Feudal Oppression in Hyderabad* (n.p., 1939), 7–11, for a

Meanwhile, curtailment of the old Mughlai departments continued, and Asman Jahi budgets show that the Gaurs had become relatively insignificant in management of the estate. A Brahmo-khatri from a family long in Paigah service headed the Managing Committee, and his relatives and Maharashtrians held more positions than did the Gaurs. Modern administrative departments already included half the estate's positions: *talukdars, tehsildars* (subordinate revenue officials), deputy *tehsildars,* education and medical officers, and so forth.[65] These departments grew at the expense of the Mughlai sections. By 1914, most of the old *serrishtahdar* positions had been abolished, including those held by Khub Chand and Kubir Chand. By 1916, the old treasury officials were merged into the new Accounts Office.[66]

Summary

In all these cases of decline, certain common factors have been noted. Most old-city Kayasths were affected by increasing supervision of their positions, whether under the modern administration, the Nizam's personal estate, or the Paigahs, and many positions were lost. *Mansabs* and *jagirs* were divided among heirs, and even if the amounts were not reduced in transmission, a fixed amount once allocated to one man was divided among several. When the Saksena Hira Lal inherited a *mansab* of 2,640 rupees per year from his father-in-law in 1864, it was a good income; but 220 rupees per month divided among three sons was less adequate at the end of the century. His sons could not inherit from their fathers-in-law, and they provided one of many instances of indebtedness among the Kayasths.

The way in which Kayasth families controlled positions changed too. Earlier in the nineteenth century, one central figure had often informally controlled several positions, distributing them bilaterally among kinsmen and redistributing them in the next generation. By the end of the nineteenth century, such arrangements had become less common. This was partly because each position was worth less and there were fewer positions; men competed for them and were reluctant to allocate them even to close

summary of the investigations; and *Paigah Committee Report,* 68–69. The latter shows, for example, that Zafar Jung had 19 concubines, Imam Jung 21, and Khurshed Jah 28, all looked after by 41 attendants and settled in about 59 houses.

65. Najmuddin, *Taqvim 1333 H.* [1913–1914], listed 98 positions, including 18 revenue officials and 12 police officials in the *jagirs.* The elephant stables and cart department vanished; buggy and motor departments remained, headed by a Muslim.

66. Reorganizations from 1911 to 1916 resulted chiefly in cuts in the military *serrishtahs* and the *karkhanahs*: Najmuddin, *Taqvim 1329 H., Taqvim 1330 H.,* and *Taqvim 1335 H.*

relatives. The development of the modern judicial system also made demographic factors even more crucial than in the past. With the increasing subjection of hereditary grants and positions to scrutiny by the modern administration and the application of Brahmanical law to Hindu inheritance cases, sons-in-law became inadmissable as legal heirs. There was great concern to secure legitimate heirs, and many adoptions occurred, some posthumously, to retain control of positions and other resources. In the late nineteenth century, *khanahdamad* or *ghardamad,* terms used for a son-in-law who lived with his father-in-law, acquired connotations of lower status even if the man held a position. Earlier, such men had been potential heirs to whom positions could be passed bilaterally within the kin group; they had often been set up in separate residences. Patrilineal inheritance now became the legal norm, and its enforcement by the government disrupted customary practices and aggravated the Kayasths' economic problems.

All of these new circumstances emphasized the importance of family and kin group control of marriages. Conflict within families and kin groups or between descendants of varying legitimacy occurred. Sometimes adoptions and marriages brought in outsiders, persons without local kinsmen, to reduce rivalry. Men and women sought to avoid known competitors or to enhance economically beneficial connections. The conflict between Gaur families, where the widowed daughters of Balmukund and their cousin-brother tried to recover economic and social dominance from Devi Pershad, is the best example of this. There were many similar cases among the Kayasths by the end of the nineteenth century, as the kin groups tried to adapt to the unfavorable economic conditions.

CHAPTER 11

Kayasth Participation
in Public Life

The period from the 1870's into the second decade of the twentieth century was one of political, economic, and social instability for most Kayasths in Hyderabad. The new administration and the Westernizing society were expanding, offering opportunities to those who had the resources (including education) to participate in that arena. But for most of the old-city Kayasths, the environment was disruptive and constricting, one of narrowing opportunities. They were hard pressed to retain the specialized hereditary positions acquired during the previous period of Mughlai administrative expansion and consolidation. The Asthanas and some Mathurs built new kin groups based upon the modern administration and without reliance on noble status. In contrast, the Malwalas, dependent Mathurs, Bansi Raja, and many other Kayasths struggled to retain control of economic and social resources based upon the older Mughlai system. Efforts to control family and kin group boundaries sometimes failed as the positions and property that had reinforced kin group solidarity dwindled.

The changes of status by this time can be seen in the classification of Kayasths in a turn-of-the-century Hyderabad publication, a two-volume history and collection of biographies. This book listed "nobles" and "officeholders" as two separate categories; the two had been the same in Makhan Lal's comparable work of the 1820's. The nobles were those who had held high positions in the Mughlai administration, and the officeholders were the Western-educated men in the modern administration, largely newcomers to Hyderabad.[1] (See Table 16.)

1. Khan, *Tuzuk,* II. This history is particularly valuable for an analysis of the old-city Kayasths and others of their background, since it concentrated on participants in the city's

TABLE 16:
Biographies in Tuzuk-i Mahbubiyah *(1902)*

Categories	Total	Non-Muslims	Kayasths
Nobles	337	59	19
Officeholders	58	23	1
Lawyers	38	6	2
Doctors	39	4	1
Poets	100	5	4
Religious leaders	17	0	0
Moulvis	15	0	0
Total	603	97	27

Source: Ghulam Samdani Khan, *Tuzuk-i Mahbubiyah* (2 vols., Hyderabad, 1902), II. Each category is separately paginated: for example, the nobles section, pages 1–504 plus a supplement of 28 pages, is followed by an officeholders section, pages 1–74. This volume totals some 1020 pages.

The sole Kayasth officeholder in Hyderabad here was Rae Murlidhar of the Asthana family. One of the lawyers was his cousin-brother Hemchander; the other lawyer was a Srivastava Arya Samajist newcomer from North India. Of the nineteen Kayasth nobles, fully thirteen were Mathurs and twelve of them were Malwala family members.[2] The thirteenth was Lalta Pershad. The other two non-Malwala Mathurs listed were Lalta Pershad's nephews. One was the only Kayasth doctor; the other, listed as a poet, had studied English to the eighth class and worked in the Accountant General's office. The other three listed as poets were another Malwala, Bansi Raja, and a Saksena from Shahalibanda.[3]

This profile of Kayasth professional and literary activities accurately reflected the limited diversification at that time. It also pointed to two of

Mughlai culture. Few residents of Secunderabad or the new city of Hyderabad were included. Large numbers of recent immigrants appeared only in the officeholder category, and of the 23 non-Muslims there, 12 were English and 7 were Parsis.

2. The other six nobles were the Srivastava Chain Rae, the Bhatnagar Durga Pershad, and four Saksenas: Bansi Raja, his nephew Sri Pershad, Isri Pershad, and Mohan Lal. Bansi Raja was double-listed as a noble and a poet.

3. Khan, *Tuzuk*, II. No Gaurs or Nigams were included (none had been listed as nobles or leading figures in Lal, *Yadgar*, in the 1820's either, though some had been listed as *mansabdars*). The Mathur doctor was Krpa Shanker, a Hakim who knew both Western and traditional medicine; the poet was Bankipat Pershad. The Malwala poet was Bhagwan Sahae, and the other Saksena poet was Sital Pershad.

the three organized public activities in which Kayasths had become leading participants: Urdu and Persian literary activities and the Arya Samaj. The third area of participation was that of Kayasth associations. The fact that associations that were specifically Kayasth did form in Hyderabad at this time, combined with the adverse circumstances for most Kayasths, raises the question of whether or not caste unification was occurring as an adaptive strategy. Rather than focus only on the Kayasth associations, Kayasth membership and participation in all three new types of activity will be examined here.

All three activities were new and drew the Hyderabad Kayasths, at least theoretically, into organizations based outside the borders of the state. Both the Kayasth associations and the Arya Samaj utilized Western associational models to some extent. The late-nineteenth-century literary activity also relied upon new methods: the publication of journals and the extension of poetry recitations to audiences larger and more diverse than had been customary. Despite the opportunities for change implicit in all of these activities, they reflected rather than altered existing social and economic patterns among the Kayasths.

Urdu and Persian Literary Activities

Urdu and Persian literature enjoyed a renaissance in Hyderabad under Mahbub Ali Khan, Nizam and poet, who became one of the major patrons of Persian and Urdu poetry in India. Famous poets flocked to the Hyderabad court. Poetry journals were published locally, some under Kayasth management. Hyderabad poets contributed to the lively Urdu journals published in North India in the late nineteenth century. The Saksena Bansi Raja and his friend Raja Kishen Pershad, from the Khatri family of Chandu Lal, were the two major links between literary activities in Hyderabad and North India. Both men introduced poets to the Nizam and secured support for them in Hyderabad.[4]

Among the Kayasths, Bansi Raja was the leading literary figure. Renowned as one of the best Persian poets ever produced in the city, he often commemorated court functions with his own compositions. His pen name was Baqi; he was prolific, producing some thirty books and major poems.[5]

4. Among those whom Bansi Raja introduced to the Nizam was Nawab Mirza Dagh, the much-admired Delhi poet who became Hyderabad's highest-ranking poet: Ram Babu Saksena, *History of Urdu Literature* (Allahabad, 1927), 187, 199–204. As poet laureate of the Nizam, Nawab Mirza Dagh received a thousand rupees per month: *Deccan Budget*, Sept. 28, 1894 (CC).

5. Most of his compositions were privately printed and are with his descendant Nar Har

Like other poets of the time, Bansi Raja was heavily influenced by Sufi thought. This fact, in conjunction with his adherence to such literary conventions as prefacing poems with the Arabic *bismillah* and composing tributes to the Prophet Muhammad, gave him an audience as far away as Persia.[6] Other Kayasths, particularly Saksenas, enjoyed good but more local reputations.[7]

It was Bansi Raja who achieved recognition in North Indian centers of Urdu journalism. He corresponded in Persian verse with Muslim and Hindu scholars in Lucknow, Bhopal, Gwalior, and elsewhere. Some of the finest Urdu literary journals of the time were edited by Lucknow Kayasths, and Bansi Raja's connections with the Saksenas in Lucknow were particularly close.[8] Although his contacts were essentially literary, he knew men active in North Indian Kayasth politics, too. He attended the All-India Kayasth Conference (hereafter, AIKC) in 1895 in Damravan state, where he read a Persian poem he had composed for the occasion.[9]

Through Bansi Raja, other Hyderabad Kayasths participated in some of these activities. When he introduced a famed Lucknow poet, Dwarka Pershad Ufuq (a Saksena), to the Nizam, Ufuq (his pen name) was entertained by the Malwala family. Ufuq's principal local connections were with Saksena Kayasths, but he wrote Urdu biographies of Raja Shiv Raj and of Raja Murli Manohar; these and his Persian biography of Bansi Raja were published in his Urdu newspaper in Lucknow. He was very

---

Raj or with Professor Mahender Raj Suxena (who has written about the Kayasth poets of Hyderabad). One of his poems commemorated a ball at the British Residency, noting that the delicacy of formal English manners contrasted strangely with the wanton appearance of the English women, with their loose hair and makeup. He disapproved of the dancing as "embracing between those not husband and wife." A later encounter with the Residency recorded changes in dress. The *sherwani* and other new fashions had become popular, but Bansi Raja still wore the long Deccani skirted robes; when his old-fashioned court dress was likened by the Resident to that of English ladies, he replied that his dress was more similar to that of clergymen and was therefore worthy of respect. Girdhari Pershad, "Maktubat-i Muazzamah," in *Kulliyat*, 32–37, for "Dance of the Westerners"; Raj, *Dard-i Baqi*, 35, for the *sherwani* story.

6. Girdhari Pershad (Bansi Raja), *Haft Band* (Delhi, 1894–1895), written at the request of a Muslim Nawab, was praised in Persia. His Hindu devotional poem praising Krishna (written in the North Indian Hindi dialect of *braj bhasha* but in Urdu script) was prefaced by the *bismillah*: Girdhari Pershad, *Bhagvat Sar* (Hyderabad, 1890–1891).

7. See Hashimi, *Dakhini Hindu*, 44; Raj, *Dard-i Baqi*, 12–13; Mahender Raj Suxena, "Chand Kayasth Shora," 7, 11.

8. The Lucknow publisher and editor Naubat Rae Nazr, connected with the journals *Tammadun, Zamanah,* and *Adib,* put out a special journal to honor the Nizam's birthday called *Khadang-i Nazr.* Dwarka Pershad Ufuq, editor of the Lucknow newspaper *Nazm-i Akhbar,* came to Hyderabad through Bansi Raja.

9. Raj, *Dard-i Baqi*, 25–26. This is the only mention I found of the AIKC in the extensive literature by and about Bansi Raja.

active in the AIKC, writing poems calling for reformation and modernization and compiling reports of the first few annual conferences (1888 to
1890).[10]

The patronage of poetry in Hyderabad in the 1890's came primarily
from the Nizam himself and from Maharajah Kishen Pershad. The latter
sponsored a monthly publication at the turn of the century called *Dabdabah-i Asafi*. Managed by a Saksena Kayasth, the journal published the
work of Hyderabad and North Indian poets. Among them were several
Mathurs, men who were also active in the AIKC and who were the chief
poets at Mathur poetry gatherings held in the 1890's.[11] There was, then,
no simple contrast between Bansi Raja and other "traditional" Kayasths
engaging in Urdu literary activities, and a few "modern" Western-educated Mathurs supporting subcaste and caste activities. The same men
engaged in both these activities in the old city, though their personal
involvements may have emphasized one more than the other.

Kayasth Associations at the Turn of the Century

Organizational efforts based upon the status of Kayasth began in Hyderabad in the 1890's. The impetus came from outside, through Bansi
Raja and Murli Manohar and their contacts with North Indian Chitragupta Kayasths and the AIKC. Within Hyderabad, the limited success
of these efforts stressed the differences between Kayasths; the idea that
caste unification was being attempted for either instrumental or expressive
purposes at this time cannot be sustained. The efforts show instead the
continuing importance of kin groups and residential localities in social
organization.

The AIKC was organized in 1887, following the early efforts of Munshi
Kali Pershad to unify the North Indian Chitragupta Kayasths. He had
founded the Kayasth Pathshala (college) in Allahabad in 1873 as a first
step in that unification. The AIKC began to hold annual meetings, and
it encouraged the formation of provincial and local affiliates throughout
India. By 1893 there were thirteen provincial *sabhas* or societies, with

10. Pershad, *Hiyat-i Baqi Manzum*; Ufuq Centenary Committee, *Poet Laureate Late
M. Dwarka Pershad Ufuq of Lucknow* (Delhi, 1964); and ed. Bisheshwar Munnavar
Pershad, ed., *Lamat-i Ufuq* (Delhi, 1964).
11. Kishen Pershad's *Dababah-i Asafi* was managed by a Saksena, Thakur Pershad;
another journal, *Mahbub ul Kalam*, was also managed by a Saksena, Hira Lal. See Rao,
Bustan, II, 698 and passim. Some copies of these journals are in Roy Mahboob Narayan's
BGVS library; interviews with him and Hakim Vicerai.

some three hundred local branches; at least nine Kayasth journals were being published.[12]

Munshi Kali Pershad's early efforts had aimed at social reform through Sanskritization of the Kayasth community. But by the end of the nineteenth century, organizations and publications pointed somewhat tentatively toward Western education and political reform. The journal of the Kayasth Pathshala Trust, *Kayastha Samachar* (initially published in Urdu but in English from 1899), began to include articles on nationalist political activities. Topics limited to the Kayasths, such as specific social reforms, continued to be debated. Kayasth publications discussed such controversial issues as the social status of the barrister returned from England, the extent to which interdining and intermarriage reforms should be pursued, and the pros and cons of those customs which some considered degrading to Kayasths. But exhortations to wear the sacred thread and apply sandalwood powder to the forehead were matched by exhortations to move beyond a narrow concern with caste and enter modern politics.[13]

Hyderabad Kayasths were remote from these developments, both geographically and culturally. There were among them as yet no barristers back from England or promoters of Sanskritization. But members of the Malwala family who accompanied the Nizam on occasional visits to North India and participated in Hyderabad's new social life knew of the AIKC. Moreover, the Malwalas, holders of high positions in the Hyderabad administration and members of the nobility, easily won recognition from North Indian Kayasths. Raja Murli Manohar conveyed the Nizam's best wishes to the AIKC in 1889; a Delhi Mathur family publicly recognized the Malwalas as a long-lost branch; and Raja Murli Manohar was honored as President of the AIKC in 1892.[14]

12. *A Short Account of the Aims, Objects, Achievements, and Proceedings of the Kayastha Conference* (Allahabad, 1893); Ram Dyal Srivastava, "A Brief Memoir and Reminiscences of the late Munshi Kali Prasad," in *Kayastha Samachar,* IV, no. 2 (1901), 174–176; and Lucy Carroll, "Caste, Social Change, and The Social Scientist," 63–84.

13. Pershad, *Ittehad al Akhwan,* is an exhaustive discussion of customs and their origins, combined with pleas for "Sanskritization." I am aware of the objections of Carroll (cited in preceding note) to the change of orientation suggested by William L. Rowe ("Mobility in the Nineteenth-century caste system," in Singer and Cohn, *Structure and Change,* 204–205). But I view her article as furnishing details which qualify rather than contradict his brief references. The contents of the *Kayastha Samachar* (later titled also the *Hindustan Review*) from 1901–1906 include articles on the Indian National Congress and Sir Syed Ahmed Khan; contributors included Lala Lajpat Rae, Tej Bahadur Sapru, Alfred Nundy, and Annie Besant. In the book reviews, English books outnumbered Urdu and Hindi ones.

14. For the Delhi Mathur family, see [Lal], *A Short Account of the Life of Rai Jeewan Lal Bahadur,* 1–7. For Murli Manohar's role in the AIKC, see *A Short Account . . . of the Kayastha Conference,* 9.

Raja Murli Manohar's sudden North Indian prominence appears to have had some institutional base in Hyderabad. The AIKC publication listed a Hyderabad provincial *sabha* in 1893; and the Malwala Palace school was listed as a Kayasth school.[15] The Malwala family donated large sums to the AIKC. Murli Manohar even secured donations of a semi-official nature from Hyderabad state by asking the Diwan for a personal contribution of one hundred rupees each year.[16] Termed, in 1893, the "feudatory noble of His Highness the Nizam," Murli Manohar was featured in a North Indian Kayasth journal in 1896, and his English pamphlets on social reform were published and circulated in the mid-1890's.[17] In 1897, Murli Manohar's son Raja Inder Karan was elected president of the AIKC.[18] A typical North Indian view of the Hyderabad Kayasths was that of a fund-collecting committee for the Allahabad Kayasth Pathshala, which in 1901 wrote of its forthcoming visit to Hyderabad: ". . . it expects to achieve great success in its efforts to collect funds . . . from the existence in the Nizam's dominions of a large number of Kayasths in well-to-do and flourishing condition, pre-eminent . . . is Murli Manohar . . . [and his] son Inder Karan."[19]

While English-language Kayasth publications mentioned only the Malwala nobles from Hyderabad, Urdu reports provided further information. The Saksena Bansi Raja was also known to North Indian Kayasths and to the AIKC, as has been mentioned. And according to one of the Urdu reports there were actually three groups in Hyderabad in 1892: the Kayasth Sadr Sabha, the Mathur Sabha, and the Srivastava Sabha. The report elaborated as follows:

According to the opinion of last year, because circumstances of the Hyderabad province were not known and it was thought there were no men of the brotherhood in Hyderabad save in the city, the city sabha was affiliated as the Sadr Sabha of Hyderabad . . . In place of a provincial sabha therefore it is really only a local

15. *A Short Account . . . of the Kayastha Conference,* 2-3.
16. Murli Manohar gave 1,000 rupees for social reform activities: *A Short Account . . . of the Kayastha Conference,* 5. For his 1893 solicitation of the Diwan Asman Jah, FCS, installment 11, list 1, serial no. 144, file Nc/c2 (the Private Secretary refused to make it a regular annual contribution).
17. *A Short Account . . . of the Kayastha Conference,* 3, for the quotation; "Rajai Rajman Maharaj Nawazwant Raja Murli Manohar Bahadur, Asaf Jahi of Hyd., Dn.," in B. Avadh Behari Lal, ed., *Kayastha* (Agra), I, no. 3 (1896), 1-3. Murli Manohar's book *The Industries of Ancient India* includes essays on: early marriage, a proposed poorhouse and orphanage, and local funds for education.
18. His hasty election was the result of dissension among the North Indian Kayasths. A telegram was sent to him as a compromise candidate, though he was then barely out of his teens, and he arrived late. Comment by S. Sinha, ed., *Kayastha Samachar,* VIII, no. 6 (1903), 613-614.
19. *Kayastha Samachar,* IV, no. 2 (1901), 169.

sabha. But in Hyderabad, three sabhas have been discovered: the Kayasth General Sabha; the Rae Sabha, or Mathur Sabha; the Srivastava Sabha . . . Of these, only the Mathur Sabha is serving the community . . . There is the Dharmwant Oriental College and the youth are keeping away from wine; a Young Mens Improvement Society has been started in which lectures are given and books are being kept . . . There has been no report from the Srivastava Sabha because the secretary has left Hyderabad . . . Save for the Mathurs, there is no interest in teaching English to the children.[20]

This first, supposedly general Sadr Sabha was limited in both membership and functions; in fact, it appears to be the same as the Mathur Sabha. Raja Murli Manohar was named president of the Hyderabad Sadr Sabha, with Munshi Raj Bali and Munshi Lakshmi Narayan (both Mathurs) as secretaries.[21] Comparing the lists of local officers, conference delegates, and subscribers to the *Kayastha Conference Gazette* (Urdu), it is evident that a few Western-educated Mathurs were the active force. Further, these men were relatives by marriage, members of Lalta Pershad's kin group.[22]

The functions of the general organization evident from the only surviving minutes of this early Kayasth Sadr Sabha were rather narrow. Their sole concern was with the presentation of the Nizam's annual birthday address on behalf of the Kayasth community in 1898 and 1899. Along with preparation of the speech, Murli Manohar wanted the *sabha* to collect funds to establish a poorhouse memorializing the Nizam's birthday. Just before the birthday, the *sabha* put out a circular informing Kayasths of the date and place of tribute presentation, asking all to come in the court dress of *jama nima* (long-skirted costume) and *dastar*.[23] In 1899, the Nizam replied to the Kayasths as follows: "You have had an uninterrupted connection with the Muslims both in State service and social intercourse . . . I always view your loyal services and submissive behavior with an appreciative eye."[24] Such mutual professions of loyalty

20. *Report Kayasth Sadr Sabha Hind,* (n.p., 1893), 22, translation from 51–52.
21. *Report Kayasth Sadr Sabha,* 3. A later reference named Raja Shiv Raj as president of the Kayasth Sadr Sabha, with Murli Manohar and Raja Girdhari Pershad (Bansi Raja) as vice-presidents: "Qaumi Report," *KH,* II, nos. 1–4 (1942), 16.
22. *Report Kayasth Sadr Sabha,* 3, 51, 89–91, and pt. 3, app. 3, for delegates. Murli Manohar, Janaki Chand, Bhagwan Sahae, Inder Karan, and Bhasker Pratab were listed as delegates to annual conferences; Raja Bhagwan Sahae, Raja Shiv Raj, Murli Manohar, Gur Pratab, and Janaki Chand were listed as subscribers to the *Gazette.*
23. The minutes, in draft and final form, were kept by the secretary, Krpa Shanker, and preserved by his son, Hakim Vicerai. All members mentioned in these minutes were Mathurs.
24. This English translation is in Kadiri Syed Murtaza, *Translation of a Review on the Addresses presented to H. H. Asif Jah . . .* (Hyderabad, 1899), 18 (APSA). The Kayasth addresses are in Ghulam Samdani Khan, *Darbar-i Asaf* (Hyderabad, 1900), 1221, 1257.

and appreciation were major features of the Nizam's birthday celebrations in 1898 and 1899; after that the custom declined.[25]

The Sadr Sabha appeared to have no strong local organization or ongoing activities. A major book on Kayasth social reform, published in 1895, printed a lengthy letter from Murli Manohar but did not include Hyderabad in its detailed survey of local attitudes towards specific reforms. Hyderabad Kayasths were not recorded either as agreeing to interdining or being opposed to it, though many Kayasths from other parts of India were named on both sides of the controversy.[26] Local recollections of a Mathur young mens' reform society at this time credit it with little activity and a brief span of existence.[27] It was not included in Kayasth reform publications.

A major center of Kayasth social reform activity in the 1890's was Gwalior, home of Munshi Kamta Pershad, editor of the *Kayasth Hitkari* and general secretary of the Kayasth Temperance Society. Other Hyderabad Kayasths, initially Saksenas, figure in his publications.[28] A series of reform pamphlets listed Kayasth abstainers and printed reports from provincial temperance societies. A Hyderabad Temperance Society, known locally as the Bazm-i Tehzib, was started in 1894; it was a Husaini Alam group led by young teachers. The group submitted a rather frank report for inclusion in an 1898 publication that listed abstainers from wine, *bhang* (hemp), and opium; its report was the only one that did not list meetings or converts to abstinence. It estimated that perhaps ten or fifteen of a community of over a thousand could be termed "temperates." Under the heading "social functions held without liquor," the Hyderabad entry read "not a one." Under the heading "Holi celebration," the Hyderabad comment was that local Kayasths had drunk very heavily. No attendance

25. Leonard, "Cultural Change and Bureaucratic Modernization," in Joshi, *Studies*, 453–454.

26. Pershad, *Ittehad al Akhwan*, II, 192–194, for his letter. Dated 1894, it advocated all possible reforms but at a later date, following educational preparation. See *Ittehad*, 111, 114, 173 for three lists: of individuals in favor of reform; individuals in favor of reform listed by place; and individuals opposed to reform listed by place.

27. Interviews with Ramchander Narayan and Hakim Vicerai. Whether they were the Sadr Sabha or the Mathur Sabha or a more specific reform group, they were kinsmen to Lalta Pershad.

28. Munshi Kamta Pershad's temperance reform series included not only annual reports, but such pamphlets as the Kayasth Temperance Societies Hind's *Report Khandan Parhezgaran* (Agra, 1899), *Report Taqriban Khushi* (Agra, 1899), and *Holi Report Hindustan* (Agra, 1900). These listed Kayasths who abstained from wine, *bhang* (hemp), and opium, both in general (the first report) and particularly on happy occasions and Holi (second and third reports respectively). Thakur Pershad and Bherun Pershad, Husaini Alam Saksenas, were listed as president and secretary: in Kayasth Temperance Societies Hind, *General Report 1898* (Agra, 1899), 22, and *General Report 1899* (Agra, 1900), 32.

figures were given, and no lectures were reported.[29] In an 1899 report only two names were given as pledged abstainers, one Saksena and one Srivastava. Although the active members of this small temperance society were all Saksenas and Srivastavas, the only donor of money to the Gwalior-based society was Raja Murli Manohar, one of fifty-three donors listed in 1898; he gave again in 1899.[30]

In the 1890's, then, Mathur Kayasths led by Raja Murli Manohar were organizing, essentially on a subcaste basis. It was they who affiliated with the AIKC as the Hyderabad branch. The Srivastava Sabha mentioned in national publications had apparently lapsed by 1893; it had depended upon those Western-educated newcomer Srivastavas who did not settle in Hyderabad. The small Husaini Alam temperance society was the first issue-oriented local Kayasth organization, led by young and relatively unknown men.[31]

While the leadership of the Mathur Sabha had greater potential, with educational and financial resources and a reform goal, it was evidently sidetracked by the celebrations of the Nizam's birthday into representing Kayasths in appeals to the Nizam. This function could have united local Kayasths under Mathur leadership, if other and poorer Kayasths had seen the *sabha* as a potentially useful vehicle for their interests. But there is no contemporary evidence that the organization in fact served Kayasths other than Mathurs, and by 1905 it explicitly spoke only for them in its birthday address.[32] Even among the Mathurs, a small group of Western-educated kinsmen formed the working core of the group. Their interests may have inclined more towards social reform and the all-India organization than to the local and limited appeals to the Nizam on his birthday; but the *sabha*'s local efforts at reform were evidently limited by Raja Shiv Raj's disapproval of reform efforts among Mathurs.

These Kayasth organizations did not recruit members from the caste as a whole, and their goals were not directly concerned with the caste. The Mathur Sabha and the Sadr Sabha, actually the same group of men, were concerned locally with the Dharmvant Anglo-Vernacular School and the

29. *General Report 1898,* 19–22; the secretary noted that on every happy occasion wine was drunk and temperates were teased and cursed. An old photograph of the seven members of the Bazm-i Tehzib is in the possession of a descendant, Gurucharan Das Saxena.

30. *General Report 1898,* 14, 27, and *General Report 1899,* 26–27, mention donations for social reform from Murli Manohar.

31. One was the Arya Samaj leader Gaya Pershad, whose efforts will be discussed shortly.

32. Thus in 1905, on the occasion of Nizam Mahbub Ali Khan's Silver Jubilee, the "Kayasth" address began, "We, the sacrificing hereditary slaves, Mathur Kayasths of Hyderabad, scions and relations of Raja Shiv Raj Dharmvant . . .": Government of Hyderabad, *Majmua Sipasnamajat o Ishadat-i Khusrana* (Hyderabad [1936]), 92–94.

annual celebration of the Nizam's birthday. When they directed themselves to the AIKC, Raja Murli Manohar and the names of Raja Shiv Raj
and perhaps Bansi Raja were put forward. Locally they were the same
Mathurs active in the Urdu and Persian activities, where Bansi Raja
functioned importantly as a leader and participants came from diverse
castes and communities. Finally, the few Srivastavas and Saksenas active
in the temperance movement began work with the Gwalior Kayasth
Temperance Society, but they soon shifted their efforts to the local Arya
Samaj.

Arya Samaj Leaders and Followers

The Arya Samaj ultimately involved a different set of Kayasths, for
newly arrived Srivastava leaders recruited members from the poorer and
allegedly *suratval* families in the city. Illegitimacy and poverty facilitated
the recruitment. In the first decades of Arya Samaj activity in Hyderabad,
the movement was anti-caste and emphasized purification and social
reform. The early leaders were newcomers, without family traditions of
service to the Nizam.

Although the Arya Samaj in Hyderabad state was first established in
the Marathwara districts in 1891, a branch was begun in the city in 1892
by newcomers from North India. Kayasths, Maharashtrian Brahmans,
and Marwaris were prominent early members. The three early leaders
most effective in reaching local Kayasths were all Srivastavas, self-made
men breaking away from relatives and developing careers associated with
the modern administration and professions. Two of the three were clerks
in the Military Accounts Office; the third was a leading lawyer of the
High Court. They had not known one another before arrival in Hyderabad, and there they related to each other chiefly through the Arya Samaj;
they did not reside in the same locality or become kinsmen.

These three Arya Samaj Kayasth preachers differed in their initial contacts with local Kayasths and in their places of residence in the city, but
they worked with the same lower class and/or *suratval* population. Their
lack of commitment to the established patterns governing interaction between Kayasths in Hyderabad was evident in several ways. They ignored
or defied kin group boundaries and appealed to those for whom religious
and social reform held special promise. They refused to conform to many
local social customs, and all three educated their sons in Arya Samaj
schools outside of Hyderabad. The basis of their appeal to their *suratval*
converts is clear from a review of their careers.

The most prominent of the early leaders was Rae Kunwar Bahadur, a Dusre Srivastava from the Lucknow area. Kunwar Bahadur arrived in Hyderabad in the 1880's and moved into the Mathur locality through friendship with a recently arrived Mathur family from Lucknow. Trained as a lawyer, he began his career in the districts, but he soon returned to Hyderabad and rented a house in the new city. He became one of the leading lawyers at the High Court and one of the most popular speakers of the day.[33] While some Mathurs were said to be influenced by Kunwar Bahadur, Raja Shiv Raj was opposed to the Arya Samaj, and no Mathurs joined it.[34] Kunwar Bahadur's converts came instead from among the poorer Srivastavas and Saksenas. He died early, before 1910; his younger brother, whom he had brought down, continued to work with the Arya Samaj.[35]

Another early Arya Samaj leader, Krishen Pershadji, came from Lucknow as a soldier in the British Contingent. He lived in Dabirpura, where many Srivastava *suratvals* lived, and he left the military to become a clerk. Another Kayasth clerk taught him Persian; he was hired as secretary to a Muslim Nawab, where a Muslim cleric discussed Islam with him constantly. About to convert to Islam, he secured a copy of Swami Dayanand's *Satyarth Prakash,* and its powerful Urdu prose restored his faith in Hinduism. He got a good job in the brigadier's office, became an Arya Samaj preacher, and joined Rae Kunwar Bahadur in speaking to Saksenas and Srivastavas in the Husaini Alam area.[36] They made several converts, one of whom, Gaya Pershad, continued the emphasis on social reform after Kunwar Bahadur's death.

Of the three, it was Gaya Pershad who knew Hyderabad Kayasth society best. He had come to Hyderabad as a boy of eight, "adopted" by an uncle employed in the Finance and Revenue Department. This family of Khare Srivastavas lived in Husaini Alam, and Gaya Pershad was unfavorably impressed with the "decadence" of local noble families in declining cir-

33. Khan, *Tuzuk,* II (Lawyers), 40.
34. Interview with Hakim Vicerai.
35. But this brother, Bakht Bahadur, went into the Revenue Department and associated with non-Srivastava Kayasths, mostly Mathurs. Consequently, he joined the Arya Samaj branch that had little to do with local *suratval* converts and did not prohibit meat and wine. (Most *suratvals* joined the stricter Gurukul branch of the Arya Samaj, which prohibited meat and wine.) Kunwar Bahadur's son went to Gurukul Kangri (school) in Hardwar. Interviews with Narinder Srivastava; Gajadhar Pershad; Bakht Bahadur; and Sohan Lal Arya.
36. Krishen Pershadji's son Surya Pratap went north to the Dayanand Anglo-Vedic High School in Dehra Dun, and then to the Kayasth Pathshala in Allahabad and Maharajah's College, Jaipur. Returning to Hyderabad, he became an Arya Samaj and Kayasth Association leader. Interviews with Captain Surya Pratap.

cumstances.[37] He first studied in the nearby Nizamia School; when it changed to an entirely Islamic curriculum, he went to Dar ul Ulum, which offered some English instruction.

Gaya Pershad's first contact with the Arya Samaj came through his job in the brigadier's office. A fellow Kayasth employee—Krishen Pershadji —gave him *Satyarth Prakash*. Then Rae Kunwar Bahadur and a Saksena teacher from Husaini Alam (one of the temperance society leaders) persuaded Gaya Pershad to stop eating meat and drinking wine. These decisions led to separate household arrangements and a break with his uncle. A public debate between Sanatan Dharm (a society defending orthodox Hinduism) and Arya Samaj spokesmen persuaded him to become an Arya Samaj member in 1901. One of his first steps was to bring his wife out of *purdah,* the first of many actions which resulted in his social boycott.[38]

Gaya Pershad's vigorous reform efforts increasingly alienated him from Kayasths who were relatively well-off and conservative. He tried to abolish the Kayasths' use of wine and other intoxicants. According to his memoirs, it was he who wrote to Munshi Kamta Pershad (*Kayasth Hitkari* editor in Gwalior) and started the local Kayasth temperance society. When Kamta Pershad replied that the Malwala Raja Murli Manohar was already a patron, Gaya Pershad contacted the latter and made him local president. He arranged a meeting of forty Kayasths in the Malwala palace, and the speakers seemed well received. But he learned that all the men who had attended still drank wine, so he stopped working with that Mathur society and started a local Husaini Alam one. When it, too, proved unsatisfactory, he turned to the Arya Samaj directly and held weekly gatherings on "a firm Vedic base."[39]

Gaya Pershad's next major effort was for flood relief in 1908, when he worked to organize the distribution of medicine and food. He did this again during the plague and influenza epidemics of 1916, 1917, and 1924. Unlike others who did relief work, he personally collected dead bodies for burial or cremation. These services, done in the name of the

37. He frequented the large neighboring residence of the Srivastava noble family of Rajas Mohan Lal and Murari Lal. The rajas often sponsored music parties, and they celebrated religious festivals quite elaborately, with splendid idols. Gaya Pershad's uncle, perhaps influenced by Islam, detested idol worship, and Gaya Pershad also came to disapprove of "ostentatiousness and decadence": Gaya Pershad, "Halat-i Gaya Pershad Aryah," 11–12 (Urdu manuscript given me by his son R. K. Khare).

38. Pershad, "Halat," 16–19.

39. Pershad, "Halat," 37–39. His account adds considerably to the knowledge available from the printed records of Munshi Kamta Pershad presented earlier in this chapter.

Arya Samaj, earned government cooperation and approval.[40] Gaya Pershad also started schools for girls and for untouchables. He believed in equality for women and celebrated publicly the sacred thread ceremony for his daughter, the first such Vedic rite performed for a female in Hyderabad.[41] (This initiation into the pure, or twice-born, state and stage of study of sacred texts was customary only for males of the top three *varnas*.)

Gaya Pershad's uncompromising beliefs and actions led to conflicts, but they also brought many local converts to the Arya Samaj.[42] Several families of Saksenas living near Husaini Alam, in the locality of dancing girls, musicians, and other entertainers, joined it at the turn of the century. Some of them were accomplished poets and *tabla* players; they played and sang at Arya Samaj meetings.[43] A typical conversion story is that of Ghausi Lal, named after the Ghausi *alam* (relic) he kept in his home for Muharram. A musician heavily influenced by Islam, he came to the Arya Samaj through domestic tragedies: three wives in succession died in childbirth, despite the Muslim *hakims* and charms he had employed. After visits from Gaya Pershad and receipt of the *Satyarth Prakash* from another Kayasth, Ghausi Lal embraced the Arya Samaj. He then renamed his sons: Habib Roy became Dharm Raj, and Khurshed Roy became Deo Raj.[44]

Another locality where converts were made was across the river in Dhulpet, where many soldiers and other lower-class employees lived. One Srivastava here, Sohan Lal, was the only Hindu pupil studying in the local mosque; his conversion to the Arya Samaj was effected by Gaya Pershad.[45]

Among the poor Kayasths of mixed ancestry in these old city areas, the message of social and religious reform—that those who followed the Vedic teachings and rites would achieve equality within a growing Arya Samaj

40. "Halat," 25–35, for Gaya Pershad's account. The Prime Minister awarded him a gold watch and a medal in 1917.

41. Rao, *Bustan*, IV, 302, records this occasion of 1921. Gaya Pershad does not refer to it in his autobiography, which seems to have been written earlier. He had no son until late in life, and he sent his children north to school. His daughters married out of Hyderabad; his son attended the Hardwar Gurukul and later married a Konkani Brahman whom he met in the Poona Arya Samaj. Interview with R. K. Khare.

42. People remonstrated with him when he exposed his wife and infant daughters to the plague by staying in the city to help remove dead bodies: "Halat," 30–32. He also refused to participate in his grandmother's funeral rites: *ibid.*, 20. At one point he moved to the new city; after a dispute with the Arya Samajists there he moved back to Husaini Alam; later he moved again to the new city.

43. These were the families of Mukhtar Rae, Saheb Rae, and Ghausi Lal in Mehbub Ki Mehndi: interviews with Captain Surya Pratap, Harish Chandra, and Manohar Lal.

44. Interview with Dharm Raj.

45. Interview with Sohan Lal Arya. He joined the Gurukul branch, abstaining from meat and wine; as with Gaya Pershad and others, his relatives resented the disturbance of cooking arrangements. They accused him of becoming a Brahman and evicted him.

community—had an obvious appeal. As economic decline limited the capabilities of many families to arrange marriages within orthodox boundaries, membership in the Arya Samaj widened the eligible pool of local marriage partners. At least two Srivastava-Bhatnagar marriages occurred in the 1890's between Arya Samaj members, and several more marriages across subcaste boundaries before 1920 involved Arya Samaj Kayasths.[46] Such marriages were still rare and were not sanctioned beyond the Arya Samaj membership.

The Arya Samaj reforms were opposed by Raja Shiv Raj and other Hindu nobles, who upheld orthodox Hinduism by establishing a Sanatan Dharm Sabha in the city. This organization had the tacit approval of the Nizam as well;[47] and the early cleavage along class lines reflected in the differing Kayasth membership in the Arya Samaj and Sanatan Dharm Sabha was later transformed into a political cleavage between challengers and supporters of the Nizam's rule in Hyderabad. But in the first decade of the twentieth century, the Kayasths and others joining the Arya Samaj shared economic and social problems, not political views.

Hyderabad Kayasths were active participants in several new kinds of public activities at the turn of the century. All these activities featured relations across kin group and subcaste lines to some extent, although the organizational efforts using the caste name were the most superficial in that respect. The various Kayasth organizations certainly did not represent an attempt at caste unification. In the case of the Mathur and Kayasth *sabhas,* the social reform and educational goals of the young, active, Western-educated members were limited by the conservatism of Raja Shiv Raj. Their activities were deflected into affirmations of political loyalty to the Nizam similar to those of other groups constituted for that purpose at the annual birthday celebrations in Hyderabad. Neither the Urdu and Persian literary activities nor the Arya Samaj social work and reform activities were based on caste or subcaste membership. The Arya Samaj teachings denied caste, and although each leader recruited new members of his own caste, he recruited many others as well. Kayasth temperance association affiliation was rejected in favor of other bases. The city Arya Samaj recruited from the lower classes of Urdu-speakers in Hyderabad, and problems of social legitimacy and poverty facilitated recruitment of many *suratval* Kayasths. The Urdu and Persian literary activities drew participants from higher levels of those same Urdu-speaking groups and represented a reaffirmation of the Mughlai heritage, a heritage that was rapidly losing its economic base at this time.

46. See Chapter 15.
47. Interviews with Hakim Vicerai and Eknath Pershad; see also Rao, *Bustan,* II, 758.

PART FOUR

Incorporation
into India

CHAPTER 12

The Kayasths and
Twentieth-Century Political
Developments

The period from the second decade of the twentieth century to the present has been very unstable for Hyderabad city and state. The changes of government in both 1948 and 1956 have brought new people to political power, and the dominant linguistic and cultural models have also changed. Educational and occupational opportunities have continued to expand throughout this period for Kayasths and most other Hyderabad citizens. But the conditions set by successive governments for participation in politics and society have differed significantly, requiring successive adaptations on the part of citizens.

This modern period has been marked by conflict and a restructuring of kin groups among the Kayasths. The chapters in this section trace Kayasth involvement in politics, their educational and occupational diversification, and the new patterns of leadership and authority developed through caste-based social reform activities. The final chapter discusses the recent constitution of new marriage networks across the former endogamous boundaries.

Administrative Policies and Cultural Nationalisms

Under the Nizam until 1948, the process of administrative modernization in the state accelerated. But the government's political vision proved limited; control remained with an administrative elite composed largely of outsiders.[1] Decision-making in Hyderabad, in an increasingly tense political setting, rested with these administrators. Nationalist

1. Leonard, "The Mulki—non-Mulki Conflict," in Jeffrey, *People, Princes,* for composition over time.

[215

mobilization in British India began to influence Hyderabad state directly, as the Indian National Congress and other religious and political movements exerted pressures against the Nizam's Muslim regime. Nizam Osman Ali Khan succeeded Nizam Mahbub Ali Khan in 1911. He and the modern administrators made little provision for public participation in politics, despite considerable evidence of unrest.

The administration failed to decentralize existing governmental structures or to initiate new and broader political institutions and processes.[2] Government regulations limited and repressed political activities. These regulations stemmed from the Khilifat agitation in the state, a Muslim movement defending the Caliph in Turkey after WWI, but they were renewed against the Arya Samaj Hindu revivalism, which was a major concern to the Hyderabad government and to the British Resident.[3] From the 1920's, a series of regulations subjected all public meetings to government approval, and at times public speeches were subject to prior censorship by government officials.[4] Lists of proscribed periodicals and books were issued and reissued periodically.[5] When communal problems or incidents occurred, for example, when Muslim and Hindu religious functions fell upon the same day, the government responded with committees to investigate and formulate new policies. Almost invariably, the Hindu members appointed to such committees were Kayasths and other Urdu-speakers from the old city, showing the government's preference for a certain type of loyal Hindu subject and leading to results more acceptable to the government than to some of the Nizam's other Hindu subjects.[6]

The government usually represented the interests of Hyderabad city rather than the state as a whole. Census figures for 1921 illustrate the

2. H. K. Sherwani, "The Evolution of the Legislature in Hyderabad," *Indian Journal of Political Science*, I (1940), 424–438, argues that there was some devolution.

3. Rao, *Bustan*, V, 254, 272, lists political exiles. Before the 1920's, Residency officials warned Hyderabad of the Swadeshi movement coming from Maharashtra through the *jagirs* of the Paigah, Vikar ul Umra: F.C.S., installment 22, list 5, serial no. 70, file H11/117, confidential reports from 1909; installment 22, list 15, serial no. 102, file H11/1 17, confidential reports from 1911. Later, the *Fortnightly Reports* (Government of India, Political Department) focused on the Arya Samaj: for example, those for 1937 (IOL).

4. For 1921, *A Peep into Hyderabad*, collected articles from the *Tribune* of Lahore, June 5, 6, 7 [1939], 26; for 1926, D. Raghavendra Rao, *Misrule of the Nizam* (n.p., 1926), 99–100; and for 1938 changes in the well-known circular no. 53 of 1930 (stating that all public meetings needed prior government permission), see the *Deccan Chronicle*, July 10, 1938 and later issues (in the newspaper's office in Secunderabad).

5. Rao, *Bustan*, IV, 226–228 for a 1920 list; Rao, *Misrule*, 26, and 111–112 for lists covering 1903 and 1923.

6. For 1924–1925, see Rao, *Bustan*, V, 153, and VI, 251–253; Rao, *Misrule*, 56–57. Among the members of such a commission appointed in December of 1925 were Rai Balmukund (the first Mulki B.A.), and Rai Rup Lal and Raja Narsing Raj, old-city *serrishtahdars*: Rao, *Bustan*, VI, 253.

TABLE 17:
Religions and Languages, 1921

	Hyderabad city	Urban areas[a]	State
Religions:			
Hindu	52%	62%	84%
Muslim	43%	34%	10%
Languages:			
Urdu	50%	——	10%
Telugu	39%	——	48%
Tamil	3%	——	——
Marathi	3%	——	26%
Kannada	——	——	12%

Sources: Government of Hyderabad, *Decennial Report on the Administration of H.E.H. the Nizam's Dominions 1322 to 1331 Fasli* [1912-1922] (Hyderabad, 1930), 60, 64, for the urban areas and state; *Census of India, 1921, XXI, Hyderabad State* (Hyderabad, 1921), pt. 1, 74, 192, for the city.

[a]Over 5,000 population.

contrasts well (see Table 17). The differences go far to explain the administration's actions with respect to education, cultural nationalism, and political mobilization in these decades. The educational system was expanded rapidly in the second decade of the twentieth century, with the establishment in 1918 of the Urdu-medium Osmania University and an increase in Urdu-medium secondary schools to feed it.[7] The decision to favor Urdu increased educational advantages for Muslims, intensified the insider-outsider conflict by equipping more local students for government service, and resulted in the formulation of conflicting cultural nationalisms that had taken organizational form in Hyderabad by the 1940's.

The government officials who founded Osmania University chose Urdu not only because it was the official state language, but because it was the

7. Harlan N. Henson, in "Elites, Language Policy and Political Integration in Hyderabad" (Ph.D. diss., University of Illinois, 1974), 55, quotes a former official to the effect that Osmania's establishment put priority on Urdu-medium high schools at the expense of primary education. See also S. Rama Char, "Education in Hyderabad," *Modern Review,* LXVI (1939), 177-181; Patrick Lacey, "The Medium of Instruction in Indian Universities," *Asian Review,* n.s., XXXIV (1938), 534-542; *A Peep into Hyderabad*; B. De, "The Educational Systems Adopted and the Results Achieved in the More Important Native States in India," *Modern Review,* IX (1911), 61-71; and H. K. Sherwani, "The Osmania University First Phase: The Urdu Medium (1917-1948)," in Sherwani, ed. *Studies in Indian Culture* (Hyderabad, 1966), 237-247.

only vernacular "more or less understood throughout the Dominions, especially in those urban areas from which His Highness's subjects who generally take to secondary education are mainly drawn . . ." English, however, was a compulsory subject, because graduates of the new university "should not be inferior to those of the existing Indian Universities as regards their practical acquaintance with a language which has become essential in every department of life."[8] The students were to come from an urban, Urdu-speaking environment. Furthermore, the Nizam's government officially stated that Osmania examinations were to be considered equivalent to those of other universities in India for purposes of employment, departmental service, and educational scholarships.[9] Osmania, then, seemed to promise opportunities for more local men to enter government service.

Yet since English was now "essential in every department of life," an Osmania education still ranked below that afforded by English-medium institutions. Accordingly, most modern administrators appear to have sent their sons and daughters to English-medium schools. While Osmania had a larger student body from its initiation, Nizam College continued to attract the best students in the state.

The inauguration of Osmania University contributed immediately to the intensification of the long-standing insider-outsider conflict in the state. The first problem came with the Translation Bureau and the preparation of textbooks for the university. Since the head of this bureau and many of the translators were outsiders, they utilized North Indian rather than Hyderabad Urdu.[10] This "pure" form drew upon classical Persian and Arabic sources when naming or translating technical terms for scientific texts. (Hyderabadis advocated use of a more localized Urdu, drawing upon Deccani Urdu and the vernaculars indigenous to the Deccan.) Thus North Indian Urdu became the standard for both texts and lectures, to the disadvantage of local Urdu-speakers.

From this early disagreement, factions developed within the faculty, and the argument moved beyond language to broader cultural and historical questions. Local scholars, led by Dr. Syed Mehiuddin Qadri Zore of the Urdu department, developed the idea of a "Deccani synthesis,"

8. FCS, installment 36, list 5, serial no. 11: Memorandum of Sir Akbar Hydari, then home secretary, in 1917 to the Nizam (quoted by numerous later sources).

9. Rao, *Bustan*, IV, 81, citing the notification of April 4, 1920, in the government's official gazette (*Jarida Ulamiyah*) V, no. 40 (April 19, 1920).

10. Moulvi Abdul Haq headed the Bureau of Translation, with a staff of eight; descriptions of the early endeavors and faculty members are in Sherwani, "The Osmania University," 243–246, and *Decennial Report on the Administration of H.E.H. the Nizam's Dominions 1322 to 1331 Fasli* [1912 to 1922] (Hyderabad, 1930), 197–200.

composed of Hindu and Muslim cultural elements and fostered by tolerant Muslim rule in the Deccan. Dr. Zore had been a student in the Malwala-sponsored Dharmvant School in the old city, and Kayasths were prominent among his followers.[11] These local scholars established a local library and research institution called the Idara-e Adabiyat-e Urdu (IAU), in about 1930, with both Hindu and Muslim members. The IAU collected and published materials supporting the idea of a Deccani synthesis.[12] This assigned a major creative role to the Muslim rulers in the Deccan for their patronage of Deccani Urdu and their development of a category of loyal subjects that cut across religious and caste lines. Hyderabad state was viewed as a unique and well-integrated society, which, like earlier Deccani kingdoms, had to defend itself against intolerant and narrow-minded outsiders. Saksena Urdu scholars from families moving out of Mughlai occupations were leaders in these cultural and literary activities.[13]

The Mulki Movement, a Hyderabadi nationalist movement inaugurated in Hyderabad in 1935, was the political expression of these ideas. It had an ideology and membership including all major elements of the population, and a long-standing grievance against the outsiders, non-*mulkis*, who controlled the administration. Loyalty to the Nizam and to a Deccan culture and language were basic tenets. It had many Muslim participants, men who had studied at Osmania or in England. The movement focused upon replacing outsiders with Hyderabadis in a responsible government, avoiding British advice and pressure, and retaining the Nizam and the old aristocracy as allies.[14] But the administration did not respond favorably to the group and its requests. It responded even more unfavorably to its apparent continuation in the Hyderabad State Congress, which was formed and officially banned in 1938.[15]

11. Interviews with Dr. Mohammed Khalidi (department of history, Osmania) and Roy Mahboob Narayan; subsequent comments, written and verbal, from Professor H. K. Sherwani, Professor Mahender Raj Suxena, and Roy Mahboob Narayan. There were generational and academic differences between the two sides, exemplified by Dr. Zore (born in 1905, had a London Ph.D.) and Moulvi Abdul Haq (born in 1871, had a B.A. and traditional degrees). Another Dr. Abdul Haq, head of the Arabic department and a Mulki, was with Dr. Zore; Dr. Habib ur Rahman of the Persian department was with Moulvi Abdul Haq.
12. The IAU publishes *Sabras*, a magazine titled after the first Deccani Urdu prose piece, and sponsors an annual commemoration of the ruler Muhammad Quli Qutb Shah, who patronized the language. See my article "The Deccani Synthesis," 205–218.
13. These men were Ragunandan Raj and Mahender Raj Suxena (brothers) and Satguru Pershad and Ragubir Pershad (the Wala Jahi family): Syed Mehiuddin Qadri Zore, *Dastan-i Adab-i Hyderabad* (Hyderabad, 1951), 194–195; Mahender Raj Suxena, "Chand Kayasth Shora," 15–16.
14. Syed Abid Hasan, *Whither Hyderabad* (Madras, 1935).
15. Swami Ramanand Tirtha, *First Class Tragedy* (Poona, 1940), and *Memoirs*; further

Those who opposed the Deccani synthesis theme were originally non-indigenous scholars at Osmania University; but Hyderabad Muslims also became prominent in the political movement, which emphasized the special position of Islam and Muslims in Deccani history. Several local institutions and organizations contributed to this, foremost among them the Anjuman-i Taraqqi Urdu, founded to promote "popularisation of the Urdu language among the masses of the people."[16] The Kayasth prominent in this organization was a Srivastava scholar of *suratval* origin, with few ties at the time to other local Kayasths.[17] After its headquarters moved to Delhi in 1936, the branch of the Anjuman that was left in Hyderabad, Urdu Hall, was linked to the Ittehad ul Muslimin, a Muslim cultural organization which became militant in the 1940's.[18]

In the 1930's, the divisive cultural nationalisms stimulated by the initiation of Osmania University were developed further. These ideologies—a concept of Deccani nationalism supported by native Hyderabadis and a concept of Muslim sovereignty in the Deccan supported initially by recently-arrived Muslims—became institutionalized in political movements. The movements dominated intellectual and political discussion in the capital city during the crucial decade preceding Indian independence and inspired a fervor that obscured the political realities confronting Hyderabad state. They allowed the reinterpretation of the insider-outsider conflict along communal lines. Furthermore, both ideologies were elitist, firmly focused upon the administration and its political control of the state.

The controversy between these two Urdu-speaking groups helped to blind the members of both to the pressure for political participation from the non-Urdu-speaking rural population of the state. In the Hyderabad

details in my article "The Mulki—non-Mulki Conflict" and in Carolyn M. Elliott, "Decline of a Patrimonial Regime," *JAS*, XXXIV, no. 1 (1974), 27–47.

16. See the brief notes by Fazlur Rahman, "Andjuman (India and Pakistan)," in *Encyclopedia of Islam*, I (new ed., London, 1960), 505–506; and see *Islamic Culture*, XIII, no. 2 (1939).

17. Interview with Khwaja/Rae Janaki Pershad (he was called by either the Muslim or Hindu term of address).

18. The Ittehad was founded in 1927 by the local Mulki Muslim Nawab Bahadur Yar Jung, who organized branches in the Hyderabad districts. After his death in 1944 the movement became overtly political; its militant wing, the Razakar terrorist movement, influenced public and Nizam in the delicate negotiations with the British, the Indian and Pakistani nationalists, and ultimately the Indian union. See *Tarikh-i Majlis Ittehad ul Muslimin, 1928–40* (Hyderabad, 1941). For the 1947–1948 negotiations, see [Ali Yavar Jung], *Hyderabad in Retrospect* (Bombay, 1949), Sadath Ali Khan, *Brief Thanksgiving* (Bombay, 1959), and Sir Arthur Cunningham Lothian, *Kingdoms of Yesterday* (London, 1951).

220]

districts, Western-educated activists were building mass political organizations directly linked to the Indian National Congress in British India. They pressed for responsible government and civil liberties within Hyderabad state, invoking their native-born status and asking for greater participation. But these Hyderabadis from the districts did not share the cultural assumptions of the urban Hyderabadi nationalist movement, and the political leadership of the two movements never fully coalesced. Throughout the 1930's, the Nizam and the government concentrated on administrative efficiency and the maintenance of law and order. A Reforms Committee was appointed, but its 1938 recommendations to perpetuate Muslim dominance helped provoke the great Satyagraha of that year.[19]

Kayasth Roles in Politics

Kayasths had two choices: to remain loyal citizens of the Nizam or to join political activities directed against the government. The communal criticisms leveled at the Hyderabad government led it to recognize and reward some of the high-ranking Hindus loyal to the Nizam, and the Malwalas benefitted from this. Less well-off Kayasths received no rewards for loyalty, yet most of them publicly supported the Nizam's government until 1948. There were few who participated in activities explicitly critical of the government.

Hyderabad was a princely state where the Congress party was outlawed and, even more than in British India, social and religious reform activities often expressed political allegiances. Participants in such diverse activities as the temperance movement, Hindi-medium education, gymnastic drills, and the spinning and weaving of *khadi* (cloth made from hand-spun yarn, associated with Gandhi) felt they were expressing political views. Another indication of changing orientation was in naming patterns. Names, particularly those given to men, have consistently reflected the ruling political culture of Hyderabad. Among the Kayasths, names like Jehangir Pershad, Mahbub Karan, or Iqbal Chand, and nicknames like Pasha, were not uncommon. In this period, some Kayasth parents, though not politically involved with the Indian nationalist movement, named their sons Rammohan Roy, Rabindranath, and so forth.

Only a few Kayasths were openly active politically. One or two may have been in the Hyderabad State Congress, which was linked to the

19. My article "The Mulki—non-Mulki Conflict" has a fuller discussion and further references.

Indian National Congress, and they were not well-known leaders. Far better known were those in the now overtly political Arya Samaj movement; local Kayasths were among its most effective leaders. Kayasths in the more militant political and religious movements tended to have marginal economic and social status.[20]

The Arya Samaj was growing and changing in terms of its membership and political goals. The Hyderabad government became concerned with the rapid expansion of the districts' membership and the connections with Maharashtrian and North Indian Arya Samajists. Arya Samaj membership in the Hyderabad districts rose from under 10 in 1921 to 3,700 in 1931, while membership in the city fell from 539 to 400 in the same decade.[21] Newly created Arya Samaj schools and gymnasiums became centers of anti-government propaganda, and they were no doubt a major cause of the government's new and strict regulations governing the recognition of private schools in 1924.[22] There was increasing coordination between Hyderabadi Arya Samajists and those outside the state. Pamphlets produced by outsiders about Hyderabad were distributed widely within the state, and their inflammatory nature was cited by the government as reason to censor printed materials entering the state.[23]

Arya Samaj membership in the late 1920's meant something quite different than it had at the turn of the century. The young men whom the Srivastava Gaya Pershad converted in the 1920's were a different generation, too. Those who had seen the Arya Samaj as a social and religious reform movement, and worked with converts of all social origins, lost control of the organization to those who saw it as one arm of a political movement against the Nizam's continued rule in the Deccan.[24]

20. See Chapter 11; interviews with Dadey Pershad, Benkat Prasad, Gurucharan Das Saxena, and Shakamber Raj Saxena.

21. Government of Hyderabad, *Report of the Reforms Committee 1938* (Hyderabad, 1939), app. 1, p. 4, summarizing census reports from 1911, 1921, 1931.

22. Rao, *Misrule,* 94, citing the *Indian Daily Mail* of April 20, 1926; *Hyderabad men Arya Samaj ki Tehrik* (Hyderabad [1939]), 82–86, reprints the rules for establishment of private schools.

23. The Hindu Mission Press, New Delhi, published the report of a committee sent down in 1934; Ganpath Rai, *Report on the position of the Hindu Communities in the Nizam's Dominions* (New Delhi [1935]). In rebuttal, Mir Zahid Ali Kamil wrote *The Communal Problem in Hyderabad* (Hyderabad [1935]). Then the International Aryan League published *Riyasat-i Hyderabad men Arya Samaj ka Muqqadama* (Delhi [1938]), and the Government of Hyderabad published *Hyderabad men Arya Samaj ki Tehrik* (Hyderabad [1939]). The International Aryan League responded with *Nizam Defense Examined and Exposed* (Delhi [1940]).

24. Captain Surya Pratap, *The Tragedy of Arya Samaj* (Hyderabad, 1960), discusses factions within the city branch. Pandit Narinderji, active in the 1930's and winner of the struggle for control, was writing a history of this branch; he died in 1976 and I do not know if it was completed.

One of Gaya Pershad's converts who became a leader of the new politicized movement was a young Shahalibanda Saksena Narinder Pershad, or Pandit Narinderji. He was the chief Hyderabad Arya Samaj leader in the 1938 Satyagraha, the mass civil disobedience action that resulted in nine thousand arrests in the city. From a respectable but low income *mansabdari* family, Narinder Pershad had joined the Arya Samaj in 1927 and gone to Lahore for three years' training as a preacher. He worked as a social reformer and leader in the local temperance movement, but his outstanding talent lay in public speaking.[25] In earlier years his mentor, Gaya Pershad, had performed social services and proudly accepted a gold watch and medal from Hyderabad's prime minister. But Pandit Narinderji called publicly for Hindu patriotism and the economic boycott of Muslim merchants; his speeches included such phrases as "Hindus! Rise and tear out the root of the tree of Hyderabad . . ."[26]

In the 1930's, Pandit Narinderji and several other Kayasths earned government retaliation for their Arya Samaj activities. Captain Surya Pratap (son of the early leader Krishen Pershadji) used a pseudonym to write essays, in Urdu, attacking Urdu imperialism. When this was discovered, he nearly lost his job in the Military Accounts Office.[27] Sohan Lal, a Srivastava from Dhulpet, was, like Pandit Narinderji, a master orator in Urdu. When he spoke at a 1938 public meeting in Dhulpet, a riot resulted in which two Muslims were killed; Sohan Lal was sentenced to twenty years in jail for provoking it.[28] Pandit Narinderji lost his hereditary *mansab*. The government considered him a major danger, and in the late 1930's he was restricted in speech and movements. In 1938, restrictions were placed upon the public speeches of two local leaders, Bahadur Yar Jung of the Ittehad ul Muslimin and Pandit Narinderji of the Arya Samaj. But a slight relaxation of the rules allowed Pandit Narinderji to lead a Dasserah procession of twenty thousand, sponsored by the Arya Samaj, through the city—an event that stimulated the Satyagraha of 1938[29] and led to Narinderji's imprisonment for fifteen months.[30]

25. Interviews with Pandit Narinderji and Gurucharan Das Saxena.
26. *Hyderabad men Arya Samaj ki Tehrik*, 9.
27. They were published as *Hamari Zaban*; interview with Captain Surya Pratap.
28. Interview with Sohan Lal Arya; Jaidev Sharma Vidyalanker et al., *Hyderabad Satyagraha ka Raktaranjit Itihas* (Ajmer, 1947). A photograph, pp. 86–87 of this Hindi book, shows Sohan Lal and specifies the sentence for the Dhulpet case.
29. For the government's specific orders against their delivering public addresses for 12 months, see the *Deccan Chronicle*, May 15, 1938, p. 9. This change in the regulations concerning public meetings appears in *ibid.*, July 10, 1938. Bahadur Yar Jung's proposed speech at Id was prohibited: *ibid.*, May 29, 1938, p. 13; for the Arya Samaj Dasserah procession, *ibid.*, Oct. 9, 1938, p. 22.
30. *Ibid.*, Dec. 4, 1938, for Narinderji's arrest. Jailed again in 1947, he was also active in the Hindi Prachar Sabha and the Hyderabad State Congress.

The Satyagraha marked a political turning point for Hyderabad; it inaugurated a state of political crisis that was not resolved for another ten years. While the takeover of the state by India in 1948 and the inclusion of its Telugu-speaking areas in Andhra Pradesh in 1956 were also traumatic political events, they were far more predictable and their consequences were certain and irreversible. Only a few Arya Samaj Kayasths risked participation in the Satyagraha, which coincided with the height of internal conflict among the Kayasths (see Chapter 14). At that time, almost all other Kayasths involved themselves in caste association politics. These contrasting commitments illustrate the extremity of the few political choices open then.

Though the Hyderabad State Congress and the Hindu Civil Liberties Union initiated the Satyagraha, its leadership passed to the Arya Samaj, whose out-of-state members provided the largest number of volunteer Satyagrahis.[31] The Government of Hyderabad ultimately arrested some nine thousand people, more than eighty percent of them non-Hyderabadis.[32] Because of heavy participation by outsiders, government officials viewed all predominantly Hindu political organizations in the state as dominated by outside politicians. The ban on the Hyderabad State Congress was not lifted; the reforms recommended by the Reforms Committee Report of 1938 were not implemented, allegedly postponed because of World War II.[33] The Satyagraha testified to existing political divisions and further consolidated them, highlighting the vastly different political goals of the central administrators and the district political leaders.

At this point, the Nizam and his leading administrators firmly committed themselves to a political ideology stressing the special role of Islam and the Muslim community. The local Ittehad ul Muslimin fell under the control of Muslim communalists, some of whom held high government positions. These "ruthless fanatics" have been held responsible for the Hyderabad government's mismanaged negotiations with the newly independent Government of India in 1947–1948,[34] when an acceptable permanent settlement between Hyderabad and India could not be reached.

31. *Deccan Chronicle,* Oct. 23, 1938; Tirtha, *Memoirs,* 91 and passim; [Jung], *Hyderabad in Retrospect,* 4–5. Abdus Salam, *Hyderabad Struggle* (Bombay, 1941), 70–75, stresses the Arya Samaj's increasing role.
32. Salam, *Hyderabad Struggle,* 75; S. T. Hollins, *No Ten Commandments* (London, 1958), 237.
33. Hyderabad State Committee for History of the Freedom Movements, *Freedom Struggle in Hyderabad* (Hyderabad, 1966), IV, 196, cites the role of the Ittehad ul Muslimin in keeping the State Congress banned. Lothian, *Kingdoms of Yesterday,* 184, states that the Nizam's government used the war as an excuse to delay the reforms, as both the Ittehad and the Congress opposed various aspects of them.
34. Wilfred Cantwell Smith, "Hyderabad: Muslim Tragedy," *The Middle East Journal,* IV, no. 1 (1950), 50; his view is shared by [Jung], *Hyderabad in Retrospect.*

In the meantime, Muslim refugees from the 1947 partition of India and Pakistan were welcomed in Hyderabad; Jinnah and others from the Muslim League were advisors to the Nizam, and Hyderabad's prime minister at the time of India's 1948 Police Action was on special loan from the government of Pakistan.[35]

Many Kayasths and other Hyderabad Hindus continued to support the Nizam's government despite its increasingly pro-Muslim ideology and actions.[36] Public support of the government was the official policy of the local Kayasth organization and newspaper down to 1948, and prominent individual Kayasths conformed to it conspicuously. They were in fact often called upon to do so by the Nizam's government, which had become skilled at using leading representatives of the indigenous Hindu communities for political purposes.

There were many Kayasths placed in delicate positions in the 1930's and 1940's. In the 1930's, the Ecclesiastical Department set up separate Hindu officials for Hindu temples and religious institutions in Hyderabad city, and a Saksena was chosen as their chief administrator.[37] At Osmania University each hostel had a special hall for Hindu prayers and separate Hindu dining halls and kitchens. These were put under the supervision of a Hindu hostel warden, a Mathur who was a lecturer in Hindu philosophy. He and several other Kayasths had received government scholarships for higher studies, abroad in some cases.[38] In 1945, three of the twenty-three young men sent for study abroad by the government were Kayasths.[39]

Raja Dharm Karan, head of the Malwala Mathur family in the 1940's, was the leading Kayasth spokesman, and he spoke from many platforms. In the 1940's, the government initiated and encouraged a number of associations in the city, putting forward leaders like Dharm Karan as their officers and patrons. One was the Mansabdars Association, which

35. For the refugees: Smith, "Hyderabad: Muslim Tragedy," 45; C. Sri Kishen, *45 Years a Rebel* (Hyderabad [1953]), 146, 164. For Jinnah, and Pakistan's loan of Mir Laik Ali: V. P. Menon, *The Story of the Integration of the Indian States,* (Bombay, 1956), 333; [Jung], *Hyderabad in Retrospect,* 6–11.

36. Chandu Lal's descendant Maharajah Kishen Pershad made a major Urdu defense of the regime in his speech "Hindu Bhaaio see Khitaab" on April 10, 1939 (reprinted in Urdu by the Government Press and translated into English in Salam, *Hyderabad Struggle,* 113–120).

37. This was Jagdish Narayan, succeeded by his son, Lakshmi Narayan (the Wala Jahi Saksena family): Kamil, *The Communal Problem,* 43.

38. The Philosophy lecturer was Professor Shiv Mohan Lal. The others included Dr. Brij Mohan Lal (later principal of Osmania Medical College), Dr. Mahender Raj Suxena (later chairman of the botany department), Maheshwar Raj Saxena, and Balobir Prosad (they later taught chemistry and education, respectively).

39. They were K. C. Asthana, A. N. Mathur, and Krishen Dayal Mathur: *KH,* IV–V, nos. 1–3 (1945), 13.

held a dinner at the Malwala palace in 1943 with Dharm Karan as chief guest. This event featured speeches on communal unity and toasts to the Prince of Berar, the Nizam's eldest son and heir. (Raja Mahbub Karan, Dharm Karan's younger brother, was the Prince's personal secretary and constant companion.)[40] Another was the Religious Leaders Association, predominantly Muslim but including Parsi, Christian, and Hindu figures as well, intended to foster unity. Dharm Karan was asked to lend his public support to this group, and he did so.[41]

Raja Dharm Karan appeared to represent the sentiments of most Kayasths. In 1943, the local Kayasth association published a collection of its addresses to the Nizams and the eloquent reply of the Nizam Mahbub Ali Khan, who had died in 1911.[42] A Mathur poet composed a national anthem for Hyderabad and sent it to the Nizam.[43] Dharm Karan served as president of the All-India Kayasth Conference in Delhi in 1945, and his presidential address praised the Nizam of Hyderabad, terming him a participant in the AIKC through his patronage of Kayasths in Hyderabad. He also made an eloquent plea for mutual love among members of different communities in India.[44] In 1947, when an assassination attempt upon the Nizam failed, the Kayasth association passed a resolution of loyalty and support, thanking God that the offender was not a Hyderabad subject and stating: "The entire Kayasth *qaum* of Hyderabad offers its unshakable faith and devotion to the royal court; we shall not hesitate to sacrifice our lives, kin, and wealth."[45] Immediately after India's independence the Nizam declared Hyderabad a sovereign and independent state, in June 1947. Raja Dharm Karan publicly welcomed the declaration, saying that his exalted highness thereby "fulfilled the political aspirations of his subjects, who pledged loyalty to his throne and person irrespective of caste, creed, or community."[46]

In the late 1940's, several Kayasths were elevated to key positions in the government. Table 18 summarizes the situation, according to the last civil list before Police Action.

Just before Police Action, then, Kayasths were prominent in the Nizam's government in responsible and delicate positions; some were prominent

40. Interviews with Mahbub Karan and Ramchander Narayan.
41. See note 46 below; and *Islamic Culture*, XIX, no. 4 (1945), 384.
42. Kayasth Sadr Sabha, Hyderabad, *Irshadat Salatin Asafiyah* (Hyderabad [1943]).
43. Hakim Vicerai wrote the anthem for the Dharmvant High School annual function.
44. The text is with Captain Surya Pratap (actual author of the speech).
45. *KH*, VII-VIII (1947-1948), 1 (translation).
46. As head of the Religious Leaders Association, he hailed the "statesmanlike move." Speech reported in the Urdu daily *Payam*, XXII, no. 6, (1947) preserved in the IAU Library; repr. in English in *New Hyderabad*, Government Public Relations Office, I, nos. 6 & 7 (1947), 6.

TABLE 18:
High-Ranking Kayasths in the Hyderabad Administration, 1948

Position	Holder's name and subcaste
Secretary of Revenue	Kunj Behari Lal, Asthana
Secretary of Supplies	Ramchander Asthana
Director of Food Supplies	K. I. Vidyasagar, Mathur
Director of Rationing	Jagjivan Chand, Mathur
Senior Deputy Commissioner of Police, Secunderabad	Shiv Kumar Lal, Srivastava
Secretary to the Nizam's Agent General, Delhi	Nagendra Bahadur, Asthana
Secretary to the Nizam's Agent General, London	Iqbal Chand, Mathur
Personal Physician to the Nizam	Dr. Benkat Chandra, Mathur
Personal Legal Advisor to the Nizam	Benkat Prasad, Saksena
Personal Secretary to the Prince of Berar	Raja Mahbub Karan, Mathur

Source: Government of Hyderabad, Office of the Accountant General, *The Classified List of Officers of the Civil Departments of H.E.H. the Nizam's Government* (Hyderabad, 1948).

in the cultural societies linked to the Hyderabad nationalist movement or to Urdu education; and a few were leaders of the Arya Samaj. The loyalty of most Kayasths resulted in relative safety for them in 1947–1948. Muslim terrorist (Razakar) activities increased in the last year before Police Action, and the city became a dangerous place for many Hindus. But no Kayasths left their old-city homes, even in the most dangerous days of Razakar activity. Some other Hindus left, and many Kayasths took care to stay inside their houses most of the time, but in fact none were harmed.[47] Those who served in the districts at that time sometimes passed as Muslims to save their lives during Razakar raids.[48]

As some Muslims say about Kayasths, "like the cat on the wall, they can fall to either side";[49] and when the Indian Army came into Hyderabad in 1948, many shed their *sherwanis* (high-collared coats) so that they would not be mistaken for Muslims.[50] The Government of India, after

47. Interviews with Hakim Vicerai, Eknath Pershad, Gurucharan Das Saxena, and Roy Mahboob Narayan.
48. Shamsher Bahadur (Srivastava) "passed" three times, traveling on trains to reach his family in the city (interview with him).
49. I heard this first from Ziauddin Ahmad Shakeb of the APSA.
50. Interview with Narinder Srivastava.

the collapse of negotiations and the Nizam's declaration of independence, sent in the Indian Army. After Police Action, a military administration was set up for an interim period.[51] The Muslim elite of Hyderabad state was dispersed; many officials and wealthy Muslims went to Pakistan and others were displaced by the military administration. New political leaders came to power in Hyderabad state, which was incorporated into India. The Hyderabad State Congress was praised for its role in the nationalist movement, and the Arya Samaj and its leaders were also acclaimed as Indian nationalists.[52]

The situation for most Kayasths improved somewhat after the secular Government of India assumed military control of Hyderabad. Placed on the defensive, however, they were required to repudiate or defend their previous allegiance to the Nizam. Since they were Hindus and their mother tongue could be termed Hindi rather than Urdu or Hindustani, the new government did accept many Kayasths as mediators between the old and new administrations. Until 1956 Hyderabad state continued to exist, nominally under the Nizam (retitled the Raj Pramukh) but with considerable restructuring of the government.

But in 1956, the "linguistic states reorganization" broke up the state, putting Hyderabad city and the Telangana districts into the Telugu-speaking state of Andhra Pradesh.[53] The former territories of Hyderabad state were permanently divided among the three neighboring states of Maharashtra, Mysore, and Andhra Pradesh. The former leaders of the Hyderabad State Congress were assigned accordingly, and many of them became residents of Maharashtra or Mysore. Hyderabad city became the capital of Andhra Pradesh.

These changes of government in 1948 and 1956 altered both individually and collectively the political, economic, and social position of Kayasths in Hyderabad. For those well equipped by education and occupational diversification (and not too closely connected to the Nizam's last efforts at independence), their standing as North Indian Hindus who spoke Hindi helped them, especially from 1948 to 1956. Some repudiated their Hydera-badi past and did well;[54] others energetically defended it and asked for a

51. See Menon, *Story of the Integration*, 36.
52. Pandit Narinderji and Captain Surya Pratap were so acclaimed, and Sohan Lal Arya was pardoned.
53. John G. Leonard, "Politics and Social Change in South India: A Study of the Andhra Movement," *Journal of Commonwealth Political Studies*, V, no. 1 (1967), 60–77; Jyotindira Das Gupta, *Language Conflict and National Development* (Berkeley, 1970).
54. Captain Surya Pratap, for example, was made head of *jagiridari* abolition; another Srivastava, Shiv Kumar Lal, became commissioner of police (his family had come at the turn of the century).

continuation of that eclectic tradition. Thus, immediately after Police Action, the familiar Hyderabadi complaint was raised: a local Hindu wrote to the presiding Indian Army general protesting the alienation of jobs to non-Hyderabadis and defending the city's Urdu culture.[55]

The discontinuities were greater after 1956, and Kayasths and other native Hyderabadis again found themselves a minority dominated by outside administrators, this time Telugu-speakers from the Andhra districts. They are now members of a linguistic rather than a religious minority. The insider-outsider terminology has been revived and applied to the current conflicts between residents of Telangana (formerly in Hyderabad state) and the other regions of Andhra.[56] Economic issues, once confined to administrative positions and now broadened to include the overall allocation of economic resources within Andhra Pradesh, continue to be central. The old theme of an eclectic Deccani culture is present in the contemporary version of the conflict, recalling the cosmopolitan culture romantically associated with the former Hyderabad city and state.[57] Most Kayasths are ambivalent about this cultural heritage, which has proved of diminishing usefulness since the late nineteenth century. Yet it still has significance to most Kayasth individuals and families, and its potential contribution to the Government of India's goal of national integration is great.

55. Barrister C. Sri Kishen's letters to Sardar Vallabhai Patel (in charge of the new military administration) of July, 1949: "You are bringing in non-Hyderabadis from outside discharging all local talents, and are getting the Public Service Commission to give preferences to outsiders . . ." And "there has been an attempt to retrench in the name of efficiency, and because to aid the new personnel, instead of the Urdu knowing staff, persons with knowledge of English and the regional languages were required." Quotations from *45 Years a Rebel*, pp. 202, 217.

56. K. V. N. Rao, "Separate Telangana State?" *Journal of the Society for the Study of State Government*, Benares Hindu University (1969), 129–143. For the continuing use of the concept with respect to educational institutions in Telangana, see Carolyn M. Elliott, "The Problem of Autonomy: the Osmania University Case," in Susanne H. & Lloyd I. Rudolph, *Education and Politics in India* (Cambridge, Mass. 1972), 277.

57. The latest version of this theme is by Harriet Ronken Lynton and Mohini Rajan, *Days of the Beloved* (Berkeley, 1974).

CHAPTER 13

Changing Educational
and Occupational Patterns

The development of Kayasth-sponsored schools in the old city and the establishment of Osmania University in the second decade of the twentieth century gave more Kayasths access to Western education. By the 1930's, many men were moving into the modern administrative service and other new professions, usually with the aid of kinsmen. Others, however, found themselves trapped in their traditional positions, and their circumstances worsened.

Two important changes occurred in the 1920's. The Asthanas began to associate with some of the old-city Kayasths, and, to outsiders, they became assimilated to "old Hyderabadi" culture. And Raja Shiv Raj's death altered the economic circumstances for Mathurs, spurring many to seek alternative means of support. Finally, the establishment of girls' schools in the 1930's and 1940's produced the first generation of educated Kayasth women, in the 1960's, from certain families and kin groups.

New Educational Institutions

The uneven development of educational facilities offering English and other modern subjects in Hyderabad city has been discussed in Chapters 7 and 12. Only a few old-city Kayasths, backed by kinsmen or wealth, had secured an education which equipped them to enter the modern administration or new professions like law and medicine. The growing recognition of a need for modern primary and secondary education in the old city led several castes and communities to establish or expand schools there. These were neighborhood lower schools, associated with different

Kayasth kin groups and subcastes. Saksenas started the Kayasth Pathshala in Husaini Alam in 1914, and the Malwala school expanded in Chowk Maidan Khan in 1915. Both soon secured government aid.[1]

The Kayasth Pathshala began without a wealthy patron, although Bansi Raja's son provided a building attached to his residence. The school depended upon student fees, and supporting families also donated one handful of rice a day, which was sold in the bazaar. The first eight students were all Husaini Alam Saksenas. Almost immediately however, Kayasths elsewhere in the old city and non-Kayasths in the neighborhood sent students to the Pathshala. It grew rapidly, enrolling one hundred thirty students in 1917. At first classes were conducted in Urdu, but English classes were added later and the school was classified as an Anglo-vernacular middle school in 1918.[2]

In the Mathur neighborhood, the Malwala palace school expanded in 1915, moving to larger quarters and admitting students other than Mathur Kayasths. It continued to be partially supported by the Malwala family but received government aid. It too was an Anglo-vernacular middle school. Not until 1921 was a local Kayasth appointed to serve as headmaster—a Mathur who had gone to the Allahabad Kayasth Pathshala and Calcutta University. Under him, Dharmvant became a higher secondary school in 1926. He estimated that one-third of the three hundred students during this decade were Mathurs.[3]

Only a few old-city Kayasths went on for higher education before the opening in 1918 of Osmania University. A comparison of the birthdates of those attaining the first higher degrees, old-city Kayasths with one another and with Asthanas, shows considerable differences in timing. The Asthanas were the earliest in all categories. Asthana men born in the 1870's earned B.A. degrees, while those born in the 1880's and 1890's earned degrees as doctors, engineers, and lawyers.[4] The Mathurs were

1. Interviews with Prithvi Raj, Eknath Pershad, Dadey Pershad (current headmaster of Dharmvant), and Jadubanth Pershad (past headmaster of Dharmvant). See Government of Hyderabad, *Report on Public Instruction in H.E.H. the Nizam's Dominions* (APSA), annual reports 1915 on, for figures.

2. Government of Hyderabad, *Report on Public Instruction* for 1917-1918, 22; interview with Prithvi Raj.

3. Interview with Jadubanth Pershad, the first local headmaster. Early headmasters had been a Madrasi, from 1901 to 1910, followed by a Maharashtrian to 1921. There had been 500 students each year from 1915, until the plague and the opening of more schools in the old city brought the enrollment down in the 1920's: *Report on Public Instruction*, annual reports from 1915-1930.

4. Jag Mohan Lal and Harish Chander were the first B.A.'s, followed by Dr. Brij Mohan Lal, Lokendra Bahadur (engineer), and Mahendra Kishore, Hemchander, and Kalicharan (lawyers). For degrees and birthdates, see the Hyderabad government civil lists (confirmed in interviews).

next. Like the founder of the Asthana family (Manu Lal, in the 1870's), the earliest Mathurs entered the modern administration before finishing matriculation or B.A. courses.[5] The earliest B.A.'s among the Mathurs were held by men born in the late 1890's or the first decade of the twentieth century, and their degrees were obtained before Osmania University opened.[6] Among the other subcastes in the old city, men born in the first or second decade of the twentieth century received the first B.A.'s, and almost all of them earned their degrees at Osmania.[7]

Only those Mathurs with wealth or patronage could afford to attend college. Raja Murli Manohar's son Dharm Karen and a few other Mathurs attended the Kayasth Pathshala in Allahabad; that school (begun in 1873 by the founder of the AIKC) began to offer a B.A. in affiliation with Allahabad University in 1914.[8] A few others took B.A.'s from Poona, Lahore, Mewar Central College, or the local English-medium Nizam College.[9]

Despite the importance of wealth, young men from Mathur families in Lalta Pershad's kin group, rather than members of the Malwala family, secured the "first" B.A.'s among the old-city Kayasths.[10] A majority of them shared one characteristic: their fathers had moved to transitional occupations, for example, jobs utilizing Urdu but in the modern administration. In many cases their fathers had died, leaving them or their older brothers to direct their educations and careers.[11]

After Osmania began accepting students in 1918, secondary schools in the old city became feeder institutions for it. More old-city Kayasths earned B.A.'s and some went further. Graduate degrees had to be earned elsewhere, since Osmania's higher degree programs were not yet developed. Only Aligarh, Dacca, and Calcutta Universities accepted the Os-

5. The men (and families, in Table 7) here were Lalta Pershad (6); Janaki Chand, Nutan Chand, and Girdhar Chand (21); Bhagwan Sahae (2); Rameshwar Pratab (5); Tulja Pershad (26); Hari Mohan Lal and Ram Mohan Lal (13).

6. These were Bhasker Anand Pershad (Madras), Nar Narayan Pershad (Mewar Central College), Tara Pershad (Kayasth Pathshala), Benkat Chandra (Poona University), and Janardhan Chand (Lahore). Interviews with Hakim Vicerai and Dr. Benkat Chandra.

7. Based on the *Classified Civil Lists* and all relevant interviews with Saksenas, Srivastavas, Bhatnagars, Nigams, and Gaurs. Exceptions are Inder Karan Bhatnagar, with a Nizam College B.A., and the newcomer Professor K. C. Roy Saksena, who had earned a B.A. in Lucknow before coming to Hyderabad in 1921.

8. Kayasth Pathshala, *Golden Jubilee 1873–1923* (Allahabad [1924]), 3.

9. Interviews with Hakim Vicerai and Maharaj Karan; see note 6 above.

10. Interviews in note 9 above, and the list of Mathur B.A.'s in Saksena, *Kul Hind Kayasth Conference.*

11. The majority were from families 21, 13, 6, and 26 (Table 7). Those whose fathers died when they were young included Shiv Mohan Lal (13); Ragubir Bali (10); Jadubans Chand, Harbans Chand, and Dr. Benkat Chandra (21).

TABLE 19:

Higher Educational Degrees by Subcaste, 1938

| | Bachelor's degree | Master's degree | Other higher degrees | | | Total |
			Medical doctors	Lawyers	Engineers	
Asthana	2	0	1	1	1	5
Bhatnagar	0	1	0	1	0	2
Gaur	0	0	0	1	0	1
Mathur	11	3	1	3	0	18
Saksena	1	2	0	1	0	4
Srivastava	1	1	0	0	0	2
Total	15	7	2	7	1	32

Sources: K. C. Roy Saksena, *Kul Hind Kayasth Conference* (Hyderabad, 1938), supplemented by the relevant civil lists and interviews.

mania B.A. degree in the 1920's. Three Mathurs studied in Aligarh and Calcutta, at least one sponsored by the Hyderabad government.[12]

By the late 1930's there were at least thirty-two local men with B.A.'s and higher degrees, grouped by subcaste (see Table 19). Many of these educated pioneers assisted younger Kayasths by helping them find part-time jobs or financial assistance to continue their educations.[13] This was particularly welcomed among the Mathurs, who still had to contend with the disapproval of the elderly Raja Shiv Raj. Several men still remember the first time an educated young Mathur refused to remove his turban at the annual *durbar* in the Malwala palace.[14] Such gestures of defiance and independence were important examples to others.

As young educated Kayasths increased in numbers and qualifications, they joined the growing group of citizens competing for jobs with the "outsiders," the administrators who dominated society and politics in Hyderabad. This indigenous Western-educated group was expanding and diversifying in the early twentieth century.[15] Its members had differential access to administrative and political resources. Kayasths from the

12. Professor Shiv Mohan Lal and Ganesh Chand went to Aligarh, and Jadubanth Pershad took a Calcutta B.A. Interviews with the first and last.

13. Nar Narayan Pershad and Narinder Pershad were noted for this among the Mathurs; Satguru Pershad and Karan Pershad among the Saksenas; Nageshri Pershad among the Bhatnagars.

14. This was Narinder Pershad: interviews with Sri Rang Pershad, Hakim Vicerai, Dr. Benkat Chandra, and Ramchander Narayan.

15. The citizen or *mulki* category now legally included: 1) people whose families had

old city had some advantages over citizens from the rural areas in this competition. Their major advantage derived from Osmania's accessibility to city residents literate in Urdu, and the possibility of going on to Aligarh or Dacca. There were also government scholarships for overseas study, initiated in the 1890's; it was originally specified that recipients should know Persian and Urdu, thereby favoring Muslims and Hyderabadi Hindus. The new educational system culminating with Osmania perpetuated that favoritism. An additional encouragement to Kayasth students was the presence of a young Saksena Kayasth on the Osmania faculty, a history teacher named K. C. Roy, who was recruited from Lucknow in 1921.[16] This was particularly true when Roy became acquainted with the Hyderabad Kayasths and tried to effect social reforms among them in the 1930's (see the next chapter).

Occupational Mobility and Stagnation

Kayasths began to move into several new occupational areas, particularly the modern administration and the legal, medical, and educational professions. These upwardly mobile Kayasths were still a small, but relatively conspicuous proportion. The larger proportion, those still dependent upon more traditional skills or resources, suffered further reductions and abolitions of income from the 1920's to the 1940's.

The modern administration continued to expand. While the state language was legally Urdu, English was also extensively used, and official reports and documents were printed in both languages. Kayasths who knew only Urdu could find employment in the lower levels of the bureaucracy. For the higher, gazetted, positions, an English-language education was essential. Table 20 lists Kayasths in gazetted service and shows the representation at that level over time.

The Asthanas were well represented early and continued thus. The abiding success of Rae Murlidhar and his kinsmen, combined with the entry of old-city Kayasths into modern occupations, resulted in greater contact between the Asthana kin group and other Kayasths. Rae Murlidhar built an enviable reputation as an efficient, honest, and courageous

---

been resident in the old city of Hyderabad for generations; 2) people from rural Hyderabad moving into urban administrative and professional positions; 3) people whose forebears had come to Hyderabad as non-*mulkis* in the nineteenth century; 4) more recent immigrants who had been able to secure *mulki* certificates. See my article "The Mulki—non-Mulki Conflict," in Jeffrey, *People, Princes*.

16. Roy was a widower who served as warden of the Hindu hostel until his second marriage: several testified to his influence (Roy Mahboob Narayan, Eknath Pershad, Gurucharan Das Saxena).

TABLE 20:

Kayasths in the Modern Administration, 1895–1949

| | Civil lists: gazetted officers[a] | | | | | | | |
	1895	1905	1915	1925	1931	1940	1948	1949
Asthanas	1	3	4	6	7	5	8	9
Bhatnagars	0	0	0	0	0	0	2	4
Gaur	0	0	0	0	0	0	0	0
Mathur	2	4	4	11	18	14	22	39
Nigam	0	0	0	0	0	0	0	0
Saksena	0	0	0	0	3	3	9	7
Srivastava	1	0	0	1	1	4	5	6

Sources: Government of Hyderabad, *The Classified List of Officers of the Civil Departments of H.E.H. the Nizam's Government,* for years indicated (APSA).

[a]The civil lists were first compiled jointly with military lists in the Finance Office and printed quarterly in Urdu and English from 1884; the military list was printed separately from 1907. From 1895, both lists were printed half-yearly and from 1925 annually; the Accountant General's office compiled them from 1922. (Rao, *Bustan,* VI, 41; but there are exceptions to his summary.) First to be titled H.E.H. (His Exalted Highness) was Mir Osman Ali Khan Asaf Jah VII, Nizam from 1911; earlier government titles used H.H. (His Highness). I have used only one bibliographic entry for these lists for reasons of simplicity and space.

administrator. Called by one contemporary "the most influential man in State service after the Prime Minister,"[17] he is said to have resigned upon seventeen different occasions, but the Nizam always called him back to service.[18] When he retired from the modern administration in about 1913, he accepted an appointment to supervise the Nizam's personal estate, where he worked with more Kayasths from old-city families. He introduced the modern pay scale into the estate on his own initiative, without the Nizam's sanction, which provoked a reaction that caused one of his famous resignations. On another occasion, when the Nizam refused to sanction *mansab* payments for a period of six months, Murlidhar decided to pay the *mansabdars* anyway. The Nizam sent the Commissioner of Police to stop the payments. Murlidhar imprisoned him in a room until informed that the treasurers had finished, whereupon he released the Commissioner and sent his own resignation to the Nizam. He was restored to favor when the Nizam returned it unsanctioned, with a gold coin.[19]

17. Mohamed Abdul Rahman Khan, *My Life and Experience* (Hyderabad, 1951), 66, quoting a letter from Mr. Seaton.
18. Interview and documents with Kunj Behari Lal.
19. Interviews with Kung Behari Lal and Nar Har Raj.

The Asthanas had entered Hyderabad as outsiders. Yet they gradually became identified not only with old Hyderabad but with the Kayasths in the old city. Rae Murlidhar died in 1929, and two recollections of him from that time testify to the lessening distance. The first, by a Muslim colleague in the modern administration, called him a "naturalized Hyderabadi" and stated that "there was the stamp of old Hyderabad on him, and though an orthodox Hindu, he looked like a Moulvi of the earlier regime—his well-kempt beard completed the illusion! In him, Hyderabad lost a memorable type of Hindu gentleman, a type that had helped to bring about a brotherly feeling between the two communities."[20]

Murlidhar's commemoration ceremony was held in the Malwala palace, an important fact in itself; on that occasion another Muslim colleague, a newcomer, linked him to the Malwala *daftardar* Raja Shiv Raj:

[Murlidhar] was representative of the best of Indian culture produced on Indian soil over centuries. I knew him not from Hyderabad, but was introduced to him in Aligarh and Agra. After his arrival in Hyderabad I met him twice, once officially and once as a friend, and thereafter I met him often in both capacities . . . I judged him a fine man . . . He worked without distinction of caste or creed . . . In the period India is passing through, these qualities should be kept in mind. It is appropriate to hold his condolence meeting here, where Shiv Raj's condolence meeting was held. He and Murlidhar possessed the same qualities. Both, being broadminded, benefitted the public as well as their own families . . . Shiv Raj looked after both temple and mosque . . . as he arranged pujas and the cleaning of temples, he arranged the lighting of mosques. The examples of both fine old men are before you; I hope you follow them.[21]

The views above were those of men without knowledge of the historical differences between the various Kayasth kin groups in the city. But they point to the increasing contacts, both occupational and social, between Asthanas and old-city Kayasths. The Asthanas' continued prosperity made them the crucial group in the Kayasth social and political conflicts of the 1930's and in the marriages across subcaste lines of the 1940's.

Table 20 shows that employment in the modern administration grew most steadily among the Mathurs. But one kin group accounted for most of the individual office-holders. Even in 1949, two-thirds of the Mathur gazetted officers were members of only five families.[22] Mathur placement

20. Zahir Ahmed, *Life's Yesterdays* (Bombay, 1945), 236, quoting Nizamat Jung, then political secretary.
21. Nawab Sadr Yar Jung, head of the Ecclesiastical Department, April 1, 1929, speech to commemorate Murlidhar's death (meeting arranged by the Kayasth Young Men's Union; manuscript with Gurucharan Das Saxena).
22. Most were in the kin group of Lalta Pershad. The five families were 6, 21, 13, 12, and a branch of 2.

of family members in service contrasted with that of the Asthanas, who worked in different departments.[23] Mathurs tended to cluster in one department, wherever a member of the Malwala family was put in a prominent position. When Raja Murli Manohar was accountant general, and when his son Raja Inder Karan was commissioner of customs, several Mathurs joined those administrative units. In the 1920's, several closely related Mathurs entered the Land Revenue Department, which Murli Manohar's second son Raja Dharm Karan had joined in 1917. One other Mathur, Satguru Narayan, was in the same department, and four more Mathurs joined it from 1922 to 1929: Satguru Narayan's brother, married to Dharm Karan's sister; two brothers of Dharm Karan's wife; and the young son-in-law of Inder Karan.[24]

There were good reasons for Mathurs to enter government service in the 1920's. In 1922, after years of delay, an official investigation into the Daftar-i Mal had commenced, as discussed in Chapter 9. This investigation, combined with Shiv Raj's age and imminent death, and the deaths of his son and two younger brothers (Murli Manohar and Lochan Chand), aroused apprehensions about the future and inheritance of the *daftar*. Then, about 1923, the Nizam embarked upon a series of formal visits to the family residence, provoking further uncertainty. Such visitations were, from one point of view, a great honor; but they may have been motivated by greed for the large tributes a family so honored had to present. Some reported an even more specific motive: the Nizam had allegedly demanded a large amount of money from Raja Shiv Raj to guarantee succession to the man of Shiv Raj's choice after his death, but he had refused to pay. The Nizam visited every day for two months, accepting formal homage and two thousand to five thousand rupees each time until he had received the figure demanded, said to be either two or three *lakhs* (200,000 or 300,000 rupees).[25] The Nizam paid similar visits to the Rae Rayan and Paigah residences during the same period—both estates were then under the Court of Wards and seeking favorable releases to heirs.[26]

23. They were in Settlement, the Medical School, the Grants Department, the Public Works Department, the Judicial Department, Commerce and Industry, and the Financial Department: *Classified Civil List*, 1931.

24. For dates of entry to service, *Classified Civil List*, 1931; for relationships, the genealogies. These men were Ramchander Narayan (3), two sons of Janaki Chand (21), and Raj Pershad (12).

25. Interviews with Hakim Vicerai, Syed Mohiuddin Pasha, and Hind Kishore; also, an article from the Poona *Dnana Prakash*, March 22, 1925, repr. in Rao, *Misrule*, 73.

26. No special enmity was seen in this pattern by local people, since the Nizam was known as a miser. But some outside comments termed it exploitation of Hindus: Rao, *Misrule*, 82, 85.

When Raja Shiv Raj died in 1925, and the *daftar* was finally transferred to the Finance Department,[27] it was chiefly the prestige of the Malwala family that was affected. But the other Mathur families faced more severe consequences. Without an abundance of power and wealth, how could the patron family provide for the rest? Were the Malwalas, in fact, obliged to continue their support? Would Shiv Raj's contending successors honor their traditional obligations, and, even if they wished to do so, would those obligations be carried out by the government-constituted Managing Committee and later the Court of Wards?

The Mathur *jagirdar* families decided to organize to protect their rights. They used Salar Jung's 1875 recognition of Raja Inderjit's right to alienate parts of the Malwala estate to his sons-in-law to substantiate their claims as sub-*jagir* holders. The marriage contracts signed and sealed by earlier Malwalas were produced to substantiate the dependent families' claims. When the *daftar* was attacked before Shiv Raj's death (in a 1922 *farman* or royal decree criticizing it and putting it under state supervision), the Committee of Jagirdars of the Brotherhood sent Shiv Raj a petition: "You called our ancestors who left everything and came; we are all dependent on you. Don't let this relationship be broken." Shiv Raj signed this in 1924, saying "I agree with all you say and approve this petition. Your rights in my estate are accepted by me." After his death, the committee secured similar endorsements from most senior members of all collateral branches of the Malwala family.[28]

The death of Raja Shiv Raj placed the Malwala estate under direct government supervision, since the inheritance was hotly contested. The government immediately issued instructions for an investigation according to the rules of the Grants Department; the estate had previously been exempted from such inquiries by the Nizam's personal orders.[29] The estate was described as being "in chaotic condition overburdened with debts and family disputes." A Managing Committee was set up with Raja Inder Karan as its nominal head. Inder Karan, Murli Manohar's eldest son,

27. The Daftar's Mansab, Khitab, and Mavahir sections (lists of *mansabs,* titles, and seals) were still being transferred a year later: Rao, *Bustan,* V, 264, 292.

28. Shiv Raj endorsed the petition Dec. 27, 1924, shortly before his death. Murli Manohar's first two sons, Inder Karan and Dharm Karan, did not sign, but Mahbub Karan, the third, did; other signers were Manohar Raj, Vinayak Raj, Gur Karan, and Rani Shiv Raj (all in July of 1930). The committee consisted of *jagirdar* families from the early nineteenth century, also the affines of Murli Manohar and Shiv Raj (documents with Hakim Vicerai).

29. See Ali, *Anvar-i Asafiyah,* 235, and FCS, installment 79, list 3, file 575, serial no. 109, of the Finance Department.

was thus recognized as best claimant, but he died in 1934 without having received the official title.[30]

Inder Karan's death left the succession question wide open again. Legal battles began, and the estate was put under the Court of Wards pending a decision. The contestants included Dhiraj Karan, Inder Karan's son; Dharm Karan, the second son of Murli Manohar; and Manohar Rani, the only surviving daughter of Raja Shiv Raj. The three claimants engaged leading lawyers from northern India,[31] but the final decision was the Nizam's. He personally intervened and issued a *farman* naming Raja Dharm Karan Bahadur heir to the estate, effective June 1, 1946. As Dharm Karan was by this time a member of the Executive Council and a strong political supporter of the Nizam, the decision was not surprising.[32]

In effect, the Malwala estate was under outside supervision for twenty years, from 1925 to 1946. In 1930, the Managing Committee presided over the "abolition" or settlement of the estate, and control of the Malwala family over other Mathurs was greatly lessened. The distribution of allowances and property within the subcaste was recorded and subjected to government supervision. The practices customary in the modern administration, the reduction of *mansabs* by one-quarter with each succession, began to be applied within the Malwala estate. When the amounts

30. Interviews with Mahbub Karan and Maharaj Karan; quote from Mudiraj, *Pictorial Hyderabad*, II, 417; Managing Committee from Rao, *Bustan*, V, 291, and Ali, *Anvar-i Asafiyah*, 180.

31. They were Sir Tej Bahadur Sapru for Dharm Karan, B. L. Mehra for Dhiraj Karan, and Sir Vazir Hussain for Manohar Rani: interviews with Ragukul Pershad, Sri Rang Pershad, and Hakim Vicerai.

32. Dharm Karan was named head of the family, though the income was to be divided into four shares after administrative fees: APSA (Interim Depository), Register of Copies of Faramin Mubarak [royal orders] connected with Mohtamad-i Mal for 1359, 60, and 61 H. [1940-1942], and confidential file 87/17. Dharm Karan's recognition as chief heir in 1946 caused divisions within the Malwala family, greatly widened by the succession decision following his death in 1947. Here the Nizam overrode his Executive Council, which voted to take the Malwala *jagirs* under government control and investigate them systematically according to Grants Department regulations. Dharm Karan had not entered the particulars of his *jagir* on the proper government list, and there were no papers on file when he died. Despite this ambiguous situation, the Nizam wrote his Executive Council that Mahbub Karan, younger brother of Dharm Karan, should clearly inherit and that a quick decision should be made. While the Executive Council equivocated, Mahbub Karan drew out 82,553 rupees, closing the estate's account with the Hyderabad State Bank. The Nizam then ordered Mahbub Karan to be named successor, though the other contestants included Dharm Karan's own sons as well as descendants of the lines of Inder Karan, Lochan Chand, and Moti Pershad Kirat Bahadur. But Mahbub Karan, like his older brother, Dharm Karan, was a crony of the Nizam; he was also private secretary to the Nizam's elder son, the Prince of Berar. Principles such as seniority, senior branch of a lineage, or ability were subordinated to closeness to the reigning Nizam.

distributed in 1925 were recorded, that froze the incomes of families and branches of families, even of Malwala family members.[33] Even those families who successfully established claims on the estate recognized that it would be a decreasing income. During this twenty-year period, the Mathur *jagirdar* families found themselves dealing with government committees and the Court of Wards; the latter handled between 55 and 74 appeals against its decisions concerning the Malwala estate in the late 1930's.[34]

While some Mathurs tried to retain incomes from the Malwala estate, others sought more modern alternatives. Many joined the modern administration, as Table 20 shows. By 1931 there were more Mathurs than Asthanas listed as gazetted officers, but their qualifications and pay still differed considerably. Four of the seven Asthanas had B.A. degrees, and three of them held higher degrees. All seven, born from 1875 to 1893, were career men, and by 1931 their salary average was 646 rupees per month. No two Asthanas were in the same department. In 1931, the eighteen Mathurs in gazetted positions had an average salary of 378 rupees a month, and they were clustered in the Land Revenue, Judicial, and Financial departments.[35]

The second area into which Mathurs moved in the 1920's was the legal profession; some entered independently and some via the Judicial Department. A member of Lalta Pershad's family was the first Mathur *vakil* or lawyer. The next two to enter legal professions were from the families of Janaki Chand and Hari Mohan Lal (numbers 21 and 13 in Table 7). These first three *vakils* and *munsifs* (subordinate judges) were born in the nineteenth century, but in the 1920's several more Mathurs took judicial degrees and certificates.[36] Some served in the districts, where they formed friendships with Asthana and Saksena colleagues.

A third new area of Mathur employment in the 1920's was the medical profession. Again a member of Lalta Pershad's family preceded others[37]

33. For example, Ali, *Anvar-i Asafiyah,* 276, where Mahbub Karan got 4,200 rupees a year (350 rupees a month) in 1930; and Muntakhab Mansabdaran (APSA, Section R1), Register 1, no. 199, *muntakhab* (award) no. 2 in the *serrishtah* of Sunder Lal, releasing a monthly sum of 271 rupees (after reduction) to the deceased Manohar Raj's seven-year-old son, with the provision that he care for the widow and his unmarried sisters and arrange marriages for the latter (1938).

34. Government of Hyderabad, *Report on the Administration of the Court of Wards Department for the Year 1348 F.* [1938–1939], APSA (Hyderabad, 1940), 25.

35. *Classified Civil List,* 1931.

36. The first three were Jairam Pershad (6), Nar Singh Pershad (21), and Brij Mohan Lal (13). The next group included Madhori Pershad (17); Bindbasni Pershad and Hind Kishore (16); Vasudev Pershad (12); Digamber Pershad (4); and Niranjan Pershad (1). Interviews with Hakim Vicerai, Hind Kishore, Shiv Mohan Lal, and Sri Rang Pershad.

37. Born in 1858, Dr. Kripa Shanker was trained in both Yunani and Western medicine.

and the next doctors came from the family of Janaki Chand. Respect for the new profession was epitomized by a 1927 marriage: Janaki Chand's son Dr. Benkat Chandra, a recent medical graduate, was chosen as bridegroom of the late Raja Nim Chand's daughter. Nim Chand's widow was the first Hindu widow in Hyderabad to legally inherit her husband's property, and her son-in-law thus had access to considerable resources (some 60,000 rupees in 1930).[38] Dr. Benkat Chandra earned an additional medical degree in London, and the Nizam became one of his patients. His success firmly established medicine as the preferred profession for younger men and women in his immediate family, which included 9 of the 34 Mathur doctors in 1970; 3 more were affines.[39]

After the inauguration of Osmania University in 1918, a few Mathurs took higher degrees and returned to teach there, coming into contact with the first Saksenas and Asthanas in the academic profession. The first Mathur to go beyond the B.A. and secure an academic position at Osmania was Shiv Mohan Lal (family 13), who took an Aligarh degree and became a professor of philosophy.[40] As one of the few Hyderabadi Hindus on the faculty, he was well placed to encourage other Mathurs and Kayasths in their studies and careers. He and other Kayasths at Osmania were leaders in the social reform, caste association, and intersubcaste marriage conflicts in the 1930's.

Occupational changes for Mathurs can be summarized from the 1870's, when most men were dependents. Lalta Pershad joined the modern administration in 1877; Murli Manohar was appointed Accountant General in 1893, and the influx of kinsmen began. Until 1920, however, only seven families were represented in gazetted positions.[41] In the 1920's, the acquisition of higher education and uncertainties about the future of the Malwala estate led many Mathurs to join the modern administration. The

38. Ali, *Anvar-i Asafiyah*, 242; Kamil, *The Communal Problem in Hyderabad*, 60; for the income, *Report on the Administration of the Court of Wards . . . for 1339 Fasli* [1929–1930] (Hyderabad, 1931), 2.

39. Interview with Dr. Benkat Chandra.

40. Having lost his father at a young age, he was impelled to consider carefully the ways in which he might support his young wife, who encouraged him to choose a career of his liking. Also crucial was the personal encouragement and partial financial support offered by Nar Narayan Pershad, one of the first Mathurs to hold a B.A. and a career civil service man, who arranged a part-time teaching job at the Dharmvant High School for Shiv Mohan Lal while he took courses at Osmania. The latter then accepted a Hyderabad government scholarship to go on for the M.A. in philosophy at Aligarh, where he prudently studied for a traditional Sanskrit degree as well. In 1926, he overcame his closest rival, a Maharashtrian Brahman also from the old city, for the newly created position in philosophy at Osmania by securing the Vice Chancellor as his patron: interviews with Professor Shiv Mohan Lal.

41. See note 22 above for five families; the others were those of Narinder Pershad (family 17) and Ramchander Narayan (3): *Classified Civil List*, 1931.

range of occupations broadened, and young men from several families became lawyers and doctors. These new professions proved particularly attractive to those allied with junior or dissident Malwalas; others depended upon close connections with family leaders to enter government service. Residential patterns reflected the divergence between those who remained dependents and those who joined the modern administration or newer professions. The former stayed in the old city, while the latter began to establish residences in the new city, particularly from the 1930's.[42]

Those families or branches of families that held sub-*jagirs* and allowances tended to remain dependents. Elder brothers retained positions within the Malwala estate, while younger ones received better educations and embarked upon modern careers. Reasons for this pattern of diversification were economic. Some of the families had grown quite large, and income was divided among several brothers or cousin-brothers. Furthermore, after the Malwala estate was settled in 1930, these hereditary grants were reduced by one-fourth with each succession.[43] Strikingly, those families or men receiving allowances took fewer risks, moving slowly into the new educational and occupational patterns.[44]

Few of the other Kayasths achieved government positions at the gazetted level, although many were employed in the modern administration below that level before the 1920's. The transition was slower, as men with limited resources worked to provide better educations and careers for their sons.

Among the Saksenas, the Accountant General's office was the starting point for this transition. Members of several families were placed there, in positions that did not require knowledge of English, by the early twentieth century. Most had moved from positions with Bansi Raja, perhaps through his advisory services to Raja Murli Manohar during the latter's tenure as Accountant General. Once placed, three of these families surpassed Bansi Raja's in terms of education and career diversification of both sons and daughters. The families were closely related by marriage, and this kin group produced the first lawyers, doctors, and educators among the Saksenas.[45]

42. Lalta Pershad, Shiv Mohan Lal, Dr. Benkat Chandra, Nar Singh Pershad, Jairam Pershad, Narinder Pershad, and Nar Narayan Pershad are good examples of those who moved; all were lawyers, doctors, or the first modern administrators in their families.

43. See page 239.

44. The Mathurs receiving allowances came from those branches of their families most closely connected by marriage with the Malwalas: for example, the sons of Shiv Raj's sisters (family 11), or Dharm Karan's son-in-law Rang Pershad (1).

45. These were the three families of Karan Pershad, Dan Chand and Kishen Lal (brothers), and one branch of the Wala Jahis. Karan Pershad and Dan Chand were

The three Saksenas in the civil lists of 1925 and 1931 illustrate the changes in status among Saksena families. In 1931, the highest salaried Saksena was a newcomer from Lucknow, Professor K. C. Roy Saksena, the history teacher at Osmania University. He earned 350 rupees a month in 1925 and 600 a month in 1931, when he was 37 years of age. Rae Karan Pershad, son of a man brought to Hyderabad and formerly employed by Bansi Raja, was in the Accounts Office, where he earned 200 rupees a month in 1925 and 510 rupees in 1931, when he was 54. The third man, Bansi Raja's son, Nar Singh Raj, had joined service in 1929. He was earning 300 rupees a month as a postal inspector in 1931, when he was 37.[46] A generation earlier, Bansi Raja had ranked far above his kinsman and employee, Karan Pershad's father,[47] and there had been neither university graduates nor teachers among the Saksenas.

Those Saksena families whose members moved earliest into modern service, then out into the newer and more independent professions, characteristically had come to Hyderabad in the late nineteenth century as sons-in-law of Bansi Raja. They did not hold hereditary *mansabs*. As among the Mathurs, those who held *mansabs* tended to change their educational and occupational patterns more slowly.[48] Those Saksenas who began their careers in district service, like their Mathur counterparts, were more open to social change. Particularly in the Police and Judicial departments, Saksenas in the districts formed friendships with non-Saksenas which facilitated the first intersubcaste marriages of the 1940's and 1950's.[49]

Many of the same patterns characterized the Bhatnagar and Srivastava families. The Bhatnagars had all been employed in the Nizam's estate. The first Bhatnagar graduates, all from Osmania and all born in the first decade of the twentieth century, were not from the wealthiest family. Four of them became lawyers and the fifth an engineer. Among them, Nageshri Pershad was the first Kayasth (and Hindu) to be selected for the Hyderabad Civil Service (begun in 1926 and modelled on the British Indian Civil Service). His starting salary in 1929 was 1,100 rupees a month, in contrast with the *mansabs* of 100 to 300 rupees a month held by other Bhatnagars in the 1920's.[50]

---

brothers-in-law. Karan Pershad's younger brothers, Kishen Lal's sons, and Balkishen's two sons (one of whom was married to Kishen Lal's daughter) were the first professionals.

46. *Classified Civil Lists*, 1925, 1931.

47. He was Narayan Das.

48. The Muntakhab Mansabdaran records (APSA) include descendants of Bansi Raja, the Wala Jahis, Hira Lal, Mohan Lal, and Khushal Rae (all older families).

49. The sons of Balkishen, Balaji Sahae, Ramchander Sahae, and Govind Raj are good examples: interview with Maheshwar Raj Saxena.

50. Nageshri Pershad became a lawyer and judge: *Classified Civil List*, 1949. For the

Similarly, Srivastavas from older *serrishtahdar* and noble families changed their educational and occupational patterns more slowly than did more recent immigrants. Of the six Srivastavas listed in the civil lists of the late 1940's, four were from families that had moved to Hyderabad in the late nineteenth or early twentieth centuries; the other two were local *suratvals,* self-made men unconnected with one another by marriage.[51] Many poorer Srivastavas served in the Police, Army, and Postal departments; many Bhatnagars also served in the Police.

The Gaur and Nigam Kayasths, without representation at higher levels of the modern administration, moved into it at lower levels as their hereditary positions were reduced or abolished. Property, *jagirs,* and special services in the Nizam's household supported leading Nigam family members, until Saksena in-laws in the 1940's helped place men in the Excise Department.[52] Saksena relatives also proved instrumental to Gaur Kayasths, who lost hereditary positions with the Paigah family and the Arab chief Ghalib Jung rather suddenly. The mortgage of property and jewelry, lawsuits between brothers, and marriage strategies designed to conserve resources characterized the early-twentieth-century Gaur residents of Shahalibanda.[53] Most still held jobs that used Urdu; or, they depended upon decreasing hereditary *mansabs.* (For example, reduction of *mansabs* resulted in the inheritance of only 34 rupees a month by a descendant of Balmukund in 1921.[54]) But the first lawyer among the Gaurs was educated and encouraged by his Saksena in-laws after he became one of the first to participate in an intersubcaste marriage in 1931.[55]

The discussion so far has emphasized occupational mobility, the conspicuous movement of young educated men into modern careers. It has

---

mansabs, see Kamta Pershad, *Chitragupta Vamsi Kayasth Qaum Directory* (Agra, 1926). Of the three sons of Bansidhar (the "Majlis Rae" family), the first held the reduced *mansab* of 300 rupees a month, and the others, Inder Karan and Chander Lal, became a lawyer and an engineer, respectively. Sham Sunder and Manohar Pershad, sons of Ram Pershad, became lawyers. Interviews with Dr. R. C. Bhatnagar and Balobir Prosad.

51. These six were Shiv Kumar Lal, Lal Mohan Srivastava, Madan Mohan Lal, Shamsher Bahadur, Janaki Pershad, and Dr. Kanval Chander (the latter two from the old city.) Rae or Khwaja Janaki Pershad's mother may have been Muslim; and Dr. Kanval Chander's mother was Bhatnagar: interviews with the last three named, Balobir Prosad, and Dr. R. C. Bhatnagar.

52. Interviews with Dwarka Pershad Nigam and Somnath Pershad.

53. Interviews with Jagdish Pershad, Ram Mohan Roy, and Roy Mahboob Narayan, whose statements differed in detail but not in general.

54. Interviews with Onker Pershad and Jagdish Pershad (the latter inherited the 34 rupees).

55. Onker Pershad, first of three Kayasths to attend St. George's Grammar School (with two Saksenas). Other Gaurs married to Saksena women (Roy Mahboob Narayan, for example) were matriculates and leaders in Kayasth association and literary activities: interviews with Ram Mohan Roy, Mahboob Narayan, and Eknath Pershad.

TABLE 21:
Mansab Inheritance, 1930–1955: Average Monthly Incomes

	Malwalas	Other Mathurs	All other Kayasths
Before 1930	Rs. 270 (10)[a]	Rs. 55 (8)	——
1930–1939	——	Rs. 20 (22)	Rs. 61 (8)
1940–1949	Rs. 96 (10)	Rs. 15 (15)	Rs. 30 (9)
1950–1955	——	——	Rs. 13 (8)

Source: Compiled from all Kayasth cases in the Muntakhab Mansabdaran records, Section R1, APSA.

[a]Figures in parentheses are the number of males who inherited shares in each period.

been hinted that they would play a key role in social and political changes including the extension of marriage networks across subcaste boundaries. But such men were still in the minority before 1948. While Kayasths in the modern administration and those entering legal or medical careers could expect a monthly income of at least 300 rupees, other men earned well below that. A Kayasth publication with information about positions and salaries in 1920 gives an average of 215 rupees a month for men in the Nizam's estate and in other hereditary positions.[56] These hereditary stipends continued to decline. The cases registered in the Inheritance of Grants files show customary reductions being enforced with each transmission. Since all male heirs divided each *mansab* equally, this soon resulted in each heir being awarded a very small sum. This had also become true for Mathur dependents of the state-administered Malwala estate. Table 21 averages individual monthly incomes from *mansabs* by decades to show the rapidity of the decline and the differing economic levels for members of the Malwala family, dependent Mathurs, and other Kayasths. These figures indicate that dependent Mathurs were slightly less well-off than other Kayasths in the *mansab* inheritance files.

In 1942 or 1943, a final blow fell for the *serrishtahdars* in the Nizam's estate: their paymaster functions were abolished. These *serrishtahdars* were pensioned off at full salary, but their positions could no longer be inherited.[57] Some of the positions had been passed down within kin groups since the eighteenth century; they had been preserved until 1942 only by their placement in that backward administrative division.

56. Pershad, *Kayasth Qaum Directory* (eight men whose monthly salaries ranged from 117 to 397 rupees).
57. One story attributes this to embezzlement, which the government used as a pretext to abolish the paymaster function: interviews with Balobir Prosad and Vijay Mohan Lal.

[245

As a result of impoverishment there were disputes, cases of desertion, and other tragedies. The paltry sums awarded after *mansab* reductions led to disputes among brothers and caused at least two men to desert their families.[58] There were instances of alleged deception and even murder in order to secure inheritances.[59] Feuds dating from the 1930's and 1940's still influence relations among members of Kayasth families.

Changing Roles for Women

This book so far has dealt directly with the occupations and activities of men. Kayasth women have come into the analysis indirectly, as persons through whom positions or other economic assets might be inherited or through whom men might gain access to the support or resources of other men. Women transmitted resources indirectly, either vertically through descent in the older bilateral system, or horizontally through close relationships between affinal kinsmen. Their value depended upon that of the men to whom they were related; and the arrangement of marriages reflected assessments of the economic resources of those men who were to become relatives.

Once marriages had taken place, women could make substantial contributions to family welfare. Most important was a woman's function as a mother, the producer of children, and particularly sons; but women could also exert considerable influence within the household realm. Among the Kayasths, many women are remembered for contributing to family stability through institution of religious rituals or events. Others have acted decisively to end the abuse of drink or drugs by their men. Several such women are said to have "been like saints," upholding family purity in implicit but obvious contrast to the men of their families.[60]

Until the twentieth century, with a few exceptions in the late nineteenth, individual Kayasth women were little known outside their own households. Married between the ages of five and ten and secluded afterwards, women of earlier generations associated only with close relatives and children. They were designated by nicknames or "house names," of which there

58. The families were those of Sohan Lal and Mohan Lal, and Bansidhar and Thakur Pershad: interviews with Gurucharan Das and Dhiraj Kumar; for Sohan Lal and Mohan Lal, Muntakhab Mansabdaran, Register 2, no. 660, *muntakhabs* no. 40 of 1944, 30 of 1950, 47 of 1951, and 34 of 1955.

59. For instance, there is the tale of the Muslim concubine of Keshav Pershad (Srivastava). She allegedly had his legal heir murdered in a mosque so that her son could secure a share of the *mansab*: interview with Jagdish Pershad (Gaur); *mansab* award to her son, Muntakhab Mansabdaran, Register 2, no. 619, *muntakhab* no. 73 of 1938.

60. Interviews with Gurucharan Das Saxena, Shiv Lal, and Manohar Lal.

were a limited number in use among the Kayasths. Women were most commonly identified as the daughters, wives, or mothers of particular men.[61]

Even though women often proved instrumental in the transfer of resources, their role was seldom publicly acknowledged. In one case in the Malwala family, the widow of Raja Inderjit is said to have personally interceded with Diwan Salar Jung I to secure the inheritance to her son Raja Shiv Raj.[62] Similarly, among the Gaur Kayasths, the "daughters of Balmukund" acted to preserve the family inheritance by seeking appropriate marriage alliances, as mentioned in Chapter 10. Even in these instances the women acted as agents. Their role was temporary, and the resources were permanently vested in men.

In the nineteenth century, the one Kayasth woman who became a public figure was a *sanyasin*, a female ascetic who was not subject to societal norms. Widowed at a young age and guided by her devout mother, this Saksena girl studied Sanskrit and took vows from a Maharashtrian Brahman guru. As the *sanyasin* Nijyanandi, she became famous in the old city for her original Sanskrit devotional poetry and singing. Her principal patron and devotee, a Maharashtrian Brahman administrator, established her residence and place of devotions in the old temple of Raja Maya Ram in Shahalibanda. As a religious figure she had a considerable Maharashtrian following in the locality, and her death by plague in 1907 was greatly mourned.[63]

After the turn of the century, the deepening impoverishment increased the vulnerability and dependence of Kayasth women. Some women were left without resources in terms of property or relatives. In one case, a Srivastava man converted to Islam in order to marry a Muslim woman as his second wife. Without parents wealthy enough to take her back, his Kayasth wife converted too, although she sent her son back to her parents to be raised as a Hindu.[64] Widows, prevented from remarrying, resorted to domestic service or disposed of property to support the family until young sons grew old enough to earn a living. In one case, impoverished and widowed women used valuable old manuscripts to make baskets to sell in the marketplace.[65] In another, a young Saksena

61. This practice hardly varied, and even for the last generation the existence of women or their names on genealogies had to be ascertained by direct questioning.
62. Interviews with Hakim Vicerai and Sri Rang Pershad.
63. Interview with Gurucharan Das Saxena; also, her compositions in Nijanand Das Bramhanand, *Sri Guru Nijanand Maharajance Caritra* (Hyderabad [1910]).
64. Interviews with Shiv Lal and Dharminder Pershad.
65. Interviews with Shakamber Raj Saxena and his mother, and Mahender Raj Suxena.

widow involved in disputes with relatives took her sons and moved to the Mathur neighborhood, concealing her origins and becoming a domestic servant in a Mathur household.[66]

Legal changes in the late nineteenth century meant that daughters or widows could inherit if there were no male heirs; this emphasized the potential value of women descended from *jagirdars* or *mansabdars*. The Malwala family provided the first example in Hyderabad of a Hindu widow awarded title and management of her husband's estate: in 1930, the Court of Wards gave the widow of Raja Nim Chand control of an estate with *jagirs* paying 60,000 rupees annually.[67] Later in the 1930's, the only surviving child of Raja Shiv Raj, a daughter, sued his nephews for title to the Malwala estate; she lost, though she secured a portion of the estate's income during her lifetime.[68] But in most inheritance cases, females were to be provided for by the male heirs until they died or were married.[69]

Kayasth men showed awareness of the new and more direct access of women to property and positions by putting them forward publicly to claim their new rights. In a number of instances, illiterate women were the apparent petitioners to the Nizam for the inheritance of their fathers, though their husbands and sons-in-law had prepared the petitions and documents. The case of the Srivastava family of Raja Mohan Lal and Raja Murari Lal was particularly striking: the Gaur husband of one of the surviving daughters fought hard to secure his wife's inheritance of the family *mansab* (fifty rupees a month). He also prepared a petition for his mother-in-law, the widow of the last male heir, imploring the Nizam to grant her 250 rupees to pay for her own funeral.[70]

In times when even small inheritances were bitterly fought over, some women appear to have played more direct roles. A Srivastava woman tried to recover a *mansab* for her husband by taking her husband's brother's cousin-son to make a personal plea to the Nizam.[71] In other cases it was not wives, but the concubines of Kayasth men who intervened. These stories concerning concubines have parallels in many communities

66. Interviews with Prof. Shiv Mohan Lal, Gurucharan Das Saxena, and Roy Mahboob Narayan.

67. See her biography in Samsam Shirazi, *Mushir-i Alam Directory* (Hyderabad, 1947), 233.

68. APSA (Interim Depository), Register of copies of Faramin Mubarak connected with the Revenue Department for 1359–6141, *farman* of 4 Ramzan 1359 H. [October, 1940]; interviews with Ragukul Pershad and Sri Rang Pershad.

69. All awards specify this, in the APSA Muntakhab Mansabdaran files.

70. Documents with Jagdish Pershad (Gaur). The petition cited her small *mansab*, 40 years' residence in a rented house, and her unemployed son-in-law (who drafted the petition).

and at all levels of Hyderabadi society, but in this period among the Kayasths they are not so much tales of intrigue as of competition for survival.

In the early twentieth century, then, women came to have new importance because of legal changes giving them direct access to property when there were no male heirs. In situations of dwindling traditional resources women could be used to play, or could themselves play, more active roles to secure resources for their sons or other relatives.

By the 1930's, several other trends had begun which significantly altered the position of women in family and society. The age at marriage was rising and girls' education was winning acceptance. While the normative age at marriage for girls in the nineteenth century was between five and ten (and the cases for which there is accurate information conform to that norm), in the twentieth century the marriage age rose. It also varied widely, as poverty or continuing education became respectable justifications for delaying a girl's marriage.

Schools for Kayasth girls were started in the 1930's and 1940's. The first female B.A. holders were born in the early 1940's and graduated in the late 1950's. Kayasth women first earned higher degrees, including medical ones, in the 1960's. Among the Asthanas, always a generation ahead of the old-city Kayasths, one woman took a position teaching school in the 1930's; and in the 1960's, employment for women outside the home began to be generally sanctioned by Kayasth families.[72] Young Kayasth women now work as schoolteachers and in a variety of other occupations. Of 102 Mathur teachers in 1971, 70 were women.[73] Other occupations considered particularly appropriate for women are medicine, both traditional and modern, and the arts. The most prestigious and admired young women are those studying medicine and embarking upon careers as doctors.[74] These recent educational and occupational changes for Kayasth women are related to the new marriage patterns discussed in Chapter 15.

The changing educational and occupational patterns among Hyderabad Kayasths show certain common characteristics. Those Kayasths who

71. Interview with Ram Mohan Roy, the young boy taken along.
72. The Asthana teacher was Shillo, daughter of Vidyasagar, first to break *purdah*: interview with Dr. Brij Mohan Lal, and his manuscript, "Our Ancestry," 28. See my article, "Women and Social Change," 117–130.
73. Interview with T. R. Mathur; list copied for a conference in the Malwala palace of the education subcommittee of the Hyderabad Mathur Kayasths, August, 1971.
74. Most of the young women doctors come from the families of Dr. Benkat Chandra (Mathur) and Professor Mahender Raj Suxena; when they enter the *purdah* section at a wedding, young girls rush to talk to them.

retained hereditary positions and allowances lagged behind others in attaining Western education and taking up modern professions; when such families did begin to change, the younger brothers usually made the transition. At higher levels of the modern administration, influential members of noble families helped place relatives, notably among the Mathurs. But the greater independence and income which could be achieved by private practice as a lawyer or doctor attracted more of those without influential relatives. The inauguration of neighborhood secondary schools and Osmania University made higher education accessible to more Kayasths and to youth of diverse backgrounds, so that *suratvals* were relatively prominent among the early graduates and new professional men.[75] Although these *suratval* Kayasths were not members of the Kayasth neighborhood associations begun in 1916, they were drawn into the political conflict of the 1930's and 1940's, to which the next chapter turns.

75. High achievers here include Dr. Kanval Chandra, the lawyer Benkat Prasad, Captain Surya Pratap, and Janaki Pershad: interviews with all of them.

CHAPTER **14**

New Patterns of
Leadership and Authority

The initiation of modern educational institutions in the old city and the expansion of education led to the founding of Kayasth associations by young Saksenas in Husaini Alam and young Mathurs in Chowk Maidan Khan. The associations were started by the educated young men and posed challenges to the control by elders of families and kin groups. Generational conflict shaped the development of the associations over time. The first associations (of the second decade of the twentieth century) lapsed after a few years, but they were started again a decade later and became increasingly active. By the 1930's, they had produced new leaders and new sources of authority for Kayasths in Hyderabad. Mobilization and conflict through the Kayasth associations reached a climax in 1938, followed by a series of compromises among Kayasths and with the Hyderabad government. The significance of the associational activities lies in their direct relationship to the changing occupational and kinship patterns among Kayasths. In particular, the new marriage networks which cross subcaste boundaries are derived from these activities.

Young Men's Kayasth Associations: The First Attempts

At the turn of the century there was organizational activity among young men in the Mathur and Saksena neighborhoods (Chapter 11). In Husaini Alam, where Saksenas predominated, the temperance issue involved some Arya Samaj members and others from the locality. In Chowk Maidan Khan, a few young Mathurs with modern educations and employment had joined together, but whatever reform goals they may have had were subordinated to the presentation of annual birthday tributes to the Nizam.

In 1915–1916, with the development of modern educational institutions in the old city, young men in both neighborhoods organized again. Their associations emphasized Western education and social reforms. Both groups tutored younger men studying for exams, and the Saksenas sponsored home tutoring of some girls in Hindi. The Saksenas also worked to encourage diversification of professions among the young men. The two associations did not compete directly for members, though there was consciousness of a general rivalry.[1]

Both associations confronted the authority of elders. Raja Shiv Raj, now in his sixties, still presided over the Mathur community (until 1925). While all Mathurs profited to some extent from the Raja's prestige in Hyderabad, he did not favor social reform. The Saksenas also met resistance from the neighborhood elders, including Bansi Raja's son. The two associations worked with this problem in ways that reflected the economic and social differences between the two memberships and the two sets of elders.

The Young Men's Kayasth Club of Husaini Alam was organized and led by young Saksenas moving into modern professions, notably lawyers. It had as its stated purpose the reawakening of the Kayasth community and the reversal of a perceived economic and cultural decline.[2] The Club attacked this central problem in several perhaps contradictory ways. Leaders made a concerted effort to instill in young Kayasths pride in their Mughlai heritage, stressing the Persian and Urdu literary skills for which Saksenas especially had been noted. Other efforts encouraged social change. The Club gave financial aid to poor Kayasth students, established a library and reading room with contemporary Urdu and English publications, and sponsored speeches and discussions on temperance, marriage reform, and other current issues. The Club also bought equipment for popular new recreations like card playing, Ping-Pong, and badminton.[3]

The Kayasth Club seems to have deliberately chosen to organize without the help of older and established men. Not only did it have no wealthy and respected patron backing it, it aroused the opposition of Kayasth

1. Both organizations published annual Urdu reports: for the Mathurs, *Kayasth Association Fatehullah Baig* (a gully off Chowk Maidan Khan), second annual report for 1917; for the Saksenas, *Kayasth Club Husaini Alam ka Pahla Sal,* 1974 sanvat [1915], also second and third years. The Husaini Alam association began with about 40 members and stayed that size (although there was turnover). The lower incomes in Husaini Alam necessitated setting separate fees for club membership, library use, and gymnasium use. The Mathur membership initially numbered 30 and increased to 60; the Mathurs had a larger budget and library.

2. *Kayasth Club, Pahla Sal,* 7.

3. See the three reports cited in note 1 above.

elders in the neighborhood, notably Bansi Raja's son Raja Nar Singh Raj. Among the Saksenas in Husaini Alam, conflict was quite open, and the records of the association mention the "opponents," the "enemy," and "opposition by the influential people."[4] To overcome the difficulties created by financial insecurity and opposition, the Club almost immediately opened "associate membership" to non-Kayasths, both Hindu and Muslim, in the neighborhood. It solicited funds and meeting and library space from all potential local donors.[5] Thus, though basically Kayasth in membership and stated goals, the Kayasth Club functioned as a young men's neighborhood association.

Leadership of this association was firmly in the hands of young men working in the Accountant General's office or embarking on careers as lawyers. Particular families, sets of brothers and brothers-in-law, provided the Club's officers; they constituted an emerging "modern" kin group. Financial donations came largely from members of the same families.[6] When the Club decided to accept membership and financial support from non-Kayasths, conspicuous among those who joined were other lawyers, colleagues of the Club's leaders.[7]

Within a year of the founding of the Husaini Alam Kayasth Club, a Kayasth Association was established by young Mathurs in Chowk Maidan Khan. This association had no non-Kayasth members; indeed, there were only two or three non-Mathur members. It too was founded by Western-educated youths and emphasized social reform. But it met for the first time in the Malwala palace and accepted the leadership and patronage of the Malwala family. The Association placed little or no emphasis on Kayasth literary and cultural traditions, and less emphasis than did the Saksenas on securing education and employment for its members. But it, too, established a library and reading room, heard speakers on contemporary issues (often high officials in the Hyderabad government), discussed temperance and marriage reform, and engaged in new recreations like tennis.[8]

4. *Kayasth Club, Dusra Sal,* 18–21.
5. The leaders of the *qaum* who promised support are listed in *Kayasth Club, Dusra Sal,* 12; member and nonmember donors are listed each year. For the decision to open membership, *ibid.,* 10.
6. The Wala Jahi family and that of Kishen Lal and Dan Chand were the major sources of support; other families were those of Nar Hari Pershad, Karan Pershad, and Bhavani Pershad.
7. These included Rai Devi Singh, Nawab Tilawat Ali Mirza, and Muhammed Varsi.
8. *Kayasth Association Fatehullah Baig.* The Malwala patron chosen by the young men was their peer, Raja Shanker Raj. The name was originally Kayasth Club, but they changed it to Association because of confusion with the Husaini Alam Kayasth Club, already in

Although outwardly more accommodating to elders, the Mathur young men's association also challenged the leadership and authority of the elder generation. It did not confront Raja Shiv Raj directly, but it publicly assumed new responsibilities for the subcaste and locality; and its members undertook reforms in secret.

The Association took over the Chitragupta temple and expanded its activities. The temple, near Shahalibanda, dedicated to the patron deity and mythical ancestor of all Kayasths, had been constructed by a Srivastava noble family. That family's last representative, Lal Pershad, had died without an heir in the late nineteenth century, and the temple had gone under government supervision. After ten years, people claiming to be heirs came forward, but the government did not recognize them. Instead, the temple was turned over to Raja Shiv Raj, apparently as the representative of all the Kayasths. Around 1916, the Kayasth Association requested and received permission to manage the temple, and it did so for several years. It sponsored an annual temple festival, sought funds, and invited a wider attendance.[9]

The Association undertook another major task when the government enlisted local organizations to help with the influenza and plague epidemics in 1917 and 1918. The Husaini Alam Kayasth Club (and the Arya Samaj, for that matter) also worked hard supervising the distribution of medicines and gruel in the old-city neighborhoods.[10] These activities were sanctioned by the government and carried out in conjunction with its officials. The work could not be viewed with public disapproval by family or subcaste elders, and it involved the young men in service work and contact with a wide range of people.

The stands of the two Kayasth associations on social reform issues most clearly demonstrate the theme of consistent challenge to the control of elders in families and kin groups. In both neighborhoods, excessive drinking was a social problem. For Kayasths who still had resources it was an indulgence; for those without resources, it threatened family welfare. Older Mathur men enjoyed frequent drinking parties. Marriages featured them, but the Malwala palace hosted them as well.[11] The Mathur elders, then, generally approved of drinking, but they were strongly opposed to interdining—sitting and eating with men from other subcastes or castes.

---

existence. The non-Mathur members were Bhatnagars (Mahabir Pershad and Ranjit Prakash Lal).

9. *Ibid.*, 7-8.

10. *Ibid.*, 5-6, for the Mathur activities in Mogulpura ward; for Husaini Alam, *Kayasth Club, Dusra Sal*, 13-14.

11. Interviews with Ramchander Narayan, Hakim Vicerai, Roy Mahboob Narayan, Sri Rang Pershad, and Gurucharan Das Saxena.

The Association membership unanimously supported interdining between members of different Kayasth subcastes and secretly held a festival dinner outside the old city to carry out the reform. Only a few non-Mathur Kayasths were present, and the event was kept secret from nonparticipants. The occasion evidenced a split on the temperance issue, however, with the "less progressive" (largely non-Mathur) members drinking and the "progressive" faction taking an oath never to drink liquor.[12] Having accepted financial support and leadership from the Malwalas, the Mathur young men undertook these symbolic reform actions secretly, and internal solidarity was high.

In the case of the Saksenas, the temperance movement was not espoused by the young men in the Kayasth Club, but by Raja Nar Singh Raj (Bansi Raja's son) and Arya Samajists. These were older men, and they were the leading opponents of the Kayasth Club in Husaini Alam. Furthermore, their temperance efforts involved the strengthening of family controls as they persuaded other older men, often those who drank heavily, to sign oaths committing their very young sons to total, lifelong abstinence. The Kayasth Club members refused to join this kind of campaign. They seem instead to have approved of the moderate use of alcohol, denying, however, that Club members were drunkards.[13] At any rate, temperance was not a reform issue for this Kayasth Club, nor was interdining.

Comparing these two early associations, it is clear that more extensive mobilization of a wider range of people occurred in Husaini Alam. The generational conflict there was quite open; and, at least on the temperance issue, the Club's "enemies" were also reformers, claiming to be more "progressive" than Club members. Both sides in Husaini Alam, then, were advocating some social changes. In the Mathur locality, the patronage of the Malwala leaders was accepted and the pressures against reform were strong. The young men challenged the control of their elders less directly and openly, but with a strong sense of daring and unity. Both associations lapsed after a few years because of insufficient funds, declining memberships, and the impact of the plague and influenza epidemics on city life.[14]

12. Interviews with Sri Rang Pershad and Roy Mahboob Narayan. The latter (a Gaur), one Nigam, and four Bhatnagars attended. The dinner took place outside the city walls, in the Tej Rae garden by the old Idgah (place where Muslims gathered to pray at the end of the two annual Id commemorations).

13. Interviews with Pandit Narinderji, Eknath Pershad, and Gurucharan Das Saxena; *Kayasth Club, Dusra Sal,* 18–20.

14. An estimated 19 percent of the old city population perished between 1911 and 1921; *Kayasth Club, Tisra Sal,* 9, reports that activities ceased for four months since most members had fled to camps in gardens and temple grounds outside the city.

New Leadership and the Young Men's Kayasth Union

Ten years later, in 1926, Husaini Alam Saksenas organized their young men again. Circumstances had changed considerably. The new educational institutions were now capped by Osmania University, and leaders of the earlier associations had established successful careers. Raja Shiv Raj had died, but since no Mathur association was immediately revived in Chowk Maidan Khan, some Mathurs joined the new Husaini Alam Young Men's Kayasth Union. Reconciliations had been effected among Husaini Alam Saksenas, so that the first reconvening took place in the Kayasth Pathshala, under the patronage of Raja Nar Singh Raj, Bansi Raja's son.[15] Not only did the Union secure the backing of Nar Singh Raj, it enlisted leading Asthanas and Mathurs, men who ranked high in the modern administration.

The man responsible for reconvening the Union, Satguru Pershad, had been active in the Kayasth Club of the previous decade; he was now a lawyer at the High Court and a recognized civic leader. Many other former participants in the Kayasth Club or their younger brothers became officers and members of the new association. First titled the Young Men's Kayasth Saksena Union, in 1927 its name was changed to the Young Men's Kayasth Union. The members and officers reflected the broader representation, and a Bhatnagar lawyer at the High Court was elected president.[16]

The theme of the Union was that the fate of the community rested with its young men and that education was necessary for progress. In contrast to the views of the Kayasth Club of 1915, the Union's secretary said in 1933: "whatever might be the past of Kayasths, we do not like to sing the songs of its grand past; our object is to discuss its present condition."[17] Individual members might still be poets in Persian and Urdu, but the Union's focus on modern education and occupations was clear.

To carry out serious efforts at education, reform, and mobilization, the Union had several advantages over the earlier organizations. Membership was open for the first time to all Kayasths in all localities, and a branch was established in Shahalibanda. Meetings alternated between different localities and residences, including the palaces of Nar Singh Raj and the Malwalas.[18] Leaders from the Asthana and Mathur kin groups

15. Raja Nar Singh Raj's son, Nar Har Raj, was a member. Annual Urdu reports for six years, 1927-1933, are with Gurucharan Das Saxena.

16. The president was Inder Karan; the 117 members of the library were: 44 Saksenas, 25 Srivastavas, 25 non-Kayasths, 18 Bhatnagars, 5 Gaurs, 4 Mathurs, and 1 Nigam. See Young Men's Kayasth Union, *Report Salanah 1927–28* (Hyderabad, 1928), 5, 7.

17. Young Men's Kayasth Union, *Report Salanah 1932–33* (Hyderabad, 1933), 1, quoting Mahender Raj Suxena.

18. The Shahalibanda branch was run by *suratval* sons of a Gaur Kayasth for some time.

in modern professions were members. These men, notably Rai Jag Mohan Lal, son of Rae Murlidhar Asthana, and two Mathurs, Nar Narayan Pershad and Harbans Chand, presided over meetings in 1927 and 1928.[19] The expanded membership and the prominence of some members, including several High Court lawyers and Mathur and Srivastava doctors who had studied abroad, enabled the Union to secure major speakers for its meetings.[20]

By 1930–1931, the Union had succeeded in greatly diversifying its activities[21] and had inspired the formation of other caste-based organizations in the old city. These included Boy Scout and Girl Guide units,[22] a short-lived Mathur reform organization,[23] and two Kayasth cooperative societies, one limited to Mathur members.[24]

The Union opened the first Kayasth girls' school, in Husaini Alam, in 1931. This Hindi-medium primary school, the Shakti Kanya Pathshala, was located in Bansi Raja's palace. A local Brahman served as headmaster. Originally a domestic science school, it added a regular academic curriculum in 1940.[25] The Malwala Girls' School (officially, the Dharm Karan Industrial Girls' School) opened in 1939, with both Malwala and government patronage, but it had a different purpose and constituency. It was an Urdu-medium *purdah* institution, intended to help poor girls

19. Nar Narayan Pershad's first wife was the sister of Harbans Chand, and both men worked in the Accountant General's office.

20. Speakers included Nawab Akbar Yar Jung, judge of the High Court (on Hindu-Muslim unity, 1930) and Nawab Bahadur Yar Jung, founder of the Anjuman Ittehad ul Muslimin (on social service, 1931).

21. See the annual reports: the library had acquired 3,000 books by 1929; 50 *purdah* ladies were registered as lending library members.

22. A Boy Scout troop begun in 1929 by the Union was registered in 1931 as the Sri Chitragupta Rovers, with Gaur and Bhatnagar scoutmasters, and a Girl Guide unit was also started then: Young Men's Kayasth Union, *Report Salanah 1930–31*, 10–11. A Mathur-led Scout troop affiliated with the Dharmvant school began at almost the same time: interviews with Chitamber Narayan and Hakim Vicerai.

23. This Anjuman Ittehad ul Amal of 1927–1928 had less than 15 members and tried to implement marriage reforms: cutting short the ceremony; decreasing the expenditure on invitations, clothes, and feasting; eliminating or reducing drinking; setting the age at marriage above 11. Widow marriage and intermarriage (between members of different Kayasth subcastes) were also discussed: interviews with Hakim Vicerai, Ramchander Narayan and Sri Rang Pershad.

24. The first was established in 1930, the second (Mathur) in 1931. Both still exist. Loans are advanced on surety of two other members, to three times their share value; the interest, initially 13 percent per year, is now 6 percent. Interviews with Jivan Pershad, Raj Pershad, and Gurucharan Das Saxena; "Report on Qaumi Institutions," *KH*, II, nos. 1–4 (1942), 18–19.

25. It became a middle school in 1944, when its examinations began to be conducted by the Hindi Pracher Sabha. *Ibid.*, 16–17, and interviews with Roy Mahboob Narayan, Shakamber Raj Saxena, Eknath Pershad, and Prithvi Raj; Inder Karan, "Shakti Kanya Pathshala," *KH*, IV, no. 3 (1944), 4.

over twelve years of age increase the income of their families through such work in the home as sewing, knitting, tailoring, and canework.[26] For an academic education, Mathur girls could attend the nearby Mufid ul Anam (Khatri) Girls' School or be tutored at home.

By the mid-1930's, the Young Men's Kayasth Union and several smaller organizations and institutions had been created by Kayasths in Hyderabad. All of them reflected the efforts of new leaders to educate and modernize their membership. The caste and subcaste basis of associational activities was secondary to the occupational mobility of the young leaders, men of local parentage who had achieved professional standing in modern occupations.

Conflict and Compromise

In the 1930's, as generational differences subsided and new leadership consolidated the social changes under way, another kind of Kayasth politics intervened. Men from the Young Men's Kayasth Union became active in the AIKC, and the resumption of this all-India connection had unexpected local consequences. In 1936, three Hyderabad men were members of the AIKC Central Working Committee: a Saksena, a Nigam, and an Asthana, residents of Husaini Alam, Chowk Maidan Khan, and the new city respectively.[27] They represented well the new leadership and expanded membership of the Union. But another new leader had become important in the city, and he was an "outsider." This was Professor K. C. Roy Saksena, recruited from Lucknow for the Osmania history department in 1921,[28] whose efforts to unite and modernize the Hyderabad Kayasths were based largely upon his view of the Malwalas as backward, retrogressive leaders who had to be rejected. Given the high status of the Malwalas and the political developments in Hyderabad state at this time, the conflicts he provoked had political overtones.

K. C. Roy became an enthusiastic participant in the activities of the Young Men's Kayasth Union. He first appeared in Union records in 1928, presiding over a condolence meeting at the Malwala palace for the death of Rae Murlidhar Asthana. That occasion linked the Malwala noble family, the Asthana modern administrators, and the educated young

26. "Report on Qaumi Institutions," 17; interviews with Balobir Prosad and Jadubanth Pershad. This school had ten students initially, and the Malwala family provided a building and *purdah* conveyances.
27. They were Raja Nar Singh Raj, Dwarka Pershad Nigam, and Jogender Bahadur Asthana: *Resolutions of the 1936 Kayasth Conference* (Bareilly, n.d.), 6–7.
28. Interview with Professor Haroon Khan Sherwani, then a member of the history department; *Classified Civil List,* 1931, for appointment.

Saksenas.[29] It was apparently K. C. Roy who affiliated the Union to the AIKC as the Hyderabad branch, and he arranged for local printing and distribution of North Indian Kayasth literature. As resident housefellow in Osmania's Hindu hostel he earned the admiration of Kayasth youths studying there.[30]

K. C. Roy first aroused controversy in 1933, when he set an example of social reform through marriage to a woman of another subcaste, a local Mathur. This "reform" marriage is often said to be the first of its kind among respectable Hyderabad Kayasths. K. C. Roy's first wife had died, and this second marriage was arranged with the help of Mathur brothers, members of a short-lived 1928 Mathur reform organization. These young men, left in charge of their siblings at the death of their father, arranged their sister's marriage with the Saksena reformer. The intersubcaste marriage was opposed by many Mathurs and older people of other subcastes.[31]

This controversy initiated a period of conflict that diffused the goals and achievements of the Kayasth Union even as it narrowed the issues and membership to a caste constituency. Acting as president of the local affiliate of the AIKC, K. C. Roy invited the national organization to hold its 1938 annual conference in Hyderabad. Members of three local Kayasth groups (a newly active Mathur *sabha,* the Young Men's Kayasth Union, and the Kayasth Cooperative Society) voted to extend the invitation. The AIKC, pleased to expand its influence and membership in the southern parts of the subcontinent, accepted; the Nizam's government, plagued by communal incidents, readily gave its permission to the Hindu organization.[32]

The Malwala family and most Mathur Kayasths expressed opposition to holding the 1938 AIKC in Hyderabad. For one thing, few Mathurs were active members of the Young Men's Kayasth Union. Even more crucial, the Malwala estate was then under control of the Court of Wards. This meant that the family could not assume its "rightful" place as host

29. Young Men's Kayasth Union, *Report Salanah 1928–29* (Hyderabad, 1929), 4.
30. Interviews with Eknath Pershad, Gurucharan Das Saxena, Roy Mahboob Narayan, and Shakamber Raj Saxena.
31. The Mathur brothers were Madhori Pershad, a lawyer, and Dr. Rup Karan. Interviews with Professor H. K. Sherwani (who attended the wedding), Hakim Vicerai, Sri Rang Pershad, Eknath Pershad, and Nar Har Raj.
32. Sources include K. C. Roy Saksena, *Report Kul Hind Kayasth Conference* (Hyderabad, 1939); *The Kayastha* (New Delhi), V, nos. 10, 11 (1938); *Resolutions passed in the 42nd session of the AIKC . . . 1938* (Hyderabad, n.d.); *Deccan Chronicle,* Dec. 18, Dec. 25, 1938, and Jan. 1, 1939; interviews with Nar Har Raj, Balobir Prosad, Sri Rang Pershad, Lokendra Bahadur, Gurucharan Das Saxena, Benkat Prasad, Roy Mahboob Narayan, and Dwarka Pershad Nigam.

to the AIKC. Mathurs charged that K. C. Roy's association did not represent the community as a whole, and that it was not led by the "natural" leaders of the Kayasths, the Malwalas, who had founded the first Kayasth *sabha* in the 1890's. K. C. Roy asked the Malwala Raja Dharm Karan to accept presidency of the Young Men's Kayasth Union and to send the official invitation to the AIKC. Dharm Karan refused this compromise.[33]

The conflict within Hyderabad quickly split the North Indian organization into opposing factions as well, and letters and petitions flew back and forth. While K. C. Roy had the support of the Bengali Kayasths and the vice presidents of the Executive Council, Dharm Karan got the president of the Executive Council to wire the Hyderabad government that the AIKC would consider any conference held in Hyderabad illegal. Undaunted by the opposition of nearly all the Mathurs, K. C. Roy collected the signatures of 72 Saksenas, 33 Bhatnagars, 28 Asthanas, 31 Srivastavas, 6 Gaurs, and 1 Nigam, and his list included several *suratvals*. He petitioned the Nizam's government not to withdraw permission for the conference.[34]

The conference was held in Hyderabad as scheduled, December 27–29, but it was a costly victory for K. C. Roy. Even in the event compromises were evident. The Maharajah of Santosh, who was to preside, "got sick," and an eminent local Asthana presided in his place.[35] Raja Nar Singh Raj served as chairman of the Reception Committee, and two non-Kayasth nobles, Maharajahs Kishen Pershad and Rae Rayan, gave receptions in place of the Malawa family. Only five Mathurs attended the conference, a long-standing member of the Kayasth Young Men's Union and his relatives, none of them dependent upon the Malwalas.[36]

Resolutions at the conference reflected the local political conflicts.[37]

33. Saksena, *Report Kul Kayasth,* 25–26.
34. *Ibid.,* apps., esp. app. 16, 99–101, for the names of the petition-signers to the AIKC and app. 18, 102–106, for those to the Nizam's government; *The Kayastha,* V, no. 11, 22–24, for this exchange from the Malwala point of view.
35. Although the Malwalas besieged officials, even the Resident, the Hyderabad government did not withdraw its permission. But the authorized meeting place was changed from the Town Hall to the West End Talkies; K. C. Roy had to improvise dormitory arrangements at his home for the large Bengali delegation; and the Maharajah was persuaded not to come by the Malwalas and their allies. Lokendra Bahadur, an Asthana engineer, presided: interviews with him and Sri Rang Pershad.
36. They were Nar Narayan Pershad, his wife, his son (Sri Kishen Sinha), Har Govind Sahae (the latter's father-in-law), and Mrs. Narayan Chand (Husaini Alam, non-Mathur wife of a Mathur).
37. National political issues were well represented: the Bengali delegates opened the session with a singing of the patriotic, nationalist "Bande Mataram," and one of the resolutions expressed "deep and respectful gratitude to his Exalted Highness, the Nizam of Hyderabad and Berar." Others congratulated Subhas Chandra Bose (just elected

One resolution enjoined all Kayasths to observe the injunctions regarding marriages as laid out in orthodox Hindu law, the Dharmashastras; and the application of this in Hyderabad did follow. Another stated that only one affiliated provincial branch of the AIKC could be recognized, and that where more than one existed, adjudication and amalgamation should be brought about by the AIKC Working Committee.[38]

K. C. Roy pointedly admonished the Malwalas in his lengthy report afterward:

Ever since its inception in 1886, it had been the long-cherished ambition of both the father and the son, the later Raja Murli Manohar Asafnawaz Want and Raja Inder Karan, Asafjahis, to invite the Conference to Hyderabad . . . But as chance would have it, their wishes did not materialize in their lifetime. Therefore the souls of the departed must have all the more derived a touching satisfaction from the fulfillment of their desire, not at the hands of those who claim to be and are the rightful claimants to their inheritance. As we all know, children are, after all, mere speculation—they may or may not care to walk in the footsteps left by their forefathers . . . Every cloud, however, has a silver lining and this ostensible dereliction of duty was, to all intents and purposes, more than made up for by the entertainments given by the two premier nobles Maharajas Kishen Pershad and Rae Rayan.[39]

While the conference mobilized many more local Kayasths, even enlisting the support of *suratvals* and women, than had previous efforts, it did not lead to unity or acceptance of the self-proclaimed leader. K. C. Roy had prevailed, but his views were not those of local men. He began publishing a local Kayasth journal, which he edited himself.[40] He then attacked the Mathurs again, over a marriage performed in September, 1939, in which the bride and groom were closely related, so that their marriage was prohibited according to the Dharmashastras and North Indian Kayasth regulations. This particular marriage was variously justified: as a love marriage, as a pact made by the parents out of mutual affection, and as a means of preserving the *jagirs* undivided.[41] Using the resolution passed at the 1938 conference enjoining Kayasths to follow the Shastric injunctions regarding the arrangement of marriages, K. C. Roy

---

president of the Indian National Congress) and censured the AIKC president's effort to declare the Hyderabad conference illegal. *Resolutions passed . . . 1938.*

38. *Ibid.* Both resolutions were sources of further feuding in Hyderabad.

39. Saksena, *Report Kul Kayasth,* app. 2.

40. Interviews with Sri Rang Pershad and Gurucharan Das Saxena.

41. There are two or three such marriages between the two families involved, and oral tradition differs on which one K. C. Roy objected to. Many assert that it aroused controversy chiefly because it was the first such marriage, and that it was progressive since the Shastras are outdated. It was *not* the first such marriage in any of the Hyderabad subcastes; it may have been the first to come to the notice of K. C. Roy.

began formal protest proceedings to the AIKC regarding this marriage.[42] But his attempts to use the AIKC against the Malwala family and oust them from a leadership position in Hyderabad were unsuccessful.

At this point, other Kayasths intervened to effect a settlement, and the consequence of the disputes became clearer. The earlier "neighborhood" openness to non-Kayasth membership was one casualty of the events of 1938, although mobilization on a caste basis broadened recruitment from within the Kayasth caste. A Hyderabad Kayasth association was reconstituted under new leadership, with members of all subcastes in the city participating. K. C. Roy himself became another casualty, when he was forced to resign following the conference. Opinion went against him as an outsider and a disrupter of local relations. A series of meetings over a three-year period reinstated the former leaders of the Kayasth Union.[43]

K. C. Roy did not give up immediately. He attempted to form another local branch and affiliate it to the AIKC, and he persisted in efforts to censure the cousin marriage performed in 1939. But a young Malwala, Raja Mahbub Karan, was elected president of the local Kayasth association in May, 1941, and the Kayasth Union leader of the 1920's and 1930's (the advocate Satguru Pershad) became secretary. This solidarity was buttressed by regular publication of the new *Kayasth Herald* (now edited by a local Saksena, Gurucharan Das) from July, 1941. Finally, the AIKC's exclusive recognition of the reconstituted *sabha* thwarted K. C. Roy's attempts to re-establish himself.[44] The final blow came in 1942,

42. *KH*, I, no. 1 (1941), for the 1940 action, taken at a Jabalpur Working Committee meeting chaired by K. C. Roy.

43. In December, 1939, a general meeting passed three resolutions: the Kayasth Sadr Sabha (the new name for the Union) was the only central organization of the community and was to strive for unity; a recent general meeting held by K. C. Roy with less than 10 percent of the membership was unconstitutional and the officers elected at the meeting (including K. C. Roy as president) had to resign; a provisional committee to hold fresh elections and affiliate correctly with the AIKC would be formed. The provisional committee duly elected had representatives from all subcastes, headed by Raja Nar Singh Raj. K. C. Roy and the other officers resigned. In February, 1940, a revised and elaborate constitution with Upper and Lower Houses was approved by a general meeting of the Sadr Sabha. The Lower House had representatives of "subcaste associations": 12 Mathurs, 6 Saksenas, 4 Asthanas, 3 Bhatnagars, 3 Srivastavas, 2 Gaurs, 1 Nigam, and 1 Chandraseni Kayasth. The Upper House was elected from the Lower House: 2 each from the Mathurs, Saksenas and Asthanas, 1 each from the others. Raja Mahbub Karan, younger brother of Raja Dharm Karan, presided over a January meeting in 1941 which again approved this constitution. See *Proceedings of the Kayasth Sadr Sabha, Hyderabad-Dn.* (Hyderabad, 1939) and reports in *KH*, esp. II, no. 1-4 (1942).

44. In 1940, the AIKC Working Committee chaired by K. C. Roy cleverly made its recognition of a provincial branch in Hyderabad contingent upon the branch's acquiescence in disapproving of the 1939 cousin marriage (note 42 above). In January, 1941, the Hyderabad Sadr Sabha decided to get that AIKC disapproval withdrawn and to take

when the AIKC elected the Malwala Raja Dharm Karan president for the next national conference. Dharm Karan, made Minister for Public Works in June, 1940, and thereby a member of the State Executive Council, inherited the estate of Raja Shiv Raj a few months later.[45] Thus the Raja Dharm Karan was rewarded both locally and nationally for symbolizing the support of Hindu nobles for the Nizam.

Following the Malwala lead, the Kayasth *sabha* functioned primarily as a political loyalist organization in the 1940's. A local Hyderabad Kayasth conference was held during the Muslim vacation for Id uz Zoha in 1942: major themes were the glorification of Dharm Karan and protestations of loyalty to the Nizam. Speeches centered upon the Kayasths' contributions to communal unity and their broad cosmopolitan heritage and outlook. There was rhetorical stress upon the advantages of education and the need to diversify occupationally, but the conference proceedings evidence little vigorous reform activity. One resolution called for the maintenance of hereditary *serrishtahdar* positions in the Nizam's estate, but no further action was taken. Another resolved to seek official recognition of the birthday of Chitragupta,[46] and in 1944, a delegation asked the government to declare his birthday a partial holiday for Kayasth employees. Refused, they resolved to try again, arguing that other communities had gained recognition for their special holidays.[47] Thus, they were seeking a minor reward, and that rather timidly.

As the *sabha* gained in visibility, at the all-India level and with the Nizam's government, local meetings became irregular. The federal structure did not work and had to be revised.[48] A 1946 local Kayasth conference, again held at the Malwala palace and hosted by Raja Dharm Karan, was again primarily concerned with expressing loyalty to the Nizam.[49]

---

action against K. C. Roy's so-called Provincial Sabha. In February, 1941, K. C. Roy finally resigned from the Sadr Sabha and *KH* editorship. A Sadr Sabha delegation sent to the AIKC Working Committee in May, 1941, succeeded in revoking the offensive resolution and having the Sadr Sabha recognized as the "district" branch: *KH*, I (1941); Satguru Pershad, ed., *Report for 1352 Fasli of the Hyderabad Sadr Sahba, Provincial Sabha* (Hyderabad [1943]), in Urdu.

45. *Hyderabad Bulletin*, June 12, 1940 (CC), for his appointment and Kayasth celebrations of this "honor to the community"; Bipin Chand, "Raja Dharm Karan," *KH*, VII-VIII (1947-1948), 2-4. For the inheritance, see Chapter 13.

46. "A Synopsis of Hyderabad Kayastha Conference," in *The Kayastha*, X, no. 1 (1942), 14-16; *The Deccan Chronicle*, Dec. 13, 21, 27, 1942, and January 3, 1943.

47. "Yamdutya Kartik Sadidooj" (Holiday for Kayasths), *KH*, IV, no. 3 (1944), 1.

48. Since few if any subcaste associations were operating, the 1946 revisions allowed for individual memberships as well as memberships through affiliated subcaste associations. Changes in the membership of the Upper House decreased the representatives from 32 to 13: *KH*, VI, no. 3 (1946) and VII-VIII (1947-1948).

49. See *KH*, V, no. 4, and VI (1946). In connection with this, a women's session and a women's Kayasth association were planned but not held.

In 1946 also, the annual Dasserah observance of the Mathur Kayasths illustrated the peculiar social and political compromises being made by Kayasths. Formerly Mathurs alone had met to pay tribute to the head of the Malwala family, but in 1946, the Kayasth Sadr Sabha held a general meeting on Dasserah, with Dharm Karan presiding. A speech on unity was delivered by Captain Surya Pratap, a Shahalibanda resident whose parentage was both Srivastava and Bhatnagar.[50] The striking features of this Dasserah meeting, then, were the extension of a Mathur observance to all Kayasths, continued deference to the Malwala family, and the inclusion of Kayasths formerly considered marginal. Even though social boundaries had been expanded by the Kayasth Union and conflicts generated by K. C. Roy, political conditions in Hyderabad forced most Kayasths to maintain or adopt rather old-fashioned forms and allegiances.

A few Kayasths did challenge the status quo in the 1940's in various ways. K. C. Roy, like many who were ultimately dependent upon government jobs, put his energy into social reform activities. His rival Kayasth association, composed chiefly of young Husaini Alam Saksenas, and claiming recognition as the AIKC provincial branch, published its own literature and advocated specific marriage reforms. This association delineated four classes of marriages, according to expenditure. The range was from 300 to 1,250 rupees per wedding, with "first-class" status awarded to the least expensive.[51] To what extent this association's recommendations were implemented, however, is uncertain; it seems to have been more important for political socialization of its young members. Association members worked together for girls' education, Hindi-medium education, temperance, and the Sanatan Dharm (orthodox Hinduism, as

50. *Ibid.* The text of the speech is with the author, Captain Surya Pratap. It was actually prepared for Dharm Karan's presidential address at the 1945 AIKC in Delhi (because of postponements, he served as AIKC President in 1942, 1943, and 1945). Another unity effort centered on the Chitragupta temple, whose management Dharm Karan turned over to the Kayasth Sadr Sabha in 1945. The appointed Managing Committee included a Saksena, a Bhatnagar and an Asthana; in 1946 the annual budget of the temple appeared in *KH*, with exhortations to attend the annual festival: "Qaumi News," *KH*, IV, no. 4, and V, nos. 1-3 (1945), 13; also VI, no. 4, and VII, no. 1, (1946-1947), 14; and Endowment Office, Serrishtah Amur-i Mazhabi, file no. 2633/2.

51. A first-class marriage was 300 rupees or less, second-class up to 600 rupees, third-class to 900 rupees, and fourth-class to 1,200 rupees; salaries of the Saksena gazetted officers in 1949 ranged from 300 to 1,250 rupees per month. Marriage rules published in 1941 called for raising marriage ages to 18 for boys and 14 for girls, stipulating that the difference in age should be between 4 and 10 years and that no man over 40 should marry a maiden under 21. Shastric injunctions regarding avoidance of both paternal and maternal lines were to be followed; but *gotras* and *als* were designated as purely fictive kinship units, to be disregarded: *Dastur-ul Amal-i Shadi Firqah-i Saksenah* (n.p., 1941), with Gurucharan Das Saxena; "Rules and Regulations for Marriages," *KH*, VI, no. 3 (1946), 17-20; interviews with Gurucharan Das Saxena, Prithvi Raj, and Eknath Pershad.

opposed to the Arya Samaj).[52] They undertook practical reforms and were chiefly responsible for the first few marriages arranged across subcaste lines. In these ventures, through K. C. Roy and a few young men who had attended St. George's Grammar School in the new city, some Husaini Alam Saksenas were influenced by secular Indian nationalists like Sarojini Naidu.[53] Thus the leadership of the association, ostensibly focusing upon specific social reforms, exposed its young members to different and exciting political alternatives.

There were those few who offered direct political challenge to the Nizam's government. After all, 1938 was not only the year of the contro-versial Hyderabad reception of the AIKC. It was also the year of the Satyagraha, in which the Arya Samaj Kayasth leaders, Sohan Lal and Pandit Narinderji, were arrested and imprisoned.[54] Government repres-sion of these dissenters contrasted with the elevation of Raja Dharm Karan to the Cabinet and his recognition as heir to the Malwala estate. But Sohan Lal, Pandit Narinderji, and their followers had little to lose, being characteristically unmarried or childless and/or of impoverished or mixed parentage.[55]

Thus it was that associational activities helped Kayasth young men to establish new patterns of leadership and authority based on modern edu-cations and occupations. In the 1930's, a series of subcaste or caste-based organizations and institutions facilitated social change for young residents of the old city. But the clarity of the initially generational conflict was confused by the passing of time, by K. C. Roy's energetic attacks on the Malwalas, and by the political need to demonstrate loyalty in the 1940's. The vigorous expansion and mobilization of the Young Men's Kayasth

52. In the temperance effort, they worked with people who opposed them on other issues: conservative older Saksenas such as Raja Nar Singh Raj, Nawab Bahadur Yar Jung, and the Arya Samajist Pandit Narinderji: *The Central Temperance Committee Report for 1946 F.* (Hyderabad, 1937).

53. Husaini Alam became quite politized in the 1930's and 1940's. The nearby Nizamia School and its orthodox Muslim founder, private tutor to Nizam Osman Ali Khan, were thought responsible for the increasingly communal views attributed to the Nizam. The Brahman schoolmaster of the Kayasth Pathshala, Bhavani Pershad, was said to be fanat-ically anti-Muslim and to have influenced some schoolboys to favor the Hindu Mahasahba. Three of the first four Kayasth boys to cross the river to St. George's all became active reformers: Gurucharan Das Saxena and Eknath Pershad (both Saksenas), and Onker Pershad (Gaur). Interviews with them and Ram Mohan Roy, Roy Mahboob Narayan, and Shakamber Raj Saxena. (The fourth, and earliest, was Raja Dharm Karan.)

54. See Chapter 12.

55. All were from impoverished Shahalibanda or Dhulpet families. Pandit Narinderji was a bachelor; Surya Pratap was of mixed parentage and his wife was a Bhatnagar; Sohan Lal's wife left him while he was imprisoned and he had no children; Raj Bahadur Gaur, a communist who helped organize the Telangana movement, was then a widower: interviews with all of them.

Union was turned into politically conditioned formal expressions of solidarity. Only a few Kayasths resisted this pressure openly.

Despite the necessarily limited and politically symbolic activities of the Hyderabad Kayasth Sadr Sabha in the 1940's, the organization contributed significantly to radical changes in marriage patterns, beginning in the 1930's. Some of the Asthana, Saksena, and Mathur families who supported K. C. Roy arranged marriages for their children across subcaste boundaries. Such marriages were numerically insignificant at first, but they marked the building of new marriage networks and a transformation in the social meaning of subcaste and caste. This transformation may have been partly a response to external perceptions and pressures—K. C. Roy, the AIKC, the Nizam's government—but it derived more fundamentally from the Kayasth associational politics of the 1930's.

CHAPTER **15**

Beyond Caste
Boundaries

Changes in marriage patterns among the Hyderabad Kayasths have been recent and striking, and the direction of change is clear. Historical factors such as subcaste designation or residential locality are still important in determining the constitution of some marriage networks, but marriages beyond subcaste, neighborhood, and even caste boundaries are increasing. A systematic survey of marriage patterns for the last two generations (since approximately 1910) shows contrasting patterns by kin groups, subcaste, and occupation and income.

There are several ways to present and analyze these new marriage patterns. First, there are descriptive accounts by informants. These emphasize the new educational and occupational connections between men and the Kayasth political alignments of the late 1930's; they also focus on key individuals and their kin groups. Then, there are statistical measures by subcaste, which give a more comprehensive but somewhat misleading idea of the broader patterns of change. Also possible are breakdowns by occupation and income, both within and across subcaste lines, which most successfully relate the kin groups of the past to the marriage networks presently being constructed. Finally, the cultural heritage of former citizens of Hyderabad has become a significant factor since the state's incorporation into India in 1948.

The First "Reform" Marriages

Which marriage was the first "reform" marriage in Hyderabad? There were many marriages before 1900 across subcaste lines, chiefly among the poorer Kayasths in Shahalibanda and Dhulpet, but the use of "reform"

[267

as a euphemism for "respectable" narrows the candidates. Only one of the earlier marriages, in 1890 between a Bhatnagar and a Srivastava, was ever spoken of as the first reform marriage. Its recognition and approval derive partly from the Arya Samaj affiliation of the participants and partly from the subsequent successful careers of several descendants and relatives.[1]

A reform marriage frequently cited as first was the Gaur-Saksena marriage celebrated by enthusiastic followers of K. C. Roy Saksena in 1931. Not only was this between members of different subcastes, but the Saksena bride was slightly older than the Gaur groom. The young man was an heir to Balmukund's positions, but his father was dead and his older cousin-brothers had just sold the ancestral property, apparently depriving their younger cousin of his fair share. The marriage was arranged by the bride's elder brother, an avid reformer along with the groom, both of whom had attended St. George's Grammar School. Encouraged by his in-laws, the young Gaur became a lawyer and won back his inheritance. Prior to 1931, at least three Gaurs had married out of subcaste, with a Srivastava, a Saksena, and a Nigam, but the marriages were not generally sanctioned. The 1931 marriage was sanctioned, as were the four others between Gaurs and Saksenas which followed almost immediately.[2]

Sometimes the first intermarriages mentioned involved Mathur Kayasths, acknowledging the greater social control exercised by members of that subcaste. Madhori Pershad, left in charge of three younger siblings by his father's death, married his two young sisters to Saksenas, K. C. Roy and Mahender Raj Suxena (younger brother of Satguru Pershad, the lawyer who led the Young Men's Kayasth Union). K. C. Roy's marriage (mentioned in the last chapter as controversial) came first, in 1933, but it was usually discounted because he was not "really" a Hyderabadi. The second marriage, because it involved the brother of an established local lawyer, was the more significant.[3] Aside from these two, at least one earlier Mathur marriage with a Saksena had occurred, but without general sanction.[4]

1. In the bride's family, descendants include the first Bhatnagar B.A., LL.B., and engineer. A son of this marriage was one of the first Kayasth doctors (Kanval Chandra), and a son-in-law (Benkat Prasad, Saksena) was one of the first Kayasth lawyers and became the Nizam's advisor. Interviews with the two men named and with Harish Chandra (Srivastava) and Dr. R. C. Bhatnagar.
2. Interviews with Onker Pershad, Roy Mahboob Narayan, Jagdish Pershad, and Shakamber Raj Saxena.
3. The groom, Mahender Raj Suxena, earned a Ph.D. in Botany.
4. The Mathur Narayan Chand's wife was probably Saksena, and Tribuan Lal (Saksena) married a Mathur woman; interviews with Sudarshan Raj Saxena and Dr. Benkat Chandra.

These first twentieth-century old-city participants in reform marriages shared several common characteristics. The grooms were almost always among the first matriculates or graduates in their kin groups and the brides among the first vernacular-educated women. In many cases the father of the bride or groom was dead, and the marriages were arranged by older brothers. In one case the bride's father was insane, and the arrangement was made by her mother's brother, the lawyer Satguru Pershad.[5] In several reform marriages, a widower took another wife from a different subcaste, reflecting his own mature commitment to social reform.[6] In all of these instances, lessened parental control was a crucial permissive factor.

The same "older brothers" were instrumental in more than one of the early reform marriages, and they shared occupational and kinship ties. Eknath Pershad, the Saksena older brother who arranged his sister's 1931 marriage to a Gaur, was *hamzulf* to Satguru Pershad, the lawyer who arranged his younger brother's marriage to a Mathur and the marriages of two of his sister's daughters to a Gaur. Lakshmi Narayan, *hamzulf* to both men and from the same (Wala Jahi) family as Eknath Pershad, took an Asthana as his second wife. Satguru Pershad's father and the great-uncle of Lakshmi Narayan and Eknath Pershad both worked in the Accounts Office. Nar Narayan Pershad, one of the first Mathur graduates and staunchest Mathur supporter of K. C. Roy in 1938, also worked in the Accounts Office. Nar Narayan Pershad and Madhori Pershad were among the few Mathur members of the Young Men's Kayasth Union of the 1930's.

Of the local marriages across subcaste lines which occurred after these first few, most were arranged by men working closely together in the modern administration and professions. Sometimes the fathers of the bride and groom served in the district town together. This was especially important for Mathur, Saksena, and Asthana lawyers, *munsifs*, and others in the Judicial and Police departments.[7] Sometimes they were professional colleagues in the city, for example, Nigams with Saksenas in

5. This bride was a sister of Shakamber Raj Saxena: interviews with him and Roy Mahboob Narayan (the groom).

6. Lakshmi Narayan and Eknath Pershad (Saksenas) and Roy Mahboob Narayan and Mahbub Rai (Gaurs) took second wives thus: an Asthana, a Bhatnagar, and two Saksenas, respectively. Interviews with men named.

7. Examples: early Saksena-Mathur marriages involved the children of Mahbub Raj, Nar Singh Raj, and Bala Pershad Farhat (Saksena) and of Darmodar Pershad, Kishori Pershad, and Harbans Pershad (Mathur). Asthana-Saksena marriages involved the children of the sons of Kalyan Rai (Asthana) and those of the Saksenas Balaji Sahae, Ramchander Sahae, Satguru Pershad (lawyers), and Arjun Pershad (brother of Karan Pershad).

the Excise Department,[8] or Bhatnagars with Saksenas, Srivastavas, and Asthanas in the modern administration. But the changing nature of occupations and career diversification within families has led not to new kin groups, but to broader marriage networks which are still in a transition stage.

New Marriage Networks

The distribution of marriages beyond subcaste boundaries (marriages that will be called outmarriages hereafter) over the past two generations is shown in Table 22, compiled from all marriage records collected. Despite the crudeness of measurement by subcaste designation, the table does accurately suggest general historical differences among Kayasth kin groups. The first notable contrast is between Asthanas and Mathurs: the Asthana proportion of outmarriages is highest and that of the Mathurs is lowest. Although members of the highly-placed Asthana families were slow to mingle socially with Kayasths from Hyderabad, their high status made them the crucial group when socially sanctioned intermarriages began. Twelve marriages of Asthanas with non-Asthanas occurred before 1940. Most were love marriages or marriages with local *suratvals*; in these cases, they were not immediately socially approved. In nine instances, Asthana men took non-Asthana women as wives: four of them were Muslim and Anglo-Indian women and four local Srivastava and Bhatnagar women. The men who arranged these marriages included one doctor, two lawyers, and three sons of a lawyer, one of whom was an independent contractor. In the ninth instance, an older brother arranged for a Bhatnagar bride from the United Provinces for his younger brother by advertising in a northern Kayastha periodical.[9]

All three marriages in which Asthana girls were given to non-Asthanas before 1940 were carefully planned and approved, and in these cases Saksenas were the chosen partners. One Asthana daughter, an educated girl, was given to a Saksena from Allahabad. He settled in the new city of Hyderabad, where both husband and wife taught school. Two Asthana daughters were given locally, one to a Wala Jahi Saksena and one to the eldest grandson of Bansi Raja. Both local Saksena grooms were well educated and in modern administrative service.[10]

8. For the Excise Department example, see note 31 below.
9. Interviews with Dr. Brij Mohan Lal and Lokendra Bahadur. The latter placed the advertisement—he was the engineer who presided over the 1938 AIKC in Hyderabad for K. C. Roy.
10. The local Saksenas were Lakshmi Narayan and Girdhar Raj, in 1936 and 1938.

TABLE 22:
*Numbers of Individuals Outmarrying by Decades
and Subcastes, 1910–1971*

	Before 1940	*1940's*	*1950's*	*1960–1971*	Total individuals outmarrying to all individuals marrying	
					Number	*Percent*
Asthana	12	25	24	25	86/130	66
Bhatnagar	12	11	8	20	51/103	50
Gaur	11	5	6	16	38/71	54
Mathur	2	4	23	37	66/626	11
Nigam	7	3	4	11	25/54	46
Saksena	28	22	25	72	147/375	39
Srivastava	28	7	20	18	73/296	25

The new pattern accelerated in the 1940's. In the past two generations, 66 percent (86 of 130) of all Asthana marrying have married with non-Asthanas. From 1940, leading Asthanas have married across subcaste lines with two major groups. The first is Srivastavas in U. P., which has given Hyderabad Asthanas access to all-India and even international administrative and professional networks. Local Saksenas and Mathurs well placed in the modern administration constitute the second group. There has been a striking imbalance in the sex ratio within Hyderabad; that is, the Asthanas have taken rather than given girls. The difference by sex was greatest in the decade of the 1940's, when the Asthanas took 13 local non-Asthana brides and gave daughters to only 4 local non-Asthana Kayasths. But their marriages with Kayasths in U. P. reflect a nearly equal exchange of brides and grooms and therefore nearly equal status of participating families.[11]

Asthana marriage patterns can be analyzed in several ways. Breaking down the 86 outmarriages by geographic area, 27 percent have occurred with non-Asthanas from outside Hyderabad, a high proportion compared to other subcastes. If all 130 individuals over the last two generations are broken down by partner's community designation, only 34 percent have married other Asthanas; 26 percent have married Saksenas (mostly local); 16 percent Srivastavas (half local and half in North India); 9 percent Bhatnagars (mostly local); and 5 percent Mathurs (all local). Ten

11. From 1940 to 1970, they took seven North Indian Srivastava women and gave five of their women; and they took four North Indian Saksena women and gave four.

Asthanas have married with non-Kayasths, constituting 12 percent of the outmarriages and 8 percent of all individuals marrying.[12] The preferences evident here are for outsiders and local Saksenas.

For the Mathur Kayasths, the pattern of marriages over the last two generations is quite different. Outmarriages have almost all occurred since 1950. The Mathur pattern differs strikingly from that of other Kayasths both in the lateness of its initiation and its rapid expansion. That the Mathurs were the most tightly organized and controlled group held true until recently; but that is clearly changing. Of the 66 recorded marriages with non-Mathurs, 91 percent have taken place since 1950 and 56 percent since 1960. Eighteen marriages with non-Kayasths have occurred since 1955, and these constitute 27 percent of all marriages with non-Mathurs. This is a higher proportion than for the Asthanas. There is another interesting contrast between the two groups. Asthanas studied overseas before Mathurs did, but no Asthana has yet married a foreign national, while three Mathurs have taken brides in England and America.[13] The Mathurs' recent rate of change has been matched by the wide expansion of boundaries.

On the other hand, while Asthanas have expanded their marriage networks to include Kayasths of other subcastes outside Hyderabad, Mathurs have not done so. There is no recorded case of such a Mathur marriage; only three Mathur men have in recent years taken even Mathur brides from outside. This contrast does not simply reflect the recent immigration of Asthanas and their continued contact with relatives and acquaintances from U.P. In fact, the Asthanas have used advertisements to make prestigious marriages primarily with Srivastava and Saksena families in U.P. This method of arranging marriages was used only by Asthanas until the 1970's.[14] The Mathurs, some of whom had social and political connections with North Indian Kayasths, have expanded their Kayasth marriage networks only within Hyderabad. They have also drawn upon local families from castes similar to the Kayasths, Urdu-speaking families of high status in the Nizam's service. Thus, Mathur marriages with non-Kayasths are being made largely with Hyderabad Urdu-speaking Hindus or foreign nationals, while the Asthana marriages with non-Kayasths have been primarily with Muslims and Indian Christians.[15] And despite the

12. See Appendix F for the breakdown on Asthanas and others.
13. These brides include one Australian (met in the U.S.) and two English women.
14. Interview with Lokendra Bahadur.
15. One such anticipated marriage, of the daughter of the Malwala Raja Mahbub Karan with Maharajah Kishen Pershad's son from the Khatri (Chandu Lal) family, would have united the leading Hindu noble families in Hyderabad. But the boy drowned in a

much earlier initiation and higher proportion of Asthana outmarriages, Mathurs have married outside the Kayasth caste proportionately more than twice as frequently (27 percent to 12 percent).

The Mathurs also differ significantly in the sex ratio characteristic of their marriages with other Kayasths. Informants frequently observed that there is a surplus of Mathur girls, a fact which has compelled Mathurs to arrange marriages with other Kayasths. This does seem possible: of the 49 Mathur marriages with other Kayasths, 36 involved Mathur women and only 13 involved Mathur men. The ratio has lessened, however, from one generation to the next, changing from 3 to 1 to 2 to 1.[16] There is also the probability that prejudice was as important as demography in producing this imbalance. Thus other Kayasths have sometimes stated that the Mathurs are not only the most closed group, but the most conservative; and there is some reluctance to send daughters into Mathur homes. The remark came most frequently from Asthana Kayasths, and their view is borne out by their recorded marriages with Mathurs. While five Asthanas have taken Mathur wives, only one Asthana daughter has been given to a Mathur, and that was very recently, in 1971.[17] A further explanation lies in the fact that the sex ratio for Mathur marriages with non-Kayasths is exactly the opposite, with 13 Mathur men but only 5 Mathur women having married non-Kayasths. Most of these are love marriages; and the pattern reflects the sex differential in educational and occupational opportunities, since these marriages almost all resulted from contacts at school or on the job.

Of the 66 Mathur marriages beyond subcaste boundaries, 49 percent have been with Saksenas, 27 percent with non-Kayasths, 14 percent with Srivastavas, and 9 percent with Asthanas. It should be remembered that individuals making these marriages constitute a low percentage of all individuals marrying since 1930: thus, those marrying with Saksenas are only 5 percent of all marrying, with non-Kayasths 3 percent, and with Srivastavas 1 percent. But the new pattern is increasing fast, particularly when measured by the numbers of families arranging such marriages.

---

boating accident; the girl later married a Bombay Marwari businessman. The Indian Christian proportion for Asthanas is almost entirely due to Dr. Brij Mohan Lal, who married a local Christian nurse in 1918 and whose daughter has also married a Christian.

16. Interviews with Gurucharan Das Saxena, Lakshmi Narayan, Eknath Pershad, and Roy Mahboob Narayan; and see Appendix F, Mathurs. It is also possible that Mathur men were making unsanctioned marriages and thus "disappeared" from the genealogies and the pool of potential husbands—see note 26 below for further comment.

17. Interviews with Lokendra Bahadur, Dr. Brij Mohan Lal, and Kunj Behari Lal; the groom was Professor Dhrubash Karan, son of the first Mathur headmaster of the Dharmvant School.

Before 1950, only 3 Mathur families accounted for the 6 marriages beyond the subcaste; now, 18 families have arranged such marriages.

The changing marriage patterns for the Kayasths, with emphasis on families within the subcastes, are summarized in Table 23. The table illustrates several further contrasts, this time chiefly between the Mathurs and the Srivastavas. As shown, the proportion of Mathur outmarriages that occurred before 1940 is only 3 percent, and the percentage of families participating in such marriages is also lowest for Mathurs. In a breakdown by family, 2 Mathur families lead the rest, with 25 to 27 percent of their members in the last two generations marrying outside the subcaste.[18] But *all* of the surviving Asthana families have married members to non-Asthanas more than 50 percent of the time for two generations.[19] Almost all families in the other subcastes have married members outside the subcaste over 25 percent of the time during the same period.[20]

The Srivastavas are at the other extreme.[21] According to all informants, the highest ratio of outmarriages should have occurred among Srivastavas at all times, and there is some evidence to support that. The Srivastavas show the highest proportion of marriages beyond subcaste occurring before 1940 and, accordingly, the most constant proportion of such marriages over time (see Table 23). The incomplete recording of Srivastava outmarriages is evident, however. While only 73 outmarriages were recorded from Srivastava informants, the genealogies of other Kayasths provided 39 additional marriages with Srivastavas.[22] Usually there was a discrepancy of only 1 to 3 marriages between the information collected from members of the subcaste involved and other informants. But all discrepancies over 5 involved the Srivastavas, indicating that the data was less complete for them.[23] The Srivastavas match the Mathurs' high pro-

18. These are the families of Anjani Shankar Lal (number 9 in Table 7) and Rameshwar Pratab (5).

19. The percentages for three families are 50–52 percent; for two, 100 percent (only one marriage each); and for seven, from 60 to 75 percent.

20. The other subcastes fall between the Mathurs and Asthanas. For the Srivastavas, five of the 33 families fall under 25 percent and the rest over. For the Gaurs, only one family falls below 50 percent; for the Bhatnagars, only one falls below 25 percent; for the Nigams, all are over 25 percent; for the Saksenas, only six fall below 25 percent.

21. Almost certainly the fragmentary genealogies recorded for Srivastavas represent fewer than the 78 separate families I have recorded; probable connections in earlier generations were not obtained.

22. I have used only the figures obtained from members of a subcaste for that subcaste in the tables; an analysis of the discrepancies cannot be included in detail here, but the Srivastava category is clearly different from the others.

23. However, in Srivastava marriages with Mathurs, five Srivastavas were under-recorded or omitted from Mathur genealogies. The Mathurs also failed to record one or two mar-

TABLE 23:
Participation in Outmarriages by Subcastes and Families, 1910–1971

Subcaste	No. outm. last two gen.	Percent outm. before 1940	Percent outm. after 1950	No. fam. outm.	Percent fam. outm.
Asthana	86	14	57	12/14	86
Bhatnagar	51	24	55	14/18	78
Gaur	38	29	63	9/10	90
Mathur	66	3	91	18/28	64
Nigam	25	28	60	5/7	71
Saksena	147	19	66	33/43	77
Srivastava[a]	73	38	52	33/78	42

Source: Compiled from Table 22 and breakdowns of marriages by families within each subcaste category (not reproduced in this book).

[a]The figures for Srivastavas are not reliable, as will be discussed in text.

portion, 27 percent, of outmarriages to non-Kayasths; significantly, this is not a recent development for them.[24] Finally, about one-quarter of Srivastava marriages over the past two generations have been with Srivastavas outside Hyderabad city, in the districts and Madras, a reminder that the number and availability of fellow subcaste members is an important consideration with respect to marriage arrangement.

To consider these demographic factors, changing norms within subcastes must also be taken into account. As marriages across nominal subcaste boundaries became accepted, the pool of eligible local marriage partners grew larger. At the same time, efforts were made to remove the restrictions on marriages within subcaste as well. The *als* were stated to be purely nominal and no longer relevant in arranging marriages.[25] And

---

riages with all other subcastes except one. The Mathur discrepancies were not due to faulty data collection: the completeness and accuracy of Mathur genealogies is probably the greatest. The discrepancies reflect, rather, stricter control of social boundaries by Mathur informants, who simply withheld information of unsanctioned marriages or alliances and no longer viewed the participants as members of the subcaste. Whereas in other kin groups the *suratvals* and "deviants" were acknowledged, if not by the family involved certainly by other families who helped fill out descent lines and marriage alliances, this did not happen among the Mathurs.

24. See Appendix F, Srivastavas.

25. Interviews with Professors Shiv Mohan Lal and Mahender Raj Suxena; note 51, Chapter 14. It is difficult to believe that the *als* had operated restrictively, in any case. Among the Mathurs, three families with the same *al* (Charchaulia) have married with one another several times since the 1850's. Among the Saksenas, I recorded no two families

the prohibited degrees of relationship were also held to be unnecessary, old-fashioned barriers to desirable marriages.[26] In effect, the intra- and inter-subcaste boundaries, breached earlier at a behavioral level by some Kayasths, expanded at a normative level.

It is possible that the percentage of outmarriages made by members of each nominal subcaste is related to the number of subcaste members in the city and state. Table 24 suggests that, while this is an important consideration, historical factors must also be taken into account.

Given the economic differences between families within each nominal subcaste, there would be fewer available partners within the smaller groups. As marriage networks expanded beyond the former endogamous limit, these smaller subcastes should have higher proportions of outmarriages as they gained access to all Kayasths at similar educational and occupational levels. Looking at the numbers alone in the table, the three largest nominal subcastes all do have an outmarriage percentage below 40 percent, and the smaller units are all over 45 percent. But the Mathur percentage is significantly lower that those of the more numerous Srivastavas and Saksenas, and the Asthana percentage is significantly higher than the comparable (smaller) Bhatnagars and Gaurs. Column 4, the proportionate representation by subcaste designation in the Lower House of the 1940 Kayasth Sabha, gives an internal view of the relative numbers of participating Kayasths at that time. According to those estimates, which obviously reflect notions of status and respectability as well as absolute numbers, the low Mathur outmarriage rate is more adequately explained.

It is possible but not very useful to construct other tables ordering information by subcaste. For example, a chart of the giving and taking of women by subcastes can be constructed, but it does not successfully show the relative ranking of subcastes, for reasons the historical data has made obvious. A breakdown by education, occupation, and income across subcaste lines does indicate relative rankings. Thus among Asthanas, Mathurs, Bhatnagars, and Saksenas in modern administrative service, the direction of movement of daughters awards the Asthanas highest status. They give their daughters to, or exchange equally with, only the local Saksenas; they take daughters locally from all the others. A list of the

---

with the same *al*. All Asthana families save one were of the same *al* (qanungo), and they denied that it had had any exogamous function.

26. Interviews with Dr. Benkat Chandra, Gurucharan Das Saxena, Mahender Raj Suxena, and Roy Mahboob Narayan.

TABLE 24:
Population Size and Outmarriages, 1910–1971

	Number of families		Total number individuals marrying 1910–1971	Number representatives (proportionate) in 1940 Kayasth Sadr Sabha Lower House[a]	Pct. individuals outmarrying to all individ. marrying, 1910–1971	Percent families outmarrying
	In 1911	In 1948				
Srivastava	58	63	296	3	25	42
Saksena	42	39	375	6	39	77
Mathur	29	26	626	12	11	64
Asthana	7	12	130	4	66	86
Bhatnagar	15	15	103	3	50	78
Gaur	11	8	71	2	54	90
Nigam	6	4	54	1	46	71

Sources: Columns 1–4 are different ways of estimating the relative size of the subcastes: Appendix A and Tables 22 and 23 for cols. 1, 2, 3, 5, and 6; for col. 4, note 43 of Chapter 14, Lower House Representatives.

[a]Proportional representation in the Lower House of the Kayasth sabha reconstituted after the resignation of K. C. Roy certainly reflected concessions to the Mathurs and status judgments, as well as sheer numbers of potential members.

most frequent outmarriage combinations by subcaste disguises significantly different patterns by class within each nominal subcaste.[27]

The new marriage networks can be more accurately described and analyzed when families and even branches of families are distinguished according to education, occupation, income, residence, and *suratval* status.[28] Those who married out of subcaste before 1930 or 1940 were generally from poorer or *suratval* families. From the 1930's, Kayasths moving into modern administrative and professional occupations began to break out of the kin groups and form broader marriage networks. Men moving away from residential localities dominated by their former kin group were particularly instrumental. Among the Mathurs, those who moved to the new city and its suburbs are chiefly responsible for the out-marriages.[29] Among the Asthanas, a few men moved to the old city and married with Saksenas, Bhatnagars, and others there.[30] A Nigam man, residing away from the locality of his ancestral home, took a (second) Saksena wife in 1940; on the same occasion, the daughter of his first wife's sister also married a Saksena. The Nigam and Saksena grooms both worked in the Excise Department.[31] The families of four young Bhatnagar lawyers began marrying about 1940 with Asthana, Saksena, and Srivastava families with similar occupational histories.[32] Among the Gaurs, the first educated men participated in the reform marriages, and the high Gaur proportion of outmarriages (Table 24) was partly due to rivalry between

27. *Outmarriages: Three Most Frequent Partners by Subcaste*

	First	Second	Third
Asthana	Saksenas, 33%	Srivastavas, 12%	Bhatnagars, 11%
Bhatnagar	Srivastavas, 31%	Saksenas, 29%	Asthanas, 11%
Gaur	Saksenas, 37% Srivastavas, 37%	Bhatnagars, 11% Non-Kayasths, 11%	
Mathur	Saksenas, 49%	Non-Kayasths, 27%	Srivastavas, 14%
Nigam	Saksenas, 40%	Non-Kayasths, 24%	Srivastavas, 16%
Saksena	Srivastavas, 24%	Mathurs, 22%	Asthanas, 19%
Srivastava	Saksenas, 29%	Non-Kayasths, 26%	Mathurs, 18%

28. Analysis by computer is necessary to fully handle this data, and such an analysis is under way.

29. They are branches of families 5, 6, 10, 13, 14–17, 21 in Table 7.

30. They were Lalta Pershad and the family of Jai Chand.

31. The Nigam was Devi Pershad; the Saksena was Tirath Raj Saksena. The former's son-in-law, Bashisht Raj Saksena, later worked in Excise also. Devi Pershad and Har Pershad Nigam were second cousins and *hamzulf*; both men remarried after their wives died.

32. Interviews with Shamsher Bahadur (Srivastava) and Dr. R. C. Bhatnagar, Balobir Prosad, Lalta Pershad, and Mahabir Pershad (all four Bhatnagar).

the two major families and their respective kin groups, ruling out many alliances between Gaurs.[33]

Features of the Marriage Networks

The new marriage networks, still evolving, have several distinctive features. First, there are changes in the naming patterns, by families and by subcaste. Second, the new networks relate quite differently to occupations than did the kin groups. Third, young women are themselves productive resources in the marriage market, rather than merely serving to transfer the resources of their patrilineages. Fourth, the marriage networks show clear preferences for former citizens of Hyderabad, those with a shared cultural heritage, above others available in the same range of occupations and income.

Names show a new emphasis on patrilineal affiliation and on subcaste. Kayasths seldom shared family names, or surnames, among all men in a lineage before 1900. Individuals in the same family might be variously named Khub Chand, Bhavani Das, Girdhari Pershad, and Chabeli Mohan. Brothers might or might not have similar names: for every Bhavani Das and Durga Das, or Hanu Lal and Manu Lal, there were brothers named Fateh Chand and Chanu Lal, or Balmukund and Gopal Rae.

Not only did members of one patrilineage not share the same surname over time, their names were not caste-specific. Men with the names given above might belong to any one of six or seven castes. In the past, the use of literary pen names and nicknames served to differentiate individuals and emphasize their personal achievements and unique attributes. This kind of usage has declined and, since 1900, naming practices are providing more mundane means of differentiation by using uniform designations for family and subcaste members.

First, families began naming their male children uniformly. Thus, a man's sons might be named Dhiraj Pratab, Dharminder Pratab, Shaminder Pratab, and so forth. From about 1930, some Kayasths began adding their subcaste designation as a surname (these did not appear in

33. See Chapter 10; interviews with Jagdish Pershad and Ram Mohan Roy; see Appendix F, Gaurs, Rivalry and lack of resources led many Gaurs to send daughters out and marry sons across subcaste lines within Hyderabad. In the last two generations, 24 percent of all marriages have been with Gaurs from central or northern India, reversing the earlier pattern when new men from outside obtained jobs and residences in Hyderabad. In one case, following expensive marriages with North Indian Gaurs for the older siblings in the 1920's, the elder brother who was arranging marriages turned to Hyderabad non-Gaurs for the younger siblings; this pattern holds for several families.

any written sources before 1930). By 1948, one-fourth to one-half of the Saksena, Mathur, and Asthana men on the civil lists of gazetted officers had adopted this usage. Daughters also were named alike, and some used the subcaste designation as a surname.[34]

The sibling naming patterns emphasize patrilineages rather than bilateral kin groups. Formerly, genealogies frequently showed women being married to men with the same or similar names as their fathers or brothers. Chabeli Mohan would marry his daughter or sister to a man named Chabeli Mohan, or perhaps Rangile Mohan. The emphasis was thus placed upon kinsmen by marriage, as much as upon patrilineage.[35]

The changes in naming patterns can be related to developments other than the outmarriages. The apparently more uniform sibling names may simply be the result of lower maternal and infant mortality; the subcaste addition may be a result of Kayasth association activities.[36] But, with some exceptions, there is a tendency for the outmarrying branches of families to adopt these usages. Given the other characteristics of these branches, the new usages may be markers for their more heterogeneous neighbors and professional colleagues in the new city. They may also reflect the effort to retain a sense of identity on the part of those whose marriage networks are expanding most rapidly.

The second feature of the new marriage networks concerns their relation to career patterns and occupational specialization. The earlier kin groups fell within subcaste boundaries and were based upon control of administrative positions, usually those in the same division of the Mughlai administration. The trend now is towards relatively unbounded marriage networks which include people in diverse occupations, so relatives can offer advice and influence in several areas. This is particularly noticeable in the families of first-generation lawyers, doctors, and educators, where some sons or daughters may follow the father's profession but others have been deliberately directed into other specializations. In contrast, those whose relatives are predominately in government service appear more likely to marry within subcaste boundaries and reside in the old city.

34. In the case of daughters, names have gained in individuality. Women are now being given distinctive personal names, not just kinship terms or brief affectionate "family" names. This evidences a shift from a primarily ascribed, private status to an achieved, public status for Kayasth women in society.
35. This change seems related to that from bilateral to patrilineal inheritance.
36. Sons by different mothers are *not* named alike; as more mothers and children have survived, the more siblings there are to form such patterns. In 1976, Gurucharan Das Saxena told me he was dropping Saxena, as requested by the AIKC for purposes of abolition of caste.

Crucial to the new strategy of occupational diversification and broader marriage networks is the rising age at marriage. This has effectively reversed the relation between marriages and occupations. When marriages occurred at earlier ages for men, their careers were determined by their marriage, by the positions available to them through bilateral inheritance. Now, men customarily acquire education and even professional placement before marriage; their marriages are determined by their initial career potential. This is even beginning to be true for some young Kayasth women.

Not only does this mean that occupational diversification can be achieved, but in some cases lucrative specializations can be concentrated in only a few families. For example, two or three families led by doctors have succeeded in training many younger family members as doctors and in recruiting other promising young doctors as affines. This strategy is illustrated in the families of Dr. Benkat Chandra and Dr. Rup Karan, the foremost Mathur doctors, and that of the Saksena Dr. Ragunandan Raj, in Figure 12.[37] Note that daughters have also become doctors and have married other doctors, in one case a Muslim.

These "doctor clusters" differ from the former kin groups in several ways. Many other occupations are represented in the same two or three families. Also the doctors who are affines do not represent families closely tied to the doctor families; they are individuals recruited for their achievements as students or practitioners of medicine. Finally, the structure of the medical profession may allow exercise of influence on behalf of relatives, but the high degree of control of shared economic resources typical of the kin groups is certainly lacking.

The third feature is the integration of qualified women into the new marriage networks on the basis of their own career potential. The striking advances in the public roles of some Kayasth women do not necessarily signify increased personal initiative and independence; but the options for women have increased.[38] There was a transition period in the 1960's when education and a career appeared to rule out marriage for women; the tendency has been for the first generation of highly educated girls in a marriage network to experience some difficulty with marriage arrangements. Among the Kayasths, there are a few cases of highly educated daughters who remained unmarried in the 1960's and who have pursued

37. Interviews with Dr. Benkat Chandra, Dr. Harish Chand, Professor Mahender Raj Suxena and Satguru Pershad. (Marriages since 1971 have added several more doctors as affines.)
38. See my article "Women and Social Change" for further discussion and references.

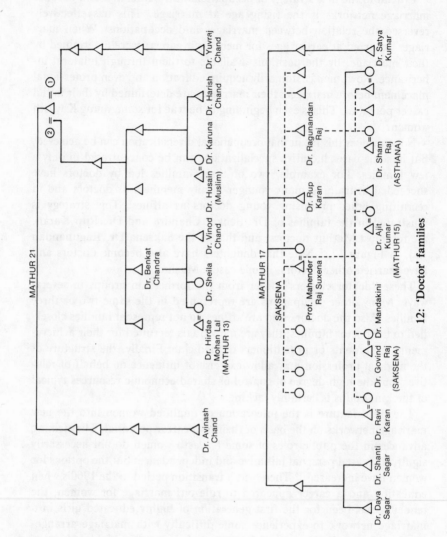

12: 'Doctor' families

careers. There have also been some very late marriages, of women close to thirty, arranged only with the help of sizable dowries.[39] This period now appears to have ended, and educated career women are being integrated into the marriage networks.

There is substantial family and community support for working wives and mothers among the Kayasths now, though family welfare rather than women's liberation is the motivation. But economic pressures and modern ideology concerning educated, employed women are producing some further changes related to marriage networks. Marriages are increasingly arranged based upon a girl's own productive capacities, and there are fewer marriages of the exchange or multiple nature.[40] The statistical incidence of love marriages for Kayasth women as well as men, and for daughters marrying out of birth order, is rising. In both cases, daughters are exerting pressures within the family regarding their prospective marriage partners. Finally, there are a few instances of divorced and remarried women, indications of individual preference rather than parental control of women.

The final feature of the new marriage networks is cultural continuity. Now that Hyderabad state has become part of India, it would seem more possible for Kayasths there to follow the Asthana example and begin to arrange marriages with Kayasths elsewhere. The political and social conditions are more similar for caste members living in different regions of the subcontinent than at any time in the recent historical past. They are citizens of the same nation, subscribing to common nationalistic sentiments and administrative principles. Yet this kind of expansion has not occurred. Instead, there has been a narrowing of geographic focus to residents of the former Hyderabad state, accompanied by broadening of the eligible subcastes, castes, and communities from which partners may be drawn. This is particularly noticeable among those Gaur, Nigam, and Bhatnagar families who formerly arranged some marriages with subcaste members outside of Hyderabad state. Many Saksenas and Mathurs who have prospered since 1948 could have initiated marriages with North Indian Kayasths. The general failure to do so cannot be attributed entirely to economic factors. In many cases, families could afford to establish the kind of long-distance marriage networks which some of the Asthanas continue to maintain. They are choosing, instead, to marry across subcaste and caste boundaries within Hyderabad city.

39. The use of dowries is supposed to have occurred for many "surplus" Mathur women: interviews with Gurucharan Das Saxena and Roy Mahboob Narayan.
40. Among the Mathurs, however, exchange marriages are still frequent.

This preference for other former citizens of Hyderabad state must be attributed to linguistic and cultural defensiveness, a revival of the native Hyderabadi sentiment after Police Action.[41] In my interviews it was stated repeatedly that Hyderabad Kayasths were marrying with members of other Kayasth subcastes at a higher ratio than North Indian Kayasths, and that a Hyderabadi was preferable to a non-Hyderabadi.[42] The political and cultural context then, is undoubtedly contributing to the movement for marriages beyond the former boundaries. The extent to which this factor, the unique cultural history of the Hindus of Hyderabad city, is truly significant can only be determined by comparative studies of other marriage networks in other contexts.

41. See my article "The Mulki—non-Mulki Conflict," in Jeffrey, *People, Princes.*
42. Interviews with Balobir Prosad, Lokendra Bahadur, Mrs. Kunj Behari Lal, Roy Mahboob Narayan and wife, Gurucharan Das Saxena, Shakamber Raj Saxena, and Dwarka Pershad Nigam (not all approved of this).

CHAPTER **16**

Conclusion:
Beyond Caste

This book has attempted to answer historical questions of fundamental significance for an understanding of social change in modern India. To what extent has a subcaste or caste been a cultural or structural unit in the past? If castes or subcastes can be shown to have operated as units, how did they adapt to changing economic and political circumstances? How did individual and family mobility occur within a particular caste, or within the caste system? What strategies could individuals and families use to maximize their opportunities and resources? While the answers found here pertain to designated members of a particular caste in the capital city of a bureaucratic state, they have a wider and comparative significance.

Throughout the four historical periods covered in this study, it has been found that families, kin groups, and marriage networks were the characteristic social units. These units and their economic strategies over time have been related to changes in the environment and to the differential access of families to economic resources. Attempts to construct or impose broader subcaste or caste units have assumed limited importance at some times of stress and conflict.

Table 25 summarizes the major findings of this book and relates the changing opportunity structure in Hyderabad over two hundred years to significant changes in social structure for Kayasths. In the first period, characterized as a military aristocracy, Kayasth immigrants from North India established themselves in the Nizam's service. As Hyderabad state became independent of the Mughal Empire, it presented opportunities to newcomers, particularly those in military positions. Migrations and marriages between northern and southern India, including other kingdoms in South India, occurred. The Saksenas and Gaurs, more numerous in central

TABLE 25:
Environment and Social Structure

Periods	Nature of environment	Characteristic social unit	Unit's degree of social control	Inheritance and succession
I 1750–1800	Politically unstable, economically expansive	Individuals, families, marriage networks	Low	Customary; bilateral
II 1800–1870	Politically unstable, economically expansive with decentralized and specialized opportunities	Kin groups (same subcaste, same administrative area)	High	Customary; bilateral
III 1870–1915	A. Mughlai administration: economic decline with constricted opportunities	Families	Low	State-regulated; patrilineal
	B. Modern administration: expansive, centralized; English education opportunities	Kin groups (same subcaste, same occupation)	High	State-regulated; patrilineal
IV 1915–1970	Modern administration: politically unstable; economically expansive, occupational diversification	Families and marriage networks (different subcastes and castes, diverse occupations)	Decreasing	State-regulated; patrilineal (to daughters, too)

and southern India than other Kayasths in the late eighteenth century, were the only two subcastes represented by marriage networks in Hyderabad city at that time. These two networks included both military men and record-keepers and, in one case, they bridged two localities. At first it was the military men who more often secured high-ranking patrons, positions, and personal wealth, but they could not always retain assets.

In the second historical period, .the consolidation of the Mughlai administration in the early nineteenth century, those who more successfully accumulated and transmitted resources to kinsmen were controllers of records, whether of the land revenue, military payrolls, or the palace departments. The Malwala Mathur family, keeper of half the state's land revenue records, best exemplified this; it ranked high in the Hyderabad nobility.. The *jagirs* and regular income provided by its resource base allowed it to recruit and support other Mathur families, constituting a large and cohesive subcaste in the city. Most Mathurs remained socially and economically dependent upon the patron Malwala family until the most recent historical period.

Other Kayasth position-holders established hereditary claims at all levels of the bureaucracy. Kin groups developed and persisted, with dominant families or heads of families allocating positions to members following a bilateral inheritance system. But some position-holders, notably a few Srivastava and Bhatnagar families, tried to maintain marriage networks drawing largely from outside Hyderabad; they did not form local kin groups.

The ability to control social boundaries depended upon economic resources. Kin groups used their resources to build and maintain social boundaries. The Malwala family exercised tight economic and social control over other Mathurs. The Gaurs recruited new kinsmen to retain their Paigah positions. Among the Saksenas, distinctions were drawn between residents of Shahalibanda and Husaini Alam, and the latter formed a kin group based on palace and other positions. The lower status of the Shahalibanda residents was due to the growing insecurity of the once-prestigious military style of life. Among the Srivastavas, older noble families refused to incorporate most newcomers into existing marriage networks, and an illegitimate category expanded steadily within the city. The Bhatnagars also showed social divisions, as two newcomer families refused to marry locally and functioned as members of kin groups in their former North Indian homes.

The third period, characterized by the development of the Anglo-Indian or modern administration in the state, was a crucial one. In this book, historical estimates of its timing and intensity are revised. Salar Jung's installation as Diwan in 1853 is usually taken to herald the inauguration of the modern civil administration and military troops, accompanied by dismantlement of the Mughlai bureaucracy and troops. In fact, it was only in the 1870's and after 1883 (Salar Jung's death) that major changes had detrimental effects upon Kayasths at all levels of the Hyderabad Mughlai administration. The state intervened and applied Anglo-Indian law to the inheritance and allocation of positions, displacing the Kayasth kin groups. The military *serrishtahdars* and others found their administrative autonomy curtailed by centralization and reforms. The political downfall of the Paigah nobles and seizure of that private estate deprived the Gaurs of protection from administrative reforms. And the Mughlai administration continued to be phased out, in a process extending well into the twentieth century.

Kayasths in the old city, hindered by lack of modern educational facilities and by regulations designed to retain the monopoly of the new administrative elite, were blocked from easy movement into the modern administration. They were also hindered by the conservatism of elders, though a few Kayasths did achieve occupational mobility in this period. One pioneering local Mathur Kayasth formed a kin group within the subcaste and encouraged kinsmen to join the modern administration, ignoring the wishes of Raja Shiv Raj. A few Saksenas gained transitional places at a lower level, chiefly in the Accountant General's office, removing themselves from Bansi Raja's kin group and forming a new one. Among the modern administrators recruited by Salar Jung was an Asthana Kayasth, representing a subcaste new to Hyderabad. He set up a powerful kin group in the new city based upon modern educational and occupational resources, and the Asthanas proved crucial to the development of new occupational and kinship patterns in the fourth period.

But most Kayasths in this third historical period experienced a steady loss of political and economic resources. Conflicts arose in several kin groups over control of decreasing resources, and affinal relatives rivaled consanguineal ones. There was an increase in "deviancies," through conversion to Islam or the Arya Samaj and through socially unsanctioned marriages and alliances. Most such instances occurred among poor or low-status families. At the same time, there was an effort to retain and champion the Kayasths' cultural identity as mediators between Hindu and Muslim culture. Persian and Urdu literary activities flourished in the old city and involved many Kayasths. The Kayasths' long-standing allegiance to the Nizam was emphasized by a primarily Mathur association, in the hope that reciprocal recognition would bring substantial rewards.

In the fourth historical period, in which Hyderabad has been incorporated into newly independent India, the majority of Kayasths have radically changed their educational, occupational, and marriage patterns. Beginning in the second decade of the twentieth century, this period has been marked by the expansion of educational facilities in the city and state and by the development of political ideologies and organizations. A turbulent and disruptive period, it has freed the Hyderabad Kayasths from dependence on the former ruling group within Hyderabad and opened new opportunities to them.

Hyderabad Kayasths participated actively in educational and social reform efforts through Kayasth voluntary associations in the 1930's and 1940's. These associations were significant because of the leadership role of the educated young men and their successful establishment of new educational and occupational models. The abrasive intervention of an "outsider" provoked conflict among Kayasths in the late 1930's; more Kayasths than had previously been acknowledged were mobilized as members of the caste, but most Mathurs were alienated. A compromise followed, achieved by the younger educated leaders from different kin groups and localities. These associational activities generated a series of "reform marriages" and then extensive new marriage networks across subcaste and even caste boundaries. At present, these new marriage networks are the most striking characteristic of the Kayasths in Hyderabad.

Succession and inheritance practices have changed radically over time. The image of stern patriarchs controlling extended or joint families and enforcing patrilineal inheritance, customary in high-ranking castes, had little relevance for the Kayasth kin groups in the eighteenth and most of the nineteenth centuries. Patrilineal inheritance was found among those few Kayasth families with landed wealth and noble status, and even there it did not strictly follow the eldest male line.[1] In the two earliest historical periods, the Kayasth kin groups practiced bilateral succession to positions. With control of positions delegated to kin groups by a decentralized administration, dominant figures acquired positions and allocated them to kinsmen, providing for all men of age in the kin group and recruiting more men as needed to occupy newly acquired or vacated positions. The effort was to provide for all male relatives of appropriate age, whether consanguineal or affinal. Sometimes those of allegedly illegitimate parentage were given positions. Affinal relatives were important economic resources; and marriages were made without dowry, for the economic

---

1. In addition to lack of adherence to seniority in the Malwala family, one of the earliest written sources for the Malwalas, Lal, *Yadgar*, 181–182, describes as affines some of the men titled around 1800. Later written and oral sources classify them as lineal descendants. In their article "A Bureaucratic Lineage in Princely India: Elite Formation and Conflict in a Patrimonial System," *JAS*, XXXIV, no. 3 (1975), 717–753, Lloyd and Susanne Rudolph discuss patrilineages competing for high-ranking bureaucratic positions, like the Malwalas and other nobles in Hyderabad.

resources women transferred through marriage were positions.[2] The importance of affinal ties was evidenced by the frequent operation of the *hamzulf* relationship, where the men married to sisters aided one another in making marriages and gaining positions for kinsmen.

The practice of bilateral succession to positions was one of the first casualties of the economic pressures at the end of the nineteenth century, as the dissension and splits in Gaur, Saksena, and other kin groups showed. State intervention at this point removed succession and inheritance from the control of kin groups and increased the Kayasths' difficulties. Inheritances were subject not only to Brahmanical law but to systematic reduction with each succession. State officials had earlier confirmed the decisions made by dominant figures in the kin groups. Now, judicial regulation narrowed the options of families and kin groups. One result was the sudden utilization of formal adoption procedures, often of a child from outside without local family members to lay claim to the properties.[3] Marriages were arranged to maximize the resources of patrilineages and to avoid conflicts with affines. Attempts to claim shares under the system of bilateral succession which provided for all men in the kin group produced severe conflicts. At this time, *suratvals* were publicly defined as illegitimate, specifically with respect to inheritance.[4]

In this stage, the confinement of legal succession to the patrilineage was somewhat balanced by the growing recognition that women could claim shares of their fathers' estates (particularly if there were no male heirs), and there were a few such claims. Affinal ties continued to be important among those making transitions to modern occupations: they provided information, access, and influence rather than property. While some of the barriers to occupational mobility for Kayasths during this last historical period were institutional (dominance by the "outsider" administrative elite and its regulation of the civil service), the inheritance practice implemented by the government, namely the equal division of resources among patrilineal heirs, was another barrier for some. The value of inherited *mansabs* was rapidly decreasing, yet those holding them took fewer risks than other Kayasths. This was especially apparent among the Mathurs. In most Mathur families, the one branch awarded allowances in 1930 (when the state took over Shiv Raj's estate) remained dependent

2. See Jack Goody and S. J. Tambiah, *Bridewealth and Dowry* (Cambridge, Eng., 1973). Among the Kayasths, gifts and expenses at the wedding were an "indirect dowry" until recently. A Persian dowry list of 1865 (Gaur, a daughter of Balmukund) included only eight cash items totalling 85 rupees, to be used at specified times in the ceremonies.

3. Recently, adoptions have again involved close relatives, to secure social progeny rather than successors to property.

4. See Chapter 11.

upon those dwindling shares, while other branches moved into modern occupations.[5]

Most family strategies in the earlier periods emphasized the retention of resources, from landed property to hereditary positions with fixed incomes. The kin groups, with exchange marriages and other "close" marriage practices, served this purpose. More recently, family strategies have focused on obtaining new resources, and the expanding marriage networks do this.[6] In many ways, the recent period is analogous to the eighteenth century, when political and economic disruption produced new opportunities, chances for men to move into new occupations and form kinship ties based on achievement in a new environment.

The modern marriage networks across subcaste and caste boundaries maximize individual and family access to resources and further diversify the occupational specialties practiced by relatives. When these marriages were first made, they drew upon associational connections among young educated men from several subcastes in the city, consolidating educational and occupational ties. The rising age at marriage has played a key role in the changed relationship between marriage and occupation upon which the marriage networks are now based. Earlier, occupation was usually determined by marriage. Fewer children survived, those who did were married before puberty, and a son-in-law would inherit a position from his own or his wife's family. Now marriages are often determined by occupations, as educated young men and women are married because of their own career prospects. Younger people have more control over educational, career, and marriage choices, and women have more formal and informal authority in both public and private spheres. Thus there has been a broadening of authority within the family, both generationally and with respect to the sexes.[7]

In all the transitions from one period to the next, the Kayasths moving into new occupations have been most characteristically on the margin, either lacking in social status and economic means or defying the social

5. See H. J. Habakkuk, "Family Structure and Economic Change in Nineteenth-Century Europe," *Journal of Economic History,* XV, no. 1 (1955), 1–12, for the general implications for mobility of single-heir inheritance practices contrasted with those of equal division.

6. A recent new strategy—a feature of the 1970's—is the placement abroad of at least one younger professional, through whom the family can educate or place other members.

7. One could apply Daniel Scott Smith's hypothesis that authority within the family has moved from lineal to conjugal emphasis; it is more promising than applying the change from extended to nuclear family that has received so much attention in the literature on India. For a brief statement of Smith's position see "Parental Power and Marriage Patterns," *Journal of Marriage and the Family,* XXXV, no. 3 (1973), 419–428. The 1970's has seen the initiation of an interesting role reversal among women in some households. Where the daughter-in-law is employed, her mother-in-law becomes responsible for care of house and children, even being sent out to district posts for this purpose in a few cases.

controls of family and subcaste. Several highly educated *suratval* professional men exemplify the former; Lalta Pershad's "civil service" Mathur kin group was the first example of the latter. Marriage networks have been constantly realigned to accord with newly won prestige and economic resources. But those successful men of marginal social status (most *suratvals* in modern professions) have not achieved integration in terms of marriage into their ascribed subcastes. Instead, they have used economic status to cross caste and community boundaries and marry with others of similar means.

Changes in the political environment have challenged Kayasth self-perceptions, raising questions not yet resolved. Few Kayasths sought political alternatives to the Nizam's rule. Most upheld their own and Hyderabad's Mughlai cultural heritage at a time when they were moving away from it educationally and occupationally. A leading Saksena literary scholar wrote in 1945: "Kayasths were first among the Hindus who learnt Persian . . . Kayasths absorbed so much of Muslim culture . . . Mutual love produced a composite culture which is the dearest wealth of India today."[8]

This view was not popular immediately after India incorporated Hyderabad in 1948, although it can be said to accord with current Indian nationalist ideals. All who were identified with the former Nizam's administration and the old Hyderabad culture came under suspicion for some time. The one element of the Kayasth cultural heritage that continued to be valued was the occupational role as administrators. Immediately following Police Action, many Kayasths felt that this functional role, devoid of cultural overtones, provided the best basis for their status in society. They supported the once-minority viewpoint expressed by an Arya Samajist Kayasth in the 1940's: "Kayasths . . . showed themselves enthusiastic followers of the Muslims . . . But we were not Muslims. We did their work. And if we imitated them, it had only so much value as an imitation . . . maybe Kayasths use English too, but that doesn't mean it is their mother tongue . . ."[9]

This was a somewhat negative view; furthermore, occupational diversification has taken many Kayasths out of administrative service. And pride in the old literary and cultural tradition has returned, perhaps spurred by the 1956 formation of Andhra Pradesh, which made the Kayasths a linguistic minority group. The opportunity structure has changed again, and Kayasths now work in the context of Telugu-medium administrative and educational institutions in Andhra Pradesh. The new marriage net-

8. Professor Mahender Raj Suxena (head of the Osmania University botany department until 1975), "Hyderabad aur Kayasth," 4.
9. Pratap, *Hamari Zaban*, 15.

works show a clear preference for relatives with a Hyderabad Mughlai background.

Finally, Kayasth associational activities have ceased now that Hyderabad is part of a modern political democracy. This is contrary to the hypotheses of many social scientists about the origins and function of associations based upon caste membership,[10] but it accords with suggestions that such associations are a defensive response to adverse administrative circumstances.[11] Caste associational activity has been shown in this book to be linked to generational conflict and the constriction, rather than the expansion, of economic and political opportunities. It was one of several activities of young Western-educated men establishing new educational and occupational patterns in the old city.[12] The associations begun in 1915 were efforts by the young educated men to play a stronger role in their communities, and their communities had neighborhood as well as subcaste and caste dimensions. As this generation achieved occupational mobility and diversification, the associational activities were revived and increased. They were most intense in the 1930's and 1940's, when political, economic, and social constraints proved very limiting for most old-city Kayasths. Despite the emphasis added by K. C. Roy, and the "communal loyalty" expressed to the Nizam by the associations of the 1940's, these activities were not directed towards caste unification.

Since 1948, Kayasths have participated in a wide variety of organizations and activities, few of which have been caste-based. Many Kayasths remain active in Urdu literary and cultural associations.[13] There was some talk of a new Hyderabad Kayasth organization in 1965, and the leading Kayasth in government service was approached to serve as president. But he decided that his position as a prominent government official precluded acceptance, and no caste organization was formed.[14] The Mathur Kayasths provide the exception, with a strong Hyderabad Mathur Kayasth Education and Welfare Society started in 1970.[15]

10. Rudolph and Rudolph, *The Modernity of Tradition*; Kothari and Maru, "Caste and Secularism," 35–50; and Hardgrave, *The Nadars of Tamilnad*—all see caste associations as tutorial experiences related to the modernization of caste-based units and to their democratic political mobilization.

11. Lucy Carroll, "Colonial Perceptions of Indian Society and the Emergence of Caste(s) Associations," *JAS*, in press; Conlon, "Caste by Association," 351–365.

12. Robert L. Kidder, "Litigation as a Strategy for Personal Mobility: The Case of Urban Caste Association Leaders," *JAS*, XXXIII, no. 2 (1974), 177–191, found this; Owen Lynch, in his work on the Agra Jatavs, has also analyzed the different types of leadership by generation.

13. These are the Idara-e-Adabiyat-e-Urdu, the Anjuman Taraqqi Urdu, and the new (all-India) Sahitya Akademi.

14. Interviews with Gurucharan Das Saxena and Kunj Behari Lal.

15. The leaders of the Mathur association reside in the old city and its patrons in the new. Some local Srivastavas are affiliated with the Srivastava-dominated Madras Kayasth

Finally, the ascriptive subcaste designations and surnames distinguishing lineages are receiving new emphasis in naming practices among the Hyderabad Kayasths. What is striking about these new usages is that they stress form rather than function. Kinship has certainly become less important in terms of succession to political and economic resources, and subcaste endogamy no longer prevails. Families, kin groups, and marriage networks have diversified occupationally and with respect to membership.

The ease with which marriages across former boundaries are accommodated is striking.[16] Marriage rituals are settled by family negotiations; usually priests from both families preside, each conducting a version of the rituals. Younger people complain that the inter-subcaste marriages are invariably longer and more complicated because of such compromises. Reciprocal kin obligations appear to have been successfully extended to individuals from different backgrounds. As one man stated, "Kayasths are like the ocean; fresh streams joining become salty."[17]

All of these changes might confirm an ideological shift from caste to ethnicity and class.[18] But adaptability, rather than conformity to accepted Brahmanical or scholarly notions about caste, has always characterized the Kayasth marriage networks and kin groups. Another transition period is under way, and it is not the first time Kayasths have changed their marriage strategies to maximize the economic and political opportunities available to them in Hyderabad.

Sabha. There are marriages between the two regions, but associational activities are minimal for the Hyderabad members. Some Saksenas are in a Marwari-dominated neighborhood association. Interviews with Benkat Prasad, Dr. Eshwar Raj Saxena, and Chander Srivastava.

16. It contrasts with data from other regions showing resistance to such marriages, for example: Harold Gould, "Some Aspects of Kinship among Business and Professional Elite in Lucknow, India," *CIS*, n.s., V (1971), 125–129; Brenda Beck, "The Boundaries of a Subcaste," in Brenda Beck, ed., *Perspectives on a Regional Culture: Essays about the Coimbatore Area of South India* (Durham, N.C., 1977); and Vatuk, *Kinship and Urbanization*.

17. Personal observance on numerous occasions; interviews with Lokendra Bahadur, Hakim Vicerai, Anjani Shanker Lal; quote from Roy Mahboob Narayan.

18. Barnett, "Approaches to Changes in Caste Ideology in South India," 149–180. Barnett shows change in the units of endogamy but asserts an increasing emphasis on substance at the caste level; the Kayasths go beyond this and appear always to have emphasized code rather than substance, contradicting his analysis in some important ways. See Beck, "Boundaries of a Subcaste," discussing an analogous emphasis on code (defined by her as professional and behavioral similarities in marriage arrangements).

Appendices

**Summary of Information
Collected about the
Hyderabad Kayasths**

	No. of families in city on specified dates[a]						Cumulative no. of families[a]	Cumulative no. of population recorded		
	1750	1800	1853	1883	1911	1948		Men	Women	Total
Asthana	0	0	0	2	7	12($\pm^{8}$)	15	156	110	266
Bhatnagar	2	2	6	6($\pm^{1}$)	15($^{+9}$)	15($\pm^{1}$)	17	161	70	231
Gaur	0	5	6($\pm^{2}_{1}$)	10($\pm^{6}$)	11($\pm^{2}_{1}$)	8($\pm^{4}$)	16	142	101	243
Mathur	3	4	14	25	29	26($_{-3}$)	29	739	564	1,303
Nigam	0	1?	3	4	6	4($\pm^{1}$)	7	53	25	78
Saksena	1?	16	19($\pm^{7}$)	47($\pm^{31}$)	42($\pm^{9}$)	39($\pm^{1}$)	59	660	443	1,094
Srivastava[b]	3	3	8	34($\pm^{28}$)	58($\pm^{29}$)	63($\pm^{14}_{9}$)	79	490	240	730
Total	9	31	56	127	168	167	221	2,398	1,547	3,945

[a]Family = patrilineage. For this table, the calculation of survival was biological, not social (legitimate). The plus and minus figures in parentheses refer to the ending of lines and the arrival of new immigrants since the previous date.

[b]The Srivastava information extends back only two or three generations in many cases: these "families" are probably related further back and are therefore probably fewer in total number. Most men listed in the "newcomer Dusre" category (Table 15) are not counted as families for this Appendix.

Mughlai Household Administration

The following *karkhanahs* and treasuries were under jurisdiction of the Khan-i Saman, or Khansaman.

Animals
    ashtarkhanah (or shutarkhana)—camels
    astabal—stables (horses)
    filkhanah—elephants
    gaokhanah—cows

Stores and Supplies
    bandikhanah (or palkikhana)—bullock carts
    buggykhanah—buggies or carriages
    chiragh o shama—lighting and lamps
    kothajat—warehouses
    mashalkhanah—torches
    rathkhanah—chariots

Factories and Production
    baghat—gardens and meadows (for grazing)
    dawakhanah (or shifakhana)—medicine
    farashkhanah—house and tenting supplies
    khusbuhkhanah—perfumes
    tambulkhanah—betel leaves, tobacco
    toshakhanah—bedding, fabrics, clothing

Court Life and Administration,
Including the Nizam's Personal Service
    abdarkhanah—water supply
    aras—*urs* administration

arbab-i nishat—dancing girls, musicians, fools and clowns
bavarchikhanah—kitchens
daftarkhanah—clerks, offices
duagoyan—religious men, prayer performers, and so on
imarat—buildings and bazars
mehlat—quarters and arrangements for women
mewahkhanah—dining, banquet arrangements
naqqarkhanah—drums
niazat—management of niaz (*fatihah*-like ceremonies)
sadqat—charities

Treasuries

mansab/rakab—to mansabdars and rakabdars (the latter were royally
  appointed suppliers)
mehlat disbursements—to residents of the palaces and properties
pensions and compassionate allowances
privy purse—to the Nizam

Source: Classification and description by Jadunath Sarkar, *Mughal Administration*
(5th ed., Calcutta, 1963), pp. 165 ff.; Manik R. V. Rao, *Bustan-i Asafiyah* (Hyderabad,
1909-1932) I, pp. 130 ff. The above is a summary of the basic units; there were others
at times.

Hamzulf Among Saksenas

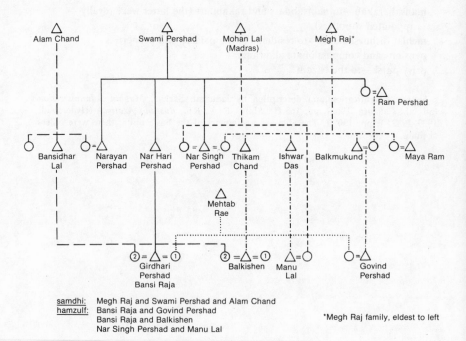

samdhi: Megh Raj and Swami Pershad and Alam Chand
hamzulf: Bansi Raja and Govind Pershad
        Bansi Raja and Balkishen
        Nar Singh Pershad and Manu Lal

*Megh Raj family, eldest to left

Legendary Kayasths of Shahalibanda

Buchar Mal's Ashurkhanah

The Saksena military *serrishtahdar* Buchar Mal held considerable property in the Shahalibanda area. It included his own large residence, 13 shops, a mosque and a temple in his yard, and an *ashurkhanah.* The *ashurkhanah,* known as Buchar Mal ki Thatti, symbolizes the end of his family. Buchar Mal's only son, Ghansur Mal, took a wife from a family related to the Bansi Raja Saksena family. Something happened to the wife which caused her mother to attempt suicide. One version is that the young bride died at 12 of cholera, and her mother tried to cut her own throat; another version says that Ghansur Mal converted to Islam and his wife did, too, so her mother took poison. Ghansur Mal himself met a dramatic end. He was a drunkard and lived well, using up all his money on liquor. Destitute, he died alone in his *ashurkhanah,* and all whom I interviewed agree that no Kayasth would take the responsibility for conducting his funeral. Finally, the family barbers took a collection and saw that the proper cremation ceremonies were carried out. The property passed first to the family of Bansi Raja "somehow related" to Buchar Mal; later, some Muslims claimed that Muslim graves were on the land and it was transferred to the management of a nearby mosque. Asked about the graves, two people said that some of the family had converted to Islam.

The Haunted Temple of Maya Ram

Raja Maya Ram, another Saksena military *serrishtahdar* of Shahalibanda, is also represented by a neighborhood landmark: an old temple inside his former residence, nearly one level below the present ground level of the area and featuring Maharashtrian-style woodwork. The temple is said to be haunted by the ghost of a Brahman. There are two versions of the origin of the ghost. One says that when a wealthy Brahman neighbor went on pilgrimage to Benares, according to

[301

the custom in those days, he left his gold with a trusted elder in the neighborhood, Raja Maya Ram. When he did not return, Maya Ram's family used the gold. Then the Brahman came back. To prevent embarrassment, the relatives of Maya Ram had him killed and put in a well; thus the temple is cursed to this day. In the other version, a brother-in-law of Maya Ram took a large loan from a Brahman money-lender and could not repay it, so the Brahman committed suicide before the house and became a devil to haunt the temple. The property is now rented out and the temple rooms except for the main shrine are used as residences. The building is owned by a Saksena family "somehow related" to Maya Ram.

APPENDIX E:

Suratval Genealogies

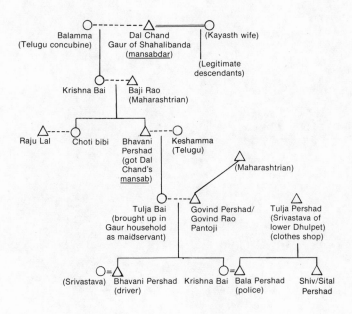

[303

Outmarriage by Subcastes

Asthana		Total	Saksena		Mathur		Nigam		Bhatnagar		Srivastava		Gaur		Non-Kayasths	
			M	F	M	F	M	F	M	F	M	F	M	F	Male	Female
Before 1929	M	4														
	F 4															1 Christian, 1 Muslim
1930–1939	M 3	8	2, 1[a]							2		2				
	F 5															1 Muslim, 1 Christian[a]
1940–1949	M 7	25	3	3, 2[a]		4			1, 1[a]	3	2[a]	1, 2[a]				
	F 18															2 Telugu, 1 Amist
1950–1959	M 11	24	6	3, 1[a]		2		1	1	1	2, 1[a]	1, 3[a]			1 Christian[a]	
	F 13															1 Maharashtrian
1960–1972	M 14	25	6, 2[a]	4, 1[a]	1		1[a]	1		1, 1[a]	2, 2[a]	1, 1[a]				
	F 11															1 Muslim
TOTAL	86		20	14	1	6	1	2	3	8	9	12	0	0	1	9
			34		7		3		11		21		0		10	

[a]North Indian

	Bhatnagar			Srivastava		Saksena		Mathur		Asthana		Gaur		Nigam		Non-Kayasths	
	M	F	Total	M	F	M	F	M	F	M	F	M	F	M	F	Male	Female
Before 1929	3	7	10		4	2	1											2 Telugu
1930–1939		2	2		1													1 Telugu
1940–1949	6	5	11		1	3	2			2	1		1	1				
1950–1959	6	2	8	3		1	2			2								
1960–1972	6	14	20		6	1	3		2	2	1	2		1	1	1 Muslim	1 Brahman
TOTAL			51	4	12	7	8	0	2	6	1	2	2	1	1	1	4
				16		15		2		7		4		2		5	

	Gaur M	Gaur F	Gaur Total	Saksena M	Saksena F	Srivastava M	Srivastava F	Asthana M	Asthana F	Bhatnagar M	Bhatnagar F	Nigam M	Nigam F	Mathur M	Mathur F	Non-Kayasths Male	Non-Kayasths Female
Before 1929		2	2														
1930–1939	2	7	9		1		1					1					
1940–1949	3	2	5		6	1	1	1		1							1 Reddy
1950–1959	3	3	6	1		1	3									1 Amist	
1960–1972	7	9	16	3	3	2	3			1	2					1 Agarwal	1 Greek (met in U.S.)
TOTAL			38	4	10	5	9	1	0	2	2	1	0	0	0	2	2
				14		14		1		4		1		0		4	

	Mathur Total	Saksena M	Saksena F	Srivastava M	Srivastava F	Asthana M	Asthana F	Bhatnagar M	Bhatnagar F	Nigam M	Nigam F	Gaur M	Gaur F	Non-Kayasths Male	Non-Kayasths Female
Before 1929 M F	1		1												
1930–1939 M F	1	1													
1940–1949 M F	4	2				2									
1950–1959 M F	23	7	6	4		2				1		1		1 Brahman 1 Punjabi-Khatri	1 Khatri
1960–1972 M F	37	10	5	5		1	1							1 Muslim 1 Marwari 1 Gujerati	1 Coorgi 2 English 1 Punjabi 2 ? 1 Australian 1 Brahman 1 Parsi 1 Tamilian 1 Khatri 1 Reddy
TOTAL	66	20	12	9	0	5	1	0	0	1	0	1	0	5	13
		32		9		6		0		1		1		18	

Nigam		Saksena		Srivastava		Asthana		Bhatnagar		Gaur		Mathur		Non-Kayasths	
	Total	M	F	M	F	M	F	M	F	M	F	M	F	Male	Female
Before 1929 M F / 1	1														
1930–1939 M F / 3 3	6		1	1							1				1 Telugu
1940–1949 M F / 1 2	3		1	2	1				1						
1950–1959 M F / 4	4		2[a] 1[b]									1			
1960–1972 M F / 4 7	11	1	3			1		1						1 Sikh	3 Telugu 1 Rajput
TOTAL	25	3	7	3	1	1	0	1	1	0	1	0	1	1	5
		10		4		1		2		1		1		6	

[a] Central Indian.
[b] Half Srivastava.

	Saksena		Gaur		Asthana		Mathur		Srivastava		Nigam		Bhatnagar		Non-Kayasths	
	Total		M	F	M	F	M	F	M	F	M	F	M	F	Male	Female
Before 1929 M 3 F 4	7								2	1						
1930–1939 M 9 F 12	21		7			2		5	2	4			1	2		1 Telugu
1940–1949 M 13 F 9	22		1		4	2	1	1	3	2	1	1	2	1	1 Brahman	1 Muslim
1950–1959 M 14 F 11	25			1	4	3	3	5	3	1	1	1	2		1 Jat	1 Muslim 1 Khatri
1960–1972 M 41 F 31	72		3	2	5	8	8	10	14	3	4	2	1	3	1 Muslim 2 Brahman 2 Jat 1 Tamilian	1 Muslim 2 Khatri
TOTAL	147		11	3	13	15	12	21	24	11	6	4	6	6	8	7
				14		28		33		35		10		12		15

	Srivastava M	Srivastava F	Total	Mathur M	Mathur F	Saksena M	Saksena F	Bhatnagar M	Bhatnagar F	Nigam M	Nigam F	Gaur M	Gaur F	Asthana M	Asthana F	Non-Kayasths Male	Non-Kayasths Female
Before 1929	3	6	9		1	1	3	1	3								1 Muslim 1 Nae 1 ?
1930–1939	7	7	14			3	3	1			2	1		1		1 Muslim	1 American 1 Telugu
1940–1949	4	3	7			1	1							1	1	1 Khatri 1 Bihari Sinha	1 *suratval*
1950–1959	6	14	20	1	5	1	1	1	3			1	1			1 Rajput 1 Maharashtrian Brahman	2 Maharashtrian Brahman 1 Anglo-Indian 1 Khatri 1 Maharashtrian
1960–1972	5	13	18		5	2	5		6					1			2 Telugu 1 Muslim
TOTAL			73	2	11	8	13	5	6	0	2	2	1	3	1	5	14
					13		21		11		2		3		4		19

Bibliography

I. REMARKS

The sources for Hyderabad's history are varied and rich. The brief discussion which follows should be supplemented by the forthcoming *Guide to the Andhra Pradesh State Archives,* edited by V. K. Bawa, and by the same author's "Some Problems in the Study of Hyderabad State," *Itihas,* I, no. 1 (1973), 145–158 (journal published by APSA).

The Hyderabad records fall into two main categories: the old Mughlai *daftars,* Persian records from the eighteenth and nineteenth centuries; and the so-called Secretariat records, those kept from the 1850's as the administration was re-modelled along British Indian lines.

There are fourteen or fifteen older Persian *daftars.* They were usually maintained by particular families and were only gradually taken over by the Nizam's Central Record Office. They differ in bulk and in chronological coverage. Most of the records are tied in bundles and stored in cupboards or on shelves, sometimes in chronological order, sometimes in a kind of topical ordering. There are ways of working with these records, although there are no real catalogues or indexes. The APSA personnel have partial reference tools for some of them, particularly the various registers of *jagirdars, mansabdars,* revenue contractors, and other employees dating from the eighteenth century. Another set of records, the *muntakhab* or inheritance case records, has partial chronological and alphabetical indexes; for the earlier *muntakhab* records there are indexes by *taluk.*

The second major category of Hyderabad records, the Secretariat records kept from the 1850's, are somewhat easier to use. First, after about 1883 most of them are in Urdu or English rather than Persian. Second, although again the sheer bulk is formidable, at least there is a sort of index: the transfer lists compiled when the APSA moved in 1966. These lists are kept in the stacks; a scholar must know about them and request to use them. There are transfer lists for fifteen or sixteen departments. The transfer lists for the Chief Secretariat alone, which handled the correspondence of the Prime Minister, are in ninety-two bound volumes or installments. Some forty-two of them contain chiefly English lists. Each installment contains from one to seventeen unrelated lists, to which there is no index. Some of the Secretariat records are kept in the Interim Depository, in the present Secretariat, where the researcher will encounter a different set of personnel and regulations.

Other valuable materials are in the APSA. There are important collections of family papers, notably the Salar Jung papers (almost catalogued). There is the room full of printed government records and reports (also almost catalogued), including such basic and barely utilized materials as the civil and military lists and the Nizam's official gazette. The APSA's Oriental Manuscripts Library (housed in the State Central Library) is well organized. There is a good library of secondary sources at the APSA.

But for both manuscripts and secondary sources, one must go beyond the APSA to fully exploit potential sources. Other useful manuscript sources are in the State Central Library, at Osmania University, in the Salar Jung Museum, and at the Idara-e-Adabiyat-e-Urdu (Institute of Urdu Literature). One must check these libraries for secondary works too, as no collection is complete. And no library has a systematic and continuing acquisition program in Decanni or Hyderabad history.

Local collections of newspapers and periodicals are a promising and barely used source for Hyderabadi history. The holdings of the Idara-e-Adabiyat-e-Urdu are the most extensive. Its collection includes files of some 735 newspapers and periodicals, 240 of them published locally. Though the collection is particularly strong from the 1930's, there are valuable earlier publications. An almost unknown local library, the Bharat Guna Vardhak Samstha, has a fine collection of late nineteenth- and early twentieth-century Urdu literary monthlies. The State Central Library has good runs of late nineteenth-century Urdu dailies. The Salar Jung Museum Library's holdings of Urdu periodicals run from the 1880's to 1940. Osmania University, with only scattered, predominantly twentieth-century holdings, has been fortunate to receive Professor K. Sajan Lal's personal collection of papers and manuscripts, which should be catalogued by now. Even the APSA, without a systematic collection of newspapers or periodicals, has a very useful clippings collection, covering 1894 to about 1901, in the Research Room. Finally, currently published newspapers have back files to which scholars can gain access without difficulty.

II. UNPUBLISHED MATERIALS

Government of Hyderabad: Archival Records

Andhra Pradesh State Archives

Asnad-i Jagir alif-ye. Two registers of *jagirdars*, nos. 1–1733. Section R2. Persian.
Daftar-i Mal, "Report of Rae Prahbu Lal, Daftar-i Mal," 36/E/ Mal 1326 F., no. 36. Urdu.

Daftar-i Mal Jagir Register. "Naqul-i asnad-i Shiv Raj" in file no. 66 of 1342 F. [1932-1933]. Section R2. Persian.

Files of the Chief Secretariat. 1793-1949. Persian, Urdu, and English. Unindexed except 92 transfer lists prepared when APSA moved.

Muntakhab Mansabdaran files, from 1876. Section R1. Persian, Urdu, and (after 1950) English.

Register Asnad-i Jagir. 18 registers, circa 1740-1913. Section R2. Persian.

Register of Copies of Faramin Mubarak (royal orders) connected with Mohtamad-i Mal for 1359, 60, and 61 H. [1940-1942]. Interim Depository. Urdu and English.

Sarfarazi Manasab o Khitabat. Section R2. Persian.

Endowment Office, Andhra Pradesh State

"Judgment of Original Suit No. 32 of 1959 (Keshovgiri temple case)." II Additional Judge. English.

Records concerning temple budgets, transferred from the Finance Department. English.

Records concerning current payments to temple managers, transferred from the Pension Payments Office. English.

Serrishtah Amur-i Mazhabi files, transferred from the *serrishtahdar.* Persian, Urdu, and English.

Statement of Endowment Register. Persian, Urdu, and English.

India Office Library

"Jagirdaran o Inamdaran Subajat-i Dakan, 1198 H. [1784]." Persian ms. 1015.4.

Sarf-i Khas Records

Arbab-i Nishat records. Sarf-i Khas files. APSA: bundle for 1280 H. (1856). Persian.

"Fehrist-i Mansabdaran muratib khizanah Private Estate H.E.H. the Nizam." A typed list of *serrishtahs* of *mansabdars,* prepared for me in February, 1965. Urdu.

Untitled. A typed list of military *serrishtahdars* prepared for me in February, 1965. Urdu.

Government of Hyderabad: Printed Records

Dunlop, A. J. *Report on the Administration of the Districts belonging to the Nawab Vikar-ul-Umra Bahadur, for the year 1293 Fasli* [1884]. Bombay, 1885. (APSA)

Glancy, R. I. R. *Report on the Claims of the Sarf-i Khas Department.* Hyderabad, 1913. (APSA)

H.H. The Nizam's Government Budget Estimate for 1304 Fasli [1894-1895]. Hyderabad, 1894.

Husain, Mazhar, ed. *Lists of Uruses, Melas, Jatras, etc.* Hyderabad, 1349 F. [1940]. (APSA)

Jang, Nawab Emad. *Report on the Administration of Justice in H.H. the Nizam's Dominions for 1299 F.* [1899-1900]. Secunderabad, 1891.

Jung, Salar. *Hyderabad State. Miscellaneous Notes on Administration.* Hyderabad [1856]. (SJL.) Published as "Administration Report of the Dominions of H.H. the Nizam, by his Excellency the Nawab Sir Salar Jung, Bahadoor, G.C.S.I." in Madhi Syed Ali, ed., *Hyderabad Affairs,* 10 vols. (Bombay, 1883-1889); handwritten copy in APSA, files of the Chief Secretariat, installment 39, list 1, serial no. 1; Al/a.

Jung, Salar II. *Confidential Memorandum of Salar Jung II.* N.p. [1886]. (SJL)

Offices of the Accountant General or of Finance. *The Classified List of Officers of the Civil and Military Departments of H.E.H. the Nizam's Government.* 1887-1948. (APSA) (The office of origin and exact titles differ slightly over the years.)

Paigah Committee Report, 1347 H. [1929]. (APSA)

(Proceedings of the Court.) "Mahkamah-i Judicial Committee, Mahbub Rae aur Brij Rani, numbers 1 aur 2 inheritance, 1343 F. [1933]." A printed copy of Hyderabad judicial records.

Report on the Administration of the Court of Wards Department, 1929-1948. Annual. 1929-1948. (APSA)

Report on the Administration of the Salar Jung Estate. Annual reports, 1896-1906. (APSA)

Report on Public Instruction in H.E.H. the Nizam's Dominions. Annual, 1896-1897 through 1946-1947. (APSA)

Sarf-i Khas. *Fehrist-i Ohadahdaran o Mulaziman Sarf-i Khas Mubarak.* 1915-1927. Printed biannually to 1919, annually to 1927.

————. *Fehrist-i Ohadahdaran-i Fauj.* 1927-1936. Printed annually.

————. *Fehrist-i Ohadahdaran Civil.* 1927-1940. Printed annually.

Statement of the Claims of Khoorshed Jah against Vikar-ul-Oomrah in respect of the Property late in the possession of Nawabs Rafee-ud-Deen Khan and Rashbee-ud-deen Khan Bahadoors. Bombay, n.d. (SJL)

Statement Showing the Names of Jagirdars Exercising Judicial Powers in His Exalted Highness the Nizam's Dominions for the year 1342 F. [1932-1933]. Hyderabad, n.d. (APSA)

Government of India: Printed Records

Foreign Department. *Nomenclature: Reports on Native Courts.* Serial no. 129 of 1814, Miscellaneous. (NAI)

Foreign Department. *Report on Reform in Nizam's Government.* Secret Consultation no. 8, Sept. 30, 1820. (NAI)

Political Department. *Hyderabad Residency Records.* Box 66, 603/92-93 and 605/92-96, concerning the Imperial Service Troops and the state administration. (IOL)

Political Department. Political Branch, Confidential. *Fortnightly Reports,* 1933–1938. (IOL)

Report on the Hyderabad Medical School, for the year 1858–1859. 1861. Selected Records India, no. 34. (BM)

Temple, Richard. *Report on the Administration of the Government of His Highness the Nizam in the Deccan.* Calcutta, 1868. Repr. by the Foreign Department from the Residency Records. (IOL and NAI)

Miscellaneous Manuscripts and Records

Arcot Diwani Records. "Persian correspondence on behalf of the Nawabs of Arcot with the Hyderabad Vakils." Tentatively numbered file 32 (1766–1855) in the private collection of Dr. Muhammad Ghaus of Madras.

Arcot Diwani Records. "Persian Records concerning titles given by the Nawab of Arcot." Tentatively numbered file 35 in the private collection of Dr. Muhammad Ghaus of Madras.

"Halat-i Khandan Rajah Rae Murlidhar." Persian obituary read at a Kayasth Union meeting. With Gurucharan Das Saxena.

Hyderabad Mathur Kayasth Welfare and Education Society. Duplicated materials for 1971 conference, and the irregularly issued journal *Profile* (1970–1976).

Jung, Nawab Sadr Yar. Speech of April 1, 1929, to Kayasth Young Men's Union meeting. With Gurucharan Das Saxena.

Lal, Dr. Brij Mohan. Letters to me of Sept. 26, Oct. 19, Nov. 12, Nov. 14, Nov. 26, and Dec. 29, 1965, and Dec. 13, 1966. English.

Lal, Dr. Brij Mohan. "Our Asthana Family Ancestry." 1953. Microfilm with me.

———. "The Story of My Life." 1956. With Kunj Behari Lal, Asthana.

Lal, Hira, and Ram Dayal. "Srimat Bhagvat." 1841. With Mahabir Pershad, Bhatnagar.

Mohan Lal and Murari Lal Srivastava family papers. With Jagdish Pershad (Gaur) and some with me.

Najmuddin, Muhammad, ed. *Taqvim 1329 H.* [1911]. Printed budget of the Paigah estate. Hyderabad, n.d.

———. *Taqvim 1330 H.* [1912]. Hyderabad, n.d.

———. *Taqvim 1333 H.* [1915]. Hyderabad, n.d.

———. *Taqvim 1335 H.* [1917]. Hyderabad, n.d.

Pershad, Gaya. "Halat-i Gaya Pershad Aryah." Manuscript Urdu autobiography, with me.

Pershad, Jagdish. Summaries of Gaur families, prepared 1971 and 1973.

[Pershad, Lalta.] "Liaqatnamajat Rai Lalta Pershad," 1893. Accession no. 2884. Persian. (SJL)

Pershad, Swami. "Insha-i Namati." Transcribed in Hyderabad, 1817. Persian ms. 608. (OUL)

Rae, Dooleh. "Munshi Malikzada." Transcribed in 1771–1772. Persian ms. 250. (APSA)

Bibliography

————. "Nigar Namah-i Munshi." Transcribed in Hyderabad, 1761. Persian ms. 1328. (OUL)

Sati stone of Girdhar Kunwar, mother of Shadi Lal (Wala Jahi Saksena), 1757-1758: Persian inscription. By graveyard at Purana Pul bridge.

Shanker, Krpa (secretary). Minutes of the Hyderabad Kayasth Sadr Sabha, 1894-1900. With Hakim Vicerai.

Vicerai, Hakim. Urdu summary of Mathur families. Prepared for me in January, 1966.

Dissertations

Bawa, V. K. "Hyderabad in Transition under Sir Salar Jung I, 1853-1883: An Indian State under British Influence." Ph.D. dissertation, Tulane University, 1968.

Henson, Harlan N. "Elites, Language Policy and Political Integration in Hyderabad." Ph.D. dissertation, University of Illinois, 1974.

Lateefunisa, Begum. "Private Enterprise in Education and the contribution of some famous private High Schools to the Advancement of Education in the cities of Hyderabad and Secunderabad." Master's dissertation, Osmania University, 1956.

Muttalib, Mohamed Abdul. "The Administration of Justice Under the Nizams, 1724-1947." Ph.D. dissertation, Osmania University, 1958.

III. PUBLISHED MATERIALS

Government of Hyderabad

Akbar, Syed Ali, ed. *Education under Asaf Jah VII: A Retrospect.* Hyderabad, 1936-1937.

Belgrami, Syed Hossain Motaman Jung. *History of the Operations of His Highness the Nizam's Educational Department for the last 30 years together with a detailed Report and Returns for 1883-84-85.* Hyderabad, 1886.

Census of H.H. the Nizam's Dominions, 1881. Bombay, 1884.

Census of India, 1891, XXIII, Hyderabad State. Hyderabad, 1893.

Census of India, 1901, XXII, Hyderabad State. Hyderabad, 1903.

Census of India, 1911, XIX, Hyderabad State. Bombay, 1913.

Census of India, 1921, XXI, Hyderabad State. Hyderabad, 1923.

Census of India, 1931, XXIII, H.E.H. The Nizam's Dominions. Hyderabad, 1933.

Census of India, 1941, XXI, H.E.H. the Nizam's Dominions. Hyderabad, 1943.

Chronology of Modern Hyderabad, 1720-1890. Central Records Office (APSA). Hyderabad, 1954.

Decennial Report on the Administration of H.E.H. the Nizam's Dominions 1322 to 1331 Fasli [1912-1922]. Hyderabad, 1930.

Department of Information and Public Relations. *Our MLAs.* Hyderabad, 1952.

————. *Some Aspects of Hyderabad 1954.* Hyderabad, 1954.

Hyderabad men Arya Samaj ki Tehrik. Hyderabad [1939].

Hyderabad State Committee for History of the Freedom Movements. *Freedom Struggle in Hyderabad.* Vols. I–IV. Hyderabad, 1956–1966.

Jung, Salar. "Financial Statement for 1288 F. [1878]," in *HA,* VI, 1–80.

————. "Translation from Persian of a Memorandum by His Excellency Nawab Mukhtar-ul-Mulk, Sir Salar Jung Bahadur, G.C.S.I., on the Financial Statement for the year 1288 Fasli [1878]," in *HA,* VI, 3–17.

[Khan], Yusuf Husain, ed. *The Diplomatic Correspondence between Mir Nizam Ali Khan and the East India Company (1780–98).* Hyderabad, 1958.

Majmua Sipasnamajat o Ishadat-i Khusrana. Hyderabad [1936].

Munn, Leonard. *Hyderabad Municipal Survey 1911.* Hyderabad, n.d.

Regulations Relating to Salary, Leave, Pension, and Travelling Allowances. Hyderabad, 1938.

Report of the Reforms Committee 1938. Hyderabad, 1939.

Report on the Administration of His Highness the Nizam's Dominions for the four years 1304 to 1307 Fasli [1894–1898]. Madras, 1899. (APSA)

Report on the Administration of H.H. the Nizam's Dominions for the four years 1316 to 1319 Fasli [1906–1910]. Madras, 1913. (APSA and IOL)

Reports on the Administration. Annually, 1912–1948. (APSA and IOL)

Statistics Department. *Diglott Calendar.* Official correspondence of Hijri, Fasli, and Christian dates, 1879–1950. 2 vols. Hyderabad, 1929, 1938.

Government of India

Nizam's Territory, Copy of all Papers relative to Territory ceded by H.H. the Nizam, in Liquidation of Debts alleged to have been due by H.H. to the British Government. Hyderabad, n.d. (Repr. in Hyderabad by request of Salar Jung I, orig. of 1854, SOAS, India Papers, 32426.)

Government of India. *Imperial Gazetteer of India.. Provincial Series. Hyderabad State.* Calcutta, 1909.

Books and Pamphlets in English

A Peep into Hyderabad. Collected articles from the *Tribune* of Lahore, June 5, 6, 7 [1939]. Lahore, n.d.

A Short Account of the Aims, Objects, Achievements, and Proceedings of the Kayastha Conference. Allahabad, 1893.

Ahmad, Aziz. *Studies in Islamic Culture in the Indian Environment.* Oxford, 1964.

Ahmed, Zahir. *Life's Yesterdays.* Bombay, 1945.

Alam, Shah Manzoor. *Hyderabad-Secunderabad.* Bombay, 1965.

al-Hassan, Syed Siraj. *Castes and Tribes in H.E.H. the Nizam's Dominions.* Bombay, 1920.

Ali, B. Sheik. *British Relations with Haider Ali* (1760–1782). Mysore, 1963.

Ali, Madhi Syed, ed. *Hyderabad Affairs.* 10 vols. Bombay, 1883–1889.

Ali, Moulavi Cheragh. *Hyderabad Under Sir Salar Jung.* 4 vols. Bombay, 1884–1886.

Bibliography

Ali, N. Athar. *The Mughal Nobility Under Aurangzeb.* New York, 1966.

Bailey, F. G. *Caste and the Economic Frontier.* Manchester, 1957.

Balfour, E. *On the Ethnology of Hyderabad in the Dekhan.* Madras, 1871.

Bhattacharya, Jogendra Nath. *Hindu Castes and Sects.* Calcutta, 1896.

Bilgrami, S. A. Asgar. *The Landmarks of the Deccan.* Hyderabad, 1927.

Bilgrami, Syed Hussain. *A Memoir of Sir Salar Jung.* Bombay, 1883.

Bilgrami, Syed Hussain, and C. Willmott. *Historical and Descriptive Sketch of the Nizam's Dominions.* 2 vols. Bombay, 1883.

Blunt, Wilfred Scawen. *India Under Ripon.* London, 1909.

Briggs, Henry George. *The Nizam: His History and Relations with the British Government.* 2 vols. London, 1861.

Burton, Major Reginald George. *A History of the Hyderabad Contingent.* Calcutta, 1905.

Cadell, Patrick, ed. *The Letters of Philip Meadows Taylor to Henry Reeve.* London, 1947.

Campbell, A. C. *Glimpses of the Nizam's Dominions.* London, 1898.

Cohn, Bernard S. *India: The Social Anthropology of a Civilization.* Englewood Cliffs, N.J., 1971.

Compton, Herbert. *A Particular Account of the European Military Adventurers of Hindustan from 1784–1803.* London, 1892.

Crofton, O. S. *List of Inscriptions on Tombs or Monuments in H.E.H. The Nizam's Dominions.* Hyderabad, 1941.

Crooke, William. *The Tribes and Castes of North-western Provinces and Oudh.* 4 vols. Calcutta, 1896.

Davies, C. Collin. *An Historical Atlas of the Indian Peninsula.* Oxford, 1959.

Farquhar, J. N. *Modern Religious Movements in India.* New York, 1918.

Fox, Richard G. *Kin, Clan, Raja, and Rule.* Berkeley, 1971.

————, ed. *Urban India: Society, Space and Image.* Durham, N.C., 1970.

Fraser, Hastings. *Memoir and Correspondence of General J. S. Fraser of the Madras Army.* London, 1885.

————. *Our Faithful Ally, the Nizam.* London, 1865.

Geary, Grattan. *Hyderabad Politics.* Bombay, 1884.

General Rules of the Hyderabad Club. Hyderabad, 1884.

Goody, Jack, and S. J. Tambiah. *Bridewealth and Dowry.* Cambridge, Eng., 1973.

Gopal, Sarvepalli. *The Viceroyalty of Lord Ripon 1880–1884.* Oxford, 1953.

Gore, M. S. *Urbanization and Family Change.* Bombay, 1968.

Gribble, J. D. B. *History of the Deccan.* 2 vols. London, 1896.

————. *History of Freemasonry in Hyderabad (Deccan).* Madras, 1910.

Gupta, Jyotindira Das. *Language Conflict and National Development.* Berkeley, 1970.

H.R.H. The Prince of Wales' Visit to India. London [1857?].

Habib, Irfan. *The Agrarian System of Mughal India.* New York, 1963.

Hardgrave, Robert. *The Nadars of Tamilnad.* Berkeley, 1969.

Hasan, Syed Abid. *Whither Hyderabad.* Madras, 1935.

Hazlehurst, L. W. *Entrepreneurship and the Merchant Castes in a Punjabi City.* Durham, N.C., 1966.

Hollins, S. T. *No Ten Commandments.* London, 1958.

Hyderabad Ripon Memorial Meeting. [Hyderabad, 1884?]

Inden, Ronald B. *Marriage and Rank in Bengali Culture.* Berkeley, 1976.

International Aryan League. *Nizam Defense Examined and Exposed.* Delhi [1940].

Jung, Ali Yavar. *Hyderabad in Retrospect.* Bombay, 1949.

Kamil, Mir Zahid Ali. *The Communal Problem in Hyderabad.* Hyderabad [1935].

Kayasth Pathshala. *Golden Jubilee, 1873–1923.* Allahabad [1924].

Kaye, J. W. *Life and Correspondence of Charles L. Metcalfe.* 2 vols. London, 1854.

————. *The Life and Correspondence of Major-General Sir John Malcolm G.C.B.* 2 vols. London, 1856.

Kessinger, Tom G. *Vilyatpur, 1848–1968.* Berkeley, 1974.

Khan, M. Fathufla. *A History of Administrative Reforms in Hyderabad State.* Secunderabad, 1935.

Khan, Mohamed Abdul Rahman. *My Life and Experience.* Hyderabad, 1951.

Khan, Sadath Ali. *Brief Thanksgiving.* Bombay, 1959.

Khan, Yusuf Husain. *The First Nizam.* 2d ed. Bombay, 1963.

Khare, R. S. *The Changing Brahmans.* Chicago, 1970.

Kirkwood, W. C. *The Story of the 97th Deccan Infantry.* Hyderabad, 1929.

Kishen, C. Sri. *45 Years a Rebel.* Hyderabad [1953].

Kurian, George, ed. *The Family in India—A Regional View.* The Hague, 1974.

Lakh Bribery Case, of Hyderabad Deccan. Bangalore, 1895.

[Lal, Lala Maharajah.] *A Short Account of the Life of Rai Jeewan Lal Bahadur, late Honorary Magistrate, Delhi, and Extracts from his diary.* Delhi, 1888. IOL pamphlet.

Leach, E. R., ed. *Aspects of Caste in South India, Ceylon, and North-west Pakistan.* Cambridge, Eng., 1969.

Lothian, Sir Arthur Cunningham. *Kingdoms of Yesterday.* London, 1951.

Lynch, Owen. *The Politics of Untouchability.* New York, 1969.

Lynton, Harriet Ronken, and Mohini Rajan. *Days of the Beloved.* Berkeley, 1974.

McAuliffe, H. P. *The Nizam.* London, 1904.

Madan, T. N. *Family and Kinship.* London, 1965.

Manohar, Murli. *The Industries of Ancient India etc.* Madras, 1897.

Mayer, Adrian C. *Caste and Kinship in Central India.* London, 1960.

Memorandum. Press extracts, 1890's. N.d., n.p. (SJL)

Menon, V. P. *The Story of the Integration of the Indian States.* Bombay, 1956.

Moodellear, M. Soobaraya. *Hyderabad Almanac and Directory, 1874.* Madras, 1873.

Mudiraj, K. Krishnaswamy. *Pictorial Hyderabad.* 2 vols. Hyderabad, 1929, 1934.

Mulla, D. F. *Principles of Hindu Law.* Bombay, 1959.

Murtaza, Kadiri Syed. *Translation of a Review on the Addresses presented to H.H. Asif Jah, Muzaffar-ul-Mamalik, Nizam-ul-Mulk, Nizam Mir Sir Mahboob Ali Khan Bahadur, Fateh Jung G.C.S.I. of Hyderabad, Deccan on the 33rd*

Anniversary of his Birthday in 1316 A.H. (and replies). Hyderabad, 1899. (APSA)

[Naidoo, P. V.] *Hyderabad in 1890 and 1891.* Bangalore, 1892.

Prasad, Munshi Kali. *The Kayastha Ethnology.* Lucknow, 1877. (IOL)

Pratap, Captain Surya. *The Tragedy of Arya Samaj.* Hyderabad, 1960.

Proceedings of the Kayasth Sadr Sabha, Hyderabad-Dn. Hyderabad, 1939.

Qureshi, Anwar Iqbal. *The Economic Development of Hyderabad.* Madras [1947].

Rai, Ganpath. *Report on the position of the Hindu Communities in the Nizam's Dominions.* New Delhi [1935].

Rao, D. Raghavendra. *Misrule of the Nizam.* N.p., 1926.

Rao, P. Setu Madhava. *Eighteenth Century Deccan.* Bombay, 1963.

Regani, Sarojini. *Nizam-British Relations 1724–1857.* Hyderabad, 1963.

Resolutions of the 1936 Kayasth Conference. Bareilly, n.d.

Resolutions passed in the 42nd session of the AIKC held at Hyderabad (Deccan), by virtue of the Royal Sanction, granted by H.E.H., on the 27th, 28th and 29th December 1938. Hyderabad, n.d.

Rudolph, Susanne H., and Lloyd Rudolph. *The Modernity of Tradition.* Chicago, 1967.

Saksena, Ram Babu. *History of Urdu Literature.* Allahabad, 1927.

Salam, Abdus. *Hyderabad Struggle.* Bombay, 1941.

Sarkar, Jadunath. *Mughal Administration.* 5th ed. Calcutta, 1963.

Sastri, J. Venkata. *The Geography of the Hyderabad Dominions.* 2nd ed. Secunderabad, 1932.

Segalen, Martine. *Nuptialite et alliance: le choix du conjoint dans une commune de l'Eure.* Paris, 1972.

Server-el-Mulk, Nawab Bahadur. *My Life.* Translated by Nawab Jivan Yar Jung Bahadur [author's son]. London, 1932.

Shah, A. M. *The Household Dimension of the Family in India.* Berkeley, 1974.

Sherwani, H. K. *Muhammad-Quli Qutb Shah: Founder of Haiderabad.* New York, 1967.

———, ed. *Studies in Indian Culture.* Hyderabad, 1966.

Siddiqui, A. H. *History of Golcunda.* Hyderabad, 1956.

Silverberg, James, ed. *Social Mobility in the Caste System in India.* The Hague, 1968.

Singer, Milton, ed. *Entrepreneurship and Modernization of Occupational Cultures in South Asia.* Durham, N.C., 1973.

Singer, Milton, and Bernard S. Cohn, eds. *Structure and Change in Indian Society.* Chicago, 1968.

Sovani, Y. K. *Feudal Oppression in Hyderabad.* N.p., 1939.

Stotherd, Major E. A. W. *History of the 30th Lancers Gordon's Horse.* London [1912].

Taylor, Philip Meadows. *The Story of My Life.* London, 1882.

Temple, Richard. *Journals Kept in Hyderabad, Kashmir, Sikkim, and Nepal.* 2 vols. London, 1887.

Thornton, Thomas H. *General Sir Richard Meade and the Feudatory States of Central and Southern India.* New York, 1898.

Tirtha, Swami Ramanand. *First Class Tragedy.* Poona, 1940.

――――. *Memoirs of the Hyderabad Freedom Struggle.* Bombay, 1971.

Ufuq Centenary Committee. *Poet Laureate Late M. Dwarka Pershad Ufuq of Lucknow.* Delhi, 1964.

Varma, Gopi Nath Sinha. *A Peep into the Origin, Status and History of the Kayasthas.* 2 vols. Bareilly, 1929, 1935.

Varma, Kumar Cheda Singh. *Kshatriyas and Would-be Kshatriyas.* N.p., 1904. Tract, in IOL.

Vatuk, Sylvia. *Kinship and Urbanization.* Berkeley, 1974.

Vidyarthi, L. P. *The Sacred Complex in Hindu Gaya.* New York, 1961.

Urdu Books and Pamphlets

Abdurrauf. *Dabdabah-i Nizam.* Hyderabad, 1904.

Ahmed, Muhammad. *Mukhtasir Sarguzasht Serrishtah-i Tappah-i Sarkar-i Ali.* Hyderabad, 1936–1937.

Ahmed, Muhammad Sayyed. *Umra-i Hinud.* Aligarh, 1910.

Ali, Sayyid Manzur. *Anvar-i Asafiyah.* Hyderabad, 1935.

――――. *Manzur ul Ikram.* Hyderabad, 1926–1927.

Bartar, Muhammad Nadir Ali. *Khandan Rajah Rae Rayan Amanatvant.* Hyderabad, 1920.

Chand, Lala Khub. *Kayasth Kul Nar Nai.* Hyderabad, 1892.

Dastur-ul Amal-i Shadi Firqah-i Saksenah. N.p., 1941.

Gaur, Ram Das. *Tazkirah-i Sucaru Vanshi.* Allahabad, 1911.

Hashimi, Nasir ud-din. *Dakhini Hindu aur Urdu.* Hyderabad [1958].

International Aryan League. *Riyasat-i Hyderabad men Arya Samaj ka Muqqadama.* Delhi [1938].

Jung, Nawab Aziz. *Khazina-i Finance va Hisab.* Hyderabad, 1909–1910.

Kayasth Association Fatehullah Baig. Second annual report for 1917. Hyderabad, 1917.

Kayasth Club Husaini Alam ka Pahla Sal. Hyderabad, 1915.

Kayasth Club Husaini Alam ka Dusra Sal. Hyderabad, 1916.

Kayasth Club Husaini Alam ka Tisra Sal. Hyderabad, 1917.

Kayasth Sadr Sabha, Hyderabad. *Irshadat Salatin Asafiyah.* Hyderabad [1943].

Kayasth Sadr Sabha Hind, *Report Kayasth Sadr Sabha Hind.* N.p., 1893.

Kayasth Temperance Societies Hind. *Holi Report Hindustan.* Agra, 1900.

――――. *General Report 1898.* Agra, 1899.

――――. *General Report 1899.* Agra, 1900.

――――. *Report Khandan Parhezgaran.* Agra, 1899.

――――. *Report Taqriban Khushi.* Agra, 1899.

Khan, Ghulam Samdani. *Darbar-i Asaf.* Hyderabad, 1900.

――――. *Hiyat-i Mah Laqa.* Hyderabad, 1906.

――――. *Tuzuk-i Mahbubiyah.* 2 vols. Hyderabad, 1902.

Bibliography

Khan, Mir Basit Ali. *Tarikh-i Adalat-i Asafi.* Hyderabad, 1937.

Lal, Lalah Javahar. *Taqvim-i Mahbubiyah.* Agra, 1915.

Pershad, Baldev. *Kayasth Kul Utpatti.* Bijnur, 1911.

Pershad, Bisheshwar Munnavar, ed. *Lamat-i Ufuq.* Delhi, 1964.

Pershad, Dwarka. *Hiyat-i Baqi Manzum.* Lucknow, 1892–1893.

Pershad, Girdhari. *Bhagvat Sar.* Hyderabad, 1890–1891.

———. *Kulliyat-i Baqi.* Hyderabad, 1887–1888. (Some of the sections are Persian poems.)

Pershad, Kamta. *Chitragupta Vamsi Kayasth Qaum Directory.* Agra, 1926.

———. *Ittehad al Akhwan.* 2 vols. Agra, 1895.

———, ed. *Patna High Court ke Faislah ka Urdu Tarjumah.* Lucknow, 1928.

Pershad, Satguru. *Farkhundah Bunyad Hyderabad.* Hyderabad, 1964.

———, ed. *Report for 1352 Fasli of the Hyderabad Sadr Sabha, Provincial Sabha.* Hyderabad [1943].

Pratap, Surya [Haq Prast]. *Hamari Zaban.* Hyderabad, 1940.

Rae, Tej. *Sahifeh-i Asman Jahi.* Hyderabad, 1904–1905.

Raj, Nar Singh. *Armaghan-i Mahbub.* Hyderabad, 1932.

———. *Dard-i Baqi o Durd-i Saqi.* Hyderabad, 1933.

Ramcharan. *Kayasth Dharm Darpan.* Translated by Lala Lalji. Lucknow, 1928.

Rao, Eshvant. *Tarikh-i Khandan-i Rajah Rao Rumbha Jivant Bahadur Nimbhalkar.* Hyderabad, 1893–1894.

Rao, Manik Rao Vithal. *Bustan-i Asafiyah.* 7 vols. Hyderabad, 1909–1932.

Saksena, K. C. Roy. *Kul Hind Kayasth Conference.* Hyderabad, 1938.

———. *Report Kul Hind Kayasth Conference.* Hyderabad, 1939.

Saksenah, Shiv Narayan. *Kayasth Sajjan Caritra.* 3 vols. Jaipur, 1912–1913.

Shirazi, Samsam. *Mushir-i Alam Directory.* Hyderabad, 1947.

Sufi ud-din, Moulvi. *Jantri Pancah Salah.* 2nd ed. Hyderabad, 1896–1897.

Tarikh-i Majlis Ittehad ul Muslimin, 1928–40. Hyderabad, 1941.

Varman, Gopinath Singh. *Mukhtasir Tarikh-i Aqvam ul-Kayasth, Prabhu, va Thakur.* 2 vols. Bareilly, 1921.

Varsi, Muhammad Ali. *Makatib Yamin-us Sultanat Kishen Pershad Bahadur.* Hyderabad, 1952.

Vicerai, Hakim. *Ramayan Manzum.* Hyderabad [1960].

Young Men's Kayasth Union. *Report Salanah 1927–28.* Hyderabad, 1928.

———. *Report Salanah 1928–29.* Hyderabad, 1929.

———. *Report Salanah 1929–30.* Hyderabad, 1930.

———. *Report Salanah 1930–31.* Hyderabad, 1931.

———. *Report Salanah 1931–32.* Hyderabad, 1932.

———. *Report Salanah 1932–33.* Hyderabad, 1933.

Zore, Syed Mehi ud-din Qadri. *Dastan-i Adab-i Hyderabad.* Hyderabad, 1951.

Persian Books

Khan, Ghulam Husain. *Tarikh-i Gulzar-i Asafiyah.* Hyderabad, 1890–1891.

Khan, Muhammad Abdul Jabbar. *Mahbub us-Zaman Tazkirah-i Shora-i Dakan.* 2 vols. Hyderabad, 1911.

Khan, Muhammad Ghaus. *Tazkirah-i Gulzar-i Azam.* Madras, 1855–1856.
Lal, Makhan. *Tarikh-i Yadgar-i Makhan Lal.* Hyderabad [1829].
Pershad, Girdhari. *Haft Band.* Delhi, 1894–1895.

Hindi and Marathi Books

Bramhanand, Nijanand Das. *Sri Guru Nijanand Maharajance Caritra.* Hyderabad [1914]. (Marathi)
Narayan, Lakshmi, ed. *Vinay Govind.* Hyderabad, 1937.
Vidyalanker, Jaidev Sharma et al., *Hyderabad Satyagraha ka Raktaranjit Itihas.* Ajmer, 1947.

English Articles

Anderson, Robert T. "Voluntary Associations in Hyderabad." *Anthropological Quarterly,* XXXVII (1964), 175–190.
Alavi, Hamza. "Kinship in West Punjab Villages." *CIS,* n.s., VI (1972), 1–12.
Barnett, Stephen A. "Approaches to Changes in Caste Ideology in South India." In Burton Stein, ed., *Essays on South India.* Honolulu, 1975.
Bawa, V. K. "Some Problems in the Study of Hyderabad State." *Itihas,* I, no. 1 (1973), 145–158.
Beck, Brenda. "The Boundaries of a Subcaste." In Brenda Beck, ed., *Perspectives on a Regional Culture: Essays about the Coimbatore Area of South India.* Durham, N.C., 1977.
Carroll, Lucy. "Caste, Social Change, and the Social Scientist: A Note on the Ahistorical Approach to Indian Social History." *JAS,* XXXV, no. 1 (1975), 63–84.
———, "Colonial Perceptions of Indian Society and the Emergence of Caste(s) Associations." *JAS,* in press.
———. "Kayastha Samachar: From a Caste to a National Newspaper." *IESHR,* X, no. 3 (1973), 280–292.
Carter, Anthony. "Caste 'boundaries' and the principle of kinship amity: a Maratha caste Purana." *CIS,* n.s., IX (1975), 123–137.
Char, S. Rama. "Education in Hyderabad." *Modern Review,* LXVI (1939), 177–181.
Cohn, Bernard S. "Notes on the History of the Study of Indian Society and Culture." In Milton Singer and Bernard S. Cohn, eds., *Structure and Change in Indian Society.* Chicago, 1968.
Conlon, Frank. "Caste by Association: The Gauda Sarasvata Brahmana Unification Movement." *JAS,* XXXIII, no. 3 (1974), 351–365.
Crozier, Dorothy. "Kinship and Occupational Succession." *Sociological Review,* III (1965), 15–43.
De, B. "The Educational Systems Adopted and the Results Achieved in the More Important Native States in India." *Modern Review,* IX (1911), 61–71.
Dumont, Louis. "Marriage in India, the Present State of the Question: III. North India in Relation to South India." *CIS,* IX (1966), 90–114.

Bibliography

Elliott, Carolyn M. "Decline of a Patrimonial Regime." *JAS,* XXXIV, no. 1 (1974), 27-47.

————. "The Problem of Autonomy: the Osmania University Case." In Susanne H. and Lloyd I. Rudolph, *Education and Politics in India.* Cambridge, Mass., 1972.

Fox, R. G. "Resiliency and Change in the Indian Caste System: The Umar of U. P." *JAS,* XXVI, no. 4 (1967), 575-587.

Gould, Harold. "Some Aspects of Kinship among Business and Professional Elite in Lucknow, India." *CIS,* n.s., V (1971), 116-130.

Goody, Jack. "Adoption in Cross-Cultural Perspective." *Comparative Studies in Society and History,* XI (1969), 55-78.

————. "Strategies of Heirship." *Comparative Studies in Society and History,* XV (1973), 3-20.

Gorst, J. F. "The Kingdom of the Nizam." *Fortnightly Review,* XXXV, n.s. (January-June 1884), 522-530.

Habakkuk, H. J. "Family Structure and Economic Change in Nineteenth-Century Europe." *Journal of Economic History,* XV, no. 1 (1955), 1-12.

Hazlehurst, Leighton W. "Multiple Status Hierarchies in Northern India." *CIS,* n.s., II (1968), 38-57.

————. "Urban Space and Activities." In Richard G. Fox, ed., *Urban India: Society, Space and Image.* Durham, N.C., 1970.

Husain, Yusuf. "Les Kayasthas, ou 'scribes,' caste hindoue iranisée, et la culture musulmane dans l'Inde." *Revue des études islamiques,* I (1927), 455-458.

Husaini, Q. S. Kalimullah. "Contribution of Hindu Poets and Writers of Hydera-bad—Deccan to Persian Literature." In *16th All-India Oriental Conference* (journal and proceedings). 1955, 165-172.

Kane, P. V. "The Kayasthas." *New Indian Antiquary,* I (1929), 739-743.

Khan, Yusuf Husain. "Anglo-Hyderabad Relations (1772-1818)." *Islamic Culture,* XXXII, no. 1 (1953), 41-57.

Khare, R. S. "A Case of Anomalous Values in Indian Civilization: Meat-eating among the Kanya-Kubja Brahmans of Katyayan Gotra." *JAS,* XXV, no. 2 (1966), 229-240.

————. "The Kanya-Kubja Brahmins and their Caste Organization." *Southwestern Journal of Anthropology,* XVI (1960), 348-367.

Kidder, Robert L. "Litigation as a Strategy for Personal Mobility: The Case of Urban Caste Association Leaders." *JAS,* XXXIII, no. 2 (1974), 177-191.

Kolenda, Pauline M. "Region, Caste and Family Structure: A Comparative Study of the Indian 'Joint' Family." In Milton Singer and Bernard S. Cohn, eds., *Structure and Change in Indian Society.* Chicago, 1968.

Kothari, R., and R. Maru. "Caste and Secularism in India." *JAS,* XXV, no. 1 (1965), 33-50.

Lacey, Patrick. "The Medium of Instruction in Indian Universities." *Asian Review,* n.s., XXXIV (1938), 534-542.

Leonard, John G. "Politics and Social Change in South India: A Study of the

Andhra Movement." *Journal of Commonwealth Political Studies*, V, no. 1 (1967), 60–77.

Leonard, Karen. "Cultural Change and Bureaucratic Modernization in Nineteenth Century Hyderabad: Mulkis, non-Mulkis, and the English." In P. M. Joshi, ed., *Studies in the Foreign Relations of India*. Hyderabad, 1975.

———. "The Deccani Synthesis in Old Hyderabad: an historiographic essay." *Journal of the Pakistan Historical Society*, XXI, no. 4 (October, 1973), 205–218.

———. "The Hyderabad Political System and its Participants." *JAS*, XXX, no. 3 (1971), 569–582.

———. "The Mulki—non-Mulki Conflict in Hyderabad State." In Robin Jeffrey, ed., *People, Princes, and Paramount Power: Society and Politics in the Indian Princely States*. Delhi, 1978.

———. "Women and Social Change in Modern India." *Feminist Studies*, III, no. 2 (Spring/Summer, 1976), 117–130.

McCormack, William C. "Caste and the British Administration of Hindu Law." *Journal of Asian and African Studies*, I, no. 1 (1966), 27–34.

Marriott, McKim. "Interactional and Attributional Theories of Caste Ranking." *Man in India*, XXXIX, no. 2 (1959), 92–107.

———. "Multiple Reference in Indian Caste Systems." In James Silverberg, ed., *Social Mobility in the Caste System in India*. The Hague, 1968.

Marriott, McKim, and Ronald Inden. "Caste Systems." In *Encyclopaedia Britannica, Macropaedia*, III. Chicago, 1974, 982–999.

Rahman, Fazlur. "Andjuman (India and Pakistan)." In *Encyclopedia of Islam*, I, new ed., London, 1960, 505–506.

[Rao, Binod.] "The Archives of Hyderabad." In Department of Information and Public Relations, *Some Aspects of Hyderabad*. Hyderabad, 1954.

Rao, K. V. N. "Separate Telangana State?" *Journal of the Society for the Study of State Government*, Benares Hindu University (1969), 129–143.

Regani, Sarojini. "The Appointment of Diwans in Hyderabad State (1803–1887)." *Andhra Historical Research Society*, XXV (1958–1960), 11–18.

Rowe, William L. "Mobility in the Nineteenth-century caste system." In Milton Singer and Bernard S. Cohn, eds., *Structure and Change in Indian Society*. Chicago, 1968.

Rudolph, Susanne Hoeber, and Lloyd I. Rudolph, with Mohan Singh. "A Bureaucratic Lineage in Princely India: Elite Formation and Conflict in a Patrimonial System." *JAS*, XXXIV, no. 3 (1975), 717–753.

Sanyal, Hitesranjan. "Continuities of Social Mobility in Traditional and Modern Society in India: Two Case Studies of Caste Mobility in Bengal." *JAS*, XXX, no. 2 (1971), 315–339.

Schneider, David M., and George C. Homans. "Kinship Terminology and the American Kinship System." *American Anthropologist*, LVII (1955), 1194–1208.

Shastri, Pandit Raghuvara Mitthulal. "A Comprehensive Study into the Origin and Status of the Kayasthas." *Man in India*, XI, no. 2 (1931), 116–159.

[327

Sherwani, H. K. "The Evolution of the Legislature in Hyderabad." *Indian Journal of Political Science,* I (1940), 424-438.

————. "The Osmania University First Phase: The Urdu Medium (1917-1948)." In H. K. Sherwani, ed., *Studies in Indian Culture* (Hyderabad, 1966), 237-247.

Smith, Daniel Scott. "Parental Power and Marriage Patterns." *Journal of Marriage and the Family,* XXXV, no. 3 (1973), 419-428.

Smith, Wilfred Cantwell. "Hyderabad: Muslim Tragedy." *Middle East Journal,* IV, no. 1 (1950), 27-51.

Srinivas, M. N. "Mobility in the Caste System." In Milton Singer and Bernard S. Cohn, eds., *Structure and Change in Indian Society.* Chicago, 1968.

Srivastava, Ram Dyal. "A Brief Memoir and Reminiscences of the late Munshi Kali Prasad." *Kayastha Samachar,* IV, no. 2 (1901), 174-176.

Stein, Burton. "Social Mobility and Medieval South Indian Sects." In James Silverberg, ed., *Social Mobility in the Caste System in India.* The Hague, 1968.

Tirmizi, A. J. "Inayat Jang Collection." *Studies in Islam,* I, no. 1 (1964), 178-190.

Vatuk, Sylvia. "A Structural Analysis of the Hindi Kinship Terminology." *CIS,* n.s., III (1969), 94-115.

————. "Trends in North Indian Urban Kinship: the 'Matrilateral Asymmetry' Hypothesis." *Southwestern Journal of Anthropology,* XXVII (1971), 287-307.

Wolf, Eric. "Kinship, Friendship, and Patron-Client Relations in Complex Societies." In Michael Banton, ed., *The Social Anthropology of Complex Societies.* New York, 1966.

Newspaper and Journal Collections

CC: Clippings Collection, APSA. Three scrapbooks of newspaper cuttings, 1890-1904.

Dabdabah-i Asafi. Urdu monthly, Hyderabad. Some holdings for 1898-1900, BGVS.

Deccan Chronicle. Back files (1930-1948) consulted in the Deccan Chronicle office, Sarojini Devi Road, Secunderabad.

Evening Mail, Bangalore. Some holdings for 1903, SCL.

Hyderabad Chronicle, Hyderabad. Some holdings for 1898, SCL.

Islamic Culture, Hyderabad. Back issues (from 1927) consulted in office, Osmania University, Hyderabad.

Kayastha. B. Avadh Behari Lal, editor. Agra, 1895-1897.

KH: Kayasth Herald. Gurucharan Das Saxena, editor. Vols. I-VII, Hyderabad, 1941-1948. (Urdu; some English and Hindi pages; with editor.)

Kayastha Samachar. Sachidananda Sinha, editor. Allahabad, 1901-1906. IOL and (1901) SJL.

Sabras. Urdu monthly, Hyderabad. Back issues (1940-1948) consulted in office, IAU, Khairatabad, Hyderabad.

IV. INTERVIEWS

Oral information from Kayasths was obtained during three periods, approximately five years apart: February, 1965 to March, 1966; December, 1970 to July,

1971; and August-September, 1976. Visits were at the convenience of those interviewed, usually informal and in their homes; there were often several family members or friends present. I made brief notes during interviews, adding information and comments later. The interviews focused initially on obtaining genealogies, but they were not structured otherwise.

I have listed here all Kayasths who provided substantial information, by subcaste; others whom I met only briefly are not included. Printing costs preclude citing here or in the footnotes the dates of the interviews (some Kayasths met with me as often as thirty or forty times), but that information is available upon request. Names are spelled as preferred in English, to the best of my knowledge. These same spellings are used for citations in all notes and bibliography, to avoid confusion created by different transliterations.

Asthana

Naresh Chandra Asthana	Dr. Brij Mohan Lal	Mrs. Kunj Behari Lal
Ramchander Asthana	Mrs. Brij Mohan Lal	Mrs. Shiv Shanker Lal
S. C. Asthana	D. B. Lal	
Lokendra Bahadur	Kunj Behari Lal	

Bhatnagar

Mrs. Inder Karan Bhatnagar	Mrs. Jag Mohan Lal	Mrs. Balobir Prosad
Dr. R. C. Bhatnagar	Mrs. Ranjit Prakash Lal	Brij Rani (Mrs. Bhavani Pershad)
Sham Karan	Lalta Pershad	
Mrs. Dori Lal	Mahabir Pershad	
	Balobir Prosad	

Gaur

Tulja Bai (Mrs. Govind Rao Pantoji)	Roy Mahboob Narayan	Jagdish Pershad
Raj Bahadur Gaur	Mrs. Roy Mahboob Narayan (daughter of	Keshav Pershad
Renuka Narayan (Mrs. Ram Narayan Agarwal)	Murlidhar Pershad, Saksena)	Onker Pershad
Reva Narayan	Bala Pershad	Mahbub Rai
		Ram Mohan Roy

Mathur

Rang Bahadur	Anjani Shanker Lal	Jivan Pershad
Mohan Chand	Shanker Mohan Lal	Ragukul Pershad
Dr. Benkat Chandra	Professor Shiv Mohan Lal	Raj Pershad
Dr. Dhareshwari (Mrs. Kishen Raj)	Bharat Kumar Mathur	Sri Rang Pershad
Maharaj Karan	C. M. Mathur	Dhan Raj Pratap
Raja Mahbub Karan	T. R. Mathur	Kishen Raj
Sham Karan	Miss Vimala Mathur	Visheshwar Raj
Sunder Karan	Huzoor Narayan	Anand Sagar
Hind Kishore	Ramchander Narayan	Mrs. Dharm Sen
		B. K. Sinha

[329

Bibliography

Pratap Kishore
Ajit Kumar
Bharat Raj Kumar
Dr. Vijay Kumar

Mrs. Dwarka Pershad
(daughter of Raja Shiv
Raj)
Jadubanth Pershad

S. K. Sinha
Hakim Vicerai

Nigam

Dwarka Pershad Nigam

Sham Kishori Nigam
(Mrs. Sri Rang
Pershad, Srivastava)

Somnath Pershad

Saksena

Mrs. Munir Chand
Dhiraj Kumar
Lakshmi Narayan
Pandit Narinderji
Eknath Pershad
Gajanand Pershad
Mrs. Murlidhar Pershad
Satguru Pershad

Vinayak Pershad
Benkat Prasad
Ghoshal Raj
Nar Har Raj
Prithvi Raj
Banarsi Das Pilibhit
Saxena
Dr. Eshwar Raj Saxena

Gurucharan Das Saxena
Maheshwar Raj Saxena
Manohar Raj Saxena
Shakamber Raj Saxena
Sudarshan Raj Saxena
Tirupati Raj Saxena
Dr. Mahender Raj
Suxena

Srivastava

Sohan Lal Arya
Bakht Bahadur
Shamsher Bahadur
Harish Chandra
Dr. Kanval Chandra
R. K. Khare
Manohar Lal

N. Inder Lal
Pyari Mohan Lal
Ram Kumar Lal
Shiv Lal
Bala Pershad
Dharminder Pershad
Gajadhar Pershad

Janaki Pershad
Dr. Manik Pershad
Captain Surya Pratap
Dharm Raj
Chander Srivastava
Narinder Srivastava
Miss Pushpa Srivastava

Miscellaneous

Mohamed ul Hussaini
(Sarf-i Khas official)
Dixit Maharaj (Kanaujya
Brahman guru)
Syed Mohiuddin Pasha
(archivist)

Dadey Pershad
(headmaster,
Dharmvant School)
Ziauddin Ahmad Shakeb
(archivist)

Dev Shanker Sharma
(Kanaujya Brahman
pandit)
Professor Haroon Khan
Sherwani (Osmania
University, historian)

Index

Index

Agra: Murlidhar as a patron in, 156; residence of Manu Lal family in, 151, 152, 154
AIKC. *See* All-India Kayasth Conference
Ajmer, 76
Al, as no longer relevant in arranging marriages, 275
Alam, 210; in the Husaini Alam neighborhood culture, 107, 109. *See also* Bik Alam
Alam, Mir, 48, 67
Aligarh University, 128, 232, 234
Allahabad, 119; college in, 154, 155, 156, 201, 231, 232
Allahabad Kayasth Pathshala, 203, 231, 232
Allahabad University, 232
All-India Kayasth Conference (AIKC): Dharm Karan as president of, 226, 263, 264n; formation of, 201–202; and literary activities, 200–201; participation of Hyderabad Kayasths in, 202–205, 207, 258–266; and social reform, 202, 205–206; and temperance, 205; and Young Men's Kayasth Union, 258–266 *passim*
Amaravati, 119
Ancestors, and naming patterns, 52
Ancestral home, 154
Ancestral property, 94
Andhra Pradesh, formation of, 224, 228, 292
Andhra Pradesh State Archives, 9
Anglo-Indian administration, 84, 128. *See also* Diwani bureaucracy
Anglo-Indian law, 160; applied to inheritance, 177–178, 288
Anglo-vernacular middle schools, 231
Anjuman Ittehad ul Amal, 257n
Anjuman-i Taraqqi Urdu, 220
Anthropologists, study of the caste system by, 6–7
Anti-caste, Arya Samajist movement as, 207, 211
Arab Court, 67
Arab mercenary troops, 59–60, 105
Arab military leaders, 114; decline of political power of, 192; political support given to Salar Jung by, 67; as revenue collectors, 61, 67
Arbab-i Nishat, 179–180, 181
Arcot Nawabship, termination ot, 98–99, 111. *See also* Nawab of Arcot
Army, 106; administration of, 25–26; modern, 104–106; monetary problems of, 60–61
Arya, Sohan Lal, 210, 223, 265

Arya Samaj, the, 160, 180; as anti-caste, 156n, 207, 211; founder of, 156n; government cooperation with, 210; and Kayasth participation in public life, 199, 207–211; and the Khilifat agitation, 216; leaders of, 207–210; and marriages of Hyderabad Asthanas, 156–157; and marriages across subcaste boundaries, 211; vs. orthodox Hinduism, 209, 211; political activities and changed membership of, 222–224; social reform activities of, 207, 208, 209–210, 211–212; *suratval* families as members of, 207, 211
Asafgarh Fort, 48
Ashurkhanahs, 80, 81; of Buchar Mal, 302
Associations, Kayasth, 169, 201–207, 251–256, 293; and caste unification, ix–x, 201, 206, 211, 259, 293; development of, accompanied by expansion of education, 149, 293; educational and social reform, efforts of, 256–258, 289; goals of, 206–207; and importance of kin groups in social organization, 201, 206, 211; and importance of residential localities in social organizations, 201, 205; government support of, 225–226; and intercaste marriages, 251, 259, 266; linked to generational conflict and reduced political and economic opportunities, 252, 255, 293; and impact of modernization, ix, 7, 262n, 293; and occupational changes, 251; as producing new leaders and new sources of authority, 251–258. *See also* Arya Samaj; Young Men's Kayasth Union; Young Men's Kayasth Club
Asthana Kayasths, 151–157; education and occupations of, 152, 154–157, 231, 234, 240; and contact with old-city Kayasths, 230, 234–236; education of women among, 249; families of, 152–153; kin groups of, 151–157, 197; marriage patterns and customs among, 152–153, 154, 156, 270–272, 276, 278; mythical origins of, 12; new kin groups of, based upon the modern administration, 197; occupational and social life of, 154–155; outmarriages among, 270–272, 276, 278; outside influences on, 156; rank of, 151, 155, 156; residential patterns of, 143, 155; temple initiation ceremony for children of, 154
Astrologers, 95
Aurangabad, 10, 20, 24, 36, 38, 46, 48, 51, 119, 160n; court shifted from, 20, 52; Gaur families from, 51, 54

Aurangzeb (Mughal Emperor), 20, 28, 38, 39
Authority of elders, 252, 254-255

Badminton, 252
Bahadur, Jung, *hamzulf* relationship of, 154
Bahadur, Keerat, 71
Bahadur, Lala (Ram Pershad), 79, 161; career and power of, 62-68, 82; conflict of power with Salar Jung, 65-68, 82; dominance and control of Mathur marriages by, 71, 74; as *daftardar,* 62, 69, 70, 111; death of and successor of, 70, 84-85; government by compared to government of Siraj ul Mulk, 64n; impact of his power on the Mathur Kayasths, 69-70, 71, 74, 82; as traditionally responsible for Salar Jung's appointment as Diwan, 65n; relationship with the Nizam, 64, 67, 83; wealth and property of, 70
Bahadur, Lokendra, 260n
Bahadur, Pratap, 71
Bahadur, Rae Kunwar, 208, 209
Baksh, Raja Ram, 98
Bali, Munshi Raj, 204
Bali, Sham, 86, 88
Balkishen, 102
Balmiks, 12
Balmukund, 114-115; marriage alliances sponsored by, 115; positions controlled by, 115-116, 189; positions of sons of, 98, 101
Balmukund family, conflict between Devi Pershad and, 190-193, 196; recruitment of relatives and sponsorship of new families by, 191-193, 196, 247
Bank, government, 67
Bankers: as "employees" of *jagirdars,* 131; financial dependence of the state on, 58; as political allies of Salar Jung, 67; political role of, 57, 61, 67; as revenue collectors, 58, 61
Bansi Raja family. *See* Raja, Bansi, family of
Bansidhar, the adopted son of Chandi Pershad, 180
Baqi (pen name of Bansi Raja), 199
Barbers, family, 14, 302
Bareilly, 119
Bawa, Dr. V. K., x, 57n, 68n, 114n
Bazm-i Tehzib, 205

Begum, Hayat Bakshi, 82n
Benares, 119, 158, 185
Bengal Kayasths, 12
Bengali language, 12
Berar, 24, 67, 119; Saksena bridegrooms from, 109
Bhatnagar, Bhavani Pershad, family of, 45-46, 179-180. *See also* Pershad, Bhavani
Bhatnagar, Majlis Rae, family of, 46, 179-180
Bhatnagar families: competition among, 94, 95, 96; "U.P."immigrant families, 94-96; marriage alliances of, 37, 45-46, 54, 93-96; occupational changes among, 243; single effective kin group not constituted by, 93, 95-96
Bhatnagars: as clerks and accountants, 95; mythical origin of, 12; in the Nizam's household service, 92-95; outmarriages of, 276, 278, 283; and purity of marriage alliances, 94-96; reduction and disinheritance of, 177, 179-181
Bhois (water carriers), 97n, 170
Bhopal, 180, 185, 200
Bidar province, 24, 51, 70, 119
Bik Alam, procession of in Chowk Maidan Khan, 82, 109; compared to the Langar procession, 123
Bilateral inheritance: and control of hereditary positions, 6, 111, 112, 195, 196, 287, 289, 290; and economic decline, 181; and marital and occupational patterns, 99, 102; vs. patrilineal inheritance, 9, 111, 196, 289; and social mobility, 103
Bilateral kin groups, 280
Birh, letter-writer of, 43, 158, 178-179
Bismillah, 185, 200
Bodyguards, 139
Books, proscribed, 216
Boy Scouts, 257
Brahmanical law, 196
Brahmans, 8, 12, 82
Brahmo-khatris, 194, 195
Brides, natal home of, 94. *See also* Affines
British East India Company, 29, 47; growing power of, 57; as initiating changes in Hyderabad's military forces, 59; repayment of the loan of, 64; treaties of, 59-60; territorial grant sought by, 61, 64
British India, 127, 155
British-Indian Madras Presidency, 163
British military forces, 59, 169
British Residency, 127, 152, 200n

Index

British Resident, 68; attitude towards land concessions to bankers, 61; in control of the Hyderabad Contingent, 59; and *daftardars,* 62; establishment of in Hyderabad, 57; Henry Russell as, 59; and Manu Lal, 152; negotiations with the Nawab, 97; reforms suggested by, 63; relationship with the Diwan and the Nizam, 58; urges reductions in the Nizam's forces, 60, 104

Burhanpur, 10, 36

Cabinet Council, 174
Calcutta University, 231, 232
Caliph in Turkey, 216
Card playing, 252
Career patterns: of Lalta Pershad and his kinsmen, 162-167, 232, 240, 292; and new marriage networks, 280-283; of women, 249, 281, 283. *See also* Professions
Carnatic Nawabship, terminated, 98-99, 111. *See also* Nawab of Arcot
Carnatic province, 24
Caste: 3, 4n; differences of income and status within, 4-5; historical assumptions in study of, ix, 6-7; marriages and activities across caste boundaries, 267-294; marriage networks, families, and kin groups as characteristic social units of, 2-3, 8, 285-294; and modernization, ix, x, 7, 293; transition to class, 3, 294; role of in Kayasth voluntary associations, ix, x, 7, 201, 206, 211, 259, 293. *See also* Anti-caste; Subcaste
Censorship, 216
Census statistics: for Arya Sanaj, 222; for late nineteenth-century Hyderabad, 140-146; for Hyderabad in 1921, 255n, 216-217; for Kayasths, 143-146
Central Treasury, 131, 133-135; pay disbursement to troops by, 182
Ceremonies, and public life, 81-82
Chaderghat: and development of voluntary associations, 149; electricity for, 170
Chaderghat Social Club, 168
Chain Rae family. *See* Rae, Chain, family of
Chand, Alam, 98, 99
Chand, Dal, 114, 115n
Chand, Dan, 186n, 242n
Chand, Girdhar, 165
Chand, Gulab, family of, 38, 173-174
Chand, Harbans, 257
Chand, Iqbal, and naming patterns, 221
Chand, Janaki, 165; family of, 240

Chand, Khub (Gaur), and cleavage among Gaur kinsmen, 192; positions held by, 191-192, 195
Chand, Khushal, 10; as a Malwala *daftardar,* 40, 69
Chand, Kubir: and cleavage among Gaur kinsmen, 192; position of as military *serrishtahdar,* 192, 195
Chand, Lala Khub, 158
Chand, Lochan, 166, 168; debts of, 171; descendants of form alliance against dominant Malwala family branch, 172
Chand, Manik, 116
Chand, Nim, 172, 241
Chand, Nutan, 165
Chand, Puran, 28
Chand, Raja Sabha, 1, 47, 183
Chand, Raja Ujagar, 76; marriage of daughter of, 75; and marriage alliances among Mathur families, 71; as the titled *daftardar,* 62, 69
Chandra, Dr. Benkat, marriage of, 241
Chandra, Harish, 268
Char Minar locality, 80, 107
Chatu Lal family. *See* Lal, Chatu, family of
Chaturbhuj, Rae, 76
Childbirth: high mortality rate in, 88, 210; mid-wife for, 156-157
Children: temple initiation ceremony for, 154. *See also* Heirs
Chitgragupta: birthday of, 263; as patron deity of the Kayasths, 44; North Indian Kayasths as descendants of, 12-13
Chitragupta Kayasth temple: 23n; constructed by Dooleh Rae family, 44, 178; management of, 254
Chowk Maidan Khan, 41, 46; Mathur subcaste in compared to Saksena kin group in Husaini Alam, 104, 107; Mathur neighborhood culture in, 79-82; Mathurs residing in, 54, 70, 76, 104, 107, 122; first Mathur to move out of, 162-163; neighborhood associations of, 251, 253-255; residence in acquired by marriage, 76; and social and residential boundaries, 123
Chowmohalla palace, 107
Citizenship status, new regulations for, 129
City High School, 146
Class, transition from caste to, 3, 294
Clerks: residences of, 95, 96, 111; Saksenas as, 48, 96
Clubs. *See* Associations; Social Clubs; Young Men's Kayasth Club

Index

administrative changes, 130–140; education and social change during, 144–150; financial dependence upon bankers during, 58, 61; military forces reorganized during, 59–61; political and economic changes in, 57–61; rise to power by recordkeepers during, 61–71, 121–122; urban-rural differences in, 140–144; wealth, status, and power of Mathur families in, 71–91

Hyderabad City: becomes capital, 20, 25; boundaries for changed, 142; as capital of Andra Pradesh, 228; government policies as favoring, 216–217; as an Islamic city, 22–23; population characteristics of, 140–144. *See also* Neighborhoods; Old-city Kayasths; Residential patterns

Hyderabad Club, 169

Hyderabad College, 146

Hyderabad Contingent, 47; as controlled by the British, 104; creation of, 59; regular source of income for, 64; salaries of, 59, 60, 61

Hyderabad Engineering College, 152, 162

Hyderabad Kayasth Sadr Sabha, 169, 204, 206, 266

Hyderabad Mathur Kayasth Education and Welfare Society, 293

Hyderabad Medical School, 127, 145, 145n–146n

Hyderabad State Congress, 219; ban on, 224; linked to the Indian National Congress, 221–222; role of in the nationalist movement, 228

Hyderabad Temperance Society, 205

Idara-e Adabiyat-e Urdu (IAU), 219

Illegitimacy, 187, 287; and recruitment of Arya Samajists, 207; and the right to inherit, 50, 178n, 189; in Shahalibanda, 103. *See also* Heirs

Immigrants: affinal ties and school friendships of, 154; Asthanas as, 151–157; and development of the Arya Samaj, 207; employment and socioeconomic status for, 118–121; imported to staff the modern administration, 127–128; in modern professions, 151–160; opportunities open to Urdu-speaking, 160; and population changes in the late nineteenth century, 142–143; residential areas of, 120, 123; Srivastava Kayasths as, 118, 119, 157–160. *See also* Migration

Inam grants, 40, 70, 71, 76

Inam Investigations (1876), 83–84, 90, 91, 172

Indebtedness: and inheritance of mansabs and jagirs, 171–172, 195; and loss of positions, 187–189; of the Paigah nobles, 194

Inderjit, Raja, as *daftardar,* 70, 161; death of, 91; dispute among relatives of, 89–90; honored by Salar Jung, 84–85; marriage of, 76–77; marriages sponsored by, 71; widow of, 247

Indian National Congress, 216, 221, 222

Influenza epidemics, 209, 254, 255

Informants, 267, 273, 274

Inheritance: impact of administrative changes on, 130–140, 177–196 *passim*; of adopted sons, 178, 180, 190; Anglo-Indian law applied to, 160, 177–178, 288; bilateral vs. patrilineal, 9, 111; Brahmanical law applied to Hindu inheritance cases, 196, 290; disputes over, 89–90, 190–193, 246; changes in the inheritance laws, 129, 132, 160, 177–178, 195–196, 245, 288, 290; from fathers-in-law, 195; among Gaur Kayasths, 116, 118, 189–195; and illegitimate children, 178n, 189; and lack of legitimate male heirs, 116, 118, 178, 180, 187, 190–191, 196, 248–249, 290; and physical afflictions, 69; and reductions in *mansab* inheritance, 239–240, 244, 245, 246, 290–291; among Saksenas, 181–189; by a widow, 241, 248. *See also* Bilateral inheritance

Inheritance of Grants files, 245

Insider-outsider conflict, in the modern administration, 229; and education of old-city Kayasths, 233–234; intensified by Urdu vs. English educational systems, 217–218; and the nationalist movements, 219–221

Inspector General of the Revenue Branch, 172

Interdining reforms, 202, 205; supported by the Kayasth Association, 254–255

International Aryan League, 222n

Interviews, x, 8–9; listed by subcaste, 330–332. *See also* Informants

Intoxicants, 181, 209. *See also* Temperance societies

Irregular Forces, 105, 106; and economic decline of Kayasth families, 186, 188; hereditary principle in blocks attempts to

Index

account of, 11-15; economic decline among, 177-196; literacy among, 143-144; marriage alliances of in the eighteenth century, 37-54; migration of to Hyderabad, 7, 36-37, 48, 71-79, 151-160; origin of, 8, 12; political activities of in the modern administration, 221-229; pronunciation of, 12; ranking of in the eighteenth century, 31-35; as record-keepers, 9, 23-25, 39-40, 57, 62-70, 81, 92, 287 (*see also Daftardars*); social units of corresponding to historical periods of Hyderabad, 2-3, 285-294; terms to describe social units of, 3-4; as a "writing caste," 7, 15. *See also* Associations; Education; Kin groups; Marriage alliances; and names of individual subcastes

Keshavgiri temple, 105n
Kessinger, Tom G., 6
Khadi, 221
Khan, Ali. *See* Nizam Ali Khan
Khan, Fakhruddin, 52, 114, 116
Khan, Ghulam Ghaus, 98
Khan, Himmat Yar, 48
Khan, Mahbub Ali. *See* Nizam Mahbub Ali Khan
Khan, Nizam Osman Ali. *See* Nizam Osman Ali Khan
Khan, Rafiuddin, 116n, 190, 193
Khan, Rashiduddin, 116n, 190, 193
Khan, Salabat, 59
Khan, Syed Ahmed, 128
Khan, Waziruddin, 190, 193
Khanahdamad, 196
Khandan, 8-9. *See also* Families
Khandesh, 24, 51
Khardla, battle of, 38n
Khare Srivastavas, 43, 44, 118; kin groups among, 158; positions held by families of, 120
Khatri caste, 50, 58n, 147
Khilifat agitation, 216
Khurram, Sital Pershad, 188
Kin groups, x; bilateral inheritance of positions encourages formation of, 6, 92, 111, 112; boundaries of, 2, 207; conflicts among for control of patrons and positions, 181, 183, 185, 190-193, 288; control of positions in the Mughlai bureaucracy, 3, 57, 92-112; demographic factors in determination of dominance among, 123; dependence upon a single patron, 113, 116, 118, 189-195; vs. "doctor clusters," 281; economic strategies of, 4, 92-

126 *passim*, 122, 127, 285-294; educational institutions established by, 231; importance of in social organizations, 201, 206; and changed marriage patterns, 177, 181, 185, 186; marital and occupational patterns emphasize strength of among Saksenas, 99-102; and naming patterns, 280; occupational and social contacts among, 236, 243; and occupational diversification, 10, 163-167, 172; and outmarriages, 270-279, 281; pioneering work on by historians of India, 6; and positions in the modern administration, 163-166, 167, 197, 237, 240, 288; and residential patterns and occupational specialization, 95, 96, 111; transition from marriage networks to kinship connections to consolidate positions, 50, 54

Kin groups, Asthana, 151-157; based upon the modern administration rather than noble status, 197; as members of the administrative elite, 155-156
Kin groups, Bhatnagar, 93, 95-96
Kin groups, Gaur, 113-118, 189-195; Balmukund's family in, 114-115, 190-193, 196; changed marriage patterns in, 115, 191-192; development of two, 192-193; as a single kin group, 113, 189
Kin groups, Mathur: compared to the Asthana kin group, 152; established by Lalta Pershad, 161, 163-166, 167, 172, 197
Kin groups, Saksena, 96-112; and definition of illegitimacy, 189; inheritance problems among, 181-189; positions lost by, 186-189
Kin groups, Srivastava, 119, 158, 160
Kinship ties, 111; categories of, 99; economic usefulness of, 49-50, 99, 103, 111; and marriages across subcaste lines, 267, 269; and Mathur marriage practices, 74-75. *See also Hamzulf; Samdhi*
Kishen, Keval, 40, 41, 74
Kishen, Ram, family of, 51-52, 114
Kitchens, supervision of, 93
Kotla Ali Jah mosque, 81
Kshatriyas, 12

Lakhi, the dancing girl, 183n
Lal, Raja Chandu: as Diwan, 58, 59, 63n, 67, 98; Khatri family of, 58n, 199; power of, 61; records kept in palace of, 111; resignation of as Diwan, 62, 63, 67
Lal, Chatu, family of, 38, 41, 74
Lal, Ghausi, 210

[341

Index

Lal, Girdhari, 179
Lal, Raja Hanu, 93
Lal, Har, 76
Lal, Hari Mohan, 232n, 240
Lal, Hira (Bhatnagar), 95
Lal, Hira (Saksena): indebtedness and loss of positions by family of, 188; *mansab* inherited by, 195
Lal, Jag Mohan (Asthana), 257
Lal, Jag Mohan (Mathur), 86, 88
Lal, Jatan, 47
Lal, Kishen, 109
Lal, Kumari, 48, 102
Lal, Manu (Asthana): English-medium school established by, 154-155; as first Kayasth to enter the modern administration, 151; as an instructor, 162; powerful kin group established by, 151, 152, 232; Western education of, 152
Lal, Raja Manu (Srivastava), 178; in the Nizam's household service, 93; move to Husaini Alam by, 94, 96
Lal, Mohan, 187
Lal, Murari, 179-
Lal, Prabhu, 154, 175
Lal, Ram, alias name of, 11
Lal, Raja Rup, 46, 47, 50, 103
Lal, Shadi, 76
Lal, Shiv Mohan, 241
Lal, Sohan (Asthana), in the British service, 151-152
Lal, Sohan (Bhatnagar), 95
Lal, Sohan (Saksena), 188
Land, public, 130n
Land concessions, to bankers and mercenaries, 61
Land revenue collection, 58; in eighteenth-century Hyderabad, 23-25; vs. military service, 29; tributes to secure land revenue contracts, 62
Land revenue offices, 62. *See also Daftar*
Land revenue records, and *daftardar* families, 23-25, 287. *See also Daftardars*
Landholders, military men as, 61
Langar procession, 109, 123, 182, 183
Languages: and education, 218, 234; of government, 8, 127, 129-130; spoken in Hyderabad, 140-144 *passim*, 217. *See also* Urdu language
Law, 127; and changed inheritance laws, 129, 132, 160, 177-178, 195-196, 245, 288, 290
Lawyers, 163, 198, 231; Arya Samajist early leader as, 208; Mathurs as, 240

Leach, Edmund R., model of the caste system by, 6-7
Leadership, and Kayasth associations, 256-266
Lectures, 149, 168
Legal profession. *See* Lawyers
Letter-writer in Birh, 43, 158, 178-179
Life-cycle ceremonies, 80
Lines of Monsieur Raymond, 20, 59n, 101, 186
Lines of the Carnatic, 101
Linewalla troops, 20, 101
Linguistic minority, 229, 292
"Linguistic states reorganization," 228
Literacy, among Kayasths, 143-144
Literary activities, 186; Kayasth participation in, 199-201, 211, 288
Literature, Urdu and Persian, 199-201
Liquor, illicit distillers of, 120. *See also* Drinking
Liverpool Agricultural College, 163
Loans, from banking firms, 58
Lodhi Khan mosques, 81
Love marriages, 261, 270, 273
Lucknow: literary activities in, 200; Mathur marriage alliances with families from, 74-75, 77, 86, 88
Luxury items, 98

Madras, 45, 98; and marriage alliances, 45, 99, 101
Madras University, 146, 147
Madrasa-i Aliya, 146, 147, 163, 168
Maharashtra, 228
Maharashtrians, 123, 207; as prominent in the Paigah estates, 194, 195
Maidan Khan mosque, 81
Maiseram Regiment, 105
Mal, Raja Buchar, 46, 47, 50, 302
Mal, Sagar, 70; death of, 40; as traditional founder of the Malwala *daftardar* family, 38-39
Males: naming of, 279-280; recorded as unmarried, 120n. *See also* Heirs
Malwala Kayasth family, 131; alliance against the dominant branch of, 90, 172; demonstration of Mathur dependency on, 81; differences within, 161, 166-172; division and inheritance of estates of, 89-90, 166, 171-172, 238-240, 242, 245; as the founding family of the Mathur subcaste in Hyderabad, 10, 38-40, 43, 54; hereditary control of the *daftardar* position by, 24, 33, 39-40, 62-71 *passim*, 76-

Index

Marriages across subcaste and caste lines, 3, 110, 121, 211, 236, 243, 267-284, 291; and career potential of women, 280, 283, 291; changed naming patterns related to, 279-280; and changing norms within subcastes, 275-276; and cultural continuity, 267, 279, 283-284; demographic factors in, 275-276; distribution of, 306-314; distinctive features of, 270-284, 291, 294; educational factors in, 269, 278, 291; geographic and residential factors in, 271, 278, 283-284; and Kayasth families, 274-275, 278-279; and kinship ties, 269, 281; for love, 270, 273; occupational ties and specialization as factor in, 236, 243, 244, 245, 267, 269, 278, 280-281, 291; and parental control, 269; population size related to, 276-277; first reform marriages, 259, 264, 267-270, 289; to reduce expenditures, 181; and the rising age for marriage, 281, 291; rituals for, 294; sex ratios related to, 271, 273

Marwaris, 207

Masonic lodges, 169

Mathur subcaste, 4; associations and organizations of, 169, 203-204, 206-207, 251, 253-255, 293; conversion to Islam among, 122n; dependency on Malwala family demonstrated, 81; diversification among, 161-176; education and new occupations among, 161-166, 167, 231-233, 238-240, 241; initial families of in Hyderabad, 38-43; formation of in Hyderabad, 69-91; genealogies, 40, 87, 167; genealogical relationships of the earliest modern administrators among, 163-167; growth of indicated by chronological summary of, 71-73; influence of Lalta Pershad on, 162-166, 167, 173, 232, 240, 292; *jagirdar* families of, 238-240; impact of Lala Bahadur's career as a *daftardar* on, 69-70, 71, 74; impact of Salar Jung on the Malwala family of, 82-85; intermarriages of, 268, 272-274, 276, 278, 283; internal conflicts among, 86-91; literary activities of, 201; marriage alliances among, 37-43, 54, 71-79, 86-88, 91; in the modern administration, 163-166, 167, 172-176, 177, 236-240; mythical origin of, 12; role of Murli Manohar in, 168-169; and neighborhood culture in Chowk Maidan Khan, 70, 79-82, 104, 107; in the professions, 240-241; schools established by, 231; wedding celebrations

among, 80-81; welfare and education society of, 293

Mayo Central College, 154, 155

Meat, abstinence from, 208n, 209, 210n

Mecca Masjid, 98

Medical profession: Mathurs in, 240-241; women in, 249. *See also* Doctors

Medical school, 127, 145

Medicinal herbs, specialists in, 181

Mehbub Ki Mehndi, 210n

Mercenary leaders, 114

Mercenary troops, 57, 58; relationship to Hyderabad nobles, 59-60; salaries of, 60-61

Mewar Central College, 232

Mid-wife, 156-157

Migration: of Asthana Kayasths to Hyderabad, 151-157; of Bhatnagar U. P. families, 94-96; of Gaur families, 50-51; and immigrants in the modern professions, 151-160; of Kayasths to Hyderabad, 2, 7, 36-37, 48; of Srivastava Kayasths, 118, 119, 157-160

Military aristocracy, 3, 19-35; opportunities and social structure of, 28-31, 285, 287; power of passes to the recordkeepers, 61-71, 103, 114, 121-122

Military expenditures, 60-61, 105

Military forces, reorganization of, 104-106, 179

Military men: replaced by bankers as revenue contractors, 58; of legendary fame, 50-51, 302-303. *See also* Military *serrishtahdars*

Military regime, administration of, 19-35; Kayasths in, 27-35; role of the army in, 25-26, 46-47, 50-51; role of land revenue collection in, 23-25; role of the Nizam's household in, 26-27

Military *serrishtahdars*: Bansi Raja as, 105, 109; impact of administrative changes on, 130-131, 133, 135-139, 182, 186, 187; Malwala family members as, 70; Mohan Das family members as, 115; relationship of to mercenary troops, 61; Saksenas as, 47, 101; of Shahalibanda, 302

Mir Alam Mandi, 80

Mitakshara law, 69, 89, 111

Modern administration: Asthana Kayasths in, 154-156, 197; Bhatnagars in, 243; censorship in, 216; and changed inheritance laws, 129, 132, 160, 177-178, 195-196, 245, 288, 290; Dusre Srivastavas in, 158; dominance of Western-educated

Index

179; residential patterns of, 120; as *surat-val*, 113, 118, 119, 120–121
Srivastava Sabha, 203, 206
Statistical measures, of outmarriages by subcaste designation, 267, 270–279, 307–314
Status: acquired by a relationship via marriage to the Malwala *daftardar*, 76–79; of families residing in Shahalibanda, 110; of the Mathur subcaste, 122; of nobles vs. officeholders, 197; of a son-in-law residing with his father-in-law, 196; of *suratvals*, 120–121; symbols of, 115. *See also* Wealth
Subcaste boundaries: and changing educational and occupational patterns, 230–250; and development and goals of voluntary associations and societies, 201–207, 251–258. *See also* Marriages across subcaste and caste lines
Subcastes: changing norms within, 275–276; defined, 3–4; food regulations of, 13; formation of the Mathur, 69–91, 122; Mathur AIKC society based on, 206; and naming patterns, 279–280; professional contacts among, 240–241, 243; origins of, 12–13; outmarriages among, 270–279, 304–314; schools for old-city Kayasths established by, 231
Suburbs: compared to the old city, 140–142; growth of, 140, 142; Lalta Pershad's move to, 163; languages spoken in, 141–142; Paigah nobles residences in, 194; and residential preferences of the modern administrative elite, 155
Sudras, 12
Sufi thought, and poetry, 200
Suratvals, 110, 118n, 120n, 189; as Arya Samaj followers, 207, 211; economic insecurity of, 120–121, 290; educational and professional status of, 250, 292; genealogies of, 304–305; and intermarriages, 270, 278; marriages of, 188, 189; among Saksenas, 50, 188; Srivastava families as, 113, 118, 119, 120–121, 158
Survey Department, 129
Suxena, Mahender Raj, 268

Tabla players, 210
Talukdars (revenue contractors), 119; Rae Murlidhar as, 155; Lalta Pershad as, 162. *See also* Revenue contractors
Taluks, assigned to bankers, 58
Tamkin, Bichu Lal, 188

Tankhah, 130
Taziyah, 82
Telangana districts, 228, 229
Telephone Department, 163
Telugu-speakers: in Hyderabad, 141, 144, 217; and the formation of Andhra Pradesh, 224, 228–229, 292
Temperance issue, and young men's neighborhood associations, 254–255
Temperance societies, 205–206, 207, 209
Temples, 23, 154; acquired by Bansi Raja, 105; haunted, 302–303; construction of as an indication of wealth and status, 93, 122; hereditary income to support, 76, 179; patronage of, 70, 181n; state income for, 187
Tent-pegging, 168
Tipu Sultan, 20
Translation Bureau, 218
Transliteration, xii
Transportation, improved systems of, 193
Treasurers: bankers as, 58
Treasury: in the modern administration, 131; of the Nizam, 119; offices established by Salar Jung for, 82. *See also* Central Treasury
Treaties, formed by the East India Company, 59–60
Treaty of 1853, 64–65
Treaty of Subsidiary Alliance (1800), 58
Troop Bazar, 152, 155
Troop reduction, and hereditary positions, 135–137
Turban, refusal to remove, 233
Turkish soldiers, 60
Tuzuk-i Mahbubiyah (G. S. Khan), 198

Uchar, 51
Ufuq, Dwarka Pershad. *See* Pershad, Dwarka
Ujjain, 51
ul Umra, Shams: as co-regent with Salar Jung, 107; as Diwan, 63–64, 68
ul Umra, Vikar, 133, 190, 194n
ul Umra II, Vikar, as Prime Minister, 188, 194
United Provinces, 151: Gaur marriage alliances with females from, 192; immigrant Bhatnagar families from, 94–96
Universities, and higher education for old-city Kayasths, 232–233
Untouchables, 210
U. P. Bhatnagar families, 111; marriage alliances of, 94–96

352]